Mind, Method, and Morality

Sir Anthony Kenny
Photograph © Russell Sach

Mind, Method, and Morality

Essays in Honour of Anthony Kenny

Edited by

John Cottingham and Peter Hacker

OXFORD

UNIVERSITY PRESS

OXFORD
UNIVERSITY PRESS

Great Clarendon Street, Oxford, OX2 6DP,
United Kingdom

Oxford University Press is a department of the University of Oxford.
It furthers the University's objective of excellence in research, scholarship,
and education by publishing worldwide. Oxford is a registered trade mark of
Oxford University Press in the UK and in certain other countries

© The several contributors 2010

The moral rights of the authors have been asserted

First Edition published in 2010

Published in the United States of America by Oxford University Press
198 Madison Avenue, New York, NY 10016, United States of America

British Library Cataloguing in Publication Data
Data available

Library of Congress Cataloging in Publication Data
Data available

ISBN 978–0–19–955612–0

Contents

Preface

Anthony Kenny is one of the most distinguished and prolific philosophers of our time. In virtue of the wide range and historical breadth of his interests, he has had a significant influence on many parts of philosophy. Diverging from the approach of many of his contemporaries who have often ignored or played down philosophy's debt to its past, Kenny's work has always been rooted in the great tradition of Western philosophical inquiry, and has been marked by meticulous scholarly attention to the texts and ideas of the canonical writers of that tradition.

Kenny's philosophical achievement over the past forty-five years has been extraordinary. In the course of this long career as a writer he has written, translated, and edited over sixty-five books and published many dozens of articles. This would be an amazing feat had teaching and writing been his sole vocation. But it is even more astonishing given that for half of these forty-five years he successively filled the roles of Master of Balliol, member of the governing council of Oxford University, Delegate to, and member of the finance committee of, Oxford University Press, Warden of Rhodes House, President of the British Academy, Chairman of the British Library Board, and Pro-Vice Chancellor for Development at the University of Oxford. It was during these twenty-three years of public service to Balliol, Oxford University, and Britain that he also wrote or edited roughly forty of his sixty-five books.

The range and depth of Anthony Kenny's writings is no less impressive than their number. The philosophical subjects closest to his heart, and to which he has made major contributions, have been the philosophy of psychology, moral psychology, and philosophy of action, on the one hand, and philosophical theology, on the other. His first philosophy book was *Action, Emotion and the Will* (1963), which rapidly became a classic in its field. It was written in the spirit of the innovatory philosophy of mind that had developed in the 1950s in the wake of Wittgenstein and Ryle—sharing the lucidity of the latter and profundity of the former. However, unlike those two masters—the one a genius, the other the finest Oxford philosopher of his day—Kenny's writings were already informed by an unusual awareness of the history of the subject. He displayed the ability to articulate the insights of great thinkers of the remote past, in this case Aristotle and Aquinas, to render them intelligible to modern readers, and to apply them to the philosophical problems that bedevil us.

Action, Emotion and the Will analysed the concepts of emotion, feeling, motive, desire, and pleasure, and then extended the analysis into the philosophical examination of actions, states, performances, and activities, culminating in a preliminary investigation of the will.

A year later Kenny published his edition of Aquinas's *Summa Theologiae* IaIIae, qu. 49–54, on the nature of action. In 1972 and 1973 he participated, together with H. C. Longuet-Higgins, J. R. Lucas, and C. H. Waddington in the Gifford Lectures, published in the two volumes *The Nature of Mind* and *The Development of Mind*, in which he focused more sharply on the intellectual powers of mankind. It was, however, the active powers that were the theme of the sequel to *Action, Emotion and the Will*, namely *Will, Freedom and Power* (1975). This examined traditional theories of will and elucidated the concepts of voluntariness and intention, explored in unprecedented detail and depth the nature of human powers, and advanced a compatibilist solution to the problem of freewill and determinism. It reintroduced the distinction between liberty of indifference and liberty of spontaneity, and argued that *both* are requisite for free action. It set out the logical features of acting for a reason and distinguished between causal and rational explanation. What is distinctive of humankind, Kenny argued in the Aristotelian tradition, is possession of will and intellect, and their mark is susceptibility to reason and the powers of reasoning. And that in turn, he held, following Wittgenstein, is a consequence of the mastery of a language.

The theme of freedom continued to preoccupy Kenny in *Four Lectures on Freewill and Responsibility* (1978) in which he developed further his account of free action and extended his discussion into the domain of responsibility and punishment. The interest in such topics in moral psychology and the philosophy of law coincided with his reading for the bar on top of all his other commitments, and led to a fruitful series of papers on criminal responsibility, the limits of the plea of duress and the definition of murder, and an investigation of the notion of expert witness. In 1979 he turned again to historical investigation and published his study of *Aristotle on the Will*, in which Aristotle's account of voluntariness, purposive choice, and practical reasoning were examined with meticulous classical scholarship and the methodological tools of analytical philosophy of psychology. His work in philosophy of mind culminated in *The Metaphysics of Mind* (1989), which was a celebration of the fortieth anniversary of Ryle's *Concept of Mind*. Here Kenny endeavoured, with conspicuous success, to give an overview of the central themes in analytic philosophy of mind—deliberately covering much the same ground as Ryle had. Seldom have so many illuminating and fruitful ideas been packed into so short a volume. Thereafter his purely analytic (non-historical) writings on philosophy of mind were limited to occasional articles. In these he was a powerful critic of contemporary philosophy of mind and cognitive science. But his main contributions to the philosophy of psychology after 1990 were within the context of his work on the history of philosophy.

Alongside his work on philosophy of mind and moral psychology lie more than half a dozen volumes on philosophical theology. In 1969 Kenny published *The Five Ways*, in which he examined Aquinas's five proofs of the existence of God, each of which he judged to be flawed. Ten years later he published *The God of the Philosophers*, in which he cast his net wider, examining the concept of God as articulated in the tradition of the monotheistic religions—in particular, but not only, in Catholic natural theology. The conclusion of the investigation was that the philosophers' conception of God as an omnipotent, omniscient, and benevolent creator was not coherent, since the three divine attributes were incompatible with one another. Moreover, the very idea of a disembodied mind, Kenny argued, was not intelligible. In his four lectures *Faith and Reason* (1983), he brought Wittgenstein's insights in *On Certainty* to bear upon the analysis of religious faith. Here he shed as much light upon Wittgenstein's last rough notes on epistemology as he did upon the notion of religious belief. His conclusion was to side with agnosticism rather than with the various forms of atheism. That conclusion was to be further explored, but not changed, in his much later collection of essays *The Unknown God* (2004). Here he argued that our thought about God is unavoidably metaphorical and that the nature of God, if there is a god, is ineffable.

Kenny's interest in poetry and in those who, like himself, had struggled so deeply with faith led him to explore the lives and work of two fine English poets associated with Balliol College, namely Clough and Hopkins. In 1988 he published *God and Two Poets: Arthur Hugh Clough and Gerard Manley Hopkins*, in 1990 he edited *The Oxford Diaries of Arthur Hugh Clough*, and in 2005 he produced a biography of Clough, *Arthur Hugh Clough: The Life of a Poet*. In these works he displayed a sensitivity both to the verse and to the predicaments of faith that informed the works and lives of these poets.

Concurrently with his works on philosophy of psychology and philosophical theology came a series of highly influential volumes on the history of philosophy. This interest was focused on four of the greatest figures: Aristotle, Aquinas, Descartes, and Wittgenstein (although he also wrote books on Wyclif, Thomas More, and Frege). He published books on Aristotelian ethics, on Aristotle on the will (as mentioned above), and on Aristotle on the good life. In the course of his work on Aristotelian ethics he became interested in the relationship between the *Eudemian Ethics* and the *Nicomachean Ethics*. In order to show that the *Eudemian Ethics* is both an authentic work of Aristotle's and indeed his primary mature work on ethics—a most radical claim—he involved himself in the budding literary science of stylometrics. A spin-off from this were three further impressive contributions to this newly emerging field. The first was an introduction to the techniques: *The Computation of Style* (1981). The second was an application of stylometric techniques to the Bible: *A Stylometric Study of the New Testament* (1986) demonstrated that the majority of St Paul's epistles are written by a single author, and that the author of the Revelation was not the same person as the author of the Fourth Gospel. The third book was the more general *Computers and the Humanities* (1991).

On Aquinas, Kenny wrote an introductory volume *Aquinas* (1980) in the Past Masters series published by Oxford University Press, followed by *Aquinas on the Mind* (1993) and *Aquinas on Being* (2002). Aquinas's reflections on philosophy of psychology in *Summa theologiae* I, qu. 75–89 display him at his very best, and in *Aquinas on the Mind* Kenny demonstrates how fruitful many of his ideas and distinctions are. Aquinas's ontology, however, was found sorely wanting. Kenny's powerful criticism in *Aquinas on Being* aimed at uncovering extensive confusions in Aquinas's influential discussion.

Aristotle and Aquinas are the two supremely systematic philosophers, writing with explicit awareness of what has already been said on the topics at hand and striving to do justice to past thinkers. Descartes and Wittgenstein are very different—the one eager to cover the tracks of his predecessors, the other with scant knowledge of any of his predecessors. Descartes, the greatest of philosophical myth-makers, with whose shade we still struggle, construed the mind as an immaterial substance, held the subjective domain of the mind to be better known than the objective domain of material things, and contended that the mental is causally and not intrinsically related to behaviour. Wittgenstein, the greatest idoloclast in the history of philosophy, set his sights against such conceptions of the mental, denying that mind is better known than matter, repudiating the primacy of consciousness, and holding the relation between the mental and its behavioural manifestations to be intrinsic. Kenny engaged intensively with both great philosophers for decades. His *Descartes: A Study of His Philosophy* (1968) gave a methodical overview of Cartesian metaphysics coupled with powerful refutations. It broke fresh ground in its treatment of the Cartesian circle, in its meticulous anatomization of Descartes's conceptions of ideas, and in its critical application of Wittgenstein's ideas to Descartes's arguments. In 1970 Kenny published his edition and translation of a selection of Descartes's letters, later incorporated into the third volume (1991) of the authoritative collection of Descartes's writings for English readers: *The Philosophical Writings of Descartes*.

Wittgenstein, however, occupies a special place in Kenny's philosophical work. Kenny was fortunate to have Elizabeth Anscombe as one of his teachers at Oxford, and it was she who brought him to realize, as he later wrote, 'the genius of her teacher Wittgenstein and his significance for the philosophy of our time'. For he, more than any other, moulded Kenny's conception of philosophy—of its legitimate goals and of the limits of its possibilities. Philosophy, according to that conception, is not a science. It is not a quest for further knowledge about the empirical world, let alone about all possible worlds, but a quest for a distinctive form of understanding. It is a quest for a general overview of the conceptual forms and structures in terms of which we articulate our knowledge of the world and of ourselves, of our reasoning concerning our goals and goal directed actions, and of our values. Kenny's main book-length contribution to Wittgenstein studies was his *Wittgenstein* (1973), in which he gave a masterly survey of the development of Wittgenstein's thought from the pre-*Tractatus* notebooks to the last notes on certainty. He argued for the continuity of Wittgenstein's early and later thought, emphasizing the persistence of what he held to be the core ideas of the picture theory of the proposition, and of the unity of the conception of philosophy, its scope and limits.

Wittgenstein's thought informed Kenny's own philosophical work, and he wrote numerous further papers on Wittgenstein and Wittgensteinian themes. In 1974 he published his translation of *Philosophical Grammar* (a compilation edited by Rush Rhees from the materials now published as *The Big Typescript*, and from the manuscripts known as the 'Umarbeitung' and the 'Grosses Format'). In 1984 he published a volume of his essays on Wittgenstein entitled *The Legacy of Wittgenstein* which included his brilliant paper 'The homunculus fallacy' and his further reflections on Wittgenstein's conception of philosophy. In 1994 he edited *The Wittgenstein Reader*, designed for undergraduate courses. The theme of Wittgenstein's metaphilosophy continued to occupy his mind, and when he published a second edition of his *Wittgenstein* in 2006 he confessed his bafflement over what he took to be an irresolvable conflict between Wittgenstein's practice and his metaphilosophical reflections, thereby raising challenging issues which have yet to be resolved.

By the 1990s Kenny's interests were more and more firmly engaged by the history of philosophy, various volumes on which he had by then edited or co-edited. In 1998 he published *A Brief History of Western Philosophy* which provided an introductory overview of the subject. On his retirement from his last public role (pro-Vice Chancellor of Oxford) in 2001, he began his magisterial *A New History of Western Philosophy* in four volumes. Volume 1, *Ancient Philosophy* was published in 2004, and the subsequent three volumes followed at yearly intervals. This grand survey, written with luminous clarity, was more concise and analytically powerful than Copleston's celebrated *History of Philosophy* and greatly surpassed Russell's best-selling *History of Western Philosophy* in scholarship, accuracy, and judgement. It combined historical and biographical survey with methodical philosophical overviews of developments in logic, metaphysics, epistemology, philosophy of mind, ethics, and political thought. Brilliantly compressed accounts of the philosophies of the great figures of the past were balanced with judicious and penetrating criticisms.

The present Festschrift, comprising sixteen essays in all, is divided into four parts, each dealing with one of the four major philosophers on whose work Kenny has focused in so many of his writings. Each part contains four papers by leading specialists in the relevant area. Strongly linked together by their focus on philosophy of mind, action, and responsibility, the papers aim to contribute to those fields of philosophy which Kenny has made particularly his own and to achieve the clarity and accessibility that are the hallmarks of his philosophical writings. The contributors—pupils, colleagues, and friends—all wish to honour the author of an outstanding body of work that has informed and inspired so many philosophers and students of philosophy, and provoked so many fruitful and lively debates over almost five decades. Clearly no single volume of essays can hope to cover the full range of Anthony Kenny's work, but it is our hope that these essays give at least some idea of the breadth and depth of his remarkable contribution to philosophy over the last forty-five years.

JGC
PMSH
March 2009

Abbreviations

Aristotle

References to Aristotle are given by the Bekker numbers (and to Plato by the Stephanus numbers), which are given in all good editions and translations. Where individual works are cited, titles are generally given in English, for the reader's convenience, and references are made to book, chapter, and section numbers that are common to all editions.

Aquinas

Summa Theologiae [1266–73]

References to parts of this work are as follows: Ia = 'Prima' (First Part); IaIIae = 'Prima Secundae' (First Part of the Second Part); IIaIIae = 'Secunda Secundae' (Second Part of the Second Part). Each part is divided into 'questions' ('qu.'), and, within questions, articles ('art.'). Sometimes further divisions are made within articles, Thus 'IaIIae, qu. 15, art. 3, ad 3' means 'Prima Secundae (First Part of the Second Part), question 15, article 3, concerning point 3'.

Other works are referred to, unless otherwise stated, by book, chapter, or section numbers that are common to all editions and translations.

Descartes

AT	refers by volume and page number to the standard Franco-Latin edition of Descartes by C. Adam and P. Tannery, *Œuvres de Descartes* (12 vols, rev. edn, Paris: Vrin/CNRS, 1964–76).
CSM	refers by volume and page number to the English translation by J. Cottingham, R. Stoothoff, and D. Murdoch, *The Philosophical Writings of Descartes*, vols I and II (Cambridge: Cambridge University Press, 1985), and
CSMK	to volume III, *The Correspondence*, by the same translators plus A. Kenny (Cambridge: Cambridge University Press, 1991).

Wittgenstein

AWL   *Wittgenstein's Lectures, Cambridge 1932–1935, from the Notes of Alice Ambrose and Margaret MacDonald*, ed. Alice Ambrose (Oxford: Blackwell, 1979).

BB   *The Blue and Brown Books* (Oxford: Blackwell, 1958).

BT   *The Big Typescript—TS 213* ed. and trans. C. G. Luckhardt and M. A. E. Aue (Oxford: Blackwell, 2005).

C   *On Certainty*, ed. G. E. M. Anscombe and G. H. von Wright, trans. D. Paul and G. E. M. Anscombe (Oxford: Blackwell, 1969).

CL   *Cambridge Letters*, ed. B. McGuinness and G. H. von Wright (Oxford: Blackwell, 1995).

LFM   *Wittgenstein's Lectures on the Foundations of Mathematics, Cambridge 1939*, ed. C. Diamond (Brighton: Harvester, 1976).

LPP   *Wittgenstein's Lectures on Philosophical Psychology 1946–1947*, ed. P. T. Geach (Hassocks: Harvester, 1988).

LW I   *Last Writings on the Philosophy of Psychology*, vol. I, ed. G. H. von Wright and H. Nyman, trans. C. G. Luckhardt and M. A. E. Aue (Oxford: Blackwell, 1982).

LWL   *Wittgenstein's Lectures, Cambridge 1930–1932, from the Notes of John King and Desmond Lee*, ed. Desmond Lee (Oxford: Blackwell, 1980).

NB   *Notebooks 1914–1916*, ed. G. H. von Wright and G. E. M. Anscombe, trans. G. E. M. Anscombe (Oxford: Blackwell, 1961).

PG   *Philosophical Grammar*, ed. R. Rhees, trans. A. J. P. Kenny (Oxford: Blackwell, 1974).

PI   *Philosophical Investigations*, ed. G. E. M. Anscombe and R. Rhees, trans. G. E. M. Anscombe, 2nd edn (Oxford: Blackwell, 1958).

PLP   *The Principles of Linguistic Philosophy*, F. Waismann, ed. R. Harré (Macmillan, London: Macmillan and New York: St Martin's Press, 1965).

PPF   *Philosophy of Psychology—A Fragment*, in L. Wittgenstein, *Philosophical Investigations*, 4th edn, ed. P. M. S. Hacker and Joachim Schulte (Oxford: Wiley-Blackwell, 2009).

PTLP   *Proto-Tractatus—An Early Version of Tractatus Logico-Philosophicus*, ed. B. F. McGuinness, T. Nyberg, G. H. von Wright, trans. D. F. Pears and B. F. McGuinness (London: Routledge and Kegan Paul, 1971).

RFM   *Remarks on the Foundations of Mathematics*, ed. G. H. von Wright, R. Rhees, G. E. M. Anscombe, rev. edn (Oxford: Blackwell, 1978).

ROC   *Remarks on Colour*, ed. G. E. M. Anscombe and G. H. von Wright (Oxford: Blackwell, 1977).

RPP I   *Remarks on the Philosophy of Psychology*, vol. I, ed. G. E. M. Anscombe and G. H. von Wright, trans. G. E. M. Anscombe (Oxford: Blackwell, 1980).

RPP II   *Remarks on the Philosophy of Psychology*, vol. II, ed. G. H. von Wright and H. Nyman, trans. C. G. Luckhardt and M. A. E. Aue (London: Blackwell, 1980).

TLP   *Tractatus Logico-Philosophicus*, trans. D. F. Pears and B. F. McGuinness (London: Routledge and Kegan Paul, 1961).

VW   *The Voices of Wittgenstein*, ed. G. P. Baker (London: Routledge, 2003).

WWK   *Ludwig Wittgenstein und der Wiener Kreis*, shorthand notes recorded by F. Waismann, ed. B. F. McGuinness (Oxford: Blackwell, 1967). The English translation, *Wittgenstein and the Vienna Circle* (Oxford: Blackwell, 1979), matches the pagination of the original edition.

Z   *Zettel*, ed. G. E. M. Anscombe and G. H. von Wright, trans. G. E. M. Anscombe (Oxford: Blackwell, 1967).

Part I

Aristotle

1

The Good, the Noble, and the Theoretical in *Eudemian Ethics* VIII.3

SARAH BROADIE

1. Introduction

It is a great pleasure to share this celebration of Anthony Kenny's magnificent contributions, practical as well as theoretical, to philosophical scholarship and to the wider academic life. My paper returns to the difficult last chapter of the *Eudemian Ethics*, 1248b8–1249b25. This text is central to the third of Anthony Kenny's three—to date—monographs on Aristotle's ethics, *Aristotle on the Perfect Life* (1992).[1] Kenny has also discussed it in chapters 7 and 8 of his first monograph on Aristotle, *The Aristotelian Ethics*.[2] *Eudemian Ethics* VIII.3 deserves considerable attention as providing a philosophically rich discussion along lines that are barely hinted at elsewhere in Aristotle.[3] Here I undertake a philosophical reading, building in part on Kenny's 1992 explication. The textual sources raise a number of problems, but I shall mostly pass them over.[4] For the most part I follow the Oxford Classical Text of Walzer and Mingay.[5]

---

[1] A. Kenny, *Aristotle on the Perfect Life* (Oxford: Clarendon Press, 1992).

[2] A. Kenny, *The Aristotelian Ethics* (Oxford: Clarendon Press, 1978).

[3] The main hint elsewhere is *Magna Moralia* II.9, which gives a significantly different sketch of *kalok'agathia* (unless it is simply confused), and mentions neither God nor the theoretical part of the soul.

[4] For detailed discussions of text and translation, see F. Dirlmeier, *Aristoteles Eudemische Ethik, übersetzt und kommentiert* (Berlin: Akademie-Verlag, 1969); W. Verdenius, 'Human Reason and God in the *Eudemian Ethics*', in P. Moraux and D. Harlfinger (eds), *Untersuchungen zur Eudemischen Ethik* (Acts of the Vth Symposium Aristotelicum) (Berlin: de Gruyter, 1971); M. Woods, *Aristotle, Eudemian Ethics, Books I, II, and VIII, translated with a commentary* (2nd edn, Oxford: Oxford University Press, 1992), as well as Kenny, *The Aristotelian Ethics*, and *Aristotle on the Perfect Life*. Reasons for choices adopted in the present essay are to be found in the above scholarship and in other works to which it refers.

[5] R. Walzer and J. Mingay (eds), *Aristotelis Ethica Eudemia* (Oxford: Oxford University Press, 1991).

Eudemian Ethics, 1248b8–1249b25 falls into two parts, the former about twice as long as the latter. The first one (ending at 1249a21) is the main body of the chapter, and the second is an important coda.[6] The main body lays out a distinction between the *good* man, the *agathos*, and the *noble-and-good* one, the *kalosk'agathos*. This is based on a prior dichotomy of 'goods that are ends...desirable for their own sake' (1248b18–26) into those that are, and those that are not, noble and praiseworthy. The non-praiseworthy ones, the *merely* good ends, are called 'the natural goods'.[7] After developing the difference between the *agathos* and the *kalosk'agathos* Aristotle moves to the coda, which raises and answers the question: what is the limit, *horos*, by which the person of excellence, *ho spoudaios* (1249a24), judges what quantity of natural goods he should acquire and possess? The answer, Aristotle says, is to be found by considering the excellent person's controlling principle, the *archê* to which he stands as slave to master. With frustrating brevity Aristotle speaks of this *archê* as God, and of the appropriate service as contemplation, *theôria*, of God.[8] The quantitative limit on the natural goods is the amount necessary and sufficient to maximize the presence of this *theôria* in human life.

2. Natural Goods and the Good Person

The first part of VIII.3 rounds off the *Eudemian Ethics* account of complete (or: perfect), *teleios*, virtue, which figures in the definition of *eudaimonia* as activity of complete vitality (*zôê*) in accordance with complete virtue (1219a35–9). In that context it was made clear that the completeness, both of vitality and of virtue, is that of a whole missing none of its parts (see also 1220a2–4; cf. 13–14). Thus the *Eudemian Ethics* is committed to the thesis

---

[6] It has not been possible in this paper to dwell on the important stretch of text, 1249a17–21, that ends the main part. Here Aristotle, alluding to points made earlier (*Eudemian Ethics* (hereafter *EE*) VII, 1235b30–1236a7; 1237a4–9; 26–7), states the coincidence between what is good, what is pleasant, and what is noble, concluding that the truly happy person will live most pleasantly. The text is problematic, and the argument elliptical: it is not clear where all its premisses come from. The preceding argument has secured the coincidence of the noble and the naturally good for the *kalosk'agathos* (and only for him); so what is new is the inclusion of the pleasant. The *kalosk'agathos* has by now been shown to be the person of 'complete virtue' (1249a16–17), in terms of which *eudaimonia* was defined at I, 1219a35–9; so including pleasure gives Aristotle the result that human beings are right to believe that the *eudaimôn* lives most pleasantly. Kenny (*Aristotle on the Perfect Life*, pp. 21–2) shows very clearly that the passage answers the Delian inscription with its implication of an inevitable divergence (cf. 1249a11 and 1237a8–9) between the beneficial, the noble, and the pleasant. The *EE* opens with an emphatic rejection of this piece of traditional wisdom (1214a1–8). Woods overlooks the connection.

[7] At 1249a12 and 1249b24 they are called 'the things that are good without qualification' (the phrase is also used at 1249a19, probably with the same reference), and at 1249a15, 'the external goods'.

[8] Keeping the MSS reading at 1249b17.

that *eudaimonia* is activity in accordance with all the many human virtues.[9]
VIII.3 begins with the statement that while the 'particular' virtues have been
discussed (*kata meros*, 1248b8), we still have to explain the virtue that 'is based
on [*ek*] them', which is *kalok'agathia* (1248b8–15). (The particular virtues
are defined by reference to the particular spheres in which they operate,
whereas *kalok'agathia* is a general attitude to virtue as such.) The explanation
concludes with the statement that *kalok'agathia* (i.e. what that quality has
now been shown to be) is complete virtue (1249a17). What is made clear
along the way is that one can have all the particular virtues, and not have
kalok'agathia.[10]

The explanation begins with a taxonomy of goods. Goods are divided into
those that are ends (*telê*) desirable for themselves and those that are not ends.
Ends are then divided into those that are noble and those that are not, the mark
of the noble being that they are proper objects of praise. For example, the
qualities of justice and moderation, from which come praiseworthy actions,
are themselves praiseworthy too. By contrast, health and physical strength, and
the exercises of them, are non-praiseworthy ends and goods (1248b16–26)[11].

But are health and physical strength and so forth really *goods*? Of course they
are: they are the things that are 'good by nature': it belongs to normal human
nature to find them desirable. Aristotle adds more examples—honour, wealth,
physical excellences in general, episodes of good fortune, capacities—with an
observation: these are 'the things that are fought over and are regarded as the
greatest goods'. In fact, he goes on, these things are very far from being good

---

[9] There is a puzzle over how such a comprehensively virtuous activity can occur. Circumstances
calling for exercise of physical courage would not normally call for exercise of liberality (to do with
getting and spending). Aristotle may mean (a) that one is not *eudaimôn* unless for each kind of situation
one is ready to manifest whichever virtue is relevant, and (b) that one's activity in each case is *eudaimonia*.
Similarly, pentathletic success in a contest accrues to someone for superb performance in each of the
five skills, if and only if he *would* also perform superbly in the others.

[10] Thus *ek* at 1248b10 cannot mean 'automatically results from them'.

[11] It is not explicit here that these are ends desirable in themselves, but since they are co-ordinate in
the taxonomy with the noble goods, and it has been said that the noble goods are a subdivision of goods
that are ends desirable in themselves, it follows that health and strength are in another subdivision of the
same. This may surprise us, given that wealth is an example of this subdivision (1248b28; cf. 1249a9;
1249b2; 18), for surely wealth is *not* to be classed as an ultimate end of human action. The puzzle
disappears if we understand that Aristotle is not using 'end desirable in itself' as entailing 'ultimate end
of human action', but rather as meaning 'objective that can be intelligently pursued without considering
what use (if any) will be made of it when achieved'. The thought is that since wealth is a single sort of
thing that can be used for indefinitely many further purposes, the work of producing it is not shaped
by any specific further objective. Thus the work focuses on it as an end and desirable *tout court*. By
contrast, a shoemaker uses different means and materials depending on the projected use of the shoes
(for football or ballet?). See S. Broadie, *Ethics with Aristotle* (New York: Oxford University Press, 1991),
p. 382 (interpretation accepted by Kenny in *Aristotle on the Perfect Life*). Cf. the discussion of deliberation
at 1227a5 ff., where wealth is coupled with pleasure as an example of an end (14–15); also 1217a36–9.

for, or in relation to,[12] every agent: in the hands of the fool, the unjust man, the immoderate person, they are damaging (to the agent himself but also indirectly to others, we are surely to think). Such people are unable to manage the natural goods properly, just as the ailing or physically weak cannot 'handle' the diet or regime that is right for the healthy individual (1248b26–34). Aristotle's use of the standard analogy between moral goodness and physical health indicates that the harm he envisages from the natural goods is moral harm. The point is not that greed, foolishness, or injustice can damage people's fortunes and reputations. For in thinking of e.g. diabetics given the same diet as the healthy, we focus only on how their illness thereby intensifies *itself*, not on how it might lead to some non-medical evil such as poverty. So the point is that the natural goods have the potential to consolidate and deepen an agent's moral deformity (more temptations available, more resources for over-reaching with, more ways of avoiding legal and social sanctions). Such a case also transmits moral damage more widely, if people are impressed by it as a model of good living.

Now we can say what it is for someone to be a *good* person: it is to be such that, possessed by him, the natural goods are not simply goods in the abstract or in general, but concretely and determinately earn their titles of 'goods' and 'ends'. They are actually good—actually add value to human living—only if the life (*zōē*) in whose orbit they appear is not being badly lived. Added to a badly lived life, they make it a worse one (more irresponsible, unjust, immoderate), removing it yet further from *eudaimonia* than it was already removed.

Before turning to the difference between the (merely) good person and the one who is noble-and-good, let us note one or two things about the account so far. It is, we may think, a rather muted account. The 'good' man has been delineated by contrast with the foolish, the unjust, the immoderate. He is simply the person who is not disposed to behave like them. Why is nothing positive said or in an obvious way implied about the good person: e.g. that he or she uses the natural goods to do just and wise things that might otherwise not be forthcoming? Could it be that what Aristotle means here by 'being (merely) good' is being somehow less than fully possessed of the virtues of justice and temperance, etc.? Is the idea that the good man has qualities that keep him out of moral trouble, but that do not live up to the

---

[12] 'In relation to' is better than 'for' (adopted by most translators). 'For' suggests that only the agent's own welfare is at stake. But the point (I take it) covers the case when use of the natural goods affects others. In bad hands they can harm even those whom the agent intends to benefit (e.g. spoiling one's children).

full meaning of 'justice', 'wisdom' etc.?[13] In response: I think that the standard conceptual connection between being a good so-and-so and having the virtue or virtues of a so-and-so is too strong to be overridden with no indication given.[14] (Where 'good', as here, is said without qualification, it is because the goodness in question is understood to be that of a rational, practical, human being as such.) That connection by itself is ground for accepting that the good man of *Eudemian Ethics* VIII.3 genuinely possesses the ordinary virtues. In addition, *kalok'agathia*, whatever exactly it is, has already been depicted as including the ordinary (the particular) virtues. Hence if the merely good man here has only watered-down versions of these, the obvious inference is that the full versions only exist when accompanied by *kalok'agathia*. But it seems very unlikely that Aristotle would have failed to make this point here (where he is carefully explaining what is involved in 'complete virtue') if it had been part of what he intends. And after all it is no small thing to be the sort of person who reliably stays out of moral trouble. How is this possible except through possession of the standard virtues? In presenting goodness through a contrast with disastrous possibilities that the natural goods place in the way of foolish, unjust, and immoderate agents, Aristotle puts uppermost the fact (no doubt implicit but not emphasized in the main *Eudemian Ethics* account of moral virtue, II. 2–5[15]) that the virtuous man is incorruptible. For what corrupts the corruptible is the prospect of having or losing some natural good.

By referring to the harm-potential of the natural goods, Aristotle taps into the ancient Greek sense, never far from the surface, of the fragility of the *goodness* of the natural goods. As witnessed in countless myths and legends, blessings can turn into curses or can turn out to have been curses all along. Life itself, and a natural lifespan, the most obvious of the natural goods, can become abominable. Such reversals of value are frightful not least because

---

[13] This is the view of Woods (*Eudemian Ethics*, p. 176); also of Rachel Barney, 'Comments on Sarah Broadie, "Virtue and Beyond in Plato and Aristotle"', *Southern Journal of Philosophy*, vol. 43, suppl. (2005), pp. 115–25. Woods's premises are: (1) that elsewhere in the *EE* (as in the *Nicomachean Ethics* (hereafter *NE*)) 'acting for the sake of the noble' is a necessary condition of courage (which must be supposed to be one of what I am calling the 'ordinary' virtues) and of virtue in general (cf. 1229a1–9; 1230a26–33), and (2) that in *EE* VIII.3 Aristotle restricts acting for the sake of the noble to the noble-and-good character. I argue below (see esp. n. 24) that the evidence of VIII.3 does not compel us to accept (2). Barney's discussion is complex and wide-ranging. I hope that mine in this and the next two sections goes some way to meet her points.

[14] Thus Aristotle does not say of the Laconian kind of people (about to be discussed) that they are *agathoi pôs*; see esp.1249a1: *agathoi men andres eisin*.

[15] This account has nothing corresponding to the *NE*'s requirement of 'a firm and unchanging disposition', 1105a33. That idea is touched on at *EE* 1238a12–14, but only as a spin-off from a discussion of firmness of friendship.

they retrospectively hollow out the efforts of those concerned. Practical life is through and through concerned with acquiring and protecting the natural goods and avoiding their opposites. If someone's life has a feature such that in its presence it becomes the case that the agent would have been better off failing than succeeding in pursuit of some good of the kind that it belongs to human nature to need, desire, hope for, plan for, work and calculate for, pray for, and be delighted to attain, then that feature makes nonsense of the person's expense of spirit in relation to that good. (At the extreme it makes nonsense of his or her practical agency *tout court*.) The presence of such a feature also makes nonsense of any expense of spirit by others in helping the agent secure the good. As long as the feature has been present, or as long as it has been developing unchecked, so long should this agent have been facing the opposite way, preferring weakness, poverty, friendlessness, early death or never to have been born; and the agent's supporters should have wanted *those* things for him or her—and possibly even for themselves rather than the resources and relationships that gave them a natural opportunity to support the person in question.[16] According to this way of looking at the natural goods, the agent's position at the extreme (even if he or she is unaware of it) is the objective correlate of the subjective perspective of the severely depressed person. Depression makes it seem as if all practical efforts on one's own behalf are pointless and may just as well fail as succeed; and on an axiological view of the sort that we are considering, the presence of whatever plays the role of X makes such a judgement true, even for an agent with no inkling that this is so, and full of energy and plans.

Such a view about the natural goods takes two main forms, which we may call archaic and enlightened. In the archaic form, X is a decree of fate or an angry divine intervention that converts A's most precious possession (Niobe's children, Oedipus' intelligence and royal status) into a source of spectacular misery. In the enlightened form, the evil demon X is A's own bad character.[17] In the latter case, the disaster of what unfolds can remain unknown throughout to A. And whereas in the archaic perspective the disaster may well have been humanly unavoidable, in the enlightened one it was not, since the character of human beings depends on the values and actions of human beings, their own and those of their fellows.

---

[16] I have discussed this more fully in my 'On the Idea of the *summum bonum*', in C. Gill (ed.), *Value, Norms, and Objectivity* (Oxford: Oxford University Press, 2005), pp. 41–58; reprinted in Broadie, *Aristotle and Beyond: Essays on Metaphysics and Ethics* (Cambridge: Cambridge University Press, 2007), ch. 9.

[17] Heraclitus B119.

3. The 'Laconian' Type (I)

It is time to turn to the difference between the merely good and the noble-and-good. Aristotle says that what makes someone noble-and-good is (a) that the goods that are noble pertain to him (*huparchein autôi*) because of themselves, and (b) that he is active (*praktikos*) about noble things, namely the virtues and their works (1248b34–7), for their own sakes. This passage does not, in my view, support the notion that Aristotle's *kalosk'agathos* is interested only in maintaining and exercising his own virtues. Clause (b) plainly allows for working to promote noble things in others and in the community; and in clause (a) what is emphasized is not that noble things are *his* attributes, but that they are realized in him on account of themselves. Moreover, *huparchein autôi*[18] is very abstract: the meaning may be only that noble things are in his life, whether as attributes of his or as objects to which he stands in some different logical relation.

Aristotle now develops the idea of the noble-and-good person through a contrast with what he calls the Laconian (i.e. Spartan) type:

There exists a certain civic disposition [*tis hexis politikê*], such as is had by the Laconians and others of that kind. This disposition is as follows. There are those who think that one must have virtue[19]—but for the sake of the natural goods. Thus they are good men, for the natural goods are good in relation to them; but they do not have noble-goodness, for it is not the case that noble things pertain to them on account of [the noble things] themselves . . . (1248b37–1249a3)[20]

How are we to understand the Laconian type? First, it clearly excludes someone who always aims to maximize the natural goods for himself, or his family and particular friends. Even if his actual actions, except for the motive, tend to match those of the virtuous person, he is not virtuous. The virtuous reliably respond to the moral shape of the situation, and the moral shape may require one to forgo natural goods for self and favourite others, e.g. when anything else would be unjust. Thus even if the character sketched never does anything wrong, in counterfactual situations not far removed from the actual we have to suppose that he would. So he is not virtuous—not 'good'. But the Laconian

---

[18] See also at 1249a2–3.

[19] This might also be translated 'one must be disposed virtuously' with *echein* picking up *hexis* at 1248b38 and the accusative understood as an internal object; similarly for *echousi* and *echoien* at 38–9.

[20] At 1249a3–4 I accept Kenny's emendation (Kenny, *Aristotle on the Perfect Life*, p. 13) whereby 2–4 reads: *ou gar huparchei autois ta kala di' hauta. <ta de kala di' hauta> {kai} prohairountai kaloik'agathoi.* 'For noble things do not belong to them on account of [the noble things] themselves. But noble-and-good men choose noble things on account of [the noble things] themselves'.

type is said to be good. Moreover, at 1249a8 Aristotle says that the Laconian disposition is 'civic':[21] it makes for decent citizens and a decent city. In some societies the civic arrangements may make it fairly unlikely that doing what the virtuous person would anyway do diverges sharply or often from individual pursuit of the natural goods. There may be in place a sensible system of easily enforceable deterrents against free-riding. But the disposition that would free-ride if one could get away with it makes no positive contribution to upholding the general system; it simply fails to damage it under the given circumstances. The same individuals can of course be expected to be positive about the civic arrangements when it comes to insisting on punishment for others who free-ride. But they are not undividedly friends of those arrangements: they are partly keen to uphold them and partly they accept them with bad grace. This mixed attitude is not what one would call 'civic' without qualification, since undivided or impartial loyalty to the system is obviously a superior candidate for that title.

So: since the Laconian type is virtuous, his particular responses are conceived and carried out in the frame of mind characteristic of virtue; he is ready to forgo the natural goods when the situation demands this of a good person, and to forgo them simply because the situation demands it. It must be, then, that where he falls short of the noble-and-good man is in his general attitude to the virtues and virtuous actions. Presumably one can be virtuous in the ordinary way without having formed a general view about the value of virtue. But if the Laconian type is pressed for a view on this, he comes up with an answer that seems to him to make sense. Or perhaps it is enough to see him as one whose view this would be if he had a view. He holds: 'One *must* have virtue'—it is a necessity, not an intrinsic good—'for the sake of the natural goods'.[22]

We can understand this in one or both of two ways,[23] or as inde-terminate between them. First, the Laconian type may in effect be a rule-consequentialist:[24] to him, the *raison d'être* of upright, courageous, tem-perate practices by everyone, and therefore of shared dispositions for these, is the consequent general prosperity in terms of the natural goods. (He knows, like everyone, that the natural goods tend to be 'fought-over' (1248b27), and regards strife in the city as one of the worst of evils.) Such a view

---

[21] Briefly discussed by Kenny (*Aristotle on the Perfect Life*, p. 10); more fully by Barney, 'Comments', pp. 120–2.

[22] Aristotle finds a number of faults with the education and outlook of the actual Laconians, including this: 'They think, rightly, that the fought-over goods come about through virtue rather than through vice; but they are mistaken in believing that these things are superior to virtue', *Politics* 1271b7–10.

[23] For the second way, see Section 4. I discussed the Laconian type, but without distinguishing the two ways, in Broadie, *Ethics with Aristotle*, pp. 373–88.

[24] Cf. Kenny, *Aristotle on the Perfect Life*, p. 14, n. 17; cf. Barney, 'Comments', p. 125, n. 6.

incorporates a reasonable efficient-causal claim linking virtuous conduct with group-prosperity. The causal link, together with the fundamental importance of the natural goods for a decent human life, makes not implausible the Laconian view that they are also the final-causal explanation of the value of virtuous conduct and virtuous dispositions. In fact, Aristotle himself would have powerful reason to draw this teleological conclusion were he studying human culture and society simply as objects of an Aristotelian natural science. Such a perspective, in a pure form, would probably smile at the judgements and feelings of some humans that the conduct which humans praise as 'virtuous' is immensely worthwhile for its own sake. The dispositions of thinking in such ways would probably seem, from that perspective, to be part of human nature's mechanism for securing group-prosperity, just as (we might suppose) ants laying down stores for winter need to treat their fetching and carrying as worthwhile in itself in order to do the work well; we might consider them capable of this sort of motivation but incapable of the planning and fear of future hunger that would otherwise be necessary to drive their efforts.[25]

However, if the Aristotelian scientist studying human culture and society regards the intellectual enterprises of natural philosophy, pure mathematics, and metaphysics as valuable in themselves for beings like him, i.e. valuable but not because engaging in them or believing in the intrinsic value of doing so helps accumulate and preserve the natural goods for his group, this scientist ought—except on one condition—to take seriously the claims of some of the humans he is studying that virtuous conduct is immensely valuable in itself. The excepting condition is that in which this natural scientist is from Mars[26]—a member of a non-human species. Such a creature might be incapable

---

[25] On the reflective level, the consequentialist Laconian type can hold such a view about the human moral attitude to human virtues and virtuous dispositions. (Meta-ethically, he is either an expressivist about that attitude, or regards it as incorporating the false judgement that its objects are valuable for themselves.) On the ground-level, he can wholeheartedly praise these and applaud them as noble. At 1248b19 ff. Aristotle treats it as a common place that virtuous actions and dispositions are praiseworthy and noble; he could not do that so easily if he thinks that many ordinary virtuous people are devoid of this attitude to virtues and virtuous dispositions! It would fit in with this to allow that, at ground-level, persons of the Laconian type act *tou kalou heneka*, 'for the sake of the noble'; actions of the particular virtues are done in this spirit, according to Aristotle (for the *EE*, see 1229a1–4; 9; 1230a27–9). But this seems to clash with 1249a15, which says that because the Laconian type thinks we must have the virtues for the sake of the external goods, he does (*prattei*) noble things *per accidens*, i.e. not because they are noble. However, rather than referring to particular episodes of action (this, I think, must be Kenny's assumption at Kenny, *Aristotle on the Perfect Life*, p. 14), the sentence may express Aristotle's comment on what the Laconian type—a reflective type—would say if interrogated *as* a reflective type: 'Why does the type that *I* am do noble things? The type that I am does (*prattô*) those things because they are necessary for the natural goods'. A similar interpretation applies to the implication of 1249a6 that what the Laconian type acts for the sake of, is not noble.

[26] For more than one reason Aristotle would find this condition absurd or incoherent.

of seeing anything important in common between those human claims and his own assumption of the intrinsic value of science for beings like himself. That condition apart, since the scientist cannot but take his own assumption seriously, he ought to take seriously claims by others of his own kind that correspondingly insist on a value independent of (even though, in the case of virtuous practical activity, often not separated from) conduciveness to the natural goods.

It may look as if I have given the above argument on the assumption that some actual Aristotelian scientist could have needed it in order to become convinced that virtuous practice is valuable in itself. But is this not an artificially imagined situation that gets things the wrong way round? For it is plausible to think that, anyway in Aristotle's day, there were those, the noble-and-good people, who already believed or were inclined to believe in the independent intrinsic value of virtuous practice, and on that basis could be brought by Aristotle to endorse by analogy the less widely accepted point that excellent theoretical activity is of great value in itself.[27] But the purpose of the argument about the Aristotelian scientist studying human beings was not to convince anyone of the intrinsic value of virtuous practice; it was to bring out the fact, surely of some interest, that if one were studying humans purely as objects of Aristotelian natural science it might be very difficult if not impossible, given the data observable from that point of view, to avoid inferring that the natural goods are in fact the *telos* of at any rate the human *group*. Aristotle's rejection of such an account of the human *telos* is rational because humans to him are fellow-beings of his—not simply objects of theoretical study—and some of these fellow-beings have an attitude to practising the practical virtues that is akin to his own to the practice of excellent theorizing. If their attitude to practical virtue is congenial to him, so that he endorses it, he cannot arrive at the theory of human nature which the facts of human behaviour would suggest if considered by an uninvolved Aristotelian theorist. This is not the familiar point that a detached theoretical perspective on human nature is different from the one we occupy when making ethical judgements. The point is directed against the thought that studying human nature from a detached perspective places no limit on what ethical judgements are available on our return to the ethical perspective. The thought is that one could in principle settle the uninvolved theoretical science of human nature, and then, resuming the ethical stance, still make any ethical judgement one had previously been disposed to make. This assumes that no ethical judgement would force rejection of the uninvolved theoretical account, whereas in the Aristotelian situation

---

[27] Cf. Broadie, *Ethics with Aristotle*, pp. 383–8.

this looks not to be so. For Aristotle's endorsement of the intrinsic value of virtuous activity commits him to dismissing a perfectly uninvolved Aristotelian scientist's most reasonable theory of human nature. This, however, is not because of the general uncombinability of ethical and theoretical perspectives in a single inquiry; it is because of the specifically *teleological* character of any Aristotelian science of a living species.

4. The 'Laconian' Type (II)

The preceding discussion arose from our first way of understanding the Laconian type's view of the value of virtuous conduct: he is a rule-consequentialist for whom the ultimate justifier of virtuous activity is adequate and secure possession by men of the natural goods. According to what I propose as a second way, the natural goods stand to the Laconian type rather as the medical objective, health, stands to the medical expert. The medical practitioner as such is constrained by various ethical requirements, e.g. confidentiality, which may, but need not, be understood by him or her in rule-consequentialist fashion, i.e. as important *solely* because consistent observance promotes health. (People are deterred from going to doctors whose discretion cannot be trusted.) I would suppose it much more common that medical practitioners take these requirements on board simply because it is right, proper, fair, respectful to practise in accordance with them—no further reason given or felt to be needed. And so with other expertises and their characteristic ethical rules.[28] The experts, I would think, are commonly deontologists about these rules, and about the particular ethical judgements made in light of them. Now, the point is that even if physicians are deontologists about such requirements on medical practice, if asked as physicians what they do, what their activity is all about, they would say: 'the promotion of health'. This promotion, and the health promoted, are what the physicians take themselves to be for. They care about the ethical requirements of their practice because this is an aspect of being a good medical practitioner, just as a good and truly professional golfer is a good loser at golf.

The professional ethical requirements are a necessary part of the framework within which the profession operates (necessary for it to be decent, worthy of respect, and perhaps possible at all in society), but, however necessary, observing them is not what the professional centrally *does*. I think that this is

---

[28] See also Barney on the virtuous agent as 'practitioner of Kuhnian "normal science"' (Barney, 'Comments', pp. 117–18).

enough to make sense of the statement: observing the ethical requirements, and reliability in observing them, is *for the sake of* practising the expertise, which (when there is a product) is in turn for the sake of the product. In a similar way, I suggest, one might think about the natural goods: they are what human life is all about, although it is not living well to pursue them or want to pursue them outside the boundaries demanded by justice, moderation, and courage. The virtue-terms become taken-for-granted adverbs on the phrases 'acquire, preserve, *A*, *B*, and *C*', where '*A*', '*B*', and '*C*' refer to natural goods. In the Laconian case, these adverbs are never missing; but they are, all the same, parenthetical. Hence *X* has done better, lived better, achieved more as a human being, than *Y* if within the deontologically accepted ethical boundaries *X* ends up with a greater measure of natural goods than *Y*. And it fits in with this, although it is not logically necessary, to allow the 'if' of the previous sentence to slip into becoming 'only if'. Thus the person who risks losing out on natural goods for the sake of pursuing some brave, imaginative, venture, or to help those to whom he has no recognized duty, or to bring about an unpopular reform which if successful would dignify the city in ways unforeseeable to most people, or to master and promote an abstruse theoretical subject, will seem rather wild, foolish, and overreaching (even if he does not risk anyone's goods but his own): not a safe model to copy, but one of whom we say 'Who does he think he is?' since he holds lightly, or even behaves as if he despises, what *we* as human beings are all about.

Aristotle, I think, does not have to choose between these models of the Laconian type, the rule-consequentialist one and the deontological one. The difference between consequentialist and deontological approaches is all-important in the debate over what makes right action right. However, Aristotle in our passage is concerned with the good, not the right, and with different ways of valuing the good of virtuous activity in relation to the natural goods. From this point of view it hardly matters whether the Laconian type is a consequentialist or a deontologist about the importance of virtuous conduct, or whether Laconians are divided between these views, or whether the views are conflated either by them or by Aristotle. The differences between these possibilities are negligible from the point of view of the question: is virtuous conduct a good that is properly valued for itself, or does it get its value from some subsidiary place it has in relation to the natural goods? For in all the cases surveyed the Laconian type endorses the second alternative.[29]

[29] 'For the sake of' is so loose that, on either model, if the Laconian view enters public discourse under the crude formula 'Virtue is for the sake of the natural goods', there is the danger of the formula's being taken up by others in a sense that sanctions moral corner-cutting when one can get away with

5. The Noble-and-Good-Person

We return to the *kalosk'agathos*. With this type as with the Laconian the
distinctive mark is not a special motive for particular decisions and actions, but
a general attitude towards the virtues and their exercise. For the *kalosk'agathos*,
these come first, and the natural goods, and our natural interest in them,
constitute opportunities and means for promoting and exercising virtue.

In the discussion so far, 'natural goods' and 'noble goods' have referred to
mutually exclusive kinds. But now Aristotle moves to complete a pattern. We
have seen (1) the good person's defining relation to the natural goods: his
ways with them are wise, just, and moderate; (2) the noble-and-good person's
defining relation to the noble goods; (3) the merely good (Laconian-like)
person's relation (attitude) to these noble goods; and now we are given (4) the
relation of the noble-and-good to the natural goods. Aristotle says of the
noble-and-good:

It is also the case that the things that are not noble by nature but are good by nature
are noble in relation to these persons. For that which is just is noble, and this [sc. that
which is just] is that which accords with worth; and this man is worthy of these things.
Also, that which is fitting is noble, and these things are fitting for this man: wealth,
good birth, power.   (1249a4–10)

In the orbit of the *kalosk'agathos*, the natural goods are themselves ennobled.
This is because there is a kind of justice and fittingness about his having them,
since he is worthy of them.

The combination 'wealth, good birth, power' suggests that the power
and wealth in question here are notable by the standards of the society.
Aristotle does not exclude from being noble-and-good individuals who lack
the combination; this would fly in the face of what he has said in defining the
noble-and-good. But here he focuses on the elements of social and economic
privilege, whose possessors are traditionally ranked *kaloik'agathoi*. And in the
context, this focus implies that tradition has it wrong: pre-eminent wealth,
pre-eminent political influence, and good family, are not what make someone
noble-and-good. They could do so only if such things were noble by nature,
but this is true only of the virtues and their exercises, whereas the former
are merely natural goods. Moreover, as he has explained, mere possession
of the goods noble by nature is not enough to make their good possessor
noble-and-good: for this, the possessor must also value the things noble by

it; see Broadie, 'Virtue and Beyond in Plato and Aristotle', *Southern Journal of Philosophy*, vol. 43, suppl.
(2005), pp. 97–114, 108–9, and Broadie, *Ethics with Aristotle*, pp. 379–81.

nature for their own sake, regarding them as noble. It is surely also implied that there is something *aischron*, ignoble, about pre-eminent wealth and status when those who possess them fall short of being *kaloik'agathoi* according to Aristotle's own definition. Furthermore, when the possessors *are* Aristotelian *kaloik'agathoi*, others should not resent their privileged position, for it is right and fitting that this should go with *kalok'agathia*. But (it is surely implied) resentment is not unreasonable when the privileged, no less than the common people, elevate the natural goods as be-all and end-all: this is paradigmatic 'vulgarity', in fact. Contrary to what many people think, good birth cannot in itself make it right and fitting and not to be resented that the well-born possess great wealth and power, for good birth is only another of the natural goods. Far from automatically ennobling wealth and power and its own possessor, good birth in itself is not noble.

In saying that the *kalosk'agathos* justly possesses good birth, wealth, and power because he is worthy of them, Aristotle invokes the idea of divine justice.[30] (*Kalok'agathia* confers no Calliclean natural right to seize an ordinary person's possessions!) But the thought cannot be that social status, wealth, and power are god-sent rewards that target *kalok'agathia*, since it is plain that non-*kalok'agathoi* and even bad men may have them too; they depend in part on luck (cf. 1248b29; 1249b3). The god by whose standard the *kaloik'agathoi* are entitled to their natural goods does not steer the course of luck in respect of such goods. This is because, as Aristotle says in a nearby passage, God's rule does not take the form of giving orders (1249b13–14). Is Aristotle here rejecting the notion of God as source of the moral law? No, the idea (I think) is rather that God does not have the function (or the power) of enforcing the divine standard. One who gives orders also controls some mechanism of sanctions. So God rules—but not by giving orders, because the implementation of the divine ethical standard is in the hands of human beings: independent initiators of action. This is why it is true *both* that the collocation of wealth, good birth, and power with genuine *kalok'agathia* accords with what is just by God's standard, *and* that it can be a matter of luck not morality who has these natural goods. (There is a conflict between the two propositions only on the assumption that it is for God to bring reality into line with the standard.) More precisely: when human beings have pre-eminent natural goods (and this is usually through the luck of birth), it is a matter for their own initiative whether or not they turn out to deserve them by God's standard of justice.

---

[30] Cf. 1233b23–6: 'Intermediate is the *nemesêtikos*, and what the ancients called *nemesis*, the <disposition> to be pained by prosperity and misfortune [of others] when undeserved, pleased when deserved; for which reason people actually think that *nemesis* is a God'.

6. The Right Quantity of Natural Goods?

I now turn to the coda (1249a21–b25). The question here is: what is the excellent (*spoudaios*[31]) person's limit or standard (*horos*) for determining what amount, great or small, of the natural goods he should have, and choose, and avoid? Something more illuminating should, and can, be said than the truism: 'What the correct prescription indicates' (1249b3–6). Aristotle's answer starts by heading in what appears to be the clear direction of saying: the right amount is whatever most facilitates devotion to one's ruling principle. However, Aristotle pauses to explain 'rule', and then plunges into some remarks about 'the theoretical' (*to theoretikon*, 1249b13) and about God and serving God. All this is notoriously obscure. But before proceeding to detailed interpretation, let us look at how the question of the right quantity of natural goods arises in the context of the main body of the chapter.[32]

Although it is obvious that both the merely good person and the *kalosk'agathos* act virtuously with respect to the natural goods, this description can fit agents who (whether for themselves or for others) obtain, hold, and operate with these goods in widely varying amounts. It is natural—certainly, tempting—to suppose that, given virtue and virtuous activity as constant over the range of variation, the lives involving more of the natural goods are *pro tanto* better human lives than those involving less. Thus the merely good live better and less well than each other depending on which of them has more, which less, of the natural goods; and similarly for the *kaloik'agathoi* as compared with one another. But this judgement risks uprooting what has been established, for it suggests that the natural goods have an axiological life of their own. If more of them makes a virtuous life, or a *kalosk'agathos* life, better—but not by making anyone more or more effectively virtuous or *kalosk'agathos*—then the whole notion that virtue is the source of the real value of the natural goods is called into question. To agree that more of them by itself makes one good life better than another is to play into the hands of anyone who thinks that simply having plenty of the natural goods is alone enough to make a life good.

The Laconian type, of course, does not think in this debased way, since he thinks that you cannot have plenty of the natural goods *alone*: you must have virtue too, for the sake of them. But what if the Laconian type realizes that the amount of natural goods can increase significantly although the level of virtue remains the same? Certainly if he is a natural-goods consequentialist about the

---

[31] From the context it is clear that this is the *kalosk'agathos*, the enthusiast for virtue and virtuous actions (*spoudê* = seriousness, dedication).

[32] Commentators have not always noted clearly that the question is about *quantity*.

value of virtue and virtuous action, he embraces the thought that a greater amount of natural goods automatically makes for a better life. In that case he should, if consistent, value whatever the non-moral means or qualities are that produce the increase in natural goods at least as much as he values virtue. So he ought to admire e.g. sheer cleverness at making money as much, and in the same way, as he admires virtue. New qualities will become human virtues in his eyes, and when there is conflict between the demands of the new values and those of the old-fashioned virtues, he has no reason to opt necessarily for the latter. Thus his hold on virtue (or its on him) is loosened, and at some point it may cease to be true that he is a good person.[33] Alternatively, if he remains strict about the demands of virtue even in the case where quite other things are reliably wealth-producing and where wealth of individuals and communities can often be seen to protect itself very effectively even at the expense of justice to other individuals or communities, then he may now feel logically forced to acknowledge that he is treating right-doing as important in itself. He is now, and consciously, a deontologist; or at any rate he is not a natural goods-consequentialist. He may still believe that, within the constraints of ordinary virtue (which he treats with a kind of piety, possibly drawn from recognized religion[34]) a greater amount of the natural goods makes life better, and thus he may go on as before except for conscious rejection of natural goods-consequentialism. On the other hand, he may be unsatisfied with that view of what makes life better, and instead pursue a better life through new and more enterprising ways of exercising and promoting recognized virtues, and perhaps through promoting and exercising less commonly recognized virtues, all for their own sakes. If so, this Laconian person has turned into a *kalosk'agathos*.

Where the degree of people's control and enjoyment of natural goods is in proportion to their adherence to the ordinary virtues, it is a natural and forgivable mistake (given the pervasive importance of the natural goods for human life) to regard the virtues as valuable only because they are necessary for the natural goods. When the balance shifts so that control and even enjoyment of natural goods is notably in excess of what could be achieved, under different circumstances, by the same adherence to virtue, the person whose virtue

---

[33] This possibility is forcefully urged by Barney ('Comments'), pp. 123–4, and she draws the conclusion that the person of Laconian type is not genuinely virtuous. However, since (see below in the text) a person of that type may also turn into a *kalosk'agathos*, are we in such a case to infer that he was never Laconian after all? I am not sure what to say here. While Aristotle emphasizes the stability of virtues and vices (see n. 15), he also says that people whom war 'compels' to be just and moderate may be made self-indulgent and arrogant by peace and prosperity (*Politics* VII, 1334a25–8).

[34] He may, of course, make sense of his earthly conduct in terms of supernatural-goods consequentialism referring to divine punishment and reward after death.

THE *EUDEMIAN ETHICS* VIII.3   19

and whose attitude towards it remain Laconian risks either compromising the requirements of virtue (the consequentialist) or taking a quasi-religious attitude towards them (the deontologist). The latter cares much more about those requirements than can be explained by his concern for the natural goods, and much more about the natural goods than can be explained by his concern for the requirements; and he cares about both very much. This may not raise our own philosophical eyebrows; but if not, that is because we do not accept Aristotle's assumption that a conjunction of intrinsically unrelated ultimate concerns is not a reasonable answer to the question 'What is *eudaimonia*?'

7. Rule and Being Ruled in the Noble-and-Good

Here is how Aristotle answers the question about quantity of natural goods:

(1) Well, then: as in other things, life should be lived with reference to that which rules, and with reference to the condition [*tên hexin*] relating to the activity of that which rules, just as a slave <lives> with reference to <that of> his master, and (2) each <thing> with reference to the rule that is proper to it.[35] And (3) since man too by nature consists of that which rules and that which is ruled, each element too should live with reference to the rule that is proper to it.[36] But (4) rule is twofold, since in one way the medical art is rule, and in another way health is; the former is for the sake of the latter. And (5) this is how it is with the theoretical <element in man> [*to theôrêtikon*]. For God [*ho theos*] does not rule by giving orders, but is that for the sake of which practical wisdom gives orders. That-for-the-sake-of-which is twofold (the distinction has been made in other writings)—<I say this> since *he* [sc. God], at least, is in need of nothing. [The distinction is between the beneficiary and the object of an activity, e.g. between the medical patient and health in the case of healing.[37]] So: whatever choice and possession of the natural goods will most conduce to the study of God [*tên tou theou theôrian*], whether they are <goods> of the body, or money, or friends, et cetera—this <choice and possession> is best, and this is the noblest limit. And whatever <choice and possession> either through deficiency or through excess gets in the way of serving and studying God [*ton theon therapeuein kai theôrein*]—this is a

---

[35] Deleting the OCT period after *despotou*, 8.

[36] Some translate 1249b11 by: 'each person should live with reference to the rule that is proper to him', but this seems to me to give a less tight argument. Still, if Aristotle means each element of the soul, why does he not say *hekateron* rather than *hekaston* at 11, since he has just made a dual distinction within the soul? The question is addressed by Verdenius, 'Human Reason and God in the *Eudemian Ethics*', p. 287; but see Kenny, *Aristotle on the Perfect Life*, p. 95, n. 18. The answer, surely, is that although the relation of rule to ruled is necessarily dyadic wherever it applies, *three* aspects of the soul are in play in the whole passage: the *alogon*, practical reason, and theoretical reason.

[37] Cf. *On the Soul* 415b2–3; 20–1; *Metaphysics* 1072b2–3; *Physics* 194a5–6.

poor one. (6) This applies to the soul, and the best standard for the soul is this: when one is least aware of the non-rational part of the soul as such.   (1249b6–23)

I shall discuss the passages more or less in the numbered order.

(1)–(2). Aristotle begins from the assumption that life must be lived with reference to that which rules. It quickly becomes clear that 'that which rules' has multiple reference, corresponding, as will emerge, to different sorts or levels of psychic functioning ('living'). The multiplicity is brought out at 1249b8–9: 'each thing <should live> with reference to the rule that is proper to it'. Aristotle also states that in cases where that which is ruled subserves the *condition* of that which rules, the subservience is geared to the *activity* of this condition (1249b7–8). He illustrates with the slave and master. Since he has said '*each* thing should live with reference to the rule that is proper to it', we have to ask what the rule is by reference to which the master should live (just as the slave lives by reference to the master's condition). Since the context is one that supposes a proper boundary on the amount of the natural goods, what rules the master cannot be simply those goods or the activity of pursuing them. Yet obviously the master has an activity other than that of giving orders to the slave; it would be absurd to have a slave obeying orders only so that the master is maintained in a good condition for telling the slave what to do. In fact, the illustration is analytically clearer if it tacitly implies that what I have just called the master's 'other' activity is the latter's only kind of activity, with orders to the slave being issued by an implied third party, a steward or mistress of the house.[38] So what rules the master? Since we are hardly to think of the master as a slave or servant of a higher master whose condition he subserves, the master's ruling factor must be the kind of object or objective that determines the activity of a free man: for instance, the object is virtuous practice, or good government in the city, and the activity is the engagement in or promotion of it.

(3)–(4). Aristotle proceeds to bring the ruler/ruled theme to bear on human nature as such: he states that the human being is composed of that which rules and that which is ruled, and he says that each of these elements should live with reference to the rule that belongs to it (1249b11). What is the rule that governs the ruling element within the human being? Well, if we think

---

[38] Cf. Dirlmeier (ed.) *Aristoteles Eudemische Ethik*, cited in n. 4, above. What is essential to being master is not giving orders, but ownership, i.e. his slave is there for him to dispose of for his own projects. The disposing may take the form of putting the slave under a third party's management. (This scenario exemplifies what becomes explicit at 1249b14–15, i.e. the role of practical wisdom, and the distinct ways of being that-for-the-sake-of-which. According to that distinction the condition for the master's activity is the *objective* of the third party's contribution, while the master himself is the *beneficiary*.)

of the ruling element within man on analogy with the art of medicine, then what rules *it* is something analogous to the medical objective, health, a good disposition of the patient. Medical art rules by giving orders, say to the patient's family, and is itself ruled by the health which these orders subserve. Health is a disposition to engage in and enjoy healthy bodily activities. Analogously, practical rationality within man rules by prescribing to the non-rational part of the soul (1219b28–31), and is ruled in turn by the disposition it promotes. This, surely, is the disposition to engage in and value for their own sake activities such as those mentioned above in connection with the master, and any other noble enterprises. Here it should be emphasized that the practical rationality in question is that of the *kalosk'agathos*, since he is our topic throughout. In his case, practical reason organizes the non-rational part of the soul (the slave) so that it is amenable not only to the demands of the ordinary virtues, but also to those of *kalok'agathia*.

The text allows us to choose whether to think of stewardly practical reason, and the internal master with his distinct activity, as different rational faculties, or as a single one that operates in different ways. It makes little or no difference on the interpretation presented here.[39] Either way, it is practical reason, and practical reason only, that prescribes to the non-rational part of the soul, while 'the master' does something else. The alternatives just mentioned are usually couched in terms of whether Aristotle here sees practical and theoretical reason as distinct parts of the soul, or postulates a single faculty with two functions. But in the contrast 'practical-theoretical', the second member is too narrow for the present purpose. We have been discussing *kalok'agathia*, and although this is the cover under which theoretic activity is introduced into the picture of complete virtue at the end of *Eudemian Ethics* VIII.3, the examples of *kaloik'agathoi* most obvious to Aristotle's immediate audience would probably not be purely theoretical philosopher-scientists like Anaxagoras,[40] but those who serve justice and political wisdom in some notable way.[41] In so doing, e.g. by engaging in legislation or political philosophy, they look beyond their own particular circumstances; their activity does not, as such, manifest the configuring of their own emotions and appetites in ways suitable for correctly responding to personal physical danger or to contexts where undisciplined people would eat or drink too much, or ones in which the irascible person would over-react.

---

[39] The difference matters if we think that Aristotle here identifies the master-element in us with God. The difficulty of thinking of a single entity as both being God and engaging in the non-divine activity of ruling by giving orders (1249b13) makes the first alternative attractive.

[40] Cf. 1215b6–14.

[41] Such as Solon, mentioned with Anaxagoras at *NE* 1179a9–16; see esp. *pepragotas ta kallista*, which by reporting Solon's own judgement shows him to be a *kalosk'agathos* as defined in the *EE*.

The quality of their noble activities may depend considerably on their exercise of ordinary virtues of restraint and good-temper, but these activities are not themselves exercises of these virtues; they are not judged as such. The moral disposition immediately exercised in activity distinctive of *kalok'agathia* consists in serious willingness to engage in it, and to do so 'because it is noble'. This applies equally to political and theoretical *kaloik'agathoi*: thus we ought not to limit the role of 'master' here to strictly theoretical reason.

(5).'The theoretical' first appears quite late in our text (on the eighth Bekker line of our eighteen-line passage). Having illustrated the two senses of 'rule' by the medicine-health example, Aristotle says: 'That is how it is with the theoretical <element of the soul>' (1249b13). He is about to explain what rules this (or: what rules it when in theoretical mode). Something must rule it, since it is part of the human being; and, as he has said at *Nicomachean Ethics* VI = *Eudemian Ethics* V, 1145a6–9, it is not the function of practical wisdom, which rules by prescription, to tell it what to do. Instead, just as the medical art is non-prescriptively ruled by its object, health, so the theoretical part is ruled by the object of its activity, which is God.[42] However, what is unnecessary to deny of health it is necessary to deny of God, namely prescriptive governance, this being commonly ascribed to God.[43]

The next clause: 'but <God> is that for the sake of which practical wisdom gives orders', is difficult. The analogies so far have suggested that practical wisdom (the steward's virtue) gives orders for the sake of (with a view to) maintaining the distinctive disposition of the *kalosk'agathos*. Now, God cannot be the element in us whose disposition this is, because the next sentence says that God is in need of nothing, and explains that he is that-for-the-sake-of-which as object, not beneficiary. This cannot be true of an element of the soul whose proper disposition depends on the ministrations of practical wisdom. Perhaps, then, God is the *activity* of that element in us? In general, Aristotle may not be hostile to this way of looking at things, but it is unlikely to be the meaning here. For the passage as a whole puts us in mind of the possibility that noble-and-good activities in general, and therefore this one, can be hindered by the presence of too much or too little of the natural goods. Even if there is some sense in which it is true that God's activity is immune from hindrance even in us (perhaps we can only be prevented from

---

[42] Keeping the MSS *theou* (subjective genitive) and *ton theon* at 1249b17 and 20 respectively. It is interesting that Aristotle can simply take it for granted here that the *thêôrêtikon* focuses on God; also that he does not regard the difference between an objective like health, and an existing object of study such as God, as mattering in this context.

[43] The fact that God does not rule us by giving us orders does not, of course, entail that God is in no way an efficient cause, e.g. of cosmic motion as in *Physics* VIII.9.

being aware of it[44]), this is surely not the meaning here: no hint of explanation is given although the context would sharply demand one. I think the best solution is to understand 'God' throughout as straightforwardly referring to God in himself, so to speak, or the god of the universe, and to take as follows the declaration about practical wisdom giving orders for the sake of (i.e. with a view to) God: God is the object studied in theoretical activity, and practical wisdom (in the *kalosk'agathos* who is involved with theoretical activity) acts so as to maintain whatever disposition or dispositions underlie *theoria*. Practical wisdom is concerned with any such disposition as basis for theoretical activity (cf. 1249b7–8); it understands this activity as having God as object; hence it itself in its own way refers to and serves God. It thinks about God in a way that makes sense of its own activity in governing the non-rational part of the soul. By combining the two common places (a) that God should be honoured, and (b) that to be ruled by God is to honour God, with (c) the Aristotelian thought that God does not rule us by issuing orders with sanctions attached, practical wisdom draws the conclusion that we, or some of us, must honour God in the only way possible for those who accept the premises of this argument, i.e. by making sure from our own initiative that some of us study the universe and its ultimate causes. We can do this by engaging in the study ourselves, or through supporting the practice of the study, or in both ways. To any would-be *kalosk'agathos* who has the resources but is looking for a project,[45] our passage sketches a protreptic argument that might well determine his practical choice. By contrast, the theoretical part of the soul, or reason in theoretical mode, neither needs nor has any room for this sort of argument; its business is to study its objects, not to justify such studies to the wider world.

In insisting that it is not the case that God gives orders to us, or can benefit from anything we do, Aristotle knocks away assumptions of traditional religion, simultaneously replacing them with an enlightened (*kalosk'agathos*) interpretation of piety that preserves its status as a virtue and its importance in human life. The present passage, as I understand it, envisages two forms of piety on the new conception: some serve God through theoretical study of first causes, etc., and some through practical measures for advancing the position of such studies in the *polis*, whether by political or financial or even legislative support, or by contributing an ethical philosophy that contains, stitched into

---

[44] Cf. *De Anima* 408b18–25.

[45] At the start of the *EE* Aristotle urges the importance of setting up a goal for living in a noble way if one is 'in a position to live according to his own choice' (1214b6 ff.); this suggests suitable conditions for noble-and-good activities, i.e. freedom from having to struggle for a livelihood, but also from having to manage some great inalienable inheritance.

it, an outline of the rationale for those studies and for supporting them. Some, like Aristotle, serve God in both ways.[46]

(6).What is meant by the culminating sentence of the coda (1249b21−3)[47]? The first clause as printed in the OCT (*echei de touto tei psuchêi*) is barely possible Greek. However, unless there is a serious lacuna, I take this to mean, or to be a corruption of something that means: 'the best standard for determining the right quantity of natural goods is also the standard for rating the soul: the soul is in an excellent or inferior state to the extent that it does or does not serve and focus on God'.[48] The rest of the sentence rephrases the standard in terms of obliviousness: the soul is at its best when the person is as unaware as possible of 'the non-rational part of the soul as such'. This is the part that would definitely be absent from the life of a god, as would all desires and emotions that originate there, even the rationally targeted ones. For someone engaged in work that is noble-and-good (whether theoretical or practical in nature), awareness of the non-rational part *as such*—even when it is not misbehaving—means division of attention between the noble and the mundane. A household runs best when its master's activity is unbroken by sight or sound of even well-disciplined slaves at their tasks.

8. Conclusion

According to *Eudemian Ethics* VIII.3, one cannot be a person of complete virtue unless one possesses a certain reflective attitude towards virtue: an attitude that consciously prizes the virtues and their activities as noble, and regards them as essentially outranking the natural goods. As we begin studying the chapter, we may be surprised at this turn of Aristotle's account. It has, of course, been obvious all along that the reflective activity of Aristotelian ethical philosophy assigns to the virtues value-precedence over the natural goods. It has also been obvious that, according to this philosophy, the genuinely virtuous person would act rightly in particular situations at the expense of natural goods where this is morally required. But this point entails nothing to suggest that Aristotle's ideal agent has a distinctive reflective attitude towards virtue in general. Hence

---

[46] This interpretation coheres with the final sentence of *EE* VIII.3 (i.e. the final sentence of the whole *EE* as we have it): 'Let this be our statement of what the standard (*horos*) is of noble-goodness, and what the target [*skopos*] is of the goods without qualification' (1249b23−5). The standard allows for exponents of noble-goodness who are not themselves theorizers.

[47] i.e. the penultimate sentence of *EE* VIII.3. The final sentence (see n. 46) seems to be a bridge to some further material either lost or re-assigned to an earlier place in the treatise.

[48] This meaning could be achieved grammatically by emending *echei* to *huparchei* at 1249b21.

we are also unprepared for the fact that Aristotle will end by insisting that the completely virtuous person, whose portrait he has been fashioning in the treatise, must share precisely the reflective attitude towards virtue that so clearly informs Aristotle's own ethical philosophizing.

This insistence of Aristotle's makes sense, however, once we realize that he has in his sights a rival reflective attitude (and, we must suppose, a prevalent one) in which the value-priorities are reversed. Aristotle cannot dismiss this as simply the view of worthless people,[49] because according to him it exists even among some who genuinely possess the standardly recognized virtues. But if genuinely good people have the wrong ideology, why should that matter, since evidently their ideology has failed to corrupt them? Well, as we have noted, the situation in which they are most clearly not vulnerable to corruption is one in which their practice of the standard virtues produces scarcely more of the natural goods than is necessary for them to keep living in their accustomed way. But a community of which this was generally true would lack the leisure and resources necessary for many fine human developments, including science and philosophy and interest in these for their own sake. And such interest can only be fostered through taking part in those activities. So if any science and philosophy swam into such a community's view, it would see these activities as pointless (and wasteful of existing natural goods) since they do not fall under the traditionally recognized virtues, and they do not help to produce natural goods. Yet simply adding wealth to this austere community opens the gate to moral corruption while leaving the cultural poverty uncured—as long as those who set the society's direction are stuck in the belief that having natural goods is what makes everything else worthwhile.[50] Where, *per contra*, the spirit of noble-goodness is present, it brings its own discipline to enhanced prosperity by generating new ends (which are also boundaries) for the natural goods to subserve.

---

[49] Cf. 1214b28–31.

[50] Cf. *Politics* 1334a11–b4. There is a lacuna in Aristotle's remarks at 1334a39–b4 about the (actual) Laconians (Spartans), but for the probable meaning see 1271b7–10, quoted in n. 22.

2

'The Opinion of Aristotle concerning Destiny and What is Up to Us'

JONATHAN BARNES

1. The Problem of Destiny

Some years ago archaeologists digging at Aphrodisias, a city in what was once
Caria and is now south-west Turkey, turned up the following inscription: 'By
the decree of the Council and People, Titus Aurelius Alexander, philosopher,
one of the Athenian professors, sets up this statue in honour of Titus Aurelius
Alexander, philosopher, his father'. The inscription dates from about AD200.
The dedicator is the philosopher hitherto known to scholars as Alexander of
Aphrodisias, a celebrated commentator on Aristotle and the leading Peripatetic
of his age.

In his essay *On Destiny* Alexander engages himself to set out 'the opinion
which Aristotle holds concerning destiny and what is up to us' (164.13–14);[1]
and since a thesis may be more clearly established if the views of its adversaries
are refuted, he 'will also argue against those who have disagreed with Aristotle
on these matters' (165.3–4). After fifty dense pages Alexander announces that he
has given an exposition of 'the chief elements' of Aristotle's opinion (212.5–6):
in truth, the exposition proper is brief, Alexander remarking after fewer than
seven pages that 'that is, in its chief elements, the opinion of the Peripatetics
about destiny' (171.16–17); and the greater part of the work is occupied with

---

[1] All references of this sort are to Alexander's *De Fato*: page and line in the edition of I. Bruns,
Alexandri Aphrodisiensis praeter commentaria scripta minora, Commentaria in Aristotelem Graeca, suppl.
II. 2, pp. 164–212 (Berlin: Reimer, 1892). The text of the work is badly preserved; and my argument
will occasionally invoke a disputed passage—but never a passage where the general sense is seriously
disputed.

the unmasking of misunderstandings, the refutation of objections, and the rebuttal of contrary opinions.

Aristotle's opinion, as Alexander expounds it, was never expressed by Aristotle himself. There are passages in the ethical works and elsewhere which say a certain amount about what is up to us; but Aristotle never speaks of destiny,[2] and he never suggests that it might be a good idea to have an opinion which, so to say, conjoins destiny with what is up to us. The opinion which Alexander sets out was constructed with material taken from the Aristotelian *corpus*;[3] but it is not an opinion which Aristotle himself ever elaborated.

Historians of philosophy continue to undertake the sort of construction-work which Alexander does in his *On Destiny*—thus the first sentence of *Aristotle's Theory of the Will* records that 'it is a commonplace of scholarship that Aristotle had no theory of the will'.[4] So what is the purpose of such labours? Well, different constructors no doubt have different purposes. In Alexander's case, it has been observed that he held the Regius Chair in Aristotelian Philosophy in Athens (164.13−15); that he was thereby obliged to expound Aristotle's opinion on the chief philosophical issues of the hour; and that one of those issues was the problem of destiny.

In modern philosophy there is something called the problem of determinism: it has seemed plain on the one hand that everything which happens is causally determined, on the other hand that our will is free, and on the third hand that those two plain truths are mutually incompatible. The problem of destiny is the ancient forerunner of the problem of determinism. 'Cicero in his book *On Destiny*, says that the question is extraordinarily obscure and intricate, and he remarks that even the philosopher Chrysippus had made no headway: "Chrysippus, he says, sweats and toils to explain how everything happens by destiny and yet some things are in our power—and he ties himself in knots" ' (Aulus Gellius, VII. ii. 15). The question was not only obscure and intricate: it

---

[2] The normal Greek word for 'destiny', namely 'εἱμαρμένη' [*heimarmenê*], is found twice in the *corpus aristotelicum*: in the spurious *De Mundo* 401b9−11, and in the *Poetics* 1455a10−12 (but the passage may not be Aristotelian, and in any event the word occurs in a quasi-quotation). An adjectival use of 'εἱμαρμένος' occurs twice: *Physics* 230a30−1 and *Meteorology* 352a28−31 (see below, p. 29). The word 'εἱμαρμένος' is the past participle of 'μείρομαι' and has the sense 'allotted'; it is common enough in Greek from Cratinus onward. The noun 'εἱμαρμένη' (presumably a brachylogy for 'ἡ εἱμαρμένη μοῖρα') is apparently first found in Plato (at *Phaedo* 115A and *Gorgias* 512E—both of which passages suggest that it was already current). The Stoics falsely derived the word from 'εἴρω' ('link'), and liked to talk of a εἱρμός—a sequence or chain of fatal causes.

[3] No doubt there were also other primary sources. If the Alexandrian *Mantissa* is anything to go by, Alexander will also have used Theophrastus' *Callisthenes, On Grief*, and the *On Destiny* of the otherwise unknown Polyzelos (*Mantissa* xxv, 186.28−31). Other Peripatetics before Alexander had discussed Aristotle's opinion on these matters; but it is unclear what Alexander may owe to that tradition.

[4] Anthony Kenny, *Aristotle's Theory of the Will* (London: Duckworth, 1979), p. vii.

was also heavy with consequence—according to Alexander, 'this doctrine is second to no philosophical doctrine; its utility extends everywhere and into every matter' (164.15–17).

Plainly, an Aristotelian must have an attitude on the matter, and since Aristotle himself had not been obliging enough to articulate one, Alexander must do so on his behalf. But it was not merely a question of constructive exegesis: as Alexander says in his piece *On the Soul*, 'just as in our other works we give first place to Aristotle's views, thinking the opinions which he has passed down to be truer than those of other men, so too in his doctrine on the soul' (*De Anima* 2.4–6). Aristotle's opinion on destiny and what is up to us will be the best solution to the problem of destiny; and that in itself is reason enough for constructing it.

Alexander is both an exegete and a philosopher: in his Aristotelian commentaries he is a philosophical exegete, his primary aim being to understand and explain the meaning of an old text. Elsewhere he is an exegetical philosopher: although he invariably starts out from Aristotelian texts, his primary aim is to resolve a philosophical problem. In *On Destiny* he draws on the *corpus aristotelicum*; but he never cites a particular text, he never offers to analyse a given passage, and he displays no particular interest in what Aristotle himself actually meant.

2. An Aristotelian Conception of Destiny

According to Alexander, when Anaxagoras affirmed that destiny is 'an empty name', he was going against 'the common belief of men' (165.21–3), and that is something which no wise philosopher will do. For 'the preconceptions of men sufficiently establish that there is such a thing as destiny and that it is the cause why certain things come about in accordance with it' (165.14–15). But if it is indisputable that destiny exists, and is a cause, it is disputable—and it was much disputed—what sort of cause it is and in what domain it functions. For there common preconceptions carry no weight.[5] (Alexander has got things upside down: common preconceptions—that is to say, the sense commonly attached to certain expressions—may tell us what destiny is; but they can scarcely show that there is such a thing as destiny.)

What sort of a cause is destiny? Alexander lists the familiar Aristotelian foursome and asserts, without argument, that 'we may properly count destiny among the productive causes [τὰ ποιητικὰ αἴτια]' (167.14–15). Alexander's

---

[5] See *Mantissa* xxiv, 176.2–5, where something similar is said about luck.

phrase '*τὰ ποιητικὰ αἴτια*' [*ta poiêtika aitia*], which does not correspond to anything in Aristotle,[6] is one of his ordinary ways of referring to what we tend to call the 'efficient' cause and what Aristotle most often calls 'that whence comes the starting-point of motion'. A productive cause is a cause which does something or sets something going.

As for the domain of destiny, another familiar Aristotelian notion distinguishes, first, between what comes about for the sake of something and what just comes about, and then, secondly, within the former class, between what comes about by reason and what comes about by nature. Plainly, destiny operates within the class of things which come about for the sake of something; 'for we always use the word "destiny" of some end, saying that it has come about by destiny' (168.27–169.2). Since 'what comes about by reason is thought to do so insofar as the man who produces it also has the power not to produce it' (169.6–7), such things do not fall under the sway of destiny. Hence 'we say that destiny is found among what comes about by nature, so that destiny and nature are one and the same thing—what is destined is natural and what is natural is destined' (169.18–20).

The *Mantissa* puts it a little more precisely: 'destiny is the proper nature of each thing' (xxv, 185.11–12); and the same text notices that destiny is limited to the sublunary world: the heavens are not subject to destiny, whose domain is 'the world of generation and corruption' (xxv, 181.16–22). Why do hornbeams lose their leaves in autumn? Because in autumn their sap congeals (*Posterior Analytics* 98b36–7). That is in the nature of hornbeams; and so it was by nature and by destiny that my hornbeams dropped their leaves last October.

The *Mantissa* allows that such a conception may seem eccentric (xxv, 186.9–10); but it can cite Aristotelian authority. A passage in the *Physics* notes that 'some comings to be are forced and not destined [*βίαιοι καὶ οὐχ εἱμαρμέναι*], to which natural generations are contrary' (*Physics* 230a31–2): what is natural is contrary to what is forced; what is forced is the same as what is not destined; so what is natural is contrary to what is not destined—and equivalent to what is destined. The *Mantissa* cites the *Physics* passage in this sense—and also, less pertinently, *Meteorology* 352a28–31 (xxv, 186.13–28).[7]

---

[6] But it is prepared for in two or three texts: see *On Generation and Corruption* 324b13; *De Anima* 430a12; *On the Generation of Animals* 729b13.

[7] 'Comings to be are forced and not in accordance with the concatenation of nature—Aristotle called them "not destined"—when things are brought to birth before their term. The commentators infer from this passage that the Peripatetics locate destiny in what is in accordance with nature' (Simplicius, *Commentary on Aristotle's Physics* 911.7–10).

3. The Problem of Destiny Resolved

What, then, of the knots of Chrysippus? How can the manifest claims of destiny be reconciled with the plain fact that many things are up to us? With the greatest of ease—and regardless of what exactly it may mean for something to be up to us.

For it is not true that everything which happens happens by destiny. First, the domain of destiny, being the same as the domain of nature, is limited: destiny has nothing to do with what comes about by reason—it has, for example, nothing to do with the arts and crafts. Hence when I write a book or build a chicken-house I do not do so by destiny; and for all that destiny has to do with it, it may be up to me whether or not I perform such pleasing activities.

There is a second point. It is by nature or by destiny that the hornbeams lose their leaves in the autumn. But they don't always do so—if the season is unusually mild, they may keep their leaves until the middle of December, or even longer. In general, what's natural doesn't always come to pass: in the world of nature, things happen (in the Peripatetic jargon) for the most part. That fact has a pertinent consequence: 'what comes about according to nature does not come about from necessity . . . For there is room in it for what is contrary to nature—and what is contrary to nature does comes about, when nature is prevented by some external cause from doing its job' (169.28–170.2). Thus even in its own natural domain, destiny is not omnipotent: although yews, by nature, grow into a sort of rounded pyramidal shape, an accidental thunderbolt or the cunning interventions of a topiarist may impose a different form. If by destiny yews become more or less pyramidal, it does not follow that it is not up to me to determine the shape of those yews in my garden.

Alexander sometimes seems to suggest that it is only when things go contrary to nature that they can be up to me;[8] but that is incoherent. By nature, men go grey. Yet I may always purchase a bottle of Dr Dorian's Special Lotion. So it's up to me whether or not I go grey. If parsimony or indolence prevail over vanity, then I shall go grey, and I shall go grey by destiny; but it is up to me whether or not I go grey.

---

[8] See e.g. 170.9–11: 'Hence a man might reasonably say that a thing's proper nature is starting-point and cause for the order of what comes about in it by nature'.

4. A Different View of Destiny

Alexander claims that 'those who have disagreed with Aristotle on these matters'
are with him at least on one point: what happens by destiny happens by nature,
and *vice versa* (192.25–6; 205.27). However that may be, the adversaries had
a view of their own about the nature of destiny. Alexander first notices it in
contrast to his own: 'There is a difference as far as action is concerned between
those who are convinced that everything comes about from necessity and in
accordance with destiny and those who think that some things come about
even though they do not have pre-established causes because of which they
will certainly come to be' (164.17–20). Thus according to the adversaries, what
happens by destiny happens certainly and by necessity. A little later Alexander
expresses the point more fully (in his usual bumbling style): 'It is by certain
precedent and antecedent causes that everything which is or comes to be is
and comes to be from necessity, each of the things which comes to be having
a pre-established cause such that when it is or has come to be it is necessary
that the thing itself is and comes to be' (173.16–19).

According to the Aristotelian opinion, destiny has a restricted range; and
within that range things may happen contrary to destiny. According to the
adversaries, destiny is ubiquitous; and it necessitates. If the adversaries are right,
then Alexander's solution to the problem of destiny is hopeless. And if the
adversaries are wrong, then his solution is at best partial. For the adversaries
will say something like this: 'Grant that destiny and nature are one, that their
domain is limited, and that they do not necessitate. It doesn't follow that
events may come about without any antecedent necessitating causes. True, it
is for the most part and hence not from necessity that hornbeams lose their
leaves in the autumn; but nonetheless, it is from necessity that these hornbeams
in my garden are now shedding their leaves—if their nature alone does not
necessitate the event, their nature and their particular circumstances, taken
together, do. As for events outside the domain of nature, you will scarcely
maintain that they come about without any antecedent causes at all—so you
must tell us how it can now be up to me whether or not I finish this sentence,
given that there are such . . .'.

Alexander claims that the adversaries' account of destiny obliges them to
deny that anything is up to us: they hold that 'there are certain pre-established
external starting-points and causes which determine that something certainly
will or will not come about—and if things were to happen like that, then

none of them would be up to us' (169.16–18). The adversaries reject the inference; and they can do so because 'they say that what is up to us is what comes about through us' (181.14). 'Since what comes about through an animal would not have come about had the animal not had an impulse to do it but comes about because the animal gives its assent and has an impulse, they say that such things are up to the animal' (183.5–8). According to the adversaries, then, something is up to me if it comes about through me—that is to say (very roughly speaking), if it comes about because I want or choose that it should come about.

Alexander does not think much of that. He remarks, first, that fire burns 'through itself', that stones fall 'through themselves', and so on; hence if something is up to so-and-so provided that when it comes about it comes about through so-and-so, then things are up to fire and up to stones and so on—and that is absurd (183.10–16). Not so, reply the adversaries, for there is a crucial difference: fire and stones have no impulses, they give no assent—something is up to so-and-so provided that, when it comes about, it comes about because so-and-so has assented to it, has had an impulse towards it.

The later philosophical tradition which occupied itself with the problem of determinism knew of two seemingly opposed accounts of what freedom of the will consists in: 'One <of them> approaches free will via the notion of wanting: we are free in doing something if and only if we do it because we want it. ...The other method approaches free will via the notion of power: we are free in doing something if and only if it is in our power not to do it: to act freely is to act in the possession of the power to act otherwise'.[9] The adversaries' account of what is up to us anticipates the first of those two approaches. Alexander's, to which it is time to turn, anticipates the second.

5. 'That Which Is Up to Us'

The Greek formula is 'Τὸ ἐφ' ἡμῖν' [to eph' hêmin]. If the nominalization is a piece of philosophical jargon,[10] the phrase 'ἐφ' ἡμῖν' is ordinary Greek: it is used by Euripides and by Isaeus; Alcidamas says that 'if we were tyrants in the cities, then it would be up to us [ἐφ' ἡμῖν] to summon juries...; but in

---

[9] Anthony Kenny, *Will, Freedom and Power* (Oxford: Blackwell, 1975), p. 122.
[10] It is not found in Aristotle, and I am not sure that it was used much before the time of Plutarch.

fact other people are in control of these things [τούτων κύριοι]' (*On Sophists* 15). And 'ἐφ' ἡμῖν' is no more than a particular case of a general type of expression: 'ἐπί' + dative may mean 'dependent upon', 'within the power of', 'in the hands of', so when Pindar says that some things οὐκ ἐπ' ἀνδράσι κεῖται he means that they are not within human power—'the god provides them' (*Pythian Odes* viii. 76).

Then what is it for something to be, in this way, up to us? Alexander offers an elucidation: 'Something is up to us if we think we have control [εἶναι ... κύριοι] both over its being done and over its not being done' (169.13–15—the 'we think' is a slip). That is the view which all right-minded men take: 'Everyone—unless he is defending a thesis—holds that something is up to us if we have control both over its being done and over its not being done, not following any external causes which may surround us or yielding to them as they lead us on' (180.4–7). Alexander often uses the term 'κύριος' [*kurios*] in this context, and even more often the term 'ἐξουσία' [*exousia*] or 'power'; and once or twice he employs the word 'ἐλεύθερος' [*eleutheros*] or 'free'.[11] He thinks that we should all agree that 'what is up to us is free and in our own power and in control of the choosing and doing of opposites' (189.10–12).[12]

Most of the things I do are in my power to do. (Not all of them: yesterday I fell off a chair, and each day I grow a day older—but it is not in my power to fall, or to grow old.[13]) Not everything which it is in my power to do is up to me to do. There are different sorts of power. According to Aristotle, 'of powers some are non-rational and some rational. ... All rational powers are powers for contraries whereas non-rational powers are one-to-one—for example, the hot is the power of heating and nothing more, whereas medicine is a power for illness and health' (*Metaphysics* 1046b1–7). Some powers are, as they say, 'one way' and some are 'two way'. My power of blushing is one way: set something embarrassing in front of me and I turn beetroot. My power of laughing is two-way: tell me a joke and I may laugh—or I may hold back my laughter.

Some powers are volitional, powers the exercise of which is a voluntary action; and it has been claimed that 'it is a mark of volitional ability, as opposed to natural power, that it should be a two-way ability'.[14] Alexander did not

---

[11] See 188.21; 189.10; 200.5. 'κύριος' and 'ἐξουσία' are Aristotelian; this use of 'ἐλεύθερος' is not.

[12] τὸ ἐφ' ἡμῖν ἐλεύθερόν τε καὶ αὐτεξούσιον καὶ κύριον τῆς τῶν ἀντικειμένων αἱρέσεώς τε καὶ πράξεως.

[13] But *Aristotle's Theory*, p. 9, cites dying and growing old as 'examples of the kinds of things which we do and which are in our power to do'.

[14] Kenny, *Will, Freedom and Power*, p. 139.

agree. His adversaries were, or at least included, the Stoic philosophers; and 'the Stoics affirmed that everything comes about by destiny, using the following example: if a dog is tied to a cart, then if it wants to follow, it is pulled along and follows, doing what is in its own power along with necessity; and if it doesn't want to follow, it will certainly be compelled to do so' (Hippolytus, *Heresies* I. xxi. 2). *ducunt volentem fata: nolentem trahunt.* Perhaps it is up to the dog whether it trots along with its tail wagging or with its tail down—but it is not up to the dog whether or not it follows the wagon. (From 'Necessarily if P then Q' and 'It is up to *x* whether or not P', you can't infer 'It's up to *x* whether or not Q'.) Now when the dog follows the cart with his tail up, he exercises a volitional ability; and Alexander allows that he acts voluntarily—'but the voluntary is not the same as what is up to us. For something is voluntary if it comes about through an unforced assent: something is up to us if it comes about with an assent in accordance with reason and judgement' (183.26–9).[15] For it is 'the sort of power which makes us capable of opposites' (180.1–2) which is needed if something is to be up to us. The possession of such a power is well expressed by way of a sentence of the form

It is up to *x* whether or not P.

The 'whether or not' is the sign that the power in question is two-way.

Alexander generally writes as though in any true instance of the schematic formula 'It is up to *x* whether or not P', the letter 'P' must be replaced by something of the form '*Fx*', where '*Fx*' says that *x* does something or other.[16] That is presumably false: it is at the moment up to me not only whether or not I open the window but also whether or not the window is opened. But perhaps where 'P' does not say that *x* does something or other, then it is up to *x* whether or not P only if (but not, of course, if) it is up to *x* to bring it about that P.

However that may be, Alexander plainly supposes that if something is up to me, then I possess certain appropriate capacities or abilities; and he tends to write as though such possession is sufficient as well as necessary. But that is hardly what he thinks. For example, at the moment, although it is (just) within my capacities to play a game of tennis, it is not in my power to do so: I've lost my racket, the court is water-logged, there's no one to play with, . . . Power

---

[15] It has been argued that in the *Eudemian Ethics* 'voluntary actions are a sub-class of actions which are in our power to do or not to do' (*Aristotle's Theory*, p. 25): Alexander holds the opposite opinion—actions which are in our power are a sub-class of voluntary actions. Better, Alexander holds that (i) if it is up to me to ϕ and I ϕ, then I ϕ voluntarily, but (ii) it is not the case that if I ϕ voluntarily then it was up to me to ϕ.

[16] For a probable exception see *Mantissa* xxiii, 175.23–4.

requires not only ability but also opportunity: the agent must be properly adjusted and so too must the environment. So perhaps a two-way power is the conjunction of a two-way ability and a two-way opportunity? After all, if a man does something which it is in his power to do, then he acts freely; and 'an agent ϕs freely at t if he has the ability and the opportunity both to ϕ and not to ϕ'.[17]

That is an attractive formulation; but on closer examination it may come to seem a little puzzling. At the moment, I have both the ability and the opportunity to consult Pauly-Wissowa: the volumes are there on the shelf, and my German is more or less up to snuff. Have I also got the ability and the opportunity not to consult Pauly-Wissowa? Well, I may manage to contrive an excuse not to consult that exhausting work; but I don't know what would count as an opportunity not to do so. Again, there are numerous things I can do to avoid taking down Band XVIII; but none of them is an ability not to consult the work. (Perhaps it's a matter not of two abilities, one to consult and the other not to consult, but rather of a single two-way ability? But there are no two-way abilities; rather, there are abilities which you may or may not exercise.)

A two-way power to ϕ requires the ability to ϕ and also the opportunity. That is not enough; but the extra item which is needed is not a further ability or a further opportunity. Rather, there must be nothing which necessitates ϕing. It's up to me, now, whether or not I check something in Pauly provided that I have the ability to consult Pauly and I have the opportunity to consult Pauly and nothing forces me to consult Pauly. (Shouldn't we add 'and nothing prevents me from consulting Pauly'? No: if something is preventing me, then I haven't got the opportunity.)

6. Action, Choice and Deliberation

Alexander frequently speaks of our having control of what we do, of our actions or $\pi\rho\acute{\alpha}\xi\epsilon\iota\varsigma$ [praxeis]. He also says that 'we have the power of choice' (190.1), and that 'we are in control of deliberating and of the choice of what emerges from the deliberation' (178.27–8). So what is up to me is implicitly restricted to what I do, what I choose, and how I deliberate.

Those three items are not independent. Alexander adopts Aristotle's narrow conception of action: 'we do not say of an infant that it acts, or of a beast, but only of someone who acts because of reasoning' (*Eudemian Ethics*

---

[17] *Will, Freedom and Power*, p. 150.

1224a28–30). Reasoning, here, is the same as deliberation; and choice or προαίρεσις [*prohairesis*] which Alexander also calls 'rational assent', is the upshot of deliberation. So we deliberate—we choose—we act. And 'it is up to men to act (inasmuch as they also have the power of not performing the very same action); for the choice of what is to be done is up to them, since deliberating and judging are up to them' (*Mantissa* xxiii, 172.30–3). So acting is up to us inasmuch as choice is up to us, and choice is up to us inasmuch as deliberation is up to us.

Cat-lovers find that account inadmissibly restrictive. Alexander is blunt about cats: 'What is up to us depends upon our rational assent—that is why what is up to us belongs only to men, since men alone among animals are rational and capable of deliberation' (*Questions* III. xiii, 107.6–8). Cats assent to things, but their assent is not rational (*Commentary on Aristotle's Prior Analytics* 73.7–10). For they act on impulse, or desire; and 'of the things which come about according to impulse those alone are up to us which are realized according to a rational impulse. And a rational impulse is one which comes about in animals capable of deliberation and choice—in other words, it is the impulse of men' (205.15–17). But surely, says the cat-lover, it's often—usually—up to Arthur whether or not he eats his Whiskas? He's got the ability, the plate's in front of him, nothing forces him to eat. The cat-lover is right; but it doesn't follow that Alexander is wrong to make what is up to us depend upon rational assent—after all, *pace* the Peripatetics, Arthur is perfectly capable of deliberation and of choice.

7. Uncaused Causes?

So according to Alexander, the fact that some things are up to us 'derives from the special characteristics of practical reasoning'.[18] Quite apart from any questions about cats, you might wonder what makes those characteristics so special: why should something's being up to us depend upon our rational assent, rather than (say) simply on our assent? An apparently crucial part of Alexander's theory has yet to be introduced: men, he says, are starting-points or ἀρχαί—and essentially so. 'Being rational is nothing other than being a starting-point of actions. For the being of different things is grounded in different items—the being of animals in the capacity for impulse, of fire in heat and the capacity to heat, ... of men, in the rational, which is equivalent to having in oneself a starting-point of choosing something and not choosing

---

[18]   *Will, Freedom and Power*, p. vi.

it' (184.15−19). Men are essentially rational, and rational things are essentially starting-points for choice and action.

The idea has a good Aristotelian pedigree.[19] But what does it mean to say that men are starting-points? In the first chapter of *Metaphysics* Delta Aristotle distinguishes among several sorts of starting-point, and he remarks that 'common to all starting-points is the fact that each is the first item from which something exists or comes to be or is known' (1013a17−19). One sort of starting-point is the 'efficient cause' of something; and Alexander says that 'men are starting-points and causes of the actions which come about through them' (185.15−16). Men are causal starting-points: they are starting-points inasmuch as they have starting-points within them ('being, for a man, is having in himself a starting-point and a cause': 185.19−21); and those starting-points are choices.

Sir Walter Raleigh sat next to his son at a grand dinner. The son made an offensive remark. 'Sir Walt, being so strangely supprized and put out of his countenance at so great a Table, gives his son a damned blow over the face; his son, as rude as he was, would not strike his father, but strikes over the face of the Gentleman that sate next to him, and sayed, *Box about, 'twill come to my Father anon*'. Sir Walter's son, or rather a choice made by Sir Walter's son, was the causal starting-point for a series of cuffs.

So 'what is up to us is the same as being a starting-point and productive cause of the things which we say are up to us' (*Mantissa* xxiii, 173.1−2). Or is it? After all, isn't the starting-point of animal action the animal itself, or something within the animal? 'My dog sees a bone, and he runs for it without anyone pushing him: the *arche* is within, it is his desire for the bone'.[20] You might expect Alexander simply to deny that my dog is a starting-point. But he doesn't. According to Aristotle, 'all substances are by nature starting-points of a sort... In addition, men alone among animals are starting-points of actions (for we would not say of any of the others that they act)' (*Eudemian Ethics* 1222b15−20). Alexander echoes the point (168.12−15). What makes rational assent special can't be the fact that it is a starting-point (since there are other starting-points), nor yet that it is a starting-point of action (for that is close to a tautology); rather, rational assent must be a special kind of starting-point.

It is a familiar Aristotelian thesis that there are causal starting-points which are themselves causeless. The second part of Book Alpha Minor of the

---

[19] For example, in the *Aristotelian Ethics* (to use Kenny's nomenclature) Aristotle says that 'three things in the soul are in control of action and of truth; perception, thought, and desire' (1139a17−18); and he argues thence to the conclusion that 'choice is either desiderative thought or reflective desire—and such starting-points are men' (1139b4−5).

[20] *Will, Freedom and Power*, p. 15.

Metaphysics is devoted to showing that 'there are certain starting-points, and the causes of the things which exist are not infinite' (*Metaphysics* 994a1–2). Alexander is echoing a part of that text when he says that 'it is reasonable to say that there is a starting-point among causes, which does not itself have some other starting-point and cause in front of it. ... For how is it not absurd to say that causes and their concatenation and their sequence go on *ad infinitum* so that none is either first or last? To say that no cause is first is to abolish causes; for if the starting-point is abolished, then necessarily what comes after it is abolished too' (195.28–196.4).[21]

So in claiming, after Aristotle, that men are the starting-points of their actions, isn't Alexander claiming that men are uncaused causes of what they do? And isn't that what makes practical reasoning so special? That view seems to be stated unequivocally in the *Mantissa*: having remarked that 'Aristotle too thinks that there are causeless movements, as he says in Book Epsilon of the *Metaphysics*' (*Mantissa* xxii, 170.9–10), the text goes on to say that 'it is the things which we choose causelessly and with no preceding cause [ἀναιτίως καὶ μὴ προϋπαρχούσης αἰτίας] that are said to be up to us' (171.22–3). Or again: 'If causes are the starting-points of the things of which they are causes, and if men are starting-points of their own actions, then men will also be causes of their actions. Now if it is absurd to seek, and to claim to find, a starting-point of a starting-point (for that of which there is some further starting-point is no longer a starting-point, without qualification), then there will be no pre-established productive cause, other than the man himself, of his choices and deliberations and judgements' (*Mantissa* xxiii, 173.10–15).

A few passages in *On Destiny* tell in the same sense. The clearest of them is this: 'Just as we do not look for some other cause why earth moves downwards in accordance with the weight which is in it, or why an animal does what it does according to impulse, inasmuch as each contributes this cause from itself to what comes about, being so by nature; in the same way, when things come about through us differently in different circumstances we should not seek any other cause apart from the man himself' (185.28–186.2). 'Why did Bernard spray his hens with weed-killer?'—'Well, he thought about it a bit, and then decided that that was the thing to do'. And that's all there is to be said: there are no further causes to be sought.

But how can choices and actions shake off the chains of causation? One answer runs like this: 'it is incorrect to think of wants as mental events which determine action. To say that someone did an act because he wanted

---

[21] For the omitted sentence see below, p. 41.

to is not to postulate a mental event as causing the action through some spiritual mechanism whose operation is as yet imperfectly understood'.[22] More generally, 'the voluntary actions of an agent are not caused by anything, neither by the agent's desires, nor by the agent himself. The movement of his limbs and muscles as he goes about his business no doubt have their own causes: but that is a different matter'.[23] Wants may explain actions: 'Because he wanted to' is a perfectly decent answer to the question 'Why did he take the third glass?'. But wants are not causes, and citing them is not giving a causal explanation. 'For an agent to have ϕd because he wanted to, it is enough that (a) he knowingly ϕd, (b) he wanted to ϕ, (c) it was in his power whether to ϕ or not to ϕ'.[24]

That is not exactly what Alexander has in mind, if only because he is concerned not with wants but with choices. Nonetheless, it might be hoped that the underlying notion that wants are not mental events—nor, of course, events of any other kind—can be adapted and applied to Alexander's case. And yet the hope must be disappointed. Perhaps you might be tempted to think that for an agent to have ϕd because he chose to it is enough that he knowingly ϕd, he chose to ϕ, and that it was in his power whether to ϕ or not to ϕ—so that, to that extent at least, choices are like wants. But that will not free choices from the causal chains. And whatever may be true of wants, and of doing something because you want to, it is plain that the deliberations and the choices which Alexander invokes are mental events. Choosing, and the preparatory deliberating, are things which we do, which take place at a time or which take time to do; and if they are events, then it must be pertinent to wonder why they do not enter into the causal nexus like any other honest event.

Perhaps Alexander simply thinks that deliberating, choosing, and acting are *sui generis*? They are events, and for that reason you might expect them to have causes. But in point of fact they do not. After all, some items (as Aristotle has shown) must be causeless—so why not these items? But there is more to be said.

8. Starting-Points

A starting-point is always a starting-point of something or other; and it is (as Aristotle puts it) a 'first item' not because there is nothing whatever before it,

---

[22] *Will, Freedom and Power*, p. 118. [23] Ibid. p. 120.
[24] Ibid.—which echoes *Eudemian Ethics* 1225b8–10 and *Nicomachean Ethics* 1135a23–5. But note that 'there is no doubt that Aristotle did delude himself with fanciful mechanisms to explain voluntary movement' (*Aristotle's Theory*, p. 165).

nor even because there is nothing of the right sort before it, but because there is nothing in the pertinent series or sequence before it: 'x is a starting-point of a sequence S' is true if and only if x is a member of S and no member of S is prior to x. That Southwark was the starting-point of their pilgrimage doesn't imply that all the pilgrims lived in Southwark; that 1942 was the first year of my life does not suggest that there was never a 1941; that the bite of a rabid dog is the first cause of hydrophobia does not mean that rabid dogs bite causelessly. So if men are, or contain, causal starting-points of certain things, that in itself doesn't imply that the starting-points are themselves somehow causeless. Sir Walter's son made a choice, and that started things off: it would be absurd to infer, from that fact alone, that the decision itself was uncaused.

Still, it can't be denied that Alexander, after Aristotle, holds that *some* causal starting-points are themselves causeless—and perhaps the decision of Sir Walter's son was a starting-point of that sort? Perhaps—but that was not in fact his master's view. In the *Ethics* Aristotle says plainly that 'the starting-point of action is choice (it is the origin of motion, not the goal), and the starting-points of choice are desire and purposive reasoning' (*Nicomachean Ethics* 1139a31–3). Choice is a causal starting-point, and itself has causal starting-points. The text offers no reason to doubt that the starting-points of choice have further starting-points, nor indeed to deny that the sequence of starting-points may go back *ad infinitum*.

As for Alexander, he reports that the adversaries of Aristotle insist that nothing can come about without a cause, and he asks the question: 'If things are thus, will something come about causelessly, and is that what our argument represents? Or can the principle that nothing comes about causelessly be saved even if things are the way we say they are?' (193.30–194.2). Alexander doesn't give the bold answer we might be expecting; he doesn't say: 'Yes, something will come about causelessly—and that is what the world is like'. The questions I have quoted are rhetorical, their answers are not 'Yes' and 'No' but 'No' and 'Yes'. And in any case Alexander has already affirmed that 'nothing comes about without a cause because of this power, because the man is cause of what comes about in this way, being himself a starting-point of what comes about by his agency' (190.19–21).

Then what of the several passages in which Alexander speaks of causeless starting-points? Different accounts must be given of different texts. In his commentary on the *Metaphysics* Alexander gives a summary of Aristotle's argument in Alpha Minor to the conclusion that there are causeless starting-points; and then adds this: 'In proving that there is not an infinity of causes... you should not think of infinity in time, considering in that way the cause of what has come to be from something. For in that way things do necessarily proceed to infinity insofar as time is infinite in that way and the universe is eternal. But in that way you will prove the infinity not of causes but rather of time: you would prove the infinity of causes if before each thing you were to take another different in form, and so *ad infinitum*—for in fact when things come to be ceaselessly in time, it can be shown that the causes are the same' (*Commentary on the Metaphysics*, 150.19–27).

That is not limpid; but what Alexander means is this. In an Aristotelian universe there will, necessarily, be temporally infinite sequences of efficient causes: this horse was sired by that horse, which had been sired by another horse—and so on *ad infinitum*. There is no first cause to that series, nor to any other series of the sort. Then what does Aristotle deny? According to Alexander, he denies the possibility of an infinitely diverse series of causes, a series in which (say) a horse is sired by an ass which is sired by an impala which is sired by an eland . . . and so on *ad infinitum*, each ancestral sire being different in kind from all his line.

Again, when the *Mantissa* refers to Book Epsilon of the *Metaphysics*, it has its mind on chance happenings; and although the text first says, explicitly, that such things are causeless, it later modifies its account: if you are digging a trench for the beans and your spade turns up a hoard of coins, then you find the coins by chance—but the digging is the cause of the finding (*Mantissa* xxiv, 178.1–5). Again, although the *Mantissa* explicitly says that deliberations and choices have no pre-established antecedent causes, it also makes it perfectly plain that nothing happens causelessly (xxiii, 174.3–12).

As for *On Destiny*, one passage seems at first sight to be clear: 'It is reasonable to say that there is a starting-point among causes, which does not itself have some other starting-point and cause in front of it. For if everything which comes about has a cause, it does not follow that there must be causes for everything—for not everything which is comes about' (195.28–196.1). That is to say, Alexander defends both the Aristotelian thesis that there are uncaused causes and also the ancient commonplace according to which every happening has a cause. The two positions are compatible insofar as there are plenty of things which are not happenings—and it is among them that any uncaused causes must be sought.[25] It is tempting to connect that remark with the claim that men are causal starting-points. After all, men are not happenings, so if men are uncaused causes it does not follow that something comes about causelessly. But if that is what Alexander had in mind, then it is scarcely

---

[25] The adversaries claim that 'nothing in the world either is or comes about causelessly' (192.8–9): Alexander implicitly rejects the first element in the disjunction.

helpful; for men are starting-points inasmuch as their deliberations and choices are starting-points—and those items are indeed happenings.

The chief passage in *On Destiny* is the one in which Alexander claims that 'we do not look for some other cause why earth moves downwards in accordance with the weight which is in it'. No doubt that is true—there is no answer to the question 'Why does its weight cause it to fall?' Similarly, perhaps, with human action: he sprayed the hens because he decided to do so—there is no answer to the question 'Why did his decision to spray the hens cause him to spray the hens?' The weight of the stone and Bernard's decision are causeless starting-points not in the straightforward sense that nothing causes them but in the refined sense that each is 'a cause whose causation has no further cause'.[26] And in any event, what Alexander says in this passage applies to stones as well as to stone-breakers—it cannot describe any pertinent peculiarity of the starting-points of action.

It may be admitted that what the Alexandrian texts says about human starting-points is less than pellucid. Nonetheless, I do not think that he maintains that deliberations and choices are uncaused causes of action. So what does make deliberation and choice different?

9. Necessitating Causes

We shall scarcely be excited by the thought that decisions and actions have their causes. After all, something is up to me provided that I have the appropriate power to act and not to act, and 'the notion of power involved here does not seem to be one which is incompatible with predictability, much less incompatible with determinism'.[27] If what I do is determined by my decisions, it would be absurd to conclude that I cannot but so act: you can't be forced to do something by your decisions, any more than you can be prevented from doing something by your desires. (Though you can, of course, be prevented by other people's desires: 'He in a few Minutes ravished this fair Creature, or at least would have ravished her, if she had not, by a timely Compliance, prevented him'.) You can't say that you were compelled to do something because you had so decided, or that you were unable to do something because you didn't want to. Nick Shadow to Tom Rakewell: 'Would you act freely? Then learn to ignore those twin tyrants of appetite and conscience. Therefore I counsel you, master, take Baba the Turk to wife.' The counsel is deliberately ridiculous.

---

[26] *Aristotle's Theory*, p. 4.   [27] *Will, Freedom and Power*, p. 143.

If my decisions have their causes, that does not imply that what I do isn't then up to me. 'Why did you decide to dine at Bofinger?'—'Because she asked me to take her there'. Do you infer that it wasn't up to me whether or not we dined there? The inference would be insane. When I unwisely took that third glass of champagne and you said to yourself 'Well, it was up to him', did you thereby imply that my taking the glass, or my decision to take the glass, was uncaused? Not for a moment. (Nor, of course, do you thereby imply that it *was* caused.)

Imagine that in point of fact there was a fatal chain of causes which led up to my choosing to accept the third glass. Does it follow that, at the crucial moment, I lacked the ability to say no? Not at all: I retained that invaluable ability but happily refrained from exercising it. (Had it been the eighth or ninth glass, things might have been different—my capacity might have been temporarily impaired.) Does it follow that I lacked the opportunity to decline the glass? No: I had every opportunity to decline—you invited me to take another glass, I accepted, you asked me if I were sure, I insisted that I was. Fatal causes or no fatal causes, I had the capacity and I had the opportunity.

But wasn't it necessary for me to take it? Didn't the fatal causes necessitate my action and so remove it from my power? According to Alexander, his adversaries hold—or are committed to holding—that fatal causes necessitate: they maintain that 'there are certain pre-established external principles and causes which determine that something certainly will or will not come about—and if things were to happen like that, then none of them would be up to us' (169.16–18). The adverb 'certainly' has the force of 'necessarily'. Again, according to the adversaries, 'it is impossible that when all the circumstances surrounding both the cause and that of which it is the cause are the same, sometimes things happen this way and sometimes they don't' (192.22–4).

Alexander denies that; in particular, he denies that in the same circumstances we always do the same things—for as a matter of fact, in the very same circumstances we will sometimes do one thing and sometimes another. After all, 'what is the advantage of deliberating?—That, having the power of choosing what we should do, we choose and do something which we would not have done had we not deliberated inasmuch as we should have yielded to first impressions and done something else—something which reason has shown to be less worth choosing' (179.8–12). That is the crucial difference between men and beasts: 'the activities in accordance with impulse of other animals are not like that—they no longer have the power not to do what is in accordance with their impulse' (205.18–20). Most causes, Alexander suggests, do necessitate their effects, in this sense: once they are in place, and the circumstances are fixed, then the effect cannot fail to come about. But not all causes are like that; and in particular the causes of rational actions are not like that—even when their causes are in place and the circumstances are fixed, the rational agent retains the power to produce the goods or not produce the goods.

Now you might well wonder if any causes necessitate their effects. The adversaries in fact denied that their fatal causes were necessitating or removed chance and contingency from the world. And when he claims that they could not consistently deny it, Alexander appears to commit a tedious fallacy: 'If the cause is in place, then the effect must come about; but the cause is in place: therefore the effect must come about or comes about from necessity.' Alexander implicitly construes the first premiss as 'If P then necessarily Q', whereas the adversaries mean it in the sense 'Necessarily (if P, then Q)'.

But that dubious argument aside, and whether or not all or some causes necessitate their effects, don't some causes take things out of our power? Alexander himself says that if 'long, long ago, even before he was born', there were certain causes which would eventually lead Paris to abduct Helen, then the abduction could not have been up to him (187.16–24). The underlying idea is this: the causes of his decision, or the causes of those causes, ..., were not and cannot have been up to Paris; for they happened long before his birth. But how can an effect of something which was not up to him be up to him? Alexander presents that as another objection to the opinion of the adversaries; but if it works against their opinion, it works equally against Aristotle's—unless, after all, the Aristotelian opinion appeals to uncaused causes.

The objection is, I think, rather seductive. But it is based on a false principle. There is a true principle of modal logic which allows the inference of 'Necessarily Q' from 'If P, then Q' and 'Necessarily P'. The objection depends on an analogous principle, a principle which allows the inference of 'It is not up to x whether or not Q' from 'If P, then Q' and 'It is not up to x whether or not P'. There is no doubt an analogy between the two principles. But there is also a difference: the second principle is false.

Perhaps, then, what really counts for Alexander—what should count for him—is not the contingency of effects but their unreliability, their irregularity. In the natural world, the same old causes bring about the same old effects: in the world of action, the same old causes bring about quite different effects. That's what makes deliberation and choice and action so special. And yet it's hard to think that that can be right. First, if in exactly the same circumstances you do make different decisions, then at least one of your decisions must have been a mistake: if the irregularity to which Alexander appeals is essential to his account, then his account entails that the decisions of perfect decision-makers are not up to them. Secondly, common experience suggests that unreliability and irregularity are as much a feature of the natural world as they are of the world of action. I pull the starting-cord of my chain-saw. Nothing happens. I pull it again. Still nothing. ... And on the tenth pull the motor fires. ('Oh, but there must have been *some* difference between the tenth pull and the others—you just didn't notice it.' It's not true that there *must* be some difference; and anything you can reasonably say in the case of the chain-saw you can reasonably say in cases of actions.)

It's up to me, now, whether or not I add a concluding paragraph: I've got the ability to do so, the opportunity is there, nothing is forcing me to write on. Does all that, as Alexander would have it, really 'derive from the special characteristics of practical reasoning'?

3

Weakness and Impetuosity

DAVID CHARLES

1. Introduction

In his essay 'The Practical Syllogism and Incontinence',[1] Anthony Kenny challenged the accepted interpretation of Aristotle's views on *acrasia* (the phenomenon of failing to do what one takes to be best) and set out a bold alternative. He argued that in his central discussion in *Nicomachean Ethics*, VII.3 (or *Eudemian Ethics* VI.3) Aristotle allows that some acratic agents have actual knowledge of the wrongness of the particular acts they do while they act. So understood, for Aristotle, some cases of *acrasia* will involve conflict. Not all are the consequence of a failure in reasoning which results in the acratic person, or *acrates*, being unaware while acting that the particular act he (or she) is engaged in is wrong (by their own lights).

In Kenny's interpretation, when Aristotle said

One acratic person does not arrive at the final proposition [*protasis*] at all, whereas another does and when he acts, utters it but does not know (or fully grasp) it, like the drunk repeating the verses of Empedocles   (1147b9–12)

he committed himself to three claims:

[A]   there are two types of *acrates*;
[B]   one (e.g.) eats this sweet voluntarily without arriving at the conclusion 'do not eat this sweet'; another arrives at that conclusion but voluntarily eats the sweet nonetheless;
[C]   the latter knows, while acting, that a specific action is not to be done. Despite having this knowledge, this type of *acrates* acts contrary to his conclusion because of the presence of an opposing desire.

[1] *Phronesis* (1966), pp. 163–84.

Most commentators, since Albert and Aquinas, have taken a different view, holding that no Aristotelian *acrates* is aware of the relevant ('good') conclusion while acting. They understood the phrase (in 1147b9) just translated as 'final proposition' to mean 'last premiss' and to refer to the minor premiss (e.g. 'This is sweet') not to the conclusion. They also believed that no one (in Aristotle's account) could arrive at a 'good' conclusion and 'voluntarily' act otherwise. Twentieth-century proponents of this, the standard view, took one *acrates* to lack the information that this is sweet, the other to fail to use it to arrive at the good conclusion. While many advocates of this interpretation regarded the resulting view of *acrasia* as deeply flawed, they saw no alternative but to attribute it to Aristotle.[2]

Kenny noted that one medieval commentator, Walter Burley, had argued that at least one of Aristotle's examples of an *acrates* arrives at and is aware of the good conclusion while acting acratically.[3] However, in subsequent discussions, St Thomas's view (as set out in the last paragraph) prevailed and Burley's was all but forgotten.[4] Kenny was practically the first to revive Burley's interpretation and I and others have subsequently followed his lead in defending a modified version of this view.[5]

Kenny, in his original article, attempted to undermine the grounds for the traditional view and to develop an alternative reading of the central texts which allows for at least one *acrates* to arrive at knowledge of the good conclusion and not act accordingly. Subsequently, in *Aristotle's Theory of the Will*,[6] he modified his views, first by taking the phrase 'the final proposition' to mean the last proposition (whatever it is) and to refer in some cases to the minor premiss and in others to the conclusion, and second by allowing that the relevant *acrates* is (in some way) ignorant of the good conclusion, at least in that his (or her) relevant belief is not operative in producing action. While some aspects of Kenny's initial essay remain controversial and others have needed

[2] For a recent statement of this view, see David Bostock's *Aristotle's Ethics* (Oxford: Oxford University Press, 2000), pp. 125 ff. He lists its main late twentieth-century proponents (p. 142): J. J. Walsh, W. F. R Hardie, R. Robinson, G. Santas, J. M. Cooper, D. Wiggins, J. O. Urmson, and M. J. Woods.
[3] For discussion of Burley's views see Risto Saarinen, *Weakness of the Will in Medieval Thought* (Leiden: Dordrecht, 1994). Burley was a Fellow of Merton College, Oxford in the early fourteenth century.
[4] Among twentieth-century writers, some of Burnet's remarks on parts of *Nicomachean Ethics* VII.3 suggest a similar view (*The Ethics of Aristotle* (London: Methuen, 1900), pp. 303 ff.). J. L. Austin (I have been reliably informed) defended a version of this view in his (unpublished) Lectures on Aristotle.
[5] I defended [A] and [B] in *Aristotle's Philosophy of Action* (London: Duckworth, 1984), ch. 3. Norman Dahl, in *Practical Reason, Aristotle and Weakness of the Will* (Minnesota: University of Minnesota Press, 1984), ch. 11, accepted [A] but not [B].
[6] (London: Duckworth, 1979).

further support, it has proved possible to defend a Burley-friendly account of the whole chapter.[7]

In the present essay, my aim is twofold. First, I shall offer further support for [A] by arguing that Aristotle's discussion in *Nicomachean Ethics* VII.3 should be seen as part of a longer discussion in Book VII as a whole, which clearly allows for at least two kinds of *acrasia*. Second, I shall discuss Kenny's earlier suggestion ([C]) that one type of *acrates* knows while acting that what he or she is doing is wrong and is led to act in this way by the presence of an unreasoning desire, and consider his later view that this kind of *acrates* is ignorant in that his (or her) belief is not operative. I shall then outline two alternatives to Kenny's suggestions which allow the weak *acrates* to be subject to conflict and aware while acting that what he (or she) is doing is wrong, but offer a different account of the relevant type of knowledge failure.

2. Two Types of *Acrates*: VII.7–10

As Kenny noted, Aristotle later comments

> There are two types of *acrasia*, impetuosity and weakness. The latter having deliberated do not stand by what they have deliberated because of passion, the former are led by passion because they have not deliberated.   (1150b19–22)

Aristotle, in fact, has more than this to say about impetuosity, separating two distinct cases of this condition (1150b25–8). In both, the acratic agents follow their imagination and do not remain within the confines of reason. One group acts in this way because they have excessive desires (Aristotle describes them as 'melancholic'), the other because of the speed of their desires ('the swift'). In the latter case their desire appears to be too quick for their reason. It intervenes and leads them to act before they have made up their minds as to what is best to do. Both types of impetuous *acrates* have (in some way) not deliberated although for different reasons.

Aristotle's distinction between the weak and the impetuous is not restricted to *Nicomachean Ethics* VII.7. In the next chapter, he returns to what is apparently the same contrast:

> Of the acratics, the best are those who are driven out of reason not those who retain their reason but do not stand by it; for the latter are beaten by less passion and unlike

---

[7] I have attempted to give a detailed reading of the chapter as a whole which supports [A] and [B] in '*Nicomachean Ethics* VII.3: Varieties of *akrasia*', in C. Natali (ed.), *Aristotle's Nicomachean Ethics VII* (Oxford: Oxford University Press, 2009). I shall refer to this book (and its chapters) using *Nicomachean* numbering, but it remains an open question whether they are best seen as part of the *Nicomochean* or the *Eudemian Ethics*.

the former have not acted without deliberation. For this *acrates* [the latter] is like those who get drunk quickly on little wine or on less wine than most.   (1151a1–5)

The first group (whom Aristotle labels 'the ecstatic') are those who have not deliberated, the second have deliberated but do not stand by their reason because of passion. Aristotle regards the second group as, like the weak, having deliberated and as being worse than the first because they are beaten by less passion. The first group will be like the impetuous in not having (in some way) deliberated, although it is not clear whether he has in mind here only the melancholic or also the 'sharp' impetuous.

In Book VII, chapter 10 Aristotle draws a similar distinction:

Of these acratics one is not prone to stand by what he has deliberated, while the other is melancholic and does not deliberate at all . . .   (1152a18–19)

The *acrates* (plural) are said (1152a10–14) to be like the practically wise in reason but to differ in their preferential choices, not to be like those who know actively but rather to resemble people who are asleep or (in some way) drunk (*oinomenos*). The melancholic is like the person asleep as far as reason is concerned. For it is inactive, shut down. They are prone to follow their imagination, as do those who are asleep, and while acratic are driven out of reason. The melancholic impetuous does not deliberate at all.

The acratic who is not prone to stand by what he has decided is the weak. He (or she), it appears, is like those who are drunk (*oinomenos*). It is important to note that their form of drunkenness (*oinomenoi*) is not that of those who are 'out on their feet' or 'closed down'. Later in the same book their state is compared with that of the young (*Nicomachean Ethics/Eudemian Ethics* 1154b10: see also *Rhetoric* 1389a18) who are optimistic, trusting, and naive, not properly influenced by the experience of life. In the *Problems*, those who are drunk in this way (*oinomenoi*) are said to be braver than those who are not (948a29). (For a similar idea, see *Nicomachean Ethics* 1117a14, where some are said to be more brave and optimistic through drink: *methuskomenoi*). Their type of drunkenness is not that of those who are dead-drunk (*methuon*), incapable of sex (*Problems* 872b15), and subject to visual illusion (see *Problems* 872b4 ff., 872a20). It is the latter who act involuntarily (*Nicomachean Ethics* 1110b26). The acratics mentioned in the present passage (*oinomenoi*) are 'tipsy' (compare the *akrothorakes* in *Problems* 871a13, 875a32 ff.), slightly drunk, 'cheerful', 'silly'.[8]

---

[8] See, for this distinction, Diogenes Laertius, *Lives of the Eminent Philosophers* 7.118: the Stoic virtuous drink in moderation (*oinousthai*) and do not engage in heavy drinking (*methusthenai*) so as to be the worse for drink. In Plutarch *Moralia* 672d, the Jews are described as taking wine on the Sabbath (*oinousthai*). Similarly, Athenaeus, *The Deipnosophists* 10.440c talks of some who taste wine without getting drunk

Those who are tipsy (*oinomenoî*) are ignorant (*agnoountes*) not because they are insensible but rather because they think they know something they do not.[9] Some may be fully aware of what they are doing or saying; their error lies in thinking that they know something they do not.

In VII.10, Aristotle continues (after a few lines) as follows:

The condition of the acratics who suffer from melancholic *acrasia* is easier to heal than that of those who deliberate and do not stand by what they deliberate ...   (1151b27–9)

The use of the term 'melancholic' connects the first group with one of the kinds of impetuosity mentioned in 1150b19 ff.: those whose reason is driven out by excessive desires. The contrast is now between this kind of impetuosity and the defect manifested by the weak, who do not stand by their deliberation.

Putting these passages together, we arrive at the following portraits of two types of *acrates*.

Type 1: the impetuous

(i)   they have not deliberated but follow their imagination;[10]
(ii) some are subject to excessive passions (the 'melancholic'), others to passions which influence their actions before they rationally make up their minds as what is best to do (the 'swift');
(iii) the melancholic do not deliberate at all;
(iv) the melancholic are easier to heal than the weak;
(v)   they (or some of them) are less bad than the weak.

In Book VII, chapter 7, their excessive or quick desires arise from (or are connected with) their imaginings and lead them not to deliberate. In passion they turn off their reasoning capacity. Those who suffer from *acrasia* brought on by excessive desires ('melancholic' impetuosity) are like those asleep: their reasoning capacity is not operative at all.

(suffering from *methe*). In the *Symposium* 176d, there is a discussion of the evils of drunkenness (*methe*), which presumably do not attend moderate drinking at a well run symposium.

[9] Philo, *Peri Methes*, distinguishes two types of ignorance: the insensibility of those who are dead drunk, 'closed down', and incapacitated (155) and the ignorance (*agnoia*) of those who think they know what they do not (162). The latter may have beliefs about what will happen (for this use of *agnoia* see *Prior Analytics* 77b18 ff.) which are either false or (even if true) not properly based on experience or reasoning. For a similar use, see *Eudemian Ethics* 1229a18 ff., where 'madmen' who act bravely but lack experience are described as ignorant of (e.g.) what snakes can do.

[10] Aristotle's idea of 'following one's imagination' requires further elucidation. Those who follow their imagination, I assume, act on how things look to them to be and not on their beliefs. For Aristotle, the sun can look to you to be a foot across even when you know its real size and are not even inclined to believe that it is so small (*De Anima* 428b). For further discussion of why these acratics may follow their imaginations, see below.

Those who have 'swift' or rapid desires seem different. Their desire is too quick for their reason in that it intervenes and influences their actions before they have completed their deliberation, leading them to act before they have reached their conclusion about what is best to do. Their reason may be inoperative in a weaker sense: they fail because of the onset of desire to arrive at the proper conclusion. If so, while for the melancholic acratic, excessive desire prevents them from reasoning at all, for the swift desire runs ahead of their reasoning and leads them to act before they have completed it.

Both kinds of impetuosity can be contrasted with the weakness of those who have completed their deliberation and do not stand by it (1150b19–22, 1151b27–9). Both will fail to be 'deliberative' in the sense in which the practically wise (1140a30–1) are described as 'practical and deliberative' (1141b26–7). For the practically wise are deliberative not in that both engage in *some* deliberation but rather in that they succeed in *completing* deliberation, in arriving at a good practical conclusion about what to do. Although both types of impetuous *acrates* will fail to be deliberative in this sense, the speedy impetuous can still engage in some deliberation provided that they do not succeed in completing it by drawing the relevant conclusion. By contrast, the melancholic acratic is so overcome by passion as not to deliberate at all. There are, it seems, two different types of impetuous acratics under consideration in these passages.[11]

Consider, by contrast, the weak.

Type 2: the weak

(i)   they deliberate, conclude their deliberation but do not stand by what they have deliberated;

(ii) they are not subject to such strong passions as the [melancholic] impetuous, being overcome by less passion than most are;

(iii) they are less easily healed than the melancholic;

(iv) they are worse than the [melancholic] impetuous;

(v)   they are like drunks (*oinomenoi*).

There are clear differences between the weak and the impetuous. Neither is persuaded that he (or she) should act as they do (1151a22 ff.) and neither constantly acts as he (or she) thinks they should (1150a34 f., 1152a19 ff.). However, the weak are in a state which is unstable, affected by weak desires (ones which do not prevent them from reasoning altogether) and 'slow-moving' desires (ones which do not race ahead of their reasoning, preventing them from completing it). They are vulnerable to desires for objects which

---

[11] I leave it open whether the person who is acratic through anger is yet a further type of impetuous acratic.

are not so strong or so swift in their operation as to disrupt their reasoning. Worse still, they do not resist these desires even when they have deliberated. By contrast, the impetuous are vulnerable only to desires sufficiently strong or 'swift' to disrupt their deliberation (1150b21). If they deliberated, they might well act on their deliberation. Their type of *acrasia* can be overcome by foresight and anticipation (1150b25 ff.). This type of cure may not work for the weak: for they have already deliberated and nonetheless do not stand by their deliberation. The mere fact of getting them to deliberate will not be sufficient to cure them.

Why are the weak worse than the (melancholic) impetuous? Aristotle gives two reasons: they have deliberated and are defeated by a less strong passion than the melancholic. But why does this make them worse? One might think that the fact that they are sufficiently rational as to deliberate makes them better than the (melancholic) impetuous. Equally, one might suspect that the fact that their sensual desires are weaker makes them more easily controllable and so less threatening. However, Aristotle does not see the matter this way. In his view, the fact that they have deliberated and are still defeated by desire shows that their reason (even when deployed) fails to control their passions (even their weak ones). In his view, this indicates that their reason is even less effective in controlling their passions than is the case for the impetuous. Their passions are more in control of what they do since they can overcome reason, even when the latter is deployed. In these ways, the weak *acrates* is closer than the impetuous to the dreadful state of those whose actions are not controlled at all by reasoning or preferential choice (1149b35 ff.). Their reason is, in the way specified, less in control of what they do than is the case for the impetuous. And this makes them worse as well as less curable.[12]

Given these differences, the ways in which the weak and the melancholic impetuous fail to be 'practical' will differ. The latter fail because their knowledge lies dormant at the time of action. They are like someone asleep as far as their knowledge of what to do is concerned. They differ in preferential choice from the practically wise in that they fail to recall the decision they have already reached.[13] By contrast, the weak can go through all the relevant reasoning, arrive at the conclusion, and still fail to be practical. If they are close in

[12] The notion of the worst kind of *acrates* is present in some difficult lines in *Nicomachean Ethics/Eudemian Ethics*, bk VI, ch. 8, 1142b18 ff., if they are interpreted in the following way: 'the *acrates*, I mean the bad *acrates*, will grasp from reasoning what he proposed he should do but has chosen a great evil...'

[13] This is why both the weak and the impetuous can be described as acting act 'against their preferential choice' (1151a6–7). For further discussion of this passage, see my *Aristotle's Philosophy of Action*, p. 141, n. 36.

reason to the practically wise, the two will march in step until they reach the final stage of their reasoning: the one which is either identical with or closer to their preferential choice. Further, elsewhere the weak are characterized as failing to stand by what they have deliberated (1150a20) or what they deliberate (1152a18–19, a28–9). These formulations give no indication that their reasoning has been forgotten (put to sleep) when they fail to stand by it, but suggest rather that it is present (in its entirety) at the same time as they fail to act appropriately.

This latter point is important: had Aristotle intended to claim that the weak *acrates'* reasoning had been shut down completely when he acted, he should have made it clear that all of the weak person's deliberation was first present and then (at the time of action) forgotten. Had this been his picture, the weak would have been, at the moment of acratic action, reduced to the state of the impetuous. Indeed, since the impetuous may well have previously considered just this type of case (although they now forget that they have done so), there would have been no real difference between the two types of *acrates*. But this seems implausible given the time and effort Aristotle spends on separating the two kinds of *acrates*.

Given these differences, the weak and the impetuous may regret their acratic actions in different ways. The weak may regret what they are doing at the time they act while the impetuous can do so only subsequently (when they come to realize that they have acted against their knowledge). If so, in the two cases, *acrasia* will be transparent in different ways. In the case of the weak, regret may be immediate, while the impetuous can only regret their actions subsequently when they come to realize that they have acted against their knowledge. However, both will be unlike the bad person whose bad action may remain concealed (even to him) because he never regrets what he has done (1150b35 f.).

3. Connections with VII.3

The distinctions we have noted between the impetuous and the weak and between various types of impetuous agents are, I wish to argue, prefigured in *Nicomachean Ethics*, Book VII, chapter 3. Some of these connections are clear, others less so.

(A) The melancholic acrates

Their plight is clearly stated in 1147a10 ff. in the case of those who 'have knowledge in a way and at the same time do not have it, like those asleep or mad' (1147a13). Melancholia requires medical treatment (1154b12 f.) as a bodily condition. In it, the sufferers are prone to excessive desires which affect the body (see 1147a15 ff.). Indeed, melancholia may be understood as a type of madness.[14] Melancholics do not deliberate, they merely follow their imagination.

(B) The swift acrates (1147a1–10)

In this passage Aristotle writes:

there is nothing to prevent one who has both types of propositions acting against his knowledge, provided that he uses the universal and not the partial one. For what is done is a particular action. There is a difference with regard to the universal. One aspect specifies the agent himself, another the subject matter.[15] Take for example:

Dry food benefits all men;
I am a man;
This kind of food is dry.

The person [who acts despite knowing better] either does not possess or does not exercise the proposition that this is of that kind [e.g. chicken].   (1146b35–1147a7)

In the agent's body of knowledge (under consideration from 1146b31 ff.),[16] one proposition fulfils the role of the major premiss: 'Dry food is good for all men.' Aristotle immediately notes a complexity: one part of the major premiss bears on the agent, another on the objects involved. This is clear in the piece of reasoning he cites:

Dry food is good for all men;
I am a man;
Such and such type of food [e.g. chicken] is dry

Here, the reasoner applies the major premiss to the two distinct partial premisses specified. From these he can deduce

Dry food is good for me

and

Such and such type of food [e.g. chicken] is good for me.

The acratic reasoner will have and use his major premiss and one specific claim ('I am a man') in the reasoning which expresses his relevant body of

[14] For a further detailed study of melancholia, see P. J. van der Eijk, *Aristoteles, Over melancholie* (Groningen: Historische Uitgeverij, 2001).

[15] Kenny takes this passage in a similar way ('The Practical Syllogism and Incontinence', p. 172).

[16] I set out this case more fully in my longer essay 'Nicomachean Ethics VII.3: Varieties of *akrasia*'.

knowledge. In this context, the *acrates* who 'either does not have or does not exercise' the claim

This is of such and such type (e.g. chicken)

will either not have it as part of his body of knowledge or have it as part of his body of knowledge but not exercise (or use) it when he acts acratically.[17]

Aristotle makes it clear that the two *acrates* mentioned in 1147a7 fail to know (in the relevant sense) that this is (e.g.) chicken (or sweet). Once we understand the terminology he employs, we can see that neither of these need fail to grasp (*eidenai*) the truth of propositions such as

This is chicken (sweet).

All they need fail to do is to grasp or use this *as part of their body of knowledge* (*epistasthai*). Perhaps they never succeed in grasping (either in the past or now) the connections between the claim 'this is chicken' and (e.g.) the requirements of the healthy diet they wish to follow. Or perhaps, under the influence of passion, that past connection is now obliterated. Either way, they do not now have (*ouk echei*) this specific claim as part of their body of knowledge. At the time of action, this claim is not part of their relevant dossier of medical or dietetic information. Alternatively, they may still retain the relevant claim as a premiss in their body of knowledge but fail to use it now (*ouk energei*) in their reasoning. (For a similar case, see *Prior Analytics* B.21, 67b7.) Although the claim still falls within their relevant dossier of medical information, the *acrates*, under the influence of passion, does not use it to draw the relevant conclusion. However, in none of these cases need they fail to grasp (*eidenai*) that this is chicken (or sweet).

Aristotle, so understood, focuses from 1146b31 to 1147a10 on two ways in which one may fail to grasp some claim *as part of one's body of knowledge*. On this reading, the person who does not have or does not exercise the claim:

This is of such and such type (e.g. chicken)

is to be understood as

[A] not having this proposition as part of his body of knowledge or as having it as part of their body of knowledge but not exercising it.

---

[17] This claim is about the minor premiss (and not the conclusion) since this is what is *used* (in the present context) in reasoning to the conclusion. *Energein* is related to the minor premiss in 1147a33 and *Prior Analytics* 67b3. The complexity introduced in the example at 1147a4 ff. allows the *acrates* to use the major premiss in some reasoning even though he does not apply it to the claim: 'This is chicken' to arrive at the conclusion: 'This is beneficial for me'.

and not as

[B] not having this proposition at all or not exercising it.

Given [A], what he fails to have or exercise is a proposition with a definite role (as a specific premiss: 1147a3) in his body of knowledge. While he can grasp (e.g.) that this food is chicken (or sweet), he fails either to have or to use this information as part of his relevant body of knowledge. In both cases, the person may be said to know (in the sense of grasp: *eidenai*) that this food is chicken. But he does so in the way a child might who has *either* not yet acquired the relevant body of knowledge about which food is healthy *or* has acquired it but for some reason fails to exercise it.

This reading of 1147a7 enjoys a decisive advantage over the standard interpretation of this passage. If one understands Aristotle as holding [A], an *acrates* can take (or avoid) this chicken knowingly (*eidos*) and 'voluntarily' (*hekôn*) even when he does not have this claim that (e.g.) this food is chicken as part of his body of knowledge.[18] So interpreted, this passage is fully consistent with Aristotle's contention that all who (e.g.) acratically eat a cake do so voluntarily (*hekontes*: 1146a7, 1136a32–5, 1152a15 f.). For that requires them to know (in the sense of grasping: *eidotes*—see, for example, *Nicomachean Ethics* 1111a22–4) that the object they eat is a cake while they eat it.[19]

By contrast, the [B] reading, itself an essential part of the standard interpretation, generates a serious inconsistency in Aristotle's thought: it requires that the *acrates* in question does not grasp (*eidenai*) that this is sweet (or chicken) while eating it voluntarily. But elsewhere Aristotle is clear that grasp of particulars of this type (*eidenai*) is required for voluntary action. As a result of its failure to pay sufficient attention to Aristotle's distinction between grasp (*eidenai*) and knowledge *(episteme)*, the standard view unnecessarily saddles him with an account of one type of acratic action which is inconsistent with his view that all *acrates* act voluntarily acratically. Charity (to Aristotle) requires that it be rejected.

Kenny saw this problem with the traditional reading clearly but (in order to avoid the difficulty just mentioned) suggested that this passage is not concerned

---

[18] This requirement is only that the *acrates* grasp (*eidenai*) that (e.g.) this is sweet when he acratically takes it. It does not require that (at that moment) that he grasp that he is acting badly (i.e. against one of his principles: see *Nicomachean Ethics/Eudemian Ethics* 1136a31 ff., 1138a9–10). It should be noted that Aristotle sometimes imposes the latter, stronger, requirement (see 1145b12).

[19] I argued for this understanding of 'voluntary' or 'intentional' action in my *Aristotle's Philosophy of Action*, pp. 57–61, 118 ff., 256–61. Agents who grasp (*eidotes*) the relevant fact before or after but not while they act do not perform that act voluntarily. Actions done in ignorance brought on by drunkenness (*methe*) are classified as blameworthy but 'involuntary' (see *Nicomachean Ethics/Eudemian Ethics* 1136a5–8) or (at least) 'non-voluntary' (*Nicomachean Ethics* 1113b30 ff.).

with *acrasia* at all.[20] However, his account seems difficult to sustain, given the initial context in which Aristotle is applying a distinction between two ways of knowing (drawn in 1146b31–3) to the case of *acrasia* (1146b33–5). Indeed, this distinction is first introduced as one of his ways to spell out the thought that *acrasia* does not occur against knowledge (1146b24–5). Since it is not clear in his initial discussion of two types of knowing which proposition the *acrates* fails to contemplate (1146b31–5), Aristotle needs to say more about his reasoning and proceeds to do so in 1147a1–10.

The reading of this passage just suggested leaves room for the case of the 'swift' *acrates*. Unlike the melancholic *acrates*, he (or she) can deliberate to some extent but still will fail to arrive at the relevant good conclusion. In the case in point, they may fail to use some information at their disposal to arrive at the appropriate conclusion although they will deliberate to some extent by using the major premises and one of their minor premises. Although in the more general (or 'logical') discussion of 1147a1–10 Aristotle does not introduce desire as the factor which prevents this acratic from using the relevant piece of information to arrive at the conclusion, the later account of the speedy desire of the sharp *acrates* fills the necessary gap. Its speed is shown by its ability to lead the *acrates* to act before he (or she) has completed his (or her) deliberation.

(C) The weak acrates

The discussion of drunkenness above has prepared us for its use in Book VII, chapter 3 in the description of the acratic who says the conclusion 'like the tipsy person repeating the verses of Empedocles' (1147b10–12). These acratics will be those who do not stay by the conclusions of their reasoning because they hold them like the tipsy drunk. They will be the weak *acrates*.

Those who are tipsy drunk in this way have been compared with the young who are optimistic and naive, not properly influenced by the experience of life. The latter can go through entire arguments, arrive at the relevant conclusions and be aware of them, but still fail to know or fully grasp them because they lack the experience required for knowledge. If so, the weak *acrates*, like the tipsy drunk, can arrive at the good conclusion of their reasoning but still fail to know it. In this their condition will be unlike that of the melancholic (who does not deliberate at all) and the sharp (who may deliberate to some degree). For both types of impetuous *acrates* will fail to arrive (in any way) at the good conclusion.

In the present context, Aristotle's comparison of those who under the influence of passions speak words without knowledge and the young students is

---

[20] 'The Practical Syllogism and Incontinence', p. 173.

important.[21] Young students can put together arguments, make long speeches, and may well be convinced (e.g. on the basis of authority) of what they have been told.[22] They can understand and present the relevant propositions clearly and lucidly. They may well think they have knowledge of the claims they put forward although they lack the appropriately based confidence (*pistis*) required for proper knowledge. When they repeat the words of their teachers, they are like those who have learned a script without properly assessing its truth. Although, when they make such speeches, the latter may believe what they say, they still lack the evidential support required for them to have rational confidence in their judgements. Their failure properly to engage with the relevant body of knowledge will consist in their lack of appropriately based (or rational) confidence (*pistis*) in the truth of what they say.

If *acrates* (pl.) make speeches in a similar fashion about the evils of drink (or cakes), they will be in a similar condition.[23] Like young students (1147a21 ff.), they fail (in some way) properly to engage with the body of beliefs (or knowledge) they repeat. In their case, drunkenness cuts them off (for a time) from a grasp (or scrutiny) of the basis for the views they express, while the young students completely lack the experience required to sustain their views (see *Nicomachean Ethics/Eudemian Ethics* 1142a20 ff.). The tipsy drunk resemble the young students more than they do the person asleep. Both fail properly to

[21] I am inclined to take the young students as cases of those who 'have and do not have knowledge'. They fail to manifest knowledge when they speak *because* they have not made the views they express their own (1147a21). However, since they have learned something (*mathontes*), they must 'have in some way' the knowledge they express (1147a12–13). While not all who say words that come from knowledge have that knowledge (e.g. a young child repeating the proofs of Euclid), the young students (as described) seem to do so. Indeed, this is probably why Aristotle uses them and not young children to make his point. However, since this point is controversial, I shall focus (in what follows) on the case of the tipsy-drunk.

[22] '*Suneirein*' means connect, compose or tie together. It is used non-pejoratively of putting together arguments: see *On Sophistical Refutations* 175a30, *Topics* 158a37, *Metaphysics* 995a16, 1093b27. Ross's translation of 'string together' is not well supported. Apparently pejorative uses fall into two categories. In one, the term is explicitly qualified in a pejorative way (with, for example, 'in one breath': see Demosthenes, 18.308). In the other, what is criticized is the putting together of two things which do not properly go together (*Metaphysics* 1090b30, *On Divination by Dreams* 464b4 f.). Neither shows that 'connect' itself has a pejorative meaning. For a somewhat similar, but less radical, view, see Myles Burnyeat's suggestion in his 'Aristotle on Learning to be Good', in Amelie Rorty (ed.), *Essays on Aristotle's Ethics* (Berkeley and Los Angeles: University of California Press, 1980), p. 89, n. 6.

[23] If the next sentence (1147a22 ff.) expresses an idea derived from the previous one (as *hoste* suggests), the *acrates* (pl.) when they speak will be like those who lack rational confidence in the arguments they deploy in their speeches (since they have not been appropriately convinced of their truth). The term '*hypokrinesthai*' (*Rhetoric* 1413b21–3) is used of orators as well as actors (*hypokritai*). Since both engage in speech making (*hypokrisei*: 1118a8), a better translation of '*hypokrinesthai*' is 'those making a speech'. The *acrates* need not be like an actor in any other respect: e.g., in saying something he does not believe or in pretending to be someone else.

engage with some body of knowledge but neither need be unaware of what they claim to believe (or know).

4. The Failure of the Weak *acrates*: The Difficulty

In the last section, in discussing the weak *acrates*, I simply assumed that the tipsy drunk mentioned in 1147a10 ff. is one who has arrived at the 'good' conclusion. While Kenny and I disagree about some of the details of the passage 1147a24–b10, we agree on this claim. Since in a recent paper, I have set out in some detail my preferred reading of the passage 1147a24–b10, I intend now to focus in more detail on the type of failure which the weak *acrates* undergoes.[24] The major issue is how to understand his failure. And it is at this point that Kenny and I disagree.

In his original article, Kenny suggested that the case mentioned in 1147b10 ff. was one where the *acrates* gets to the good conclusion, knows it, and is prevented from acting by the presence of an unreasoning desire. In this view, the condition of the weak *acrates* is to be understood in terms of two separate components: a belief (amounting to knowledge) that something is best to do (expressed in the conclusion) and a desire to act (which in this case runs contrary to his knowledge) and leads him astray. There need be no failure on the part of belief: it is merely that the belief in question is successfully opposed by sensual desire which leads him away.

This suggestion is difficult to sustain. First, as Kenny subsequently noted, it does not involve any failure of knowledge on the part of the *acrates*. But, if so, he (or she) is not in any way ignorant, although the *acrates* is so described by Aristotle in 1147b5–8.[25] Second, and more generally, there would be little point in Aristotle's attempt throughout the chapter to compare failures in theoretical reasoning (where knowledge is lacking) with those in practical reasoning (1147a16 f.), if in the latter case knowledge is present and unaffected. However, on Kenny's first suggestion, the weak *acrates* does not fail in knowledge at all: it is simply that desire successfully resists what he (or she) knows is to be done. 'Practical knowledge', so understood, turns out to be simply (and disappointingly) a label for two otherwise unconnected items: knowledge (properly speaking) and desire, which operate in the present case independently of one another. Third, Kenny's first view is difficult to

[24] In 'Nicomachean Ethics VII.3: Varieties of akrasia'.
[25] Kenny initially suggested relocating these lines as 'clearly out of place' in the present context ('The Practical Syllogism and Incontinence', p. 183).

square with the details of Aristotle's claim in 1147b9 ff. (cited above) where he writes:

Since the final proposition is an opinion about a perceptible object, and is responsible for action, this the person either does not have while influenced by passion or has in such a way that the having [in question] is not knowing but saying in the manner of the tipsy drunk who repeats the verses of Empedocles.

For if there were nothing wrong with the *acrates*' opinion (or belief), the *acrates* would continue to have it (even while acratically) in a perfectly acceptable way. However, this passage indicates that there is something wrong with the opinion in question so that the *acrates* in question is reduced to saying it but not knowing it. There is, in effect, an elliptical argument in these lines:

(1) The final proposition is an opinion and responsible for action.
(2) The *acrates* does not act on it.
(3) Hence: either the *acrates* lacks the final proposition altogether or merely says without knowledge.

But (3) only follows from (1) and (2) if one makes the further assumption that the *acrates* fails properly to grasp the relevant opinion. The passage pinpoints a failure in knowledge in addition to any failure brought on by revolt on the part of desire. Indeed, it requires that there is something amiss with the *acrates*' relevant opinion which explains why it fails to be knowledge. This is why his (or her) state is compared with that of the tipsy drunk who clearly fails in knowledge and not just in action. (Indeed, the tipsy drunk might actually act on his conclusion even though he fails to know (or even believe) it.)

Kenny returned to this passage in *Aristotle's Theory of the Will* and proposed a second reading of 1147b9–12 in which there is a failure in knowledge (and belief) as well as a revolt by opposing desire. Indeed, the failure in belief is now held to explain why the agent lacks the desire required for him (or her) to act. That is, the *acrates* lacks the relevant desire because the belief in question fails to be operative in producing it. But if the belief fails to be operative, the weak *acrates* will not properly have it because (as Kenny now suggests) it is, for Aristotle, a criterion for having this belief that it guides the subsequent desire. On this revised view, the *acrates* is ignorant in that he (or she) must in some way lack the belief in the conclusion since they fail to act accordingly. The ignorance, mentioned in 1147b5–8, is the deficiency in the *acrates*' belief which must be present since it fails to guide his (or her) action.

This interesting proposal, which is introduced in a few suggestive lines, deserves more spelling out. On one understanding, it offers merely a redescription of the condition of the weak *acrates*. The acratic agent, we assume, acts against his conclusion because of the presence of an opposed desire. This, indeed, is the fact that we are trying to explain. But if we are now told that because he acts in this way he does not really believe the conclusion, we gain no further understanding of why he fails to believe that conclusion or what that failure consists in. We have just labelled his case as one of a failure of belief simply because he (or she) does not act on it. Since, as Kenny himself has rightly emphasized,[26] Aristotle is aiming at some type of explanation of the phenomenon, at least in the last ('physical') part of the chapter, he must say more to account for the weak *acrates'* failure to act. More specifically, he needed to point to some feature of the belief in question which explains why it fails to control the relevant desire.

Kenny understood the elliptical argument in 1147b9–12 sketched above in terms of the Wittgensteinian notion of a 'criterion'. The reason why the *acrates* who fails to act lacks the relevant belief is that it is a criterion for his (or her) having that belief that he acts accordingly. However, it is far from clear that Aristotle subscribed to this notion, whose roots lie in a twentieth-century idea of how we, as interpreters, ascribe mental states to one another.

Aristotle, by contrast, seems to have approached the issue differently, assuming an account of mental states whose existence (and identity) does not depend on how we, as interpreters, understand each other. Indeed, in general, he seems to think of the operation of beliefs and desires in causal terms as real entities existing independently of our preferred mode of ascription. While Kenny himself dismisses aspects of this approach as 'fanciful', there can be little doubt that Aristotle, in so far as he was guided by it, needed to find an explanation of the failure of the *acrates* more realist than that offered by the theory of attribution, however sophisticated.

Aristotle's explanatory ambitions can be seen, in 1147b9–12, in his comparison of the weak *acrates* with one who has a proposition but does not know it but merely says it like the drunk reciting the verses of Empedocles (1147b12). Earlier the tipsy drunk was introduced as one who fails properly to know (1147a14) and is (no doubt) included amongst those who say proofs or verses without knowledge in 1147a21ff. However, the failure of the tipsy drunk is not (at least standardly) that he fails to act on what he says.[27] It is rather a failure properly to grasp the propositions in question. In 1147b9–12 Aristotle appears to be seeking a specification of a type of belief-failure characteristic of the weak *acrates* which is (in some way) like that of the tipsy drunk. If he

---

[26] *Aristotle's Theory of the Will*, p. 165.
[27] There is no evidence that the verses in question are concerned with the evils of drink. Nor will the proofs in question be!

can establish that, he will have taken an important step towards explaining the predicament of the weak *acrates*.

How is this step to be taken? If the resulting desire simply does not respond appropriately to the belief that one should (e.g.) abstain from this sweet, what occurs appears to be a failure not of belief but of desire. For if the belief has done all it can to tame the desire and still fails, why impugn its status as a belief? It has, for all that has been so far said, been arrived at by deductive steps from other beliefs the agent still holds. However, as Kenny notes, it seems preferable to locate the failure as one of belief, which in turn accounts for the resulting failure in desire. Indeed, this is what the comparison with the tipsy drunk would suggest. For the latter fails in knowledge (and belief) and it is a failure like this which is now invoked to account for the failure of the weak *acrates* to guide his desires.

But what is the type of failure in belief (or knowledge) at issue? It may seem that there could not be a failure of belief in this case. For if one derives a proposition as the deductive consequence of two other claims that one knows to be true, one must surely believe (indeed know) the conclusion (if one sees it as the conclusion). Hence, if the *acrates* knows the major premiss and combines this with a minor premiss that he (or she) also knows to form a conclusion, they must also know the conclusion to be true. Indeed, Aristotle himself seems to accept this principle in the *Analytics*. If so, it seems that there cannot be a failure (on the part of weak acratics) to know the conclusion, granted (as Kenny and I do) that they know both major and minor premisses and combine these to form a conclusion.

Confronted with this difficulty, some will be tempted to conclude that, after all, Aristotle has not properly accounted for a case in which the [weak] *acrates* arrives at the good conclusion but fails properly to believe it and so fails to act. It might be better to locate the *acrates'* failure in belief at an earlier stage in his reasoning, either as ignorance of the content of the minor premiss or as a failure to use his (or her) premisses to arrive at the good conclusion. Perhaps his failure is not explained at all but simply described (without explanatory intent) by Aristotle as a failure to use the minor premiss in the way which leads to action.[28]

---

[28] Albertus Magnus was the first to suggest that to fail to theorize (in the practical case) might simply be to fail to act on one's reasoning. His account has been recently revived by A. Mele, 'Aristotle on *Akrasia* and Knowledge', *Modern Schoolman*, 58 (1981), pp. 137–59 and S. Broadie, *Ethics with Aristotle* (Oxford: Oxford University Press, 1991), pp. 292–7. There are, however, problems with this suggestion. There are no parallels elsewhere for this use of *theorein*. Of course, when one theorizes (about building) as a builder one will go on to build. But this does not make building part of one's theorizing. Indeed, doing (*prattein*) and contemplating (*theorein*) are regularly distinguished. On this,

5. The Failure of the Weak *acrates*: Two Attempts to Resolve the Difficulty

The considerations advanced above offer two ways to address this problem. Both begin with the suggestion that the tipsy drunk, like the young students, lacks knowledge because he lacks rational confidence (*pistis*) in what he (or she) says). But, in Aristotle's view, confidence of this type is a necessary condition for opinion. In *De Anima* he writes:

confidence attends every opinion, having been persuaded attends confidence and reason attends persuasion.   (428a22 ff.)

If one lacks reason-based confidence of this type, one has not belief but some lesser type of state (*phantasia*).[29] Hence, if the weak *acrates* lacks rational confidence in the conclusion he has drawn, he will fail to accept it in the way Aristotle requires for opinion and knowledge. He may get to the conclusion, assert it and even accept it as true but still lack rational confidence in its truth. So understood, while the weak *acrates* draws a conclusion from his premises, he does not have confidence in the conclusion he draws. Lacking rational confidence in this way, he will not withstand the desires for the opposed course nor stand by what he has concluded as the best thing to do. This lack of confidence will account for his failure to act appropriately and explain why he lacks knowledge of the conclusion. Indeed, he (or she) will lack the relevant opinion (given Aristotle's understanding of the requirements for having an opinion) and so may be deemed to be ignorant (in some way) of the conclusion.

There are, however, two ways to understand the relevant lack of rational confidence and attendant failure of belief in the case of the weak *acrates*. In what follows, I shall discuss both without attempting to come to a final decision between them.

One way to develop this proposal runs as follows: the weak *acrates* suffers precisely the same type of failure that characterizes the tipsy drunk. In the case of the acratic, the appeal of the opposed course (taking the sweet) makes the best action no longer seem an attractive option. Its ceasing to appear attractive undermines his confidence in the claim that this is the best thing to

see David Bostock's persuasive criticisms (*Aristotle's Ethics*, p. 126, n. 11) of recent attempts to revive Albertus' view.

[29] Aristotle makes the connection between opinion and confidence twice in this passage of *De Anima*, first at a general level (428a19–22), second at that of each individual opinion (428a22–4). Since these passages make different but interconnected points, both should be retained.

do. Even if he still holds that claim to be true, he does so without rational confidence. As a result of this lack of confidence, he fails to withstand his desire for another action and does not stand by his judgement that it is the best option available to him. Desire, fear, lack of nerve can, on this account, undermine one's rationally based confidence that a given course is best. They do this not by making one unaware that one holds this to be true but by diminishing one's confidence in its truth. Thus, influenced by desire, the weak *acrates* may say without knowledge (or opinion) 'Do not do this' (1147a34 f.) because that desire undermines his confidence in the truth of the conclusion he has drawn.

The account just offered, like Kenny's, involves two separable components, belief and desire, where failure in the former leads to failure in the latter. It differs from his account in (i) seeing the relevant failure in belief as one in rationally based confidence in the truth of the conclusion and in (ii) suggesting an outline explanation of how the relevant confidence is undermined by the operation of sensual desire. Of course, the latter explanation is not complete. One still needs to know how rational confidence can be undermined in this way by the presence of sensual desire or the attractions of some other course of action. One might wonder how it is that intellectual confidence based on an acceptance of relevant evidence is, or can be, affected in this way. However, in reply, it may be suggested, that, as with the issue of how knowledge is restored, Aristotle's explanation runs out at this point. He is perhaps content to address both these questions to 'the students of nature' (1147b7 ff.). Perhaps he thought that there was nothing problematic with the idea that sensual desire, like drunkenness or sleep, can remove rationally based confidence by, for example, limiting or restricting one's ability to support one's claims by reason. If so, he could reasonably leave the precise details of what happens to 'the students of nature'.

There is another account of the failure in rational confidence of the weak *acrates* to be considered. This departs from the idea, on which the first proposal rests, that (i) there are two separable components, desire and belief, involved in the case of the weak *acrates* and that (ii) a failure in his belief leads to failure in his desire. Rather, on the alternative account, to see something as good (or fine) is to rationally desire it as to see something as pleasant is to sensually desire it.[30] On this model, preferential choice is not a combination of intellect and

---

[30] I set out this account in more detail in 'Aristotle's Desire' in V. Hirvonen, T. Holpaianen and M. Tuominen (eds), *Mind and Modality* (Leiden: Brill, 2006), pp. 19–40 and 'Aristotle's Weak *acrates*: In What Does Her Ignorance Consist?' in C. Bobonich and P. Destrée (eds), *Akrasia in Greek Philosophy* (Leiden: Brill, 2007), pp. 193–214.

desire but is rather a distinctive type of state: intellectual desire or desiderative intellect. It is that type of grasping what is best to do which cannot be defined except as a desiderative type of grasping or alternatively that type of desiring which cannot be defined except as intellectual type of desiring, one focused on doing what is best. From this perspective, when the weak *acrates* fails in his preferential choice, his failure is one in a distinctively desiderative type of grasping. If this is represented as a failure in opinion, it is a failure in a desire-involving type of opinion which can also be represented as a failure in intellect-involving desire. His failure in rational confidence will, on this view, not be a purely intellectual failure (i) caused by the attractions of the other course which (ii) causes him to fail in his desire for the better option. Rather it will consist in his failing to be attracted to the better course and therein failing to desire that course as he should.

The first account of failure of the weak *acrates* involves three stages:

[1] a failure in intellectual rational confidence in the conclusion that (e.g.) abstaining is best, generated by one's being drawn to the attractiveness of (e.g.) eating a sweet;

[2] a failure in belief constituted by the failure in this intellectual rational confidence;

[3] a failure in desire which results from the failure in belief.

By contrast, in the second account, there are only

[1] a failure in rational confidence (partially) constituted by one's being drawn to the attractiveness of eating the sweet

and

[2] a failure in belief which is also a failure in desire, both (partially) constituted by the failure in this distinctive type of desire-involving rational confidence.

In being attracted towards the pleasures of eating the sweet, he is less attracted to the better course, therein less confident that it is the better course and more easily led to take the other course. The greater simplicity of the second account springs from its treating practical opinion and its grounds as essentially desire-involving.

It would be a major undertaking to show that Aristotle preferred one or other of the two suggestions just canvassed. *Nicomachean Ethics*, Book VII chapter 3 appears, by itself, to be consistent with both interpretations. Even if Aristotle is clear in this chapter that one *acrates* gets to and is aware (while acting) of the good conclusion, he does not determine the precise nature of his lack of confidence or knowledge failure. Perhaps Aristotle does not need to specify more precisely the nature of the lack of confidence (*pistis*) involved to resolve the first *aporia*. Both accounts show in different ways the type of knowledge failure involved in the case of weak *acrasia*.

Nor is it clear that Aristotle favours one or other of these alternatives in the remainder of Book VII. Consider three passages that might have been thought helpful.

(1) the [weak] *acrates* differs from the practically wise in preferential choice. For he is not like one who knows actively . . . but like one who is tipsy (*oinomenos*). (1151b14–16)

However, in this passage, the relevant failure of knowledge could be the cause of the *acrates*' lack of a good preferential choice (as in the first suggestion) or, alternatively, it could be (as in the second account) identical with his having a less than ideal preferential choice.[31]

(2) the impetuous do not stay true to reason because they have quick or excessive desires because they are prone to follow their imagination. (1150b27 ff.)

However, in this passage it is not clear whether people have strong or quick desires because they are prone (intellectually) to follow their imaginations (as in the first account mentioned) or whether their being prone to follow their imagination consists in their having desires of this kind (as in the second). While both accounts seem possible, neither is required.

(3) the *acrates* is the kind of man to pursue bodily pleasures which are excessive and against good reason not because he has been convinced that this is the right thing to do . . . [rather he] is the sort of man who stands outside reason, one whom passion overcomes to the extent he does not act in accordance with good reason but not to the extent that he is convinced that he should pursue without restraint such pleasures . . . (1151a11 ff.)

This formulation seems consistent with both the accounts just offered of the way in which the weak *acrates* fails to be convinced, when he is acratic, that he should do the best action.

If Aristotle elsewhere favoured one or other of these styles of account, this will emerge in his treatment of other themes concerning virtue, self-control, desire, and practical reasoning. The differences between them are not easy to discern in his attempts in *Nicomachean Ethics*, Book VII to give an account of *acrasia* which resolves the *aporiai* raised at the beginning of the book.

---

[31] I leave aside here the relation between preferential choice and the conclusion of practical reasoning.

6. Conclusion

I have argued, following Kenny's lead, that there are two major types of acratics introduced in *Nicomachean Ethics* Book VII chapter 3, and I have suggested that they are characterized more fully in chapters 7–10. These are the *impetuous*, who fail to complete their deliberation, and the *weak*, who arrive at the good conclusion of their deliberation but do not stand by it. There are, moreover, two varieties of impetuous acratic: the sharp and the melancholic. Both fail to control their actions by reason and both (or so I have argued) are introduced, albeit implicitly, in Book VII chapter 3. Further, I have proposed an account of the knowledge failure of the weak acratic as consisting in his not being rationally persuaded (at the time of action) that he should do the best action. If this is correct, he may fail in knowledge even though he has drawn the relevant conclusion, is aware of it, and accepts that it is the best thing for him to do. What he lacks is rational confidence in the truth of his 'good' conclusion. Given this account of his knowledge failure, Aristotle's weak acratic, when confronted with a tempting sweet, may (i) draw the correct conclusion that he should abstain from it; but nevertheless (ii) take it, under the influence of a conflicting sensual desire; yet at the same time (iii) be aware, while taking it, that he should not do so.

4

An Approach to Aristotelian Actuality

CHRISTOPHER SHIELDS

Simple notions cannot be defined, since an infinite regress in definitions is impossible. But actuality is one of those simple notions. Hence, it cannot be defined.

Aquinas, *Commentary on Aristotle's Metaphysics*, Bk IX, ch. 5; 1826.

1. A Kind of Account

In asserting the indefinability of the Aristotelian notion of actuality, Aquinas appeals to two distinct methodological principles, both derived from Aristotle, one general and one specific. The general principle holds that definition must end somewhere, that the process of defining cannot carry on *ad infinitum*; the specific principle holds that since definition proceeds analytically, by breaking complex concepts into their simpler parts, no simple concept admits of definition. In this, Aquinas shows himself at ease with some tenets of Aristotelian philosophy which later found themselves rather starkly assailed. We may, for instance, contrast Aquinas's sanguinity about Aristotelian actuality with the later reaction of Gassendi, who grew dyspeptic when confronted with the same concept, as he found it deployed in Aristotle's definition of motion. According to Aristotle, motion (*kinêsis*) is not a simple concept, and may indeed be defined in terms of the notion of actuality (*entelecheia*) as the 'actuality of what is in potentiality *qua* such'.[1] Gassendi's reaction:

---

[1] *hê tou dunamei ontos entelecheia hê(i) toiouton; Physics* 201a10–11.

Great God! Is there any stomach strong enough to digest that? The explanation of a familiar thing was requested, but this is so complicated that nothing is clear anymore... The need for definitions of the words in the definitions will go on *ad infinitum*.[2]

Gassendi's response is initially understandable. We think we know what motion is, but we do not know what actuality is, and still less do we know what it is for something to be the actuality of what is in potentiality *qua* such. If we find the plain defined in terms of the obscure, then we rightly demand definitions of the obscure. If the obscure is in turn defined in terms of the still more obscure, we will never reach bedrock, and will have succeeded only in making what is familiar ever more alien, without end.

Aquinas and Gassendi thus enter into a dispute about a concept fundamental to one of several philosophical traditions Anthony Kenny has done so much to illuminate. It is thus especially welcome to contribute a chapter on the topic of Aristotelian actuality to a volume dedicated to his honour. In this chapter I seek to emulate Kenny, so far as possible, by using the techniques and methods of philosophical exploration pioneered and practised with such noteworthy success by him. In particular, Kenny has seen the appropriateness of roaming freely through the history of Aristotelianism to throw light on the sometimes intractable problems within Aristotle's own texts; and this paper follows suit by identifying and augmenting an interpretation of Aristotelian actuality (*energeia* or *entelecheia*) introduced by Aquinas but then largely neglected, to its detriment, by the tradition which followed him.

We do well to begin this exploration by sharpening the issues dividing Aquinas and Gassendi. One accuses Aristotle of obscurantism and of creating an unnecessary pressure for endless definition; the other thinks that definition comes to a close when it reaches the conceptually basic concept of actuality. Both rightly see that little of Aristotle's physics or metaphysics has a chance of being intelligible unless we can become clear about Aristotelian actuality. Aquinas thinks that we can become clear, and that clarity does not in this instance require definition; Gassendi implicitly demands definition for clarity, and sees little prospect of success in that enterprise.

In reviewing the divide between Aquinas and Gassendi, one might fairly think that each has a point. When we define motion in terms of actuality, we use a technical term to define something non-technical. So, Gassendi has a point. Still, not every technical term requires a definition, at least not a reductive definition. It is not clear, for instance, whether the fundamental

---

[2] Pierre Gassendi, *Exercises against the Aristotelians* [*Exercitationes paradoxicae adversus Aristoteleos*, 1624], II.2, 4.

modal terms of *possibility* and *necessity* may be defined, or defined reductively in wholly non-modal terms, but that does not impede their being used to great effect in metaphysics and mathematics. Less severely, if they do admit of definitions, those definitions are not universally agreed, and the lack of agreement on this point does not by itself hinder their use. So, Aquinas too has a point on his side.

The concept about which Aquinas and Gassendi clash is *actuality, actualitas* in their Latin, *energeia* or *entelecheia* in Aristotle's Greek. Both *energeia* and *entelecheia* are regularly rendered into Latin and English by a single word, since both are evidently Aristotelian neologisms[3] and they are often used interchangeably by Aristotle. We will begin without worrying about whether these words should be distinguished systematically and may speak somewhat generically of *actuality*.

Our question thus becomes whether there is an account of Aristotelian actuality available, so that Gassendi's complaint may be met. If so, a subsidiary question comes to the fore concerning the kind of account we have in view. If this account is non-reductive, then Gassendi's complaint may be countered without contravening Aquinas's strictures concerning definition, since it is clear that his contention pertains only to the indefinability of simple concepts, and especially to the impossibility of reductive definitions of such concepts.

To be sure, no definition revealing *energeia* to be equivalent to some other, more basic Aristotelian notion such as *form* (*eidos*) or *being* (*to on*) can be developed. Nor indeed can there be a canonical definition given in terms of genus and differentia; for the case of *actuality*, says Aristotle, is rather like *being* (*to on*) across the categories (*Metaphysics* 1045b26–1046a2), and certainly no reductive account of being is possible. Moreover, as is clear from Aristotle's definition of motion, there is also a second sort of impediment to reductive definition: every account of actuality will at least implicitly advert to some notion of potentiality (*dunamis*), and every account of potentiality will at least implicitly appeal to some notion of actuality. There is thus no breaking out of this interlocking circle of definition.

Bracketing worries about reducibility and circularity, we may turn to a more consequential and instructive impediment to there being a single, all-encompassing account of actuality in Aristotle: he simply does not use the term univocally. Instead, he self-consciously introduces several different, if related concepts of actuality, and sometimes even insists that his readers attend to the differences between them (*Metaphysics*, Bk IV, ch. 12). This is a fact already

---

[3] I discuss Aristotle's introduction of these neologisms in Section 2 below.

appreciated by others,[4] and is reflected in the variety of words translators have found it necessary to use when trying to render *energeia* into English and other modern languages (some English renderings in addition to *actuality* and *activity*: *act, actualization,* and in its adverbial form, *actually*).

While most agree that Aristotle uses *actuality* in several discernibly distinct ways, controversy erupts when commentators begin to specify these ways with precision and to assess their relation to one another. Some suppose the changing meanings of 'actuality' reflect developmental shifts in his thinking about actuality and potentiality;[5] others suggest that when he finds himself faced with disparate philosophical problems in different areas of inquiry—beginning with an analysis of change, and then, heading in one direction, moving to an account of the soul and its faculties, and then again, heading in another direction, to an analysis of pleasure—Aristotle simply shifts the meanings of *actuality* to suit the context of inquiry.[6]

His practice in this regard leads to an important, but difficult question: how are Aristotle's various notions of *actuality* related to one another? Naturally, this question presupposes a prior question: why does Aristotle feel compelled to distinguish different notions of *actuality*? After all, since the word *energeia* was his own coinage, he might have avoided using it in non-equivalent ways.[7]

We make some progress on this question by focusing on the two main uses of *actuality* in *Metaphysics* IX, which contains Aristotle's most protracted and intricate discussion of the correlative notions of *actuality* and *potentiality*. The best route to understanding the relation between the two notions of *actuality* distinguished in this book begins by focusing on a question given little attention in most contemporary discussions: what forces a distinction in the first instance? If we can determine clearly why Aristotle insists that there is more than one form of *actuality*, then we can also move some way towards understanding how he thinks the two notions of *actuality* are related. It emerges

---

[4] H. Bonitz, *Index Aristotelicus* (2nd edn, Berlin, 1870). See also Chung-Hwan Chen, 'Different Meanings of the Term *Energeia* in the Philosophy of Aristotle', *Philosophy and Phenomenological Research* 16 (1956), pp. 56–65.

[5] Daniel Graham, 'States and Performances: Aristotle's Test', *Philosophical Quarterly* 3 (1995), pp. 117–29; Stephen Menn, 'The Origins of Aristotle's Concept of *Energeia* and *Dunamis*', *Ancient Philosophy* 14 (1994), pp. 73–114.

[6] Charlotte Witt, *Ways of Being: Potentiality and Actuality in Aristotle's Metaphysics* (Ithaca, NY: Cornell University Press, 2003), pp. 13 and 123–4, n. 2.

[7] David Bostock, *Aristotle Ethics* (Oxford: Oxford University Press: 2000), p. 150 comments: 'I have not seen any good explanation of why Aristotle should have introduced a new word of his own, and then used it in the two apparently very different ways, which force translators into different renderings in each case. Certainly, it can be confusing.' This seems a reasonable observation, though, if the argument of this paper is correct, we will have before us a perfectly good reason for Aristotle to proceed in this way.

that although neither form is more basic than the other, both equally derive from a prior core notion, and so may be related as non-core instances of a core-dependent homonym.[8] As being (*to on*) is a core-dependent homonym,[9] so too is *actuality*. If correct, this is a welcome result not least because it provides a principled way of constraining extensions of Aristotle's notion of *actuality* relative to its main interpretative competitor, that the various notions of *energeia* in Aristotle's corpus are related no more than analogically.

2. Some Ways of Ordering Actuality

Scholars who approach the Aristotelian corpus as a whole without any preconceived notions about Aristotle's development confront an obvious problem about his introduction and use of his primary term for actuality, namely *energeia*. He uses the word frequently,[10] often in tandem with a second neologism, *entelecheia*.[11] He regularly pairs these terms and often simply uses them as interchangeable synonyms (e.g. at *Metaphysics* 1065a14–16). Thus, if we have a clear sense of *entelecheia* we will be much closer to a full understanding of *energeia*. Unfortunately, the meaning of *entelecheia* is even more disputed than the meaning of *energeia*, as is the precise question of its relation to *energeia* in their non-synonymous uses.[12] Indeed, despite its being Aristotle's own (evident) neologism, *entelecheia* has a vexing and disputed etymology.[13] By contrast, the primary meaning of *energeia* is at least reasonably clear, as is

---

[8] The terminology of 'core-dependent homonymy' derives from Christopher Shields, *Order in Multiplicity: Homonymy in the Philosophy of Aristotle* (Oxford: Oxford University Press, 1999), which prefers this locution to other, similar terms, including Owen's 'focal meaning' (G. E. L. Owen, 'Logic and Metaphysics in Some Early Works of Aristotle', *Symposium Aristotelicum* 2 (Louvain: 1960), pp. 163–90) and Irwin's 'focal connexion' (Terence Irwin, *Aristotle's First Principles* (Oxford: Oxford University Press, 1988))—all representations of Aristotle's device of *pros hen* homonymy. On the relative merits of these terms, see Shields, *Order in Multiplicity* and Julie K. Ward, *Aristotle on Homonymy: Dialectic and Science* (Cambridge: Cambridge University Press, 2007).

[9] Shields, *Order in Multiplicity*.

[10] He uses *energeia* more often than *entelecheia*, by a ratio of almost five to one (671 to 138 uses respectively).

[11] *Entelecheia* is used much less frequently by Aristotle, with most of its uses concentrated in *De Anima*, where it is used 40 times (39 of them in its second and third books), which is the highest relative frequency in all his works. Elsewhere it occurs frequently in the corpus only in *Physics* (34), *Metaphysics* (40), *On Generation and Corruption* (21), and then rarely also in *De Caelo* (3) and *On the Generation of Animals* (2), and just once each in *The Parts of Animals* and the *Meteorology*.

[12] John Ackrill, 'Aristotle's Distinction between *Energeia* and *Kinēsis*', in R. Bambrough (ed.), *New Essays on Plato and Aristotle* (New York: Humanities Press, 1965) articulates this question in an especially clear and forceful manner.

[13] For a succinct review of some of the main proposals, no one of which is indisputably correct, see Graham, 'States and Performances'.

its probable etymology: it is likely developed by Aristotle from a verbal form (*energein*) derived from the adjective *energos*, which means in ordinary Greek to be active or employed, as opposed to being inactive or idle.[14]

Beyond that reasonably straightforward etymology, however, begins a disconcerting mass of linguistic data about Aristotle's use of *energeia*. In the *Rhetoric* he subordinates *energeia* to *kinêsis* (motion or change) (*Rhetoric* 1412a9); elsewhere, and more often, he subordinates *kinêsis* to *energeia* (*Physics* 201b31; *De Anima* 431a6; *Nicomachean Ethics* 1154b27; *Metaphysics* 1065b16); still elsewhere he actively opposes *kinêsis* and *energeia* (*Metaphysics* 1048b29; cf. 1065b14–1066a26 and *Nicomachean Ethics* 1173b2). So he seems to think now that *energeia* is a kind of motion, now that motion is a kind of *energeia*. Then again he implies that *energeia* and motion can have nothing to do with one another, since the two are mutually exclusive. While careful attention to context goes a long way towards resolving these seeming contradictions, so that in the end they prove to be mainly verbal, they do illustrate the difficulties attendant upon spelling out Aristotle's dominant use of the term *energeia*.

Prima facie contradictions aside, we can appreciate the breadth of the concept of *energeia* from its extension. The many uses of the term were already thoroughly catalogued in the nineteenth century by Bonitz in his *Index Aristotelicus*,[15] and he was followed by a series of other scholars who sought to impose some order on his data by taxonomizing the various uses of the word in Aristotle.[16] Efforts at taxonomy, whatever their final worth, tend to proceed in a unitarian rather than developmental fashion, as if the totality of Aristotle's corpus were delivered at once, as a completed whole. Others have developed a much more nuanced developmental picture, issuing in greater explanatory

[14] In this I side with Daniel W. Graham, *Aristotle's Two Systems* (Oxford: Clarendon Press, 1987), pp. 185–7, and against the criticisms of G. A. Blair, *Energeia and Entelecheia: 'Act' in Aristotle* (Ottawa: Western Ontario University Press, 1993), p. 95.

[15] Here it serves to recall the remark of Bonitz in his entry on *energeia* in the *Index Aristotelicus* (1870). After introducing the distinction in *Metaphysics* 1048b8 between *energeia* where it is related either as *kinêsis* to *dunamis* or as *ousia* (substance) to *hulên* (matter): '*Quod discrimen quamquam non potest ubique accurate observari, tamen ad perlustrandam varietatem usus aptum est.*' ('This distinction cannot always be accurately observed, but it does effectively cover the various uses found.')

[16] Thus, for instance, after listing 'at least nine' separate meanings of *energeia* in Aristotle, Chen seeks to impose some order on them. Although it is unlikely that these are in fact nine discernibly distinct uses of *energeia* in Aristotle, Chen's list in nonetheless instructive: (i) *energeia* as actuality, as contrasted with *dunamis* as potentiality; (ii) *energeia* as 'being actualized' or 'being perfect' (*Generation of Animals* 734b21); (iii) *energeia* as applied to form and soul (*Metaphysics* 1043a6, 12); (iv) energeia as actualization, the sense in which it is used for defining *kinêsis* at *Physics* 210a10–11; (v) *energeia* in its application to sensation and knowledge, as in *De Anima* 431a4–5 and 417b20–1; (vi) *energeia* as used in the definition of the chief good in *Nicomachean Ethics* 1098a7; (vii) *energeia* in the sense of 'pure activity' as at *Metaphysics* 1072b18–30; (viii) *energeia* in the sense of incomplete motion (*Nicomachean Ethics* 1174a19; *Physics* 201b31–2, 257b8–9; *De Anima* 417a16–17). See Chen, 'Different Meanings of the Term *Energeia*', pp. 56–65.

power than its unitarian predecessors.[17] On the developmental approach, Aristotle moves from a reasonably non-technical use, through various phases, to fully appropriated and technical use with a home only in metaphysics.[18] This sort of developmental approach has had adherents and detractors since the advent of developmental studies of Aristotle's philosophy, inaugurated by Jaeger in the nineteenth century.[19] Neither approach supplants what might be called the textbook taxonomy,[20] according to which Aristotle simply establishes a tripartite hierarchy (however and whenever developed) such that we can distinguish, in keeping with the clear indications of *De Anima*, Bk II, ch. 1 between (i) a being with the potentiality to Φ, where that potentiality is as yet undeveloped (a first potentiality, normally called a *dunamis*); (ii) a being that has developed its potentiality to Φ, but which is not at present Φ-ing (a second potentiality = a first actuality, normally called a *hexis*); and (iii) a being which has actualized its capacity to Φ and is now occurrently Φ-ing (a second actuality, an *energeia*). Where Φ is *speaking Chinese*, a human but not a stone has a first potentiality; a human who has learned to speak Chinese but is not

[17] Menn, 'Aristotle's Concept of *Energeia* and *Dunamis*'. Daniel Graham, 'The Development of Aristotle's Concept of Actuality: Comments on a Reconstruction by Stephen Menn', *Apeiron* 15 (1995), pp. 551–64, argues forcefully that despite his (generally plausible) developmental account, Menn indefensibly overlooks some formidable developmental predecessors, including, not least, Werner Jaeger, *Aristotle: Fundamentals of the History of His Development* (1928), 2nd edn, trans. R. Robinson (Oxford: Clarendon Press, 1948).

[18] So Menn, in 'Aristotle's Concept of *Energeia* and *Dunamis*', identifies four phases: (i) First comes *energeia* as simple *activity*, a sense found in the *Protrepticus* and other early writings, and foreshadowed in Plato's *Euthydemus* and *Theaetetus*. This sense is effectively continuous with non-technical senses of activity in fifth- and fourth-century BC prose (which did, however, rely on diction other than Aristotle's neologism *energeia*). (ii) Second is *energeia* in a quasi-technical sense, as an actually existing being, contrasted with a being existing in potentiality. A being exists in potentiality when there is a genuine capacity present in an actual being to be something other than that actual being in fact is, as an actual attorney is potentially but not actually an accountant. (iii) Third in Aristotle's development comes *energeia* as the completion of a process, the end of which sees a new being in actuality. This notion of *energeia*, suggests Menn, is a pure Aristotelian innovation, and is marked by the introduction of the more problematic and distinctively Aristotelian term *entelecheia*. (iv) Finally, fourth are the so-called analogical extensions *Metaphysics* IX.6, which form part of the focus of our interest. This fourth sense, according to Menn, underpins both the first and third senses already introduced, but in a vague and generic way.

[19] Jaeger, *Aristotle: Fundamentals*. Jaeger's arguments are revisited to good effect by both John M. Rist, *The Mind of Aristotle: A Study in Philosophical Growth* (Toronto: University of Toronto Press, 1989) and Graham, 'The Development of Aristotle's Concept of Actuality'.

[20] Menn ('Aristotle's Concept of *Energeia* and *Dunamis*', p. 88) does, however, regard himself as challenging what I call the textbook taxonomy, since he thinks it tends to obscure or conflate his distinction between (i) and (iii). In this he seems mistaken, since however accurate or not his developmental hypothesis may be, it is fully consistent with the textbook taxonomy, and may even be thought of as a genetic account of how Aristotle arrived at it. For some difficulties with Menn's developmental hypothesis, and especially his treatments of (ii) and (iii) as phases in Aristotle's thinking, see Graham, 'The Development of Aristotle's Concept of Actuality', pp. 555–8.

currently doing so is in a state of second potentiality or first actuality; and, finally, a person who has learned Chinese and is now speaking Chinese is in a state of second actuality.

Now, whatever these various ways of organizing Aristotle's different notions of *energeia* may show taken individually—and there do seem to be significant problems with all of them except for the textbook taxonomy, which escapes refutation mainly by being bland—taken corporately they do point to some disarray. In these terms, we find Aristotle relying upon a host of vaguely related notions, some of them technical and some of them not—and among these, the technical uses are especially difficult to comprehend.

3. Potentiality and Actuality in *Metaphysics* IX: A Pair of Approaches

Some progress can be made if we focus on Aristotle's most mature and extended discussion of actuality (both *energeia* and *entelecheia*), in *Metaphysics*, Book IX. He introduces a basic notion of potentiality (*dunamis*) in *Metaphysics* IX.1, which despite being characterized by him as the most fundamental sort of *dunamis*, is not, says Aristotle, going to be primary concern in that book; and he implies that the same point pertains to the correlative notion of *energeia* (*Metaphysics* 1045b36–7). His primary concern is rather going to be extension of that basic notion, which he introduces only much later in the book, in *Metaphysics* IX.6. Given the introduction of a basic notion which proves to be a merely peripheral concern, there is an obvious question pertaining to Aristotle's procedure in this book. Why should Aristotle feel compelled to introduce a basic notion of actuality as basic, only to set it aside in favour of an extended sense? If the first sense is basic, or primary, then presumably it should serve as the primary focus of any investigation into the concept. Why introduce it only to set it aside?

Scholars do not seem to have come to terms with this question.[21] It is as if a contemporary philosopher investigating the nature of causation were

---

[21] S. Makin, *Aristotle: Metaphysics Book θ, translated with an introduction and commentary* (Oxford: Clarendon Press, 2006), pp. 19–20, for instance, despite his otherwise admirably thorough and incisive commentary, passes over this matter, except to observe that despite appearances to the contrary, it does not contradict the general interpretative strategy he prefers for the book as a whole. He may or may not be right about that (I discuss his strategy in the text), but even if so, that does not engage the question of why Aristotle should remark that the core notion of *energeia* is not pertinent to his primary motivation for considering *energeia* at all.

to contend that causation relates events and that we consequently need to understand the nature of events in order to understand causation—but then, after identifying the basic notion of an event, proceeded to observe that this notion is actually beside the point. Minimally, such a procedure would be puzzling; indeed, it would seem rather bizarre. So too, then, in the case of Aristotle: why should he insist that we need to understand *energeia* only to add that its core meaning 'is not the most useful for what we want now' (*Metaphysics* 1045b36–7)? What is it that we want now? Ultimately, I suggest, only by appreciating the contours of Aristotle's answer to this question can we develop a full appreciation of his most mature approach to *energeia* in *Metaphysics* IX and beyond.

We may begin by noting Aristotle's express motivation for discussing actuality in this book. He mentions two related but importantly distinct concerns.

The first surfaces in the last chapter of the previous book, *Metaphysics* VIII.6. Aristotle is concerned about the problem of substantial unity, because he wants to know how, if at all, we are to account for the existence of privileged unities. How, for instance, is a human being, though a composite of many parts, nevertheless one thing, and one thing in some way other than the way in which a mere pile or heap is one thing, by simple aggregation? Aristotle says in this regard that he wishes to explain the unity of things with 'several parts and in which the totality is not, as it were, a mere heap, but the whole is something besides the parts' (*Metaphysics* 1045a8–10). He doubts that the problem can be solved without adverting to the apparatus of form and matter, actuality and potentiality: 'One element is matter and the other is form, and one is potentially and the other is actually.' With this framework in place, he concludes, 'the question will no longer be thought a difficulty' (*Metaphysics* 1045a20–5). His solution to the puzzle of substantial unity thus requires an inquiry into actuality and potentiality, and it is to this inquiry that Aristotle turns in *Metaphysics* IX.

When beginning to undertake that inquiry Aristotle introduces his second and more general motivation for investigating *energeia*. The *energeia/dunamis* contrast, contends Aristotle, is basic to an investigation of being—akin, in fact, to the theory of categories, without which no such investigation could get underway. He says:

Since being (*to on*) is said in one way with reference to what something is, or quality or quantity, and in another way with respect to potentiality and actuality (*entelecheia*) and with respect to function, let us make determinations about potentiality and actuality—first about potentiality most properly so called, even though this is not the most useful for what we want now.   (*Metaphysics* 1045b32–1046a1)[22]

Aristotle makes two important claims in this passage. First, he accords the *actuality/potentiality* distinction the kind of centrality he normally reserves for his theory of categories, evidently because he regards actuality and potentiality as fundamental to metaphysics in a manner analogous to the theory of categories. Second, he contends that potentiality and actuality extend more widely than is the case with change, which he introduces as actuality 'most properly so called' (*legetai men malista kuriôs*; *Metaphysics* 1045b35–6). By this he means, as the ensuing chapter makes clear, that it is in its application to change that *energeia* has its first home: it is in the analysis of change that the notion of *energeia* must first be understood. This is perhaps unsurprising since in the *Physics*, Aristotle had gone so far as to define change (*kinêsis*) in terms of actuality and potentiality: 'change is the actuality of that which potentially is, *qua* such' (*hê tou dunamei ontos entelecheia hêi toiouton*; *Physics* 201a10–11).[23] Since there is change, there are also beings able to change, beings able to be changed, and beings which have changed in actuality. In short, since there is change, there are beings in states of actuality (in *energeia(i)*) and also beings in states of potentiality (in *dunamei*).

Like *energeia*, *dunamis*—unsurprisingly since it is the correlative of *energeia*—makes its way into English in different and non-equivalent ways: *capacity*, *faculty*, *power*, *potency*, *potentiality*, and in its dative form, either *in potentiality* or, adverbially, as *potentially*. All of these translations have been used by interpreters trying to come to terms with Aristotle's two main *energeia/dunamis* contrasts in *Metaphysics* IX: the most proper notion of *dunamis* and its correlative *energeia* in *Metaphysics* IX.1 and the extended, or derived of *energeia* and its correlative

---

[22] In this passage Aristotle twice uses *entelecheia* rather than *energeia*, which is relatively uncommon for him in *Metaphysics* IX. He uses *entelecheia* only six times in this entire book (1045b33–4, 1045b35, 1047a30, 1047b2, 1049a5–6, 1050a23). Here and throughout it seems to be used as a direct synonym for *energeia*, and I have accordingly rendered it as 'actuality'. Some translators prefer to mark the difference in diction by rendering *entelecheia* as 'fulfilment'.

[23] Aristotle's definition of motion has occasioned controversy of its own. The basic idea is, however, reasonably clear: an instance of change occurs when something which can be F, as a grey fence can be white, comes to be actually F, when it is painted white. The rider '*qua* such' in this definition serves various functions, including that the actualization in question must be categorically suited to the potentiality in question. Thus, if a grey fence is being lengthened even as it is being painted, the change from grey to white is a change insofar as the fence is able to be *qualitatively* altered, whereas the lengthening is a change to the fence insofar as it can be *quantitatively* altered. For a brief explication of this definition together with some of the problems pertaining to it, see Christopher Shields, *Aristotle* (London: Routledge, 2007), pp. 196–202.

dunamis in *Metaphysics* IX.6. Unfortunately, scholars have conceived the two main contrasts of *Metaphysics* IX in radically different ways.

At one end of the spectrum, Ross took Aristotle to be distinguishing between *powers* and *capacities*, and their correlatives, that is, between the power of one thing to effect a change in another and the potentiality of a single thing to move into a fulfilled state of itself.[24] The first notion of *dunamis*, which Ross renders as 'power', is what Aristotle defines as 'the source of change in another or in itself *qua* other' *(Metaphysics* 1046a11). The second notion, which Ross renders as 'capacity', is initially less easy to grasp. Aristotle introduces it by example as something moving into a full state of activity from a prior state of potentiality, as when someone who knows the Russell set-theoretic paradox, but is not at present contemplating it or the problems it poses, comes to contemplate it actively *(Metaphysics* 1048a32). On Ross's approach, the first contrast is essentially relational, since it ineliminably involves A's effecting some change in B (or A's effecting some change in A *qua* other, as when a barber shaves himself instead of one of his clients), whereas the second contrast is not essentially relational. Even if the expression of a *dunamis* considered as a capacity does result in some change in another thing (or in its subject *qua* other), this change will be incidental to its expression.[25] The actualization of a capacity does not, or need not, effect a change in another thing with a correlative passive capacity to be changed; it is rather a non-transitive development.

The contrast Ross envisages may be illustrated at least roughly as the difference between (i) the power of a painter to paint a fence white, where the white fence is the upshot or result of the painter's activity, and so is itself the relevant *energeia*, and (ii) the capacity of a painter to paint, which he actualizes when and only when he is engaged in the activity of painting, so that the relevant *energeia* is the activity of the painter painting, rather than the product, the fence. In general, on Ross's approach, the two distinctions, however related to one another, are clearly different kinds of oppositions.

A contrasting view, preferred by Makin, in his excellent Clarendon translation and commentary, would not read *Metaphysics* IX as quite so disjointed.[26]

---

[24] W. D. Ross, *Aristotle's Metaphysics* (Oxford: Oxford University Press: 1924).

[25] Ibid., vol. ii, pp. 240–1: 'Potentiality on the other hand is a potentiality of A of passing into some new state or engaging in some new activity . . . This activity may be the production of a change in B but the notion of a B to be acted on is not necessarily implied in the notion of potentiality as it is in that of power.'

[26] Makin, *Aristotle: Metaphysics Book θ.* Makin credits Michael Frede, 'Aristotle's Notion of Potentiality in *Metaphysics* Θ', in D. Scaltsas et al. (eds), *Unity, Identity and Explanation in Aristotle's Metaphysics* (Oxford: Clarendon Press, 1994) as the source of this view. Since, however, Frede is crucially unclear in several places where Makin is crystal clear, I will discuss Makin's presentation of the view.

The later chapters of the book 'do not move to a radically separate topic',[27] by leaving off a discussion of power in favour of potentiality. Rather, on this approach, Aristotle's uniform concern throughout the book is *potential being*, which extends in various ways by contrasting potential beings with different kinds of *actual beings*—fences which can be painted with painted fences, idle painters with painters who are busy painting, and then also, much more generally, bodies capable of being alive with the actually living animals whose bodies they are.

Crucially, on this approach, the two topics of *Metaphysics* IX are not distinct, but are rather analogical manifestations of a more amorphous and general notion of potentiality.[28] Here the thought is that there is some general conception of *being potentially* which covers, not as a genus but rather analogically, a full complement of potential beings, all of which are correlated with actual beings, or beings *in* actuality (*en energeia(i)*). According to this approach, Aristotle's thought is that there are fundamentally different kinds of beings, beings in actuality and beings in potentiality. These beings may be contrasted in a variety of non-equivalent ways so that the contrast between them resolves itself in analogous but discernibly distinct ways across a variety of contexts, though these resolutions never result in clear divisions or different classes of potential and active beings, as Ross seems to suggest. There is thus no general demarcation into *capacities* and *powers* or *activities* and *actual beings*. What that general notion of potential being is, however, is left permanently and purposely unspecified: Makin says that it is a *schema*. It is itself neither a power nor a capacity, but is the sort of condition which might be analogously regarded, in different contexts, as a power or as a capacity. This Ur-*dunamis*, so to speak, is amorphous potentiality.

Although the proponents of this second view do not put it this way, perhaps the schematic notions of *energeia* and *dunamis* standing behind the specific applications in *Metaphysics* IX and elsewhere are to be likened to 'journey' in 'The journey from St Pancras to Gare du Nord takes just over two hours' and 'Her life was a strange journey with some surprising destinations along the way', or again to 'recording' in 'a recording of *Tannhäuser* from Bayreuth in 1966' and 'a complete and accurate recording of all the papal bulls between the fifth and sixteenth centuries'. These sorts of cases would be illustrative, on the assumption, of course, that we would not want to say that journeys

---

[27] Makin, *Aristotle: Metaphysics Book θ*, p. 18.

[28] Ibid., p. 19. Concerning his approach, Makin says 'I do not introduce something new with this [the latter] notion of potential being over and above the capacities I started with. Rather, I extend a notion by analogy from the cases I originally started with—capacities to produce change—to new cases.'

and recordings in these instances are genera divided into different species, nor either that their uses in these instances are therefore utterly unrelated to one another. So too with Aristotelian 'actuality' or 'activity' in 'contemplation is the finest human activity', 'the soul is the actuality of the body', and 'the sculptor brought the sculpture into actuality'. In all these contexts Aristotle avails himself of some notion of actuality, though it is not precisely the same notion in each instance. There is rather some general notion which is made determinate only by its realization in specific contexts, where these precise, realized concepts bear only analogical relations to one another.

These contrasting approaches reflect different attitudes towards Aristotle's motivations for offering distinct pairs of *energeia/dunamis* oppositions in *Metaphysics* IX.1 and 6. Probably, in fact, the contrast between these two approaches has been overdrawn in the literature, since Ross nowhere contends or even implies that powers and potentialities are 'radically separate' topics of investigation.[29] Still, the two interpretations may be introduced as competing ways of conceiving Aristotle's two dominant accounts of actuality in *Metaphysics* IX, since they are in fact distinct: the first conceives Aristotle's two contrasts as positing different *kinds* of *energeiai* and *dunameis* and the second conceives these contrasts as analogically related precisifications of a more general, somewhat nebulous contrast. Just as there is no genus *journey* of which lives' courses and train rides are species, so there is no genus of actuality of which powers and potentialities are species. Still, as journeys through life and space are related to one another analogically, so too are powers and potentialities; and they are weakly unified because they equally draw upon the same general notion.

Put thus sharply for emphasis, each of the views creates difficulty for our understanding of *energeia*: neither captures adequately everything Aristotle says about *energeia* in *Metaphysics* IX, even though, to give each its due, each individually captures at least part of his intended meaning. Importantly, however, their individual partial correctness obscures a characteristically Aristotelian *tertium quid*: the two *dunamis/energeia* contrasts in the chapter are neither 'radically separate' nor related *merely* analogically—though one surely can, as Aristotle contends, grasp the meanings of the contrasts between them at best analogically (*Metaphysics* 1048a35−b9; cf. 1071a3−5). Rather, they are related

---

[29] Ross (*Aristotle's Metaphysics*, vol. ii, p. 240) speaks of powers and potentialities as 'two senses' of *dunamis*, but does not say that he thinks of these senses as in any way radically discrete from one another. On the contrary, in a manner plainly in keeping with his critics who have nonetheless disparaged him on this point, he says: 'Potentiality or actuality, like being, unity, and good, is one only *kat' analogian*, and we must be content to grasp the analogy and see the nature of the universal germ by studying the instances of it.' He also says (non-equivalently) that *kinēsis* and *energeia* 'are species of something wider for which Aristotle has no name, and for which he uses now the name of one species, now that of the other' (vol. ii, p. 251).

in the manner of core-dependent homonyms, not because one is prior to the other, but because there is a third notion prior to them both such that each of the non-core notions depends upon the core for its elucidation.

Both notions of *energeia* at work in *Metaphysics* IX are thus fully literal senses of actuality, and each has its own determinate sphere of application. As it turns out, only one of the derived, non-core notions of *energeia* pertains to the science of metaphysics, to being as such. More specifically, according to this approach, which develops a suggestion mooted but left undeveloped by Thomas Aquinas (*Commentary on Aristotle's Metaphysics* IX.5; 1770), the derived notion of *energeia* developed in *Metaphysics* IX.6 is central to metaphysics because it pertains to beings incapable of intrinsic change—and these constitute the subject matter of metaphysics, or *first philosophy* in Aristotle's own terminology. By contrast, in the basic case *energeia* of *Metaphysics* IX.1 applies to beings subject to intrinsic change; since such beings are not treated by the metaphysician except coincidentally, the kind of potentiality enjoyed by them is 'not the most useful for what we want now' (*Metaphysics* 1045b36–1046a1). As Aquinas contends, 'the principle aim of this branch of this science [viz. metaphysics] is to consider potency and actuality not insofar as they are found in mobile beings, but insofar as they attend to being in general' (*Commentary on Aristotle's Metaphysics* IX.5; 1770; cf. 1786).

To reach this conclusion, we proceed in three phases. First, we focus on the introduction of *energeia* in *Metaphysics* IX.1, where the basic and most familiar notion of *dunamis* is characterized (§4). With that complete, it becomes possible to characterize the extended notion, and, again following a clue from Aquinas,[30] by developing an account of the correlative notion of *energeia* in its derived sense (§5). As will become clear at that juncture, the two notions are related as core-dependent homonyms to a specifiable core (§6)—not as species under a single genus, to be sure, but not merely as analogous contrasts drawing upon some more general, indeterminate notion of actuality.

4. The Basic Sense of *energeia*

We began with the thought that Aquinas is right to regard *energeia* as indefinable, but only on the understanding that the definitions denied would be reductive definitions. For Aristotle plainly does offer an account of *dunamis* in *Metaphysics* IX.1, and since *energeia* may be defined in terms of that account, he also implicitly offers an account of *energeia* in that same chapter.

---

[30] *Commentary on Aristotle's Metaphysics*, IX.5; 1823.

Aristotle contends that potentiality is spoken of in many ways, though he recommends that the *merely* homonymous uses be set aside:

We have shown elsewhere that potentiality and being potential are spoken of in many ways [*legetai pollochôs*]. Of these, those that are called potentiality homonymously should be set aside (for some are so called because of some similarity, as in geometry and we speak of what is possible and impossible because things are or are not in a certain way); but those that relate to the same form [*to auto eidos*] are all sources [*archai*] and are spoken of with reference to the primary one [viz. the primary source [*archê*]], which is the source [*archê*] of change in something other than itself or in itself *qua* other. For one is the capacity [*dunamis*] of being acted upon, which is the source [*archê*] of being changed in what is itself affected and acted upon by something else or by itself *qua* another; another is the state of not being liable of being acted upon for the worse and so as to be destroyed by something else or by itself *qua* something else, that is, by a source [*archê*] of change. For there is in all these definitions the account [*logos*] of the primary capacity [*dunamis*].   (*Metaphysics* 1046a4–15)

There is then, relative to the basic notion of *dunamis*, some core sense in terms of which the basic notion must be understood (*Metaphysics* 1045b36–1046a1).

Some points of terminological clarification will help forestall misunderstanding. First, and most importantly, when Aristotle says he means to set aside the homonymous cases of *dunamis*, his example (the notion of power as it applies to geometry) makes perfectly plain that he means to set aside those instances which are *mere* homonyms, or homonyms from chance (*apo tuchês*) that is, homonyms whose accounts make no reference to one another, as, for instance is the case with the word 'key' (*kleis*), which is applied to both collar bones and to door keys (cf. *Nicomachean Ethics* 1096b26). A modern English analogue is 'bank' as it applies to savings institutions and sides of rivers. The situation regarding mere homonymy here in fact perfectly and instructively parallels Aristotle's remarks about being (*to on*) in *Metaphysics* IV.2: there he says that being is spoken of in many ways but is not a homonym, that is not a mere or chance homonym, but is rather spoken of in reference to some one source (*archê*) (*Metaphysics* 1003b5–6). Thus, the basic notion of *dunamis*, like that of being (*to on*), is a core-dependent homonym, despite the superficial appearance to the contrary.

Two further points in this passage underscore this contention. The first is also a terminological point. When Aristotle speaks of the primary *dunamis* as the sort 'most properly so called' (*Metaphysics* 1045b36–1046a1), he is not making a simple observation about linguistic propriety. Rather, the notion of being *most properly* (*malista kuriôs*; *Metaphysics* 1045b36) called a *dunamis* is a way of saying that this primary or core notion is the *controlling* sense of the term (*Categories* 2a11; *Physics* 191b7; *Generation and Corruption* 314a10, 317a33; *De*

Anima 412b9; *Nicomachean Ethics* 1144b4). Thus, if the core notion of health is an intrinsic state of a healthy organism, but the diet of that organism is called healthy because it is productive of health, the core sense *controls* the non-core sense, because any account of the non-core sense must advert to an account of the core instance. There is, then, an asymmetric dependence of accounts in cases of core and non-core instances of homonyms. This then gives way to the final prefatory point. When at the end of the passage Aristotle says 'there is in all these definitions the account (*logos*) of the primary capacity (*dunamis*)', (*Metaphysics* 1046a15–16) he is picking up on just this asymmetry. The core sense is primary (*prôtê*) relative to the non-core instances precisely because it perforce shows up in their accounts, but not *vice versa*. To advert again to the illustration of health, any account of 'healthy' as it occurs in 'healthy regimen' will need to take some such form as 'productive of health', where the appeal to health in the *definiens* will receive its own independent account. The core notion will thus 'be in' (*enesti*; *Metaphysics* 1046a15) the account of the non-core instance.

We should thus expect the account (*logos*) of the core notion of *dunamis* to be present in the accounts or definitions of all of the non-core instances. (It is noteworthy that Aristotle has no difficulty of speaking of accounts (*logoi*; *Metaphysics* 1046a16, 18, 19) and definitions (*horoi*; *Metaphysics* 1046a15) in this connection.) What, though, is that core account? Aristotle offers:

- ϕ is a core instance of *potentiality* $=_{df}$ ϕ is the source (*archê*) of change in something else or in itself *qua* other

Because this account is the primary one, it will show up in all derived accounts.

To take just one example, a passive capacity will simply be the converse of this, making an ineliminable appeal to this core notion: 'one is the capacity [*dunamis*] of being acted upon, which is the source [*archê*] of being changed in what is itself affected and acted upon by something else or by itself *qua* another' (*Metaphysics* 1046a11–13). This may seem woefully jargon-ridden at first blush, and thus to lay it open to Gassendi-style objections of obscurantism. The basic idea, however, may be paraphrased directly: a basic capacity is simply that feature of an entity in virtue of which that entity may initiate change in another entity, or, as Aristotle adds, in itself 'qua other'. The rider 'qua other' he adds in order to make clear that the feature which initiates change is not the very feature which is changed. Thus, the source of a doctor's ability to heal is his medical knowledge, and in deploying that knowledge when treating a patient, the doctor effects a change in her patient. She may, of course, be her own patient, and may treat herself as she would any other patient, say administering herself an injection. In that case, however, she effects a change in herself insofar as she is a patient, rather than insofar as she is a doctor. Insofar as she is a doctor, she remains unchanged, just as she would when dealing with any other patient.

Having thus introduced the core instance of a *dunamis* as a source of change, Aristotle notes that what is changed must have a correlative feature, a passive capacity, to be changed. In his terms, an ability to change and a correlative ability to be changed must be *categorially suited* to one another.[31] Thus, for instance, a painter's ability to paint something white must be met by a correlative capacity to be painted white, a capacity had by entities with surfaces but not by numbers. This passive ability Aristotle defines in terms of the core notion of an active *dunamis* already defined:

- ϕ is a passive *potentiality* $=_{df}$ ϕ is an *archê* categorially paired to a source (*archê*) of change in something else or in itself *qua* other

Thus, again, a passive *dunamis* such as *being able to be made white* will belong to all and only entities with surfaces—and this feature, being a surface, will be a categorical rather than dispositional feature of the entity, one which is requisite for an active capacity to effect its change. Conversely, while it will be true as a matter of the same categorial necessity that the active capacity will need to be keyed to a suitable passive capacity, Aristotle assumes that the active capacity is prior, because in it resides the agency of change. Accordingly, the account (*logos*) of the passive potentiality contains the account of the active potentiality, and not *vice versa*.[32]

With just so much in place, we should be in possession of everything needed to characterize the correlative notion of a core *energeia* emerging from *Metaphysics* IX.1. Since it is correlative to *dunamis*, the core notion of *energeia* may be stated as follows:

- ψ is a core instance of *energeia* $=_{df}$ ψ is something wrought by the expression of a core *dunamis* in another or in itself *qua* other.

---

[31] See n. 23 above on the notion of categorial suitability.

[32] Makin (*Aristotle: Metaphysics Book θ*, pp. 26, 30) reasonably wonders whether there may be a problem for Aristotle here, since the necessity pairing active and passive capacities is symmetrical, whereas the necessity relating non-core to core homonyms is asymmetrical. There being symmetrical necessities is not, however, sufficient for the symmetry of *account* dependence, and it is the asymmetry of account dependence which is at issue in cases of core-dependent homonymy, as is made clear in Aristotle's introduction of two kinds of *kath' hauto* predication in *Posterior Analytics* I.4 (73a34–b5). Thus, for instance, in saying that oddness is predicated of number *kath' hauto*, we are highlighting a metaphysically binding reciprocity between subject and predicate, though it is no part of the *logos* of number that it be odd (or indeed that it be odd or even). In these forms of necessity, we are not indicating anything essential to the subject. See also Shields, *Order in Multiplicity*, pp. 122–6.

Plainly, the definition makes use of the already defined notion of *dunamis*, though this is not a cause for concern. Aristotle exhibits no inclination to seek a reductive account of either *dunamis* or *energeia* in this chapter, and in the end, we will find one defined in terms of the other. In this he is no more blameworthy than a modal logician who takes either possibility or necessity as primitive, and then defines the other in terms of the primitive notion.

The suggestion that an *energeia* is *something wrought* may appear a bit obscure. It helps to note that the relevant sense of source (*archê*) in view in the core definition of potentiality is the sense of source according to which an *archê* is a cause (*aition*) (*Metaphysics* 983a29, 990a2, 1013a17, 1025b4, 1042a5, 1069a26). Causes are, however, essentially relational, in that a cause is always a cause of something. It follows, then, that since a potentiality is a source of change, an actuality is the result of that source's expression. This is the sense in which an actuality is something wrought.

That allowed, it is also true that 'something wrought' remains crucially ambiguous, in two different dimensions. One can conceive of the change wrought either narrowly or broadly; and one can, again, think of the change wrought as the *process* of being changed or as the *product* or end-point of that process. To illustrate, one might think of the change in the case of a grey fence painted white broadly, as the fence-made-white, or more narrowly, as the whiteness of the fence, the colour brought about by the causal process. Importantly, in the latter case, Aristotle does not think that, properly speaking, grey can be made white: grey is supplanted by white along a continuum of colour in a qualitative change (*Physics* 200b32–201a9). So, the change wrought is more appropriately construed broadly. In a similar way, one might think of the change involved in a grey fence's being painted white as the product, the white fence, or as the process leading to that product, its being painted white. (It is in this latter sense that we might speak of something's undergoing a change, where we are focusing on the process of being changed, rather than the end product of that process.) Aristotle offers little by way of concrete example in *Metaphysics* IX.1, and so does not, in that chapter at least, resolve this ambiguity.

Something is gained by considering the account of change given in *Physics* III.1, though it must be said that there is likewise controversy attendant upon that definition, indeed the same controversy.[33] That said, Aristotle does seem

---

[33] W. D. Ross, *Aristotle's Physics* (Oxford: Oxford University Press, 1936), p. 537 treats *entelecheia* in Aristotle's definition of change at *Physics* 201a10–11 as a process: '*entelecheia* must here mean "actualization", not "actuality": it is the *passage* from potentiality to actuality that is *kinêsis*'. Compare

in that context to indicate that a change is a process: 'the actualization of the buildable insofar as it is buildable is building' (*Physics* 201b10), which is Aristotle's way of saying that a passive potentiality's transition to actuality is a *process*. If that is so, then the core account of actuality involves a kind of process rather than a static event or a completed product; this process is the activity of a *dunamis* whose realization brings about a change.

Thus clarified, the core account of *energeia* is reasonably clear: an *energeia*, in its primary sense, is what is wrought by a *dunamis*, in its primary sense.

5. An Extended Sense

In *Metaphysics* IX.6, Aristotle introduces a new notion of actuality. This, unlike the sort of actuality we have been considering so far, is the actuality of primary concern to the metaphysician. To reiterate this concern: Aristotle contends that the metaphysician needs to appeal to *energeia* in order to account for privileged unity; and he also thinks more generally that *energeia* is a fundamental concept of metaphysics, on par with the notion of being in the theory of categories, so that it would in any case fall to the metaphysician to assay it. Everything in *Metaphysics* IX so far has thus been leading to the introduction of this new kind of *energeia* in the sixth chapter, and is properly regarded as propaideutic to that introduction.

Aristotle's introduction of this new notion of *energeia* contains several surprises. He claims:

Since the potentiality spoken of with respect to change has been discussed, let us now delineate actuality, both what it is and what sort of thing it is. For the potential [*to dunaton*] will become clear at the same time: it will become clear that not only do we call what naturally moves something else or is moved by another (either *simpliciter* or in a certain way) potential, but that we speak of potentiality differently as well; and

A. Kosman, 'The Activity of Being in Aristotle's *Metaphysics*', in D. Charles, D. Scaltsas, and M. L. Gill (eds), *Unity, Identity and Explanation in Aristotle's Metaphysics* (Oxford: Clarendon Press, 1994), pp. 201–2, when commenting on Aristotle's treatment of motion as a certain kind of realization: 'The well-known definition of motion in *Physics* III is stated in precisely these terms. Aristotle, however, makes clear—although commentators have had difficulty hearing this—that he does not mean by realization the *process* by which such an ability is realized; that process is precisely the entity that Aristotle means to be defining, not the concept in terms of which he means to define it. Nor, he reminds us, can he possibly mean the *product* of that realization: the physical building, for example, which results from the act of building. The realization that he wishes to define a motion to be is in fact an *activity*, the activity of a potential entity prior to its realization having been completed.' It would follow if this were correct, of course, that no activity is a process. One might wish to stipulate this, perhaps, but Kosman does not offer any compelling reason for doing so.

that is why we have run through these matters in conducting our inquiry. Actuality is *something's obtaining*, though not in the way that we speak of something's obtaining in potentiality. We say something is in potentiality when, for example, we say that Hermes is in a block of wood or that a half-line is in a whole line, because they might be separated out; and we say that the one who knows and can contemplate but is not contemplating is in potentiality, and when he does contemplate we say that he is in actuality. What we mean to say in each instance is clear by induction, and it is not necessary to seek a definition [*horos*] of everything, but also to see the point [*sunoran*] of an analogy: as the builder building is to the builder able to build, and as what is awake to what is asleep, and as seeing is to one with sight but whose eyes are closed, or as what has been separated out of the matter is to the matter, or as what has been wrought is to the unwrought. Let actuality [*energeia*] be defined [*aphôrismenê*] by one part of each of these contrasts, and potentiality [*to dunaton*] by the other. All these things are said to be in actuality not in the same way, but by analogy: as this is in that or is related to that, or as this other is in that other or is related to that other. For in some cases we have change [*kinêsis*] related to potentiality [*dunamis*], and in other cases substance [*ousia*] related to some matter.   (*Metaphysics* 1048a25–b9)

This passage moves from the familiar sense of *energeia*, the sort pertaining to beings which change (*Metaphysics* 1048a29), to another sense, which pertains instead, says Aristotle, to substance (*ousia*) and its relation to matter (*Metaphysics* 1048b9).

The first surprise is the implied contrast between the familiar case and its extension: if the first case pertains to motion, and the second to substance, then the implication is that the kind of *energeia* pertaining to substance does *not* pertain to motion. This is a point largely underappreciated by Aristotle's exegetes today, but it is a point to which Aquinas was fully alive. He rightly regards this fact as consequential for our understanding of Aristotle's basic enterprise in *Metaphysics* IX: 'Potency and actuality are referred in most cases to things in motion, because motion is the actuality of a being in potency. But the principle aim of this branch of knowledge [viz. metaphysics] is to consider potency and actuality not insofar as they are found in mobile beings, but insofar as they attend to being in general. Hence potency and actuality are also found in immobile beings, for example, in intellectual ones' (*Commentary on Aristotle's Metaphysics* IX.5; 1770; cf. 1786). Aquinas's observation, which makes ready sense of Aristotle's dominant contrast between the two notions of *energeia* of *Metaphysics* IX, rightly situates the primary difference as a difference of domain: actuality in its extended sense pertains to beings not liable to motion.

A second surprise concerns the prospects of a definition of *energeia*. Aristotle may seem to imply that no definition of *energeia* is possible, or at least that no definition is possible in its extended sense. It is unclear why this should be so. Indeed, we have already seen Aristotle offers not one but several accounts (*logoi*) and definitions (*horoi*) of several kinds of *dunameis* in *Metaphysics* IX.1, and since *energeia* is definable in terms of *dunamis*, we should expect a definition of at least the *energeia* corresponding motion to be immediately forthcoming. If that is possible, then we would need a special reason to suppose that definability gives way when we move to *energeia* in its extended sense. Aquinas, as we have seen, makes the plausible suggestion that *energeia* is simple, and thus not definable in more basic terms (*Commentary on Aristotle's Metaphysics* IX.5; 1826). It is compatible with that observation, however, that a non-reductive account be offered.

More importantly, caution is required in this matter, since it is not entirely plain that Aristotle actually *denies* that definition is possible, or still less states directly that a definition is impossible. What he says instead is rather more oblique, that 'it is not necessary to seek a definition (*horos*) of everything', and that one may instead 'see the point [*sunoran*] of an analogy' when trying to understand a challenging concept (*Metaphysics* 1048a36–7). He even then goes on to speak in this very passage of *energeia* as being defined (*aphôrismenê*; *Metaphysics* 1048b5). At most, then, he wishes to indicate that one style of definition is not possible, and he does not say even this much directly. On the contrary, he indicates that one can move towards a definition by seeing the point of the analogies he puts forward.

That said, Aristotle conspicuously does not offer a definition of *energeia* in the sense pertaining to substance, as he had done in the case of *energeia* pertaining to motion. Still, if we rely upon the instructive analogies offered and appreciate, as Aquinas recommends, that the main need to develop an extended account of *energeia* derives from the fact that the basic notion is inapplicable in the domain of interest to the metaphysician, then it is possible to hazard an account.

Aristotle's own general summary of the analogy offered in the chapter is that some instances of actuality are related as change (*kinêsis*) is to potentiality (*dunamis*), while other instances are related as substance (*ousia*) is to matter (*hulê*) (*Metaphysics* 1048a25–b9). If we accept Aquinas's contention that Aristotle means to distinguish these two kinds of actuality because of their different domains of application, then we appreciate directly the need for an extended account of actuality. Given that the basic sense pertains to motion, and is indeed *defined* in terms of a primary potentiality which is in turn defined in terms something's being an *archê* of change, the core notion of actuality simply will not apply in the domain now under investigation. Those who doubt Aquinas's contention in this matter then owe an explanation of why an extended notion is needed at all; there must be some impediment to the application of the basic sense, and Aquinas's point about domain specificity explains what that may be.

Importantly, change-enmeshed *energeia* is inapplicable to the domain of metaphysics *as opposed to* physics, which Aristotle characterizes very clearly as a science which 'concerns the kinds of beings which are able to be moved' (*Metaphysics* 1025b26–7). Metaphysics, by contrast, treats separate beings which are not able to be moved. If the substances studied by metaphysics cannot be moved, then there is sense in which *energeia* pertains to them as sources (*archai*) of their movement. So, if it is to apply at all, it will not be in its basic sense.

Further, it is significant that in the very core definition of the core notion of a basic *dunamis* Aristotle appeals to something's being a source of movement—where the very phrase 'source of motion' (*archê tês kinêseôs*) is, as Ross notes, a term for efficient causation: ' "Efficient cause" is simply the translation of Aristotle's *archê tês kinêseôs*.'[34] Evidently, then, the core definition of a basic *dunamis*, along with its correlative notion of *energeia*, is a principle restricted to the realm of efficient causation. In the illustration of its extended sense, Aristotle thus unsurprisingly selects examples in which efficient causation plays no part: the relation of substance (*ousia*) to matter (*hulê*) (*Metaphysics* 1048b9) is rather an instance of formal causation.[35] A formal cause is also a source (*archê*), as Aristotle argues in *Metaphysics* VII.17, but of a different sort: a formal cause is a source of being (*tou einai*) and not of becoming (*Metaphysics* 1041a31–2).

Taking that together, we may offer a conjectural account of *energeia* in its extended sense:

- ψ is an instance of *energeia* in the extended sense $=_{df}$ ψ is a formal cause in the domain of what is incapable of motion.

This general account explains why Aristotle thinks that *energeia* is relevant to the question of substantial unity: as *energeia* in its extended sense, *form* is *substance* (*ousia*)—and as substance, form is that which makes something potentially ψ something ψ in actuality.

---

[34] Ross, *Aristotle's Metaphysics*, vol. i, p. cxxxiv.

[35] Here again Aquinas's gloss, though unargued, is apt: 'Then he shows that the term actuality is used in different senses; and he gives two different senses in which it is used. First, actuality means action, or operation. And with a view to introducing the different senses of actuality he says, first, that we do not say that all things are actual in the same way but in different ways; and this difference can be considered according to different proportions. For a proportion can be taken as meaning that just as one thing is in another so a third thing is in a fourth; for example, just as sight is in the eye, so hearing is in the ear. And the relation of substance (i.e. of form) to matter is taken according to this kind of proportion; for form is said to be in matter' (*Commentary on Metaphysics* IX.5; 1828).

6. Relations between the Basic and Derived Senses of *energeia*

If we have come this far, then we have two accounts of *energeia* before us, one pertaining to the domain of motion and one pertaining to the domain of what is not liable to move. The first is couched in the language of efficient causality and the second, if we are to rely on Aristotle's analogical illustrations, in the language of formal causation. We may then wonder what relation, if any, obtains between them.

Some suppose that the answer to the question of the relation between the basic and extended sense is simple: there is no relation between them, beyond what one might grasp murkily by analogy. The worry, then, is that we have no clear grounding relation governing extensions of the basic notion of *energeia* to domains beyond its original home in the theory of change and mobility.[36] Indeed, it is easy to think that because the basic and extended senses are related analogically, they *cannot* be related in any more structured way. In particular, they cannot be related as instances of core-dependent homonymy, because these forms of relation are mutually exclusive.[37] After all, Aristotle treats core-dependent homonymy and analogy as mutually exclusive alternatives in *Nicomachean Ethics* I.6; so, it is unsurprising that in *Metaphysics* IX, he makes clear that any relation between the basic and derived senses are to be governed by a relation of analogy and no more.[38]

This sort of view would be compelling if we had reason to believe that Aristotle in fact argued that the only form of unity available to the kinds of *energeia* in view in Metaphysics IX is analogical. As we have seen, he does not go that far, but instead urges his readers to 'see the point' (*sunoran*) of an analogy, using a word he standardly uses to indicate the ability of a knower to grasp some item cognitively (*Sophistical Refutations* 167a38, 174a18; *Topics* 100b30; *Physics* 241b32). This falls far short of any claim to the effect that the only relations between forms of *energeia* are analogical. Consequently, there is no immediate reason to insist that the basic and extended senses, having their

[36] Makin, *Aristotle: Metaphysics Book θ*, p. 133, who does an admirable job of explicating the view that only analogical relations may obtain, forthrightly allows that it is difficult to determine how one should conceive the basis of the analogy.

[37] Ibid.: '...there are differences between the relations of change to capacity, substance to matter, and eternal thing to perishable thing. And those differences may be unsystematic. That is why the different relations are brought under a common pattern only through analogies (rather than by a focal account...)'

[38] Makin (ibid., p. 134) appeals to *Nicomachean Ethics*, Bk 1, ch. 6 1096b26–8 in this regard.

respective homes in the domains of physics and metaphysics, are not yet related in some more instructive way. If there is some such way, what might it be?

Here we must return to the question of why Aristotle had thought it sensible to spend the first five chapters of this book discussing a matter which, by his own account, 'is not the most useful for what we want now' (*Metaphysics* 1045b36–7). One thought would be that he simply wants to ground our understanding of *energeia* in its extended sense by dealing first with the familiar, basic sense which we encounter in sense perception.

Another alternative would be that the basic sense is presupposed by the extended sense, because any account of the derived sense must advert to the account of the basic sense. On this latter suggestion, the thought would be that though itself a case of core-dependent homonymy (which, indisputably it is), the basic sense itself forms the core of the extended sense, so that we have yet another instance of core-dependent homonymy. The extended sense would thus be a non-core instance of core-dependent homonymy, by depending on the basic sense as its core. This suggestion seems markedly unpromising, however, since, as we have seen, the basic notion appeals ineliminably to efficient causation and the extended notion is precluded from any such appeal in virtue of its domain of application.

Happily, however, there is a third possibility: both the basic and extended notions of *energeia* are non-core instances of a further notion to which they must appeal in the specifications of their accounts. There does indeed seem to be such a core available. The idea underpinning both the basic and the extended senses is simply: *being a source of something's being* φ. Where the *source* in question is restricted to the domain of efficient causality, we have a case of efficient causation; in this derived sense, we have a case of *energeia* in the basic, familiar way. By contrast, when the *source* in question is restricted to the domain of formal causation, which Aristotle regards as a kind of causation different from but on par with efficient causation, we have an instance of actuality in the extended sense. Neither form of actuality is exhausted by being a source, since each must be a source in some determinate way or other; and, further, neither is a source in the sense in which the other is a source. So, they are equally related to the same core.

So much would suffice for core-dependent homonymy. Any commitment in this direction would have the welcome result of offering more structure to this fundamental concept in Aristotle's metaphysical scheme than we are afforded by mere analogy. This is welcome since, one fears, bare analogy would be so open-textured, and so amorphous, as to allow forms of actuality alien to Aristotle's concerns. In this respect, at least, the core of any case of core-dependent homonymy serves as a conceptual anchor constraining the contours of Aristotelian actuality; and with such an anchor, it becomes possible to determine which extensions of the basic notion are legitimate and which are spurious.

7. Conclusions

According to Aristotle, we do not make progress in metaphysics without coming to terms with the concept of actuality. We find, for instance, that we cannot account for substantial unity without adverting to actuality; and we need more generally to think about actuality because it enjoys a fundamentality in metaphysics on par with the theory of categories. Yet when we deploy the concept of actuality in addressing the problem of substantial unity, we find that it proves unsuitably anaemic if it is restricted to its original framework, the realm of the mobile. For in this realm, physics, it serves primarily to explicate the nature of change (*kinêsis*), and the objects of metaphysics are changeless.

Accordingly, the kinds of unity to be explicated by the metaphysician require the services of formal no less than efficient causation. Since the notion of actuality in its first formulation is restricted to the domain of efficient causation, if it is to find application in the realm of interest to the metaphysician, it must be altered and extended, by being shorn of its defining ties to change. When Aristotle effects this extension in *Metaphysics* IX.6, he does so without sacrificing the orderly association of his various and non-equivalent notions of actuality: actuality, like being, an equally fundamental and indefinable notion to which it is expressly compared in the opening lines of *Metaphysics* IX, may yet exhibit unity in its variety. As a core-dependent homonym, actuality admits of an explication without requiring any form of univocal or reductive definition. Accordingly, Aristotle meets any reasonable demand for an explication of actuality Gassendi might seek to impose, and he manages to do so without violating Aquinas's observation that simple notions elude definition. Aristotelian actuality admits of at least this much elucidation, and, arguably, this is all the elucidation it needs. Actuality, says Aristotle, can be understood by the work it does in metaphysics; if this is so, it has neither more nor less claim to acceptance than the notion of being developed in his theory of categories. This notion, it is true, is replete with philosophical difficulties of its own; but this is equally true of all foundational concepts in metaphysics, and if Gassendi's complaint about actuality is really no more than an expression of his dissatisfaction with metaphysics in general, then neither Aristotle nor Aquinas need feel especially bothered.[39]

[39] An earlier version of this paper was presented at the University of Jyväskylä; I am most grateful to the members of the audience on that occasion for their enlightened and engaging questions. I thank also the editors of this volume for their insightful and instructive comments on the original version, as well as Nathanael Stein and Cissie Fu, both of whom kindly read an earlier draft and provided valuable suggestions for improvement.

Part II
Aquinas

5

The Role of Consent in Aquinas's Theory of Action

TERENCE IRWIN

1. Too Many Stages?

Throughout his work Anthony Kenny has drawn the attention of contemporary philosophers to the light they can gain from attention to Thomas Aquinas. Kenny's work on will and action includes constant references to Aquinas. To introduce his account of the will Kenny says:

The theory of the will which I will present in this book will be traditional without being Platonist. It will resemble the theory developed out of Aristotelian materials by St Thomas Aquinas and later mediaeval philosophers, rather more than it will resemble the view of classical post-renaissance philosophers. However, I shall try to free it from the Platonist elements which it incorporated in mediaeval times; and I shall try to incorporate into my presentation insights of contemporary philosophers. This will be the easier in that it was reflection on contemporary problems which brought me to see the very substantial degree of truth in the ancient theory.[1]

He discusses Aquinas on action more directly in his later book *Aquinas on Mind*.[2]

All of us who study Aristotle and Aquinas on action and will have benefited extensively from Kenny's work as interpreter and critic. I would like to take a small step on the road he has marked out for us, by considering one aspect of Aquinas's views on action.[3]

---

[1] Kenny, *Will, Freedom and Power* (Oxford: Blackwell, 1975), p. 11.
[2] (London: Routledge, 1993).
[3] I have offered a broader sketch of relevant aspects of Aquinas's views on action, in *Development of Ethics*, i (Oxford: Oxford University Press, 2007), §241–70, 292–8.

As Kenny recognizes, it is easy to be put off by some presentations of Aquinas's position. Older textbooks of Thomistic philosophy usually include a section that describes the treatise on human actions in the Prima Secundae of the *Summa Theologiae*.[4] The point of the description may be explained in this way:

Voluntary action embraces in its complexity both the end to which a man determines himself and the means by which he proposes to reach it. The philosophers of the middle ages described very concisely the successive phases of the complete free act, and distinguished the stages involved, as regards the order either of intention or of execution . . . Here is the schema of this complex process; it contains twelve acts, from the logical point of view . . .[5]

The twelve acts are: (1) Presentation of an object as good. (2) Volition. (3) Judgement recognizing the possibility of obtaining the object. (4) Intention. (5) Deliberation. (6) Consent. (7) Judgement on the most suitable means. (8) Election. (9) Command. (10) Execution. (11) Obtaining the end. (12) Enjoying the possession of the end.

We may ask when these twelve acts are supposed to happen. If every 'complete free action' requires this complex process, we may wonder how often anyone manages a complete free act. In order to act voluntarily, we have to go through a number of steps that seem to take so much time that they severely restrict our time for getting on with what we want to do. The twelve-stage description may seem too elaborate to be credible.

Readers who have found Aquinas's description difficult to take seriously as a description of the causal antecedents of an action have tried to take it another way. Perhaps we should regard it as an analytical description that indicates the different aspects that we can recognize in an action. We need not, on this view, think of intention, deliberation, and so on as temporally prior events that cause the action. Though they mark different features of an action, we need not suppose that Aquinas offers them as an over-complicated series of causal antecedents, and so we should not criticize his account for excessive causal complexity.

---

[4] The Prima Secundae is cited hereinafter as 'IaIIae'.

[5] H. Collin and R. Terribilini (eds), *Manuel de Philosophie Thomiste* (Paris: Tequi, 1949), ii.36. The same twelve-stage list may be found in A. Gardeil, 'Acte', in *Dictionnaire de théologie catholique*, i.1, 343. In saying that these are the elements of a complete act, Gardeil allows (Remark 2) that some of the intermediate stages may not be explicitly present; in such cases the act is incomplete. Alan Donagan, 'Thomas Aquinas on Human Action' in N. Kretzmann, A. Kenny, and J. Pinborg (eds), *Cambridge History of Later Mediaeval Philosophy* (Cambridge: Cambridge University Press, 1982), p. 653, offers a different list with only eight stages.

This may be what Alan Donagan has in mind in his defence of Aquinas against one of the 'vulgar objections, or rather slogans' that he takes to betray misunderstanding of Aquinas.

As for the . . . objection that the elicited acts which according to Aquinas are components of even the simplest complete human acts are too numerous to be credible, and correspond to nothing in our experience of our own acts, the reply—made also by action theorists today—must be that the components of simple human acts are ascertained, not by introspecting what happens when we perform them, but examining various cases in which an act is begun but not completed.[6]

However vulgar the objection may be, it is not clear how Donagan answers it. We may agree with his observation that sometimes acts are begun but not completed because we do not deliberate about means, or because we deliberate but do not make up our minds on the conclusion. But this observation only shows that sometimes a complete act requires the stages that Aquinas describes. It does not seem to follow that every time a desire for an end results in a voluntary action, all Aquinas's stages have come between the desire and the action.

Perhaps we should take Donagan to mean that the vulgar objection is misguided because Aquinas's 'stages' are not really preliminaries to the action, but aspects of an action. We can describe an action as intended, deliberate, and chosen (e.g.) because these are different features of the action; they need not be features of its mental antecedents.

Kenny may also believe that Aquinas's description is best understood as an interpretation of an action. He recognizes that this is not the most obvious way to understand Aquinas:

Human voluntary action, then, for Aquinas, is action that issues from a rational consideration. But what is rational consideration? Aquinas sometimes contrasts deliberate action with action on a sudden and talks as if it must be a time-taking process of deliberation. If this is his considered view, it seems wrong.[7]

If we reject a time-taking process of deliberation, what is the alternative? Kenny suggests a retrospective understanding of one's action:

If these actions are done for a reason, then there will be a pattern of reasoning which can be exhibited after the event ('I obeyed the doctor because . . .' 'I turned the steering wheel to the right because'). But the reasons which would appear in the later

---

[6] Donagan, 'Thomas Aquinas on Human Action', p. 654.
[7] Kenny, *Will, Freedom and Power*, p. 21.

formulation need not have formulated themselves in the agent's consciousness at the time in order to have been his genuine reasons.[8]

If Aquinas holds this view, we need not suppose that he belongs to the 'introvert' tradition that explains action by appeal to an 'episode in one's mental history, an item of introspective consciousness'.[9]

This alternative to a time-taking process of deliberation might be understood in different ways: (1) When an act issues from a rational consideration, it need not issue from any conscious process of formulating reasons. (2) It need not issue from a process of deliberation. (3) It need not issue from any time-taking process. (4) All that is needed is the retrospective pattern of reasoning.

These different alternatives to a time-taking process of deliberation express gradually more extreme reactions to the introverted view. The fourth view affirms that the retrospective analytical description is sufficient for an action to issue from a rational consideration. But what does this description describe, if it does not describe the causal antecedents of the action? Kenny speaks of 'the agent's sincere account of what he is doing and why' (p. 23). But what does the sincerity consist in, if it does not express the agent's belief that these are causal antecedents of the action? And how should we understand the role of deliberation if it is not a causal antecedent?

We might answer that A deliberates about whether to do x or y and decides to do y in preference to x if and only if A had a choice between x and y and did y. This answer is unsatisfactory. If we want to know what considerations A acted on, it is not enough to see what was in fact open to A. We also need to know what A was aware of, and how much the different considerations that A was aware of actually mattered to A. To explain A's doing x rather than y by reference to A's choice of x over y, we cannot simply say that a rational agent would have chosen x over y in A's circumstances; we also need to know how A in particular looked at x and y, and how A's view made a difference to what A did. But how can we answer these questions unless we consider the causation of A's action? Once we consider causation, we cannot easily avoid consideration of the causal antecedents of the action.

These remarks allude to questions about action that have sometimes been controversial. When Donald Davidson defended a causal account of action in 1963, he remarked that his view opposed that of the authors of the series of Routledge books called 'Studies in Philosophical Psychology'.[10] One of the

[8] Kenny, *Will, Freedom and Power*, p. 22.
[9] Ibid.
[10] D. Davidson, 'Actions, Reasons, and Causes' in *Essays on Actions and Events* (Oxford: OUP, 1980), p. 3 n. From *Journal of Philosophy* 60 (1963), pp. 685–700. Elsewhere (*Essays*, p. 261) Davidson speaks of 'a very strong neo-Wittgensteinian current of small red books'.

most important of these books is Anthony Kenny's *Action, Emotion and Will*, which seems to defend the non-causal account of explanation of actions.[11]

I will assume that Davidson's defence of a causal view of action and reasons is correct, and that therefore we should not welcome an interpretation or (as I would be inclined to say) a revision of Aquinas's view that removes all causal claims. Aquinas seems not to doubt that he describes the causal antecedents of action. An interpretation or revision that replaced causal claims with non-causal analytical claims would not improve his account. If he makes the causal antecedents of action too complicated, his mistake is not that he looks for causal antecedents, but that he finds the wrong ones.

If, then, Aquinas offers a causal account, we have not yet found an easy answer to the objection that he offers an over-complicated account of voluntary action. We still need to decide whether his account is indeed over-complicated, and, if it is, how we might try to remove the unwelcome complications.

I will defend some aspects of Aquinas's account on the assumptions that (i) he offers a causal account, and (ii) he is right to offer such an account. Readers who disagree with either of these assumptions may want to reinterpret what I say so as to fit a non-causal account of action.

2. Deliberation, Consent, Election

Aquinas's claims about deliberation raise an obvious question about over-complication. Does he really mean that in every voluntary action, we must previously have thought about what is to be said on each side of the question, in order to reach a conclusion on the basis of deliberative comparison of different options?

If he demands such an extensive role for deliberation, Aquinas seems to overlook one virtue of Aristotle's account, which he takes as one of his models. For Aristotle does not take deliberation to be necessary for all voluntary actions; it is necessary for actions on election (*prohairesis*), which are a proper subset of voluntary actions.[12]

---

[11] See Kenny, *Action, Emotion and Will* (London: Routledge, 1963), ch. 5. I say 'seems to defend' because the theses that Kenny specifically rejects are more specific than the general claim that explanation of action by reasons and motives is causal explanation. He argues, for instance, that 'it cannot ... be in general true that to ascribe a feeling to a particular emotion is to make a hypothesis about its cause' (p. 83).

[12] Actions on election are not the only ones that depend on deliberation. We can also, according to Aristotle, act on deliberation without election. See *Nicomachean Ethics* 1142b17–20.

Aquinas appears not to draw Aristotle's apparently helpful distinction between non-deliberate and deliberate voluntary action. He speaks as though all the stages he describes in the treatise on action are necessary for voluntary action. We might wonder, then, how he deals with the actions that Aristotle takes to be voluntary but non-deliberate.

He adds a further, and apparently unwelcome, complication to Aristotle's account of action. Aristotle seems to take election to result directly from wish (*boulêsis*) and deliberation, but Aquinas adds a step between deliberation and election.

The first reaction to deliberation is the recognition that one action or a number of actions are satisfactory (*placet*). Election is a further stage, at which we select the satisfactory action that is to be done. If we have identified only one action as satisfactory, we elect that action. If we identify several as satisfactory, we elect the one that seems best. In the second case, but not the first, we need election to eliminate all but one of the options that have been found satisfactory. In the first case, we do not need election to eliminate any options, but we need it to endorse the one satisfactory option as the best available. The fact that this task is easy does not mean that it is absent.

This introduction of consent draws on the Stoic conception of voluntary action. The Stoics may notice that Aristotle offers no clear necessary and sufficient condition for voluntary action; they fill the gap he leaves by identifying voluntary action with action that rests on assent (*sunkatathesis*) rather than simple appearance (*phantasia*).[13] Augustine takes over this Stoic analysis. Nemesius and Damascene combine it with the Aristotelian analysis, and Aquinas follows their lead.[14]

Stoic assent seems to lack two characteristics of Aristotelian election: (1) Aristotle believes that election essentially involves preference for one alternative over another (*Nicomachean Ethics* 1112a15–17; *Eudemian Ethics* 1226a5–9). He does not simply mean that in choosing one thing we forgo other things; he means that when we elect we act on a view about the merits of one course of action as opposed to another. (2) This is why he thinks election requires deliberation; for deliberation is the examination of the comparative merits of different courses of action. The Stoics do not make either of these features prominent in their account of assent. My assent to an appearance need not

---

[13] Aquinas explains the difference he intends between *consentire* and *adsentire* in IaIIae, qu. 15, art. 1, ad 3. See also Section 6 below.

[14] See O. Lottin, *Psychologie et morale aux xii et xiii siècles* (Gembloux: Duculot, 1948), i. 422–3.

result from rational reflection and consideration of alternatives.[15] Assent seems to be present in many situations where we do not consider alternatives. It is not surprising, then, that Augustine speaks of 'assent' or 'consent' as the mark of free action (*De Civitate Dei* ix 4).

Aquinas combines the Stoic doctrine of consent with the Aristotelian doctrine of election. He agrees with his Stoic-inspired sources in treating consent as a mark of rational and voluntary action. Consent is an 'application of the movement of desire towards something to be done' (IaIIae, qu. 15, art. 2). This application is an action that presupposes our control over the movement of desire, and hence non-rational animals cannot consent (qu. 15, art. 2).[16] Consent is different from election; if several means seem to promote our end, we consent to them all as being satisfactory, whereas election picks out one means as better than another (qu. 15, art. 3, ad 3). If we recognize only one thing as satisfactory, the same action is both consent and election, and they differ only in definition (*ratione tantum*).[17] Hence we act on consent if and only if we also act on election.

Why should Aquinas insist on these two stages? His fusion of the Stoic and Aristotelian views seems unwarranted because the Stoic view gives us the generality we need without the Aristotelian element. Aristotle implicitly acknowledges this. Just as he recognizes that deliberation is unnecessary for voluntary action, he also recognizes that election is unnecessary. The voluntary actions that do not depend on deliberation do not depend on election either.

---

[15] When we have a clear and striking apprehensive appearance, it 'all but grabs us by the hair and draws us into assent' (Sextus Empiricus, *Adversus Mathematicos* vii. 257). If we are uncritical and too easily impressed by appearances, we may 'yield' to them without proper reflection.

[16] '. . . consent implies an application of the movement of desire to something as to be done. Now to apply the movement of desire to the doing of something, belongs to the subject that has the movement of desire in its power; thus to touch a stone is an action suitable to a stick, but to apply the stick so that it touch the stone, belongs to one who has the power of moving the stick. But non-rational animals do not have the movement of desire in their power, but this sort of movement is in them from natural instinct. Hence the non-rational animal certainly desires, but it does not apply that movement to anything. And for this reason it is not properly said to consent: only the rational nature is said to consent, which has the movement of desire in its power, and is able to apply or not to apply it to this or that' (qu. 15, art. 2)

[17] 'Election adds beyond consent a certain relation to something in preference to which something else is elected, and therefore after consent there still remains election. For it may happen that through deliberation several things are found leading towards an end, and, given that any of them is satisfactory [*placet*], we consent to any of them; but from the many that are satisfactory, we put one ahead of the others by electing it. But if we find only one thing that is satisfactory, consent and election do not differ in reality, but only in character [*ratione*], so that it is called consent in the respect that something is satisfactory for action, but it is called election in the respect that it is put ahead of the things that are not satisfactory' (qu. 15, art. 3, ad 3).

He has no general account, however, of what actions on election and actions without election might have in common that would make them all voluntary. The Stoics seem to offer this general account; they take assent to be necessary and sufficient for voluntary action. Aquinas adds the Stoic element of assent, but he does not seem to see that this makes it unnecessary to insist on election in all voluntary action.

3. Passion and Consent

The complexity of Aquinas's description not only seems excessive in itself, but also raises difficulties for some of his other claims about voluntary action. Though he insists that action on passions is usually voluntary, he does not suggest that it requires election. He argues that it is voluntary in so far as it is 'subject to the command of reason and the will' (IaIIae, qu. 24, art. 1; qu. 42, art. 4). Though passions may arise independently of the will, they normally await the consent of the will.

Aquinas's claim about acting on passions may be contrasted with Aristotle's position. We might take Aristotle to say that acting on passion is by itself sufficient for voluntary action because passion is an internal cause. Aquinas believes that this is too simple a view about our responsibility for acting on passions. If passions submerge reason we are not responsible for acting on them, and we do not act on them voluntarily. If we act on them voluntarily, we have to consent to them.[18]

This condition is puzzling. For Aquinas takes consent to be an intermediate stage between deliberation and election. Why, then, does he not say that deliberation and election are necessary for voluntary action on passions? If we do not deliberate about acting on the passion, we do not reach any consent. And if we consent, but do not elect, the process leading to action is incomplete, and we do not act voluntarily.

But it is difficult to suppose that Aquinas's reference to consent is just an abbreviation for a reference to the whole series of deliberation, consent, and election. If he insists on the whole series, he restricts the types of action that are subject to the will. To require deliberation on each occasion is to ignore the contrast between impulsive actions and actions that result from reflection

---

[18] 'For no matter how much anger or appetite grows, a human being does not rush into action, unless the consent of rational desire is added. Further, the first claim seems inappropriate in the same way, namely someone's saying that goods that one ought to desire in accordance with passion as well [as rational desire] are not voluntary. For reason leads us through will to desire those things that we ought to' (Aquinas, *in X Libros Ethicorum Aristotelis*, §428).

and deliberation. Since many actions on passion are impulsive, but none the less voluntary, it seems unreasonable to require all voluntary action to rest on deliberation and election.

This question is not confined to action on passions. It applies equally to non-reflective actions that do not seem to depend on particular passions. If I eat when I am hungry, that may be action on passion. But if I put plates on the table when I eat and wash the dishes after eating, these actions do not result from any specific passion; nor do they seem to result from deliberation, if I habitually do the same things every day without thinking about them. Moreover, they may not be exactly what I would do if I were to deliberate about it. Deliberation might lead me to see that it would be better to do something different from what I habitually do. And yet, what I habitually do seems to be voluntary. If it were urgent to do something else before I wash the dishes, I would not find it difficult to change what I usually do, and I would not find that the 'force of habit' impels me into compulsive dishwashing.

In this case also it would be reasonable for Aquinas to maintain that some actions are voluntary even if they do not result from deliberation and election. We might suggest that this is what he means when he picks out consent as the mark of voluntary action. Perhaps he means that, even when deliberation and election do not precede an action, the action is still voluntary if consent precedes it. This suggestion conflicts with Aquinas's explicit description of consent, but it is worth exploring none the less.

4. Virtual Aiming

To see how consent might operate without deliberation, we may consider some other cases where Aquinas discusses voluntary action without deliberation.

The easiest case is virtual aiming. Aquinas argues that if we have formed a complex plan to gain some remoter end by gaining a series of more proximate ends, our aiming (*intentio*) at the remoter end may influence our pursuit of the more proximate ends even if we do not rehearse at each stage the reasoning that takes us from our first aim to our current aims. In these cases the 'power of the first aim' remains in our later aims even if we do not think of the first aim.[19]

---

[19] 'One need not always be thinking of the ultimate end, whenever one desires or does something: for the power [*virtus*] of the first aim [*intentio*], which has a view to the ultimate end, remains in any desire at all of anything, even if one is not actually thinking of the ultimate end. In this way it is not necessary for anyone who is walking along a road to be thinking of the end at every step' (IaIIae, qu. 1, art. 6, ad 3). '...though aiming always aims at an end, it need not always aim at the ultimate end' (qu. 12, art. 2) Cf. *Summa contra Gentiles* iii.138.

These cases help us to understand how we can act on an end at a particular time even though our action does not issue directly from deliberation about how to achieve that end. An architect who has to design a new centre for a city may have to design a new railway station. The task of designing the parts of the station may occupy her without any current deliberation about how to design the whole city centre. But the plan for the city centre still influences her; it explains the position, size, and shape of the station. She has not forgotten that she has to design the whole city centre, but she need not think of this overall aim at every time when this aim guides her. Consent to a particular step in the building of the station may not result immediately from all the deliberation that explains it.

5. Indirect Virtual Aiming

This example of virtual aiming does not take us very far towards an understanding of consent without deliberation, since the consent issues immediately from some deliberation. Can we relax this condition, and still adhere to Aquinas's conception of voluntary action?

To see how this is possible, we should consider how an end may influence actions that we do not undertake (as the architect does) in order to achieve the end. If I am afraid, I form an inclination to avoid an apparent danger. If I believe that the danger is a real danger and that I have no good reason to face it, I will avoid it. In this case deliberation about my ulterior ends causes me to endorse the initial tendency of my fear, even though the fear did not arise in order to promote any ulterior ends.

Aquinas's views on virtual aiming show why deliberation about ulterior ends may not be needed on this occasion. If I am going very near the edge of a cliff, and I remember that in general this is a dangerous thing to do, I avoid the edge. I do not need to recapitulate the deliberation that once convinced me that this is a dangerous thing to do. Hence the power of an ulterior end may support or oppose an action that is not undertaken for the sake of that end. No deliberation here and now seems to be needed to explain why the ulterior end exerts influence on my action.

Aquinas recognizes such cases in his discussion of indirectly voluntary action. If an action is directly voluntary, the will tends (*fertur*) towards it; if it is indirectly voluntary, the will was able (*potuit*) to prohibit it, but does not prohibit it (qu. 77, art. 7). We act voluntarily on our fear of going near the edge of a cliff in so far as our ulterior ends permit it. If it had been important to go near the edge in this case (to help someone in danger, for instance), we would have inhibited our fear and gone near the edge.

6. Deliberate Consent

In this example we do not deliberate from an ulterior end before we endorse a particular action based on a passion. But we might argue that Aquinas does not allow this possibility, because he regularly connects consent with deliberation.

The connexion with deliberation explains why consent belongs to both reason and will:

Consent is an act of the desiring power, not absolutely, but in consequence of an act of reason that deliberates and judges, as stated above. For consent ends in this, that the will tends to what has been judged by reason. Hence consent may be ascribed both to will and to reason. (IaIIae, qu. 74, art. 7, ad 1)

Aquinas refers back here to his earlier discussion of the close connexion between consent and deliberation (qu. 15, art. 3). The presence of thought preceding the act of consent explains why the term 'consent' is appropriate; the will agrees with the preceding thought.

... the determination of the will to one thing is called consent because it presupposes thought with which its sentiment agrees (*cum qua simul sentit*), while it tends towards what reason judges to be good. And that is why the will is said to consent, but intellect is said to assent. (*Scriptum super Sententiis* III, d23, qu. 2, ad 1)

If there were no preceding thought, there would be nothing for the will to agree with, and so there would be no consent.

The connexion between deliberation and consent explains why consent is necessary for a mortal sin:

Now when anyone proceeds from passion to a sinful act, or to a deliberate consent, this does not happen suddenly: and so the deliberating reason can come to the rescue here, since it can drive the passion away, or at least prevent it from having its effect... (IaIIae, qu. 77, art. 8)

The pleasure that follows thought about fornication because of the thing thought about is mortal in its genus, but only by accident it is a venial sin, in so far as it precedes deliberated consent, in which the character of mortal sin is completed. (*De Veritate*, qu. 15, art. 4, ad 2)[20]

---

[20] See the similar references to deliberate consent as a condition of mortal sin, *De Malo*, qu. 7, arts. 3–4; qu. 12, art. 3.

Here Aquinas speaks equivalently of consent and of deliberate consent.[21] The consent that marks the difference between venial and mortal sin is deliberate consent.

7. Consent without Deliberation

Not all cases of consent, however, seem to require deliberation; for Aquinas sometimes seems to allow consent without deliberation. When he discusses the effects of passion on reason and will, he suggests that a passion may be strong enough to interfere with deliberation:

> When a passion precedes (*praeveniens*) the judgement of reason, if it prevails so much in the mind (*animus*) that <the mind> consents to it, it impedes deliberation and the judgement of reason. But when it follows <the judgement of reason>, as though commanded by reason, it helps towards the execution of reason's command.   (IaIIae, qu. 59, art. 2, ad 3)

> The second act is deliberation about things to be done, which is removed by appetite [*concupiscentia*]. For Terence says in the *Eunuchus*, 'This is something that allows neither deliberation nor any measure; you cannot control it by deliberation'. He speaks of lustful love. The condition that belongs to this case is lack of consideration. The third act is judgement about things to be done, and this is also impeded by lust. For it is said in *Daniel* 13 that 'they turned away their mind [*sensus*]. . . so that they would not remember just judgements'. The condition that belongs to this case is rashness [*praecipitatio*]—that is to say, while someone is drawn rashly towards consent, without waiting for the judgement of reason.   (*De Malo*, qu. 15, art. 4)

If a passion is strong enough, it impedes deliberation, but the mind consents to it anyhow. The strength of the passion explains both the consent and the failure of deliberation. Aquinas clearly does not mean that the action on this passion is involuntary, since he affirms that the mind consents to it. He supposes, then, that consent is possible without deliberation, in the face of a strong passion.[22]

8. Consent without Election

If Aquinas allows consent without deliberation, does he suppose that in such cases election must come between consent and action? If we can reach consent

---

[21] See *Scriptum super Sententiis* II, d24, qu. 3, art. 4.

[22] This possibility is relevant to Aquinas's views on incontinence. I have discussed them in 'Will, Responsibility, and Ignorance: Aristotelian Accounts of Incontinence', in T. Hoffmann, J. Müller and M. Perkams (eds) *Das Problem der Willensschwäche im mittelalterlichen Denken* (Leuven: Peeters, 2006).

without deliberation, and we act on our consent, must we elect the action, or one of the actions, we consent to? According to the twelve-stage account, we consent to an action in so far as we judge it satisfactory, but we act only in so far as we judge that the action we have consented to is better—either better than the other options we have consented to, or better than those we have not consented to.

If Aquinas believes that consent leads to action only through election, his remarks about voluntary action on passion imply that such actions require election; for if they are voluntary actions, and such actions require election, a passion cannot lead to action except through election. If this is what he means, voluntary action on passion requires a more definite judgement than it would require if only consent were needed. If only consent is needed for voluntary action, we do not need to judge that acting on the passion is the best thing to do in the circumstances; we need only judge that it is acceptable. Consent to action prompted by fear of falling over a cliff is consistent with the judgement that it would be better not to act on this fear.

If Aquinas believes that consent alone is sufficient for voluntary action, he does not believe that we have to elect our voluntary actions, or that we have to judge them better than other options. If that is his view, his assertion that consent is necessary for voluntariness and hence for mortal sin, does not imply that all the voluntary actions we have consented to have issued from election. Hence he seems to allow voluntary action to result from consent, without deliberation or election.

We might reasonably suppose that this is what he has in mind when he speaks of the premature termination of deliberation. Even if we begin the right sort of deliberation, we may not conclude it properly.

The one who has now rejected the unchangeable good in favour of a changeable good does not now regard it as bad to be turned away from the unchangeable good, in which [sc. being turned away] the character of mortal sin is completed. Hence he is not held back from sinning by the very fact that he notices that something is a mortal sin, but he needs to go further in consideration until he reaches something that he cannot fail to regard as bad, such as misery or something of that sort. Hence before as much deliberation takes place as is needed in someone in such a condition in order to avoid mortal sin, consent to mortal sin precedes. That is why, supposing that freewill adheres to mortal sin or an end that it ought not to adhere to, it is not in its power to avoid all mortal sins, although it can avoid any particular one if it exerts itself against it, because, even though it has avoided this or that one by applying as much deliberation as is needed, still it cannot prevent consent to a mortal sin from preceding this much deliberation, since it is impossible for a human being to be always or for a long time to be as watchful as is needed for this purpose, because of the many things in which a human mind is occupied.   (*De Veritate*, qu. 24, art. 12)

This is premature consent by someone who would have reached the right conclusion if he had deliberated enough. Aquinas does not suggest that the deliberator has reached the premature conclusion that the sinful action is better than the alternatives. The premature consent seems to cut off the deliberation that would have shown why this consent was mistaken.

These remarks, however, do not settle this question about the presence or absence of election. Just as we can consent without prolonged deliberation immediately before the action we consent to, we can also elect a particular action without deliberation on that occasion. It is perhaps more difficult to suppose that we could elect precipitately without waiting for the judgement of reason (*De Malo*, qu. 15, art. 4, above); some judgement of reason seems to be needed for the conclusion that one option is better than another. But we might suppose that in this case Aquinas is speaking loosely, and simply means that we do not wait for the rational reflection that belongs to deliberation.

9. Negative Consent

It becomes more plausible, however, to suppose that Aquinas recognizes consent without election if we consider his views about what consent consists in. So far we have not questioned the description that he gives in the official account; consent seems to be an explicit positive judgement that some proposed action is satisfactory, and so it seems to require explicit endorsement. But this description does not seem to cover all the cases of consent that he recognizes.

Sometimes Aquinas envisages consent without any act of endorsement. Failure to reflect on considerations that we ought to reflect on, in circumstances where it is up to us to reflect, constitutes consent to the action that we would have rejected if we had thought about it as we ought to have.

The higher reason is said to consent, from the very fact that it fails to direct the human act according to the Divine law, whether or not it adverts to the eternal law. For if it thinks of God's law, it holds it in actual contempt: and if not, it neglects it by a kind of omission. Therefore the consent to a sinful act always proceeds from the higher reason . . .   (IaIIae, qu. 74, art. 7, ad 2)

Before reason considers its own pleasure or harm, it has no interpretative consent, even though it does not resist. But when reason is now considering the rising pleasure and the harm that follows, as when someone recognizes that he is being totally turned towards sin by pleasure of this sort and falling headlong, then, unless he expressly resists, he seems to consent. And then the sin is transferred to reason through its act, because acting and not acting when one ought to act are referred back [*reducuntur*] to the genus of act, according as a sin of omission is referred back to a sin of acting.   (*De Veritate*, qu. 15, art. 4, ad 10)

This consent can also result from habitual inclination, if it is not inhibited by enough deliberation.

Without the consent of freewill there is no act of sin. But consent follows habitual inclination, unless much deliberation is applied in advance.   (*De Veritate*, qu. 24, art. 12, ad sc. 3)

Aquinas refers back to his previous remark (quoted above) about the need for extensive deliberation to see the badness in the mortal sins that we are used to. He implies that inclination results in consent without any deliberation. Without any positive endorsement, we can follow our habitual inclination, so that we consent to the action we would have rejected on further consideration.

This negative consent is an instance of error by omission. Aquinas takes some omissions to be sufficient for sin. Since sin is voluntary and therefore presupposes consent, an error of omission is sufficient for sin. This error depends on a cause or occasion of omission that is subject to the will. In the case of omission, no positive act of endorsement is necessary.

...it is evident that then the sin of omission has indeed an act combined with, or preceding, the omission, but that this act is related accidentally to the sin of omission. ...And so it can be said more truly that some sin can be without any act. (IaIIae, qu. 71, art. 5)

Something is said to be voluntary not only because an act of the will is brought to bear on it, but also because it is in our power that it happens or does not happen, as is said in *Ethics* III. Hence even not willing can be called voluntary, in so far as it is in a human being's power to will and not to will.   (IaIIae, qu. 71, art. 5, ad 2)

The sin of omission is voluntary, because we can speak of a voluntary action as one that is up to us to do, even if we do not positively endorse our doing it.

We do not have to conjecture that Aquinas sees that his doctrine of sinful omission implies the possibility of consent without positive endorsement. He allows that we can consent either positively or negatively. To show that consent belongs to higher reason even if higher reason does not positively endorse an action, he argues that we can consent by not dissenting.

The higher reason is said to consent not only because it always moves to act, according to the eternal reasons, but also because it does not dissent according to the eternal reasons.   (IaIIae, qu. 15, art. 4, ad 3)

The purely negative consent that Aquinas intends here is also taken to be sufficient for voluntary action; for he has just said that consent makes actions voluntary (IaIIae, qu. 15, art. 4, ad 2).

The acceptance of negative consent is just one aspect of Aquinas's doctrine of 'negative causation'. He applies this doctrine to his account of the voluntary.

[One thing is from another] indirectly, from the very fact that it does not act. In this way the sinking of a ship is said to be from the pilot in so far as he stops steering. But it should be noted that what follows from lack of action is not always traced back to a cause in the agent from his not acting, but [it is traced back] only when the agent can and ought to act. For if the pilot were unable to steer the ship or the steering were not assigned to him, the sinking of the ship, which might happen through [*per*] the absence of a pilot, would not be ascribed [*imputaretur*] to him, although it might be due to his absence from the helm.   (IaIIae, qu. 6, art. 3)

The pilot of a ship may cause an accident by steering badly, but he may also cause it by allowing an incompetent passenger to steer the ship, or by staying at home and failing to do his part. In the last case the pilot might deny that he caused the accident; since he was in the wrong place, he was no part of the causal chain that led to the ship's running aground. He might also protest if it were alleged that he caused the accident because the accident would not have happened if he had been there. He might answer that if any one of many different skilled pilots had been there, the accident would not have happened, but they are not held to have caused the accident.

In this case Aquinas holds that judgements about causation depend on deontic judgements. The absence of the pilot who ought to have been present is a cause of the accident, whereas the absence of pilots who were not required to be there is not a cause, even though their absence had the same counterfactual role as the absence of the pilot who ought to have been there.

This doctrine of negative causation applies to negative consent. Not every failure to dissent constitutes negative consent. We consent negatively to actions that we are capable of consenting to or dissenting from and that we ought to consent to or dissent from. When we act on our negative consent, the action is voluntary and we are open to praise or blame for it.

Though Aquinas allows negative consent, he does not countenance negative election. We do not elect something negatively in so far as we fail to reject it. Election requires us to judge one thing better than another, and such a judgement cannot be imputed to us simply because we act in one way when we could have acted differently. Hence the possibility of negative consent implies the possibility of consent without election.

10. The Role of the Will in Consent

We have discovered that Aquinas requires consent to amount to less than we might initially have supposed, and that in particular he requires neither deliberation nor election. Consent requires no more than a failure to dissent in certain conditions. What has Aquinas left us with? Has he given us a plausible or informative condition for voluntary action? In his view, voluntary action proceeds from the will. But has he left the will any significant role in voluntary action, if negative consent makes an action voluntary?

To find a suitable analogy for the role of the will, we may return to negative causation and responsibility. An inspector in a market may have the task of examining fruit to see whether or not a particular batch is fresh. A careful and skilled inspector looks at the fruit to make sure it is fresh. An ignorant inspector looks at the wrong features of the fruit. A careless inspector looks at the fruit hastily. A negligent inspector does not even bother to open the box, but just lets the fruit go by. All of them, however, pass the fruit as fresh. It would not be a plausible defence if the negligent inspector claimed that he had not really passed it because he never bothered to look at it. By letting it go by undisputed he passed it. If he had looked at the fruit, he would have noticed (we may suppose) that it was rotten, and in that case he would have rejected it, and so he cannot be accused of asserting that the fruit was fresh. But he passed it as fresh by his inaction, because it was up to him to pass it or to reject it, and he ought to have rejected it if it was rotten.

If it is plausible in this case to say that the inspector passed the fruit by not rejecting it, we can defend Aquinas's view that the will can consent to an action by not dissenting from it, even though it does not endorse the action. We can also see the point of his distinction between consent to something as satisfactory and election of something as better than the other options. It would not be plausible to say that if we allow x rather than y, we elect x as better. It would be plausible to say only that we raise no objection to x in comparison with y. Similarly, then, the consent that finds something satisfactory, in so far as it raises no objections, is to be distinguished from the election that rests on the judgement that one option is better than others.

Is negative consent too negative to constitute a genuine role for the will? Would it be clearer to say simply that I ought to have refused to do what I did, but I did it none the less? Do we add anything to this condition if we say that I consented to what I did by not dissenting?

Aquinas might reasonably answer that consent is relevant to this case in so far as it engages the will. An agent's will is guided by his views about the ultimate good, but it does not always apply these views to a particular action. Will influences intellect in so far as we choose to deliberate or not to deliberate, and to raise some questions rather than others. When we consent, we are aware of some of what can be said for and against a particular course of action, and we go no further in deliberation. If we consent correctly, we have already gone far enough in deliberation; for we have deliberated enough to find out which options are satisfactory and which one is preferable to the others, so that we can consent and elect. But if we cease to deliberate before we have reached this point, we stop applying our views about the good to this situation.

This process would not result in action if we interrupted deliberation at a point where we were inclined no more to one action than to another. If we consent to both, we still have not determined ourselves to do either one. But when we already are inclined to one action, our consent to it allows our previous inclination to proceed unimpeded by any objections that might arise. That is why consent is especially important when we act on passion, or when we have some initial inclination as a result of habit. Aquinas appeals to consent rather than election because he believes that we can act voluntarily on an inclination without judging that action better than other options. Voluntary action only requires us to declare the action satisfactory, so that we raise no objection to the inclination that already favours one of the options.

We can see why Aquinas's view of consent is useful if we compare it with Aristotle's claims about voluntary action. Aristotle might be taken to imply that if A does x knowing that A is doing x and out of a desire for x, A does x voluntarily. If this were a sufficient condition for voluntary human action, it would be difficult to see how voluntary human action differs from voluntary action by animals in any way that is relevant to responsibility, praise, and blame. We need not consider at the moment how Aristotle answers, or might answer, this difficulty. The fact that the difficulty arises shows why Aquinas's claims about consent are relevant and useful. They offer a clear and reasonable solution to the difficulty that faces Aristotle.

Aquinas has a good reason, therefore, to maintain that many actions are voluntary in so far as the will consents to them. His claim would not be true if he spoke of election rather than consent. But if he is right on this point, we do not act on election whenever we act on consent; for the explanatory value of consent sometimes depends on the fact that we stop short of electing what we have consented to. If we are to grasp the point of Aquinas's introduction of consent, we should reject or reinterpret his apparent claim that action needs election as well as consent. Since the cases in which we need to consent without electing are prominent in Aquinas's discussion, we have some reason to reinterpret rather than to reject.

11. A Paradigm of Action

We can now return to Aquinas's twelve-stage account of the antecedents of action. His treatment of consent shows that at least two of the stages are not after all necessary conditions for voluntary action; for Aquinas recognizes voluntary actions that rest on consent without deliberation and without election. We have therefore found a partial defence of his account against the charge of over-complication; for the short cut to voluntary action that proceeds through consent implies that not all voluntary action has to follow a process of deliberation and a judgement about the comparative value of the available options.

Since Aquinas is very likely to be aware that not all cases of action fit his twelve-stage account, he should recognize that the account does not provide necessary and sufficient conditions. One might suggest that it presents a paradigm rather than a general account. A paradigm for all Fs need not include features present in every single F; it presents a set of features that different Fs embody to some degree, and they are Fs to the extent that they include some of the relevant features of the paradigm.

Perhaps, then, Aquinas intends his full description, including deliberation, consent, and election, to be a paradigm of voluntary action. An action that meets all these conditions will be voluntary to the highest degree, or most fully voluntary. Other voluntary actions will be voluntary to some degree, in so far as they meet some of the conditions that mark a fully voluntary action.

Aquinas is willing to consider the possibility that voluntariness comes in degrees. He discusses the question whether non-rational animals act voluntarily, as Aristotle claims they do. His answer is that they do not display the degree of voluntariness that we find in human beings, but voluntariness belongs to them 'in accordance with an incomplete character' (*secundum rationem imperfectam*, IaIIae, qu. 6, art. 2). Since they have no will, their actions do not reach the higher degree of voluntariness.

The example of animals, however, is not entirely suitable for the purpose I have suggested. For we might argue that, according to Aquinas's conception of the voluntary, animals do not act voluntarily. Their second degree of the voluntary is simply an approximation to the voluntary, and falls short of being voluntary. This does not seem to be his view of action on passion, however. Animals are not responsible for their actions, whereas people who act on passions are responsible for these actions. Hence these people seem to act voluntarily. They are responsible for their actions because these actions are voluntary, and they are voluntary because they engage the will. Hence the genuinely voluntary action of rational agents differs from the second degree of voluntary action in non-rational agents because it involves the will. For this reason the actions of rational agents are different from those that simply approximate to the voluntary.

But even if we concede this point, we may still believe that the voluntary actions that make rational agents responsible for what they do can allow degrees of voluntariness. For they may engage the will to different degrees. Since non-rational agents have no will, their actions cannot involve their will to any degree. But if rational desire may be involved in action to different degrees, genuinely voluntary actions may be voluntary to different degrees.

We can now state a little more precisely the suggestion that Aquinas's description of voluntary action gives us a paradigm rather than a general set of necessary and sufficient conditions. The description presents the highest degree of involvement of the will in the causation of action, but we ought not to suppose that any action that involves the will to a lesser degree is not voluntary. Action on consent without deliberation and election is less voluntary, in so far as the will has a smaller role in actions to which it simply consents than it has in actions that it elects. The minimal role for the will is negative consent.

12. Why Election?

But is action on consent less voluntary than action on election? We might think that consent, explained as we have explained it, provides a sufficient basis for voluntariness and responsibility without the further mental elements that Aquinas introduces. In particular, we may be inclined to doubt whether deliberation and election make an action more voluntary. If we raise this question, we may conclude that the Stoics are right (whether or not this was their intention) to explain voluntariness and responsibility by appeal to assent rather than Aristotelian election. For the reasons we have given, we may take Aquinas's claims about consent to develop Stoic views of assent so that they apply to all the cases that need to be covered. We may then find it puzzling that Aquinas still holds on to the extra elements derived from Aristotle. Since they are not derived from Aristotle's account of the voluntary, we may well wonder why they should intrude in an account of the voluntary. Would Aquinas not be better off without them?

The answer to this question depends on how far Aquinas is right to connect voluntariness with the involvement of the will. For he has reason to believe that the will is more involved in action on deliberation and election than in action on mere consent. Our will expresses our conception of comparative values, so that we do not act only on some conception of value, but on a conception of what matters more than what. We reach this conception most explicitly when we formulate a conception of the ultimate end; and we apply our conception of the ultimate end most precisely to action when we act on deliberation and election.

If our voluntary action skips some of the steps in Aquinas's description, it fails to apply an articulate conception of the ultimate end precisely to our action. This point is especially clear in the case of negative consent that consists in failure to dissent. The fact that we allow ourselves to do something that, if we thought about it, we would reject reveals something about our character, but it may give a misleading presentation of it. Laziness and negligence are not the same as a misguided conception of comparative value.

This is why consent alone does not provide a measure of praiseworthiness or blameworthiness. Aquinas agrees with Aristotle's conception of a virtue as an elective state (*habitus electivus, hexis prohairetike*). We can display virtue or the lack of it, in consent without election, but this display does not directly apply our conception of comparative values to our actions. If we want to know what sort of person someone is, we reasonably want to know what he cares about for its own sake and how he applies these concerns to his actions. For this purpose, we need to answer the questions that Aquinas answers in his complete account of human action.

If this is a good reason to make election a prominent and essential component of virtue, we may still wonder whether that answers our question about voluntary action. If election is essential to virtue, is it thereby paradigmatic for voluntary action? We might argue that these two roles for election are separable, and that it belongs to a theory of virtue but not to an account of action.

Aquinas rejects this attempt to separate the questions about action and responsibility from the questions about virtue. He begins the Prima Secundae with the ultimate end not only because of the overall plan of the *Summa*, but also because we need to grasp the character of the ultimate end in order to grasp the character of the will and of distinctively human action. When we think about responsibility and about virtue, we are really thinking about the will and the ultimate end, because voluntary action and virtuous action are two ways in which the will expresses its conception of the ultimate end in particular actions.

Aquinas's remarks on consent need some expansion, and perhaps some revision, if consent is to play the role that it needs to play in Aquinas's theory of action. But this expansion does not threaten the central role that Aquinas assigns to election in his account both of action and of virtue. Once we see that his account of action is more flexible than it may initially appear, we can better appreciate the unified and systematic character of his views on action, character, and virtue.

6

Kenny and Aquinas on the Metaphysics of Mind

JOHN HALDANE

If Wittgenstein was right, philosophy had been on a wrong track since the time of Descartes and should alter course in a way that would make it more sympathetic to medieval preoccupations.

Anthony Kenny, *Aquinas* (1980)

1. The Proper Study of Mankind

Anthony Kenny's contributions to philosophy are marked by their considerable range, engaging issues in epistemology and metaphysics, philosophy of mind and action, ethics and philosophy of religion, and social philosophy and philosophy of law. In addition he has contributed very significantly to the history of philosophy both in respect of the study of individuals such as Aristotle, Aquinas, Descartes, and Wittgenstein, and in regard to particular concepts, including those of existence, intentionality, and practical reasoning.

Beyond these philosophical enquiries he has exercised his questioning and clarifying habits of mind in the study of other disciplines and issues including theological, literary, political, historical, and biographical ones. In all of this his work is marked by a broad and deep humanism: a fascination with the products of human thought and action; a sympathy and admiration for human achievement, be it intellectual, moral, or in a broad sense spiritual; and a desire to understand these achievements from the 'inside' as an engaged participant.

These interests, talents, and sensibilities combine in an approach to under-standing the defining aspects of human nature that is itself humanistic in the sense that it identifies the subject matter of enquiry as being personal life: consisting in the exercise of various sensitive, affective, volitional, and intellectual powers, developed and modified through rule-governed social practices. In keeping with this view of the subject, Kenny has seen the task of philosophical study as being one of understanding the aspects of personal life at various levels of constitution and expression, and in their interrelatedness. Philosophy of mind, in this way of conceiving it, is an aspect of philosophical anthropology. It aims to arrive at general descriptions and interpretations of the psychological that make sense of it, but not only from the point of view of the theorist. Rather, allowing for the fact that philosophical illumination is achieved at a level of abstraction from ordinary modes of description, what is understood is what was already given in experience and in reflection. Comprehending the human in this sense is not a matter of fashioning a theory of sub-personal mechanisms but of discerning the meanings and purposes that shape and direct human action.

The distinction between the 'descriptive' and the 'revisionary' in metaphysics was deployed by Peter Strawson to mark a contrast between approaches to understanding the structure of our thought about the world.[1] On the one side stand those that make sense of what is identified and referred to in common discourse by placing it within a framework of categories that serves to illuminate the most general features of the world. On the other stand those that set aside the objects, attributes, and relations of ordinary experience and replace them with metaphysical entities of quite different sorts. Descriptive philosophy accepts the familiar as real, allowing for occasional illusions; the revisionary looks elsewhere for reality and in doing so rejects the familiar as deceptive.

The principal contemporary challenge to humanistic accounts of the personal comes not from advocates of esoteric metaphysical schemes, but from those who look to other non-philosophical fields of study to provide an account of the human psyche. And here there is something of a cultural divide deriving from contrasting social and intellectual histories. 'Continental' thinkers have often deployed cultural and political hermeneutics in an effort to dissolve the personal into the social, then proclaiming the latter to be a network of conflicting power relations. This is revisionary in the sense that it challenges familiar forms of self-understanding, but equally it is also recognizably humanistic in retaining categories of subjectivity, meaning, purpose, and value, and in having a familiar emancipatory intent (revealed in the common rhetoric of revelation, release, and autonomy).

---

[1] P. F. Strawson, *Individuals: An Essay in Descriptive Metaphysics* (London: Methuen, 1959).

It has long been customary for analytical philosophers to disparage such styles of thought as unrigorous, extravagant, rhapsodic, and obscurantist, not to say pretentious. Such criticisms are often merited, but it is worth noting that while they call into question the methods and quality of the thought, they generally leave unaddressed the substance of the theories, save where those involve obviously self-refuting declarations of global relativism or anti-rationalism. This attitude of non-substantive criticism might well seem apt given the oft-made claim that analytical philosophy is a style or method of thought and not a set of doctrines or an ideological outlook. As such, save where inconsistency may be involved in the statement of a theoretical position, it should have no prejudicial view regarding it.

In the last thirty years, however, things have changed considerably, and the charge that it is disingenuous to represent analytical philosophy as neutral with regard to such fundamentals as the nature of human beings is well founded, for it is here more than anywhere else in Anglo-American philosophy that the scientistic turn begun in the United States has shown itself.[2] Philosophical psychology, philosophy of thought and action, and philosophy of language have all been configured in ways that correspond to certain assumptions imported from scientific theorizing. It is worth reflecting briefly on the roots of this development, for Kenny is himself more sensitive than most of his contemporaries to the ways in which cultural forces have influenced and continue to shape the development of philosophy.

2. The Scientistic Turn

Until the 1960s it was common for British philosophers to have been educated in literary, historical, and theological traditions, so that their approach to philosophy was one that assumed that the subject was a branch of humanistic study in which contributions from past centuries might be as valuable as contemporary ones. By stages, however, the educational background and general outlook of those entering into advanced philosophical studies began to change. At the same time, the leadership of philosophy in the English-speaking world had been assumed by elite American universities in which scientific styles of thought already enjoyed high status and in some cases pre-eminence.

In addition, however, philosophy had taken its own scientific turn under the direction of Carnap, Quine, Sellars, and others. It is common enough to observe

---

[2] This development is discussed by Anthony Kenny in 'Cognitive Scientism', in *From Empedocles to Wittgenstein: Historical Essays in Philosophy* (Oxford: Clarendon Press, 2008).

the considerable influence of Quine on his contemporaries and students, but in order to understand why his combination of pragmatism, naturalism, and scientism took hold, and why his agenda of issues and methods proved so influential, one has to appreciate that philosophy was already predisposed to take a scientific turn because of the general character of American university studies in the post-war period, and because of the waning of religiously inclined idealism. Out of this cultural environment emerged a determination to make philosophy a precise, rigorous, and economical discipline informed by contemporary empirical science. In this context to speak of being 'informed by science' means more than keeping up with relevant developments in physics, cosmology, and biology, for example; it means looking to science for solutions to traditional philosophical problems. Thus, as Quine puts it, in his essay 'Epistemology Naturalized': 'Epistemology, or something like it, simply falls into place as a chapter of psychology and hence of natural science. It studies a natural phenomenon, viz., a physical human subject'.[3]

On or near to the surface in this passage are the notions that science is the only source of positive knowledge about the world, that norm-governed practices can be reconstrued and explained in terms of causal regularities, and that human beings are physical objects no different in fundamental nature from other material objects. This leaves the question of what to make of talk of mind and mental activities. Whereas Quine once supposed that intentional idiom might be dispensed with in the study of human behaviour he became largely persuaded of the view advocated by Donald Davidson that insofar as we may be interested in the behavioural phenomena of human action and language there is no practical alternative to psychology with its categories of mentalistic concepts that classify dispositions, events, and processes in point of ascribed intentional contents. This reintroduced a humanistic element, but seen from another perspective Davidson's correction to Quine's scientism is more a matter of interpretative interest than one of metaphysical difference. This emerges in the following remark of Davidson:

I agree that it is because [basic psychological] concepts operate in a conceptual domain that psychology is different [from the hard sciences] but I see this difference as due to our special interest in interpreting human agents as rational agents rather than to special powers of those agents.[4]

---

    [3] W. V. O. Quine, 'Epistemology Naturalized', in *Ontological Relativity and Other Essays* (New York: Columbia University Press, 1969), pp. 82–3.
    [4] Donald Davidson, 'Reply to Lanz', in Ralph Stoeker (ed.), *Reflecting Davidson* (Berlin: de Gruyter, 1993), p. 303.

This supports an interpretation of his anomalous monism that is rather different from what that theory has sometimes been taken to assert, and from what others have proposed under the general heading of non-reductive materialism. Here Davidson disavows the idea that rational psychology is required to describe and explain events that are in and of themselves expressions of rational powers of thought, deliberation, and action; rather psychology is a scheme constructed out of interests that we bring to the study of human animals. It looks, however, as if a transcendental argument can be constructed to refute the idea that rational psychology could simply be an interpretative imposition. For the interests of those who might construct and apply such a scheme, as well as the processes of construction and application, must themselves be exercises of cognition and intentional action. Mindedness on the part of the interpreter is a precondition of the possibility of psychological description.

Here I am not concerned to press this argument, but I do want to suggest that Davidson's distance from the reductionists and the eliminativists is less than it might seem.[5] His was an account not of intrinsic human nature but of an interpretative practice, and this difference of subject emerges both in the passage quoted above and in his reluctance to draw metaphysical conclusions from the irreducibility, by analysis or law, of intentional discourse. For all that he argued against conceptual reductionism Davidson remained a physicalist, and this ontological position was shared by most of his analytical critics. Their dispute was not about the metaphysics of mind but about the reducibility of psychological explanations.

3. Making Sense of the Intentional

It is not generally known that one of the points of departure for Davidson in developing his account of action and mind was Anthony Kenny's book *Action, Emotion and Will* (1963). Given the task of reviewing this for the *Journal of Philosophy*, Davidson found himself drawn to reflect on the matter of whether everyday descriptions and explanations of actions, motives, and reasons showed them to be logically rather than causally related. Challenged by Kenny's subtle presentation of a broadly rationalist understanding according to which reasons and actions are not separately identifiable items but rather aspects of an agent's

---

[5] For further discussion of these matters see John Haldane, 'Folk Psychology and the Explanation of Human Behaviour', *Proceedings of the Aristotelian Society*, suppl. vol. 62 (1988), and 'Theory, Realism and Common Sense: Reply to Paul Churchland', *Proceedings of the Aristotelian Society* 93/3 (1993).

ongoing life, the intended review developed into the article 'Actions, Reasons and Causes'. In this Davidson took on the general anti-causalist position of a group of philosophers influenced by Wittgenstein, including Elizabeth Anscombe, Norman Malcolm, Abraham Melden, and Peter Winch as well as Kenny himself. His critical conclusion that psychology is *both* rationalizing and causal, and the first only insofar as it is also the second, initiated the general movement towards a causal theory of mind and ironically opened the door to the idea that human psychology might in fact be made the subject of scientific study. Introducing a collection of his essays Davidson wrote as follows:

[My] thesis is that the ordinary notion of cause which enters into scientific or common sense accounts of non-psychological affairs is essential also to the understanding of what it is to act for a reason ... Cause is the cement of the universe; the concept of cause is what holds together our picture of the universe, a picture that would otherwise disintegrate into a diptych of the mental and the physical.[6]

Seen in this perspective Davidson's defence of rational psychology has been deemed uncertain, whereas his (re)introduction of a causalist understanding of the nature of mind and action has been regarded as an irreversible achievement that has paved the way for a comprehensive account of the inner causes of behaviour.

By contrast, if we follow Anthony Kenny whose course has been largely constant from the publication of *Action, Emotion and Will*, through *Will, Freedom and Power* (1975) to *The Metaphysics of Mind* (1989) we find the case being made that modern philosophy of mind repeats the errors of Cartesianism and does so culpably, having failed to learn the lessons taught by Wittgenstein and elaborated in his immediate wake by Anscombe in *Intention* and by Peter Geach in *Mental Acts*. *The Metaphysics of Mind* is Kenny's most comprehensive treatment of the subject. It builds on the earlier studies and on a number of related essays and is avowedly Wittgensteinian. As with most of his writings on philosophical psychology, however, it draws on another anti-Cartesian tradition, namely that of Thomistic-Aristotelianism. Indeed, it has been an important and repeated observation dating from Kenny's first philosophical essay 'Aquinas and Wittgenstein' published in the *Downside Review* fifty years ago[7], that with regard to central issues in philosophy of mind, action, and language these thinkers have more in common with one another than with the tradition of modern philosophy begun with Descartes and Locke and

---

[6] Donald Davidson, *Essays on Actions and Events* (Oxford: Clarendon Press, 1980), p. xi.

[7] Anthony Kenny, 'Aquinas and Wittgenstein', *Downside Review* 77 (1959). The topics on which he finds instructive parallels are 'analogy and univocity', 'hylomorphism and atomism', 'singulars and universals', and 'intellect active or passive'.

continued today in the mainstream of analytical philosophy. As Kenny has observed more recently: 'If Wittgenstein was right, philosophy had been on a wrong track since the time of Descartes and should alter course in a way that would make it more sympathetic to medieval preoccupations'.[8]

In addition, Anthony Kenny has done more than any other author to substantiate this observation, both through illustrative comparisons and contrasts offered in the course of essays, and through sustained analyses of issues as in the books mentioned. Besides these there is also his study *Aquinas on Mind* (1993) which both celebrates and criticizes Aquinas: the former for his insightful development of an Aristotelian account of human nature, the latter for what Kenny takes to be his lapses, mainly in failing to remain consistent to that account.

Since I shall be proceeding in a direction that Kenny is likely to regard as belonging to the lapsarian strand of Thomistic philosophy of mind let me make a couple of points by way of acknowledgement. When I was a student being taught philosophy in the analytical style I encountered the idea, then largely associated with Brentano, that the defining mark of the mind was intentionality. On asking one of my teachers what this meant he replied that it was something Brentano had got from medieval philosophy and to find out more he referred me to work by Roderick Chisholm. Famously Chisholm had transposed Brentano's thesis that 'aboutness' provided a criterion of the mental into a logical claim to the effect that sentences reporting intentional attitudes failed of extensionality, but Brentano wrote as follows:

Every mental phenomenon is characterized by what the Scholastics of the Middle Ages called the intentional (or mental) inexistence of an object, and what we might call, though not wholly unambiguously, reference to a content, direction toward an object (which is not to be understood here as meaning a thing), or immanent objectivity. Every mental phenomenon includes something as object within itself . . .[9]

Chisholm's gloss on this was that the scholastics believed that '[the word] "unicorn" in "John is thinking about a unicorn" . . . is being used simply to designate a unicorn . . . but a unicorn with a mode of being (intentional inexistence, immanent objectivity, or existence in the understanding) that is short of actuality but more than nothingness'.[10] Thinking this could not be right

[8] Anthony Kenny, *Aquinas* (Oxford: Oxford University Press, 1980), p. 28.

[9] Franz Brentano, *Psychology from an Empirical Standpoint*, trans. A. C. Rancurello, D. B. Terrell, and L. McAlister (London: Routledge, 1973) (2nd edn, introd. Peter Simons, 1995), p. 88. I explore Brentano's own account of intentionality, and that of Chisholm, from the perspective of Aquinas's position in John Haldane, 'Brentano's Problem', *Grazer Philosophische Studien*, 35 (1989), and 'Forms of Thought', in L. E. Hahn (ed.), *The Philosophy of Roderick Chisholm* (Chicago: Open Court, 1997).

[10] Roderick Chisholm, 'Intentionality', in Paul Edwards (ed.), *Encyclopedia of Philosophy* (London: Macmillan, 1967), vol. iv, p. 201.

I headed off to track down the medieval sources, but I struggled to make sense of Aquinas and Ockham and of modern neo-scholastic texts. Then someone mentioned a volume of essays edited by Anthony Kenny that might contain things likely to be of interest.[11] There I found Kenny's own 'Intellect and Imagination in Aquinas' which provided an exemplary treatment of Thomas's account of cognition and made it clear that the kind of existence at issue in the notion of intentional (in)existence is predicational rather than substantial. As Kenny puts it, 'when St Thomas follows Aristotle in describing the mind as *becoming* its object, the becoming must be thought of as the acquisition of a new characteristic (like *becoming red*) rather than as the turning into a new kind of thing (like *becoming a butterfly*)'.[12]

For all that has been written since on the subject of Aquinas on intentionality, including Kenny's later book, I would still recommend this early essay as the best starting point for anyone wishing to engage with St Thomas's views in a philosophically critical mode.[13] Second, and following from this assessment, while I am more favourable to Aquinas's reasoning from the intentionality of intellectual cognition to its immateriality, and from that to the immateriality of the intellect, my sense of the difficulties confronting this reasoning derives more from reflecting on criticisms made by Kenny than from any other single source.

4. Powers and their Possessors

I shall examine Aquinas's argument about the immateriality of thought and of the intellect later but I want to approach this indirectly by first exploring what Kenny appears to regard as another lapse from philosophical good sense. In this case, however, the source is not Aquinas nor any Thomist but, surprisingly, Wittgenstein. Kenny identifies the issue in the course of a recent broadly Aristotelian-cum-Wittgenstein essay, 'Cognitive Scientism', in which he argues that mind is a capacity to be distinguished, like any other power, from its *possessor*, its *exercise*, and its *vehicle*. He then objects to the failure of philosophers to observe these distinctions or to their liability to blur them in the interest of effecting reductions of mind either to behaviour ('exercise reductionism') or to bodily structures in virtue of which we possess mental powers ('vehicle

---

[11] Anthony Kenny (ed.), *Aquinas: A Collection of Critical Essays* (London: Macmillan, 1969).

[12] Kenny, 'Intellect and Imagination in Aquinas', p. 283.

[13] For convenience, and for further context, one could also read the developed version of that essay which appears as chapter 3 'Mind', in Kenny, *Aquinas* (1980).

reductionism'). Both reductions, Kenny argues, involve category mistakes, for neither behaviour nor brains are capacities, though there are conceptual and causal relations, respectively, between mindedness and its expression on the one hand, and its bodily vehicle(s) on the other.

In conclusion, Kenny then draws attention to a passage in *Zettel* where Wittgenstein writes as follows:

No supposition seems to me more natural than that there is no process in the brain correlated with associating or with thinking. ... It is perfectly possible that certain psychological phenomena *cannot* be investigated physiologically, because physiologically nothing corresponds to them. I saw this man years ago: now I have seen him again, I recognise him, I remember his name. And why does there have to be a cause of this remembering in my nervous system ... Why should there not be a psychological regularity to which *no* physiological regularity corresponds? If this upsets our concept of causality then it is high time it was upset.[14]

Kenny's gloss on this is that in countenancing a causal relation between an earlier perception and a later memory that is not mediated physiologically Wittgenstein allows 'the possibility of an Aristotelian soul or entelechy, which operates with no material vehicle, a formal or final cause to which there corresponds no mechanistic efficient cause'.[15] Leaving to one side the Aristotelian characterization of the envisaged situation, Kenny's own concern is with Wittgenstein's willingness to accept the possibility of a materially unmediated psychological process. To recognize the core of his unease one has, I think, to set aside one interpretation and response to the quoted passage. For in light of Davidson's arguments regarding the anomality of the mental someone might be inclined to read Wittgenstein as being concerned specifically with the issue of psycho-physical regularities, and to treat his example as simply telling against the requirement that if a perception and a memory are causally related then they must fall under a mental-physical law, or that there must be some systematic physical regularity corresponding to such types of mental parings. For Davidson this possibility would not impugn the underlying material basis of mind, since the claimed identity of every mental event with a physical event does not imply law-like connections between psychological and physiological event types or patterns.

The concluding remarks about the absence of physiological regularities, though intelligible in context, distract from what I take to be the real scandal for Kenny of Wittgenstein's envisaged possibility, which is the idea that mental

[14] Ludwig Wittgenstein, *Zettel* 608–10 (cf. *Remarks on Philosophy of Psychology* 903–6) as cited by Kenny in 'Cognitive Scientism', p. 161.
[15] 'Cognitive Scientism', p. 162.

processes might occur without a material medium or enabling physiological structure. It is this rejection of what might be termed 'the material foundation of mind' that is the cause of Kenny's 'queasiness' about this passage. Here, as in connection with his rejection of Aquinas's immaterialist account of intellectual activity, it is important to determine Kenny's own position on the central question of the metaphysics of mind, namely whether mind is something material.

In the familiar understanding of it, however, that question is, from Kenny's perspective, ill-formed. Following in the Aristotelian and Thomistic traditions Kenny treats mind as a power or capacity, more precisely as a capacity for acquiring, developing, and exercising various powers of cognition, deliberation and agency. As he puts it:

[T]he mind itself can be defined as the capacity for behaviour of the complicated and symbolic kinds which constitute the linguistic, social, moral, economic, scientific, cultural, and other characteristic activities of human beings in society.[16]

Here we should note several points. First, he differs from Descartes (though sides with Brentano) in making conceptual intentionality or symbolic activity, rather than introspectable phenomenal consciousness, the mark of the mental. Second, he relegates the sensory side of human psychology to the *psyche*, a domain of capacities shared with non-minded animals. Third, the characterization of mental powers makes intelligible my earlier claim that for Kenny the study of human mindedness is the work of humane interpretation rather than of scientific theory. In so far as the exercise of mental powers employs or depends upon physiological processes these may become objects of study, but to that extent the subject has changed from the interpretation of mental activities to the investigation of sub-personal parts and mechanisms. Fourth, given the classification of mind as a capacity it makes no sense to ask whether this is itself a material or immaterial entity since capacities like dispositions and attributes more generally are not things or parts of things. Allowing for this conceptual point, however, the general issue of materialism with regard to human minds can still be raised by asking the following series of questions: what is it that has a mind? is there a necessary medium of mental activity, and if so what is its nature? does mind, or the specific mental capacities acquired by it require a vehicle or vehicles, and if so what is its, or their, nature?

So far as the first of these questions is concerned Kenny has often quoted Aquinas and Wittgenstein with approval to the effect that the subject of human mental capacities is not the mind in any Cartesian substantial sense, or the

---

[16] *The Metaphysics of Mind* (Oxford: Clarendon Press, 1989), p. 7.

brain or some other bodily part, but the living human being. To that extent he disavows both central state materialism and mind–body dualism in favour of a form of *personalism* (though so far as I am aware this is not a classification he has used).

Someone might argue in reply that since human persons, so conceived, are a kind of living animal composed of matter it follows that the subject of mental capacities is a material object; but that fallaciously confuses the nature of a substantial individual and the medium of its composition. Rejecting the identification of states of mind with physical states Kenny writes:

> [W]hat counts as the same individual depends on what kind of individual is being described. The criteria for a mental state are not the same as those for a physical state. ... The materialist is right in claiming that to describe a state of mind is to describe, at a certain degree of abstraction, a physical object. But the physical object which is described by mentalistic predicates is a human being, not a human brain.[17]

Given this approach, however, Kenny could have applied the point about identity and individuation more extensively to conclude that it is incoherent to identify human beings with physical objects insofar as the latter description fails to provide any relevant sortal in terms of which to identify instances. Relatedly, reflection on the matter of personal identity provides further reason to reject the view of whole-body materialists according to which persons are identical with their entire bodies as defined by their current or historically aggregated matter.[18]

The body of Anthony Kenny is a component of a plurality of existing collections of bodily particles. Let C be the set of particles that composes his body at the time of my writing this; let C−1 be that which comprised Kenny's body a year ago; C−2 a year prior to that, and so on. Assuming that none of these component particles has passed out of existence then all of these collections continue to exist though they are spread across a range of (presumably spatially non-contiguous) places, and on this account are distributed objects. Which material body is it that Anthony Kenny is said to be identical with: is it C, or C + C−1, or C + all prior Cs? Any attempt to answer this question encounters a range of difficulties. The identification of distinct collections via yearly intervals is arbitrary and the question of how many such collections there are seems hard to resolve; but in any case the identification of a material body with its component particles

---

[17] Ibid., p. 151.

[18] The same considerations also tell against situated whole-body materialism which allows environment to be relevant to individuating or even partly constituting mental states and seeks to accommodate this by identifying persons with body-environment complexes.

presumes definiteness which the general concept of a material body fails to provide. Besides, the identity of the individual Anthony Kenny is that of a living rational animal and involves characteristics, including modal properties, that are drawn from different categories than those of material composition and organization. I conclude that human persons are not to be identified with material objects and that Kenny need not have conceded that to describe a state of mind is to describe a physical object. In saying this, however, I am not at all denying that human beings are bodily creatures.

Similarly while such natural expressions of thought and intention as speech and bodily action involve sounds and movements, it is again a mistake to infer from this that mental activity can be identified with its bodily expressions. That is an instance of the fallacy of exercise reductionism. This now brings us to the question of whether specific mental powers, and the second order capacity for acquiring these, which is the nature of mind in general, require *vehicles*. So far as sentient powers are concerned, i.e. those capacities that belong to the psyche and are shared with animals, these do have physiological vehicles, parts of the body serving as relevant organs. Thus sight depends upon the eye (and also upon the brain), hearing upon the ear, taste upon the tongue, and so on for the other senses. To that extent, while it is a category mistake to think of sense powers as themselves material, it is not a mistake to say that they are physiologically embodied, and in that respect to maintain an organicist account of them.

This is not in dispute between Kenny and Aquinas (nor between both and Wittgenstein) for although St Thomas does not speak of vehicles of cognition he does say that sense-perception involves organs. He writes:

Sensation and the acts consequent upon it manifestly take place along with a certain physical change in the body; as in seeing, colour according to its kind, affects the pupil of the eye; and the same for the other senses. So it is clear that the sense soul [or 'the powers of sensing'—*anima sensitiva*] has no proper activity of its own but that each of its acts is of the body-soul compound.[19]

Immediately prior to this, however, he observes, 'But Aristotle proved that understanding [or 'intellection'—*intelligere*] alone among the acts of the soul, took place without a physical organ'. Before considering something of the argumentation Aquinas gives in support of Aristotle's position, we still need to get clearer about the idea of a vehicle of a capacity and about the relation between these two elements in Kenny's general analysis of thought, for here I detect some tension or uncertainty.

[19] St Thomas Aquinas, *Summa Theologiae* Ia, qu. 75, art. 3, responsio; in *Summa Theologiae*, vol. xi (London: Eyre & Spottiswoode, 1970), p. 15.

5. Powers With and Without Vehicles

In Kenny's most recent discussion of these issues he gives his most abstract characterization:

The vehicle of a power is the abiding actuality in virtue of which a substance possesses a potentiality which finds expression in transitory exercises. This underlying actuality may be an ingredient, or a property or a structure.[20]

When Kenny speaks here of 'substances' it is clear that he has in mind not any kind of individual object but more restrictedly 'actualities', that is to say non-abstract objects that act or are acted upon: substances possessed of active or passive powers. On this account we need not wonder whether numbers, geometrical objects, or abstract essences have associated vehicles, but one might ask whether an immaterial actuality would require a vehicle for any capacity it might have. Though it does not say so explicitly, the description given above suggests that vehicles are deemed universally necessary for the possession of powers, but it does not state whether they must be material. Elsewhere, however, when exploring the notion of abilities, Kenny writes as follows:

The vehicle of an ability is the physical ingredient or structure in virtue of which the possessor of an ability possesses the ability and is able to exercise it. ... A vehicle is something concrete, something which can be weighed and measured. ... In the case of the mind, the connection between capacity and exercise is a conceptual connection ... The connection between capacity and vehicle on the other hand, is a contingent one, discoverable by empirical science.[21]

Here there seems no question but that abilities are taken to require material grounding and although it is also said that the connection between capacity and vehicle is 'contingent' this is naturally read as referring to the specifics of any foundation, and the manner of its sustaining a capacity, rather than to the existence of one. On that reading the concluding contrast is that whereas capacities are specified in terms of their exercises and so the relation between the contents of these is conceptually necessary and a priori, it is a contingent matter *what* serves to ground a particular ability, though it is not contingent *that* there is such a grounding. On the other hand were it Kenny's view that the existence of a vehicle is a conceptual and hence a priori matter then his response to Wittgenstein's example of the physiologically unmediated relation between mental acts would be outright rejection rather than mere 'queasiness'.

[20] 'Cognitive Scientism', pp. 155–6.   [21] *The Metaphysics of Mind*, pp. 72 and 74.

Moreover the queasiness seems to lie closer to being an empirical than a philosophical doubt. Kenny writes:

Since the time of Galileo, it has been a presumption of science that every power has a vehicle, that to every potentiality for the future there corresponds a present actuality. It is this presumption that Wittgenstein is here calling in question. He is undoubtedly correct that there is nothing conceptually incoherent in the idea of a capacity existing without a material vehicle ... Maybe Wittgenstein is right that, in Aristotelian terms, there may be formal and final causes in the absence of efficient and material ones.[22]

This is a surprising concession given the character of the corresponding discussions in the *Metaphysics of Mind* and in *Aquinas on Mind*. From the former I have quoted passages which suggest that Kenny then regarded a vehicle to be a necessary ground of a capacity, and in the case of human intellectual powers (no less than sensory ones) the vehicle to be a material one. He writes: 'The mind, as we have said, is the capacity to acquire or possess intellectual abilities. The vehicle of the human mind is, very likely, the human brain'[23] and here the modifying probability is not in response to the thought that there may be no material vehicle but in reaction to incautious or inaptly precise localizations of it. In *Aquinas on Mind*, having allowed that Thomas's general *agent-ability-exercise* analysis does not include the fourth element of *vehicle*, Kenny raises the question of whether Aquinas is not inclined to hypostatize abilities, which may be related to the worry about Wittgenstein allowing free-standing capacities.

These points raise large and quite general metaphysical questions that are beyond the scope of this essay. It is widely held that every dispositional property has to have a categorical grounding, but others have argued that there can, and perhaps must, be ungrounded dispositions. This is how the opposition is usually framed but these are in fact contraries rather than contradictories since there is a broader version of the grounded thesis to the effect that every disposition has to be grounded in something other than itself, and so formulated that would allow for the possibility of dispositions being grounded in other dispositions, or directly in substances unmediated by structuring properties. In these terms a power might be grounded in another power or be immediately possessed by an agent.

Applied to the context of intellectual capacities this would allow that, for example, the ability to engage in deliberation between alternative courses of action was grounded in the power to conceptualize situations, and that this was grounded in the ability to construct general descriptions, which itself was grounded in the capacity to form abstract universals. Matters might come to

---

[22] 'Cognitive Scientism', p. 162.
[23] *Metaphysics of Mind*, p. 73; see also the discussion on pp. 27–31.

rest there, or more intelligibly in the claim that these abilities are the direct and unmediated powers of an intellectual subject. I quoted Kenny saying that the vehicle of a power is an 'abiding actuality' and while the passage indicates that he takes this to be something other than the possessor of the power, and to be an 'ingredient, or a property or a structure', other remarks suggest that the driving metaphysical thought is the Aristotelian one that all potentialities have to be keyed to actualities. That might be interpreted as a version of the requirement of grounding, but as I have just indicated this requirement might be met other than by ingredients or structures.

6. Aquinas and the Immateriality of the Intellect

Aquinas gives a number of 'proofs' of the immateriality of the intellectual soul some of which are clearly influenced by neo-Platonic ideas, as for example his reasoning in *Summa Contra Gentiles* where he writes that 'no bodily action is self-reflexive, but in acting the intellect reflects on itself, not only as to a part, but as to the whole itself, therefore it is not a body'.[24] This echoes part of an argument developed by Plotinus in *Enneads* IV.7 regarding the unity of the soul and what he describes as the 'community of awareness' throughout it. Nonetheless the main arguments, oft repeated by Thomists, and discussed by Kenny in *Aquinas on Mind*, are those given in the *Summa Theologiae*, Prima Pars, question 75 (articles 2 and 5 respectively) which are avowedly Aristotelian and which I shall title, respectively, *the argument from conceptual omniscience* and *the argument from concepts as universals*. Aquinas writes as follows (I use Kenny's translations):

The principle of the operation of the intellect, which we call the human soul, must be said to be an incorporeal and subsistent principle. For it is plain that by his intellect a human being can know the nature of all corporeal things. But to be able to know things, what knows must have nothing of their nature in its own. If it did, what it had in its nature would hinder it from knowing other things ... But everything that is a body has some determinate nature; and so it is impossible that the intellectual principle should be a body.[25]

This argument depends on the Thomistic thesis that cognition involves reception of the form of the thing known into the intellect where it is deployed as a concept informing an intellectual act. That is a development of

---

[24] *Summa Contra Gentiles* trans. James F. Anderson (Notre Dame, Ind.: University of Notre Dame Press, 1975), II.49.8, p. 148.
[25] *Aquinas on Mind* (London: Routledge, 1993), p. 132 (*Summa Theologiae* Ia, qu. 75, art. 2).

an analogous claim made by Aristotle and adopted by Aquinas that in the case of sense-cognition the sensible form of the object is received into the sense. As previously noted, however, in the case of the latter St Thomas holds that the process of reception and the realization of the form in the sense (which come to the same thing) is a material process. In grasping the warm cup the hand receives heat and in so doing takes on the sensible form of warmth. This process of change exemplifies the general Thomistic formula according to which that which is potentially F becomes actually F through that which is already in act with respect to F. Accordingly one cannot become what one already is actually, but only what one is potentially.

Kenny raises doubts about Aquinas's account of sensation and its suitability as a model for intellectual cognition, but the main problem with this argument as I see it is that it overlooks a distinction essential for the application of the theory of form reception to the case of conceptual intentionality. As a human being I have the form humanity. If I think about the nature of butterflies I am informed by 'papilionicity', the form of butterfly. But in this event my humanity is not displaced by papilionicity. I do not become a butterfly in the respect in which I am already a man. So in addition to the idea of form inherence and reception Aquinas needs a distinction between two ways in which a form can feature in or characterize a substance, an accident, or an act; and he has such: the distinction between possession *in esse naturale* and *in esse intentionale* (with natural and with intentional being respectively).[26] I am *naturally* informed by humanity in being a man and *intentionally* informed by papilionicity in thinking of a butterfly. But that distinction having been drawn it is no longer possible to say, without qualification, that if you are already F you cannot become F, or that being F prohibits becoming G. Since a man may think of a butterfly while naturally remaining a man, why may not the intellect receive the form of butterfly while naturally being made of, or being exhaustively realized by, movements of flesh and blood? If there is a reason why that cannot be so it is not demonstrated by the first proof of intellectual immateriality.

How then stands *the argument from concepts as universals*? Aquinas writes:

Each thing is known in so far as its form is in the knower. The intellectual soul's knowledge is pure knowledge of a thing's nature; knowledge, for instance, of stone simply *qua* stone. Thus the pure form of stone is in the intellectual soul in accordance with its own formal concept. The intellectual soul, therefore, is pure form, not something composed of matter and form. For if the intellectual soul were composed of

---

[26] There are subtleties here that I cannot now pursue involving distinctions within the category of intentional being.

matter and form, the forms of things would be received in it as individual. In that case it would not have knowledge of anything except singulars, as is the case with sensory powers, which receive the forms of things in a bodily organ. For matter is the principle of individuation.[27]

For Aquinas, natures are as such neither one nor many, but many in things and one in the mind.[28] To each member of a natural kind K belongs an individualized nature: the $k$ness-of-a, the $k$ness-of-b, and so on. These natures are numerically distinct, being individuated by the diverse quantities of matter they inform; but they are formally or specifically alike, and this formal identity provides the basis for a general nature produced by the mind in abstraction from particulars. In sense experience individualized forms corresponding to those in the objects of sense are instantiated under the material conditions appropriate to the particular sense organ. In intellectual cognition, by contrast, the principle of cognition is not an individualized form but the universal. When I look at Belle the butterfly, both Belle and my eyes feature individualized sensible forms of the colours of her wings. When I think that butterflies are insects, by contrast, the content of my mental act is not a particular butterfly, or the set of existing butterflies; rather it is papilionicity per se (or some subspecies thereof). Papilionicity per se, however, is an abstract entity, an immaterial universal. So if intellection involves a cognitive faculty receiving forms in this way, then that faculty and its acts are themselves immaterial. If purely conceptual thought involves universals and is thereby immaterial, then since acting follows upon being (*agere sequitur esse*) the faculty or power is itself immaterial.

Kenny's assessment of this argument is not as a general proof of the immateriality of thought but as a would-be refutation of the position of Bonaventure and others who held that the soul is hylemorphically composed of form and spiritual matter. In general, however, he accepts Aquinas's theory of intellectual cognition as having as its proper object universals, and as involving the identity of the contents of intellectual acts (universal concepts) with these objects. He does, though, raise the question of whether a universal idea might nevertheless be individuated in the mind not by being referred to an individual object falling under it, but by being the idea of a particular thinker: individuation not by content/object but by subject.[29] Whether this troubles the main point of the argument regarding the immateriality of mental acts depends on how subject-related individuation is effected; but the notion that besides

---

[27] *Aquinas on Mind*, p. 140 (*Summa Theologiae* Ia, qu. 75, art. 5).

[28] See *De ente et essentia* and *Sententia libri Metaphysicae* V.

[29] 'Sure, my idea is not the idea of an individual object; but it is an idea belonging to an individual subject: it is *my* idea and not your idea'. *Aquinas on Mind*, p. 140.

being distinguished by content, mental acts may be further distinguished by
agent as well as by time, does not of itself imply materiality.

Unlike the previous argument this one does not depend upon an analogy
with the causality of sensation but rests instead on the pure metaphysics of form
and nature. Yet it has been criticized for committing a fallacy of equivocation
reminiscent of that with which I charged the first proof: the accusation being
that it confuses two senses of receiving a form, in this case a universal formed
by abstraction. Joseph Novak argues as follows:

> The difficulty in Aquinas's argument does not lie [in the claim that] spiritual accidents
> must have spiritual substances in which they inhere ... one can readily grant [this].
> Rather the problem lies in attributing the property of being immaterial [intentionally]
> and immaterial [ontologically] in the same sense. A representation seems to possess
> the property of being immaterial [intentionally] while the intellect itself seems to
> possess the property of being immaterial [ontologically]. Moreover, one cannot argue
> from the immaterial quality of the form as representation to its immaterial quality as
> inhering accident, since the former possesses only intentional, while the latter possesses
> ontological, immateriality.[30]

Here Novak distinguishes between representational abstraction as when
one moves from an idea of some particular f to that of Fness per se,
and metaphysical or ontological abstraction whereby a material particular is
replaced by an abstract universal. In the case of the latter there is an existential
difference between a material and an immaterial entity, while in the case of the
former the difference concerns intentional content. Granting that the process of
intellectual abstraction may effect the latter, producing universal concepts from
representations of particulars, it does not follow that in crossing this intentional
divide one has also crossed the ontological one between the material and the
immaterial.

By way of reply, first consider the distinction between thoughts as mental
acts and as intentional *contents*, i.e. between episodic 'thinkings' and what these
'thinkings' are about. Different criteria of identity and individuation apply
to each, though they may be mixed as when we say that 'John thought of
immortality while looking at the night sky' which involves subject, content,
and temporal individuation. For the materialist, whatever thoughts (as mental
acts or states) are about they themselves are certainly physical entities. For

---

[30] Joseph Novak, 'Aquinas and the Incorruptibility of the Soul', *History of Philosophy Quarterly*
4 (1987), p. 413. Robert Pasnau follows Novak in making the same argument in 'Aquinas and
the Content Fallacy', *Modern Schoolman* 75 (1998), and again in *Thomas Aquinas on Human Nature*
(Cambridge: Cambridge University Press, 2002), pp. 315–16 where he writes 'It seems to me that
Aquinas has fallen victim to what I call the content fallacy: the fallacy of conflating facts about the
content of our thoughts with facts about what shape or form those thoughts take in our mind'.

Aquinas sensory acts and what they represent exist under material conditions, individuated by the quantities or regions of matter that they characterize. In intellectual abstraction, however, particulars (states of the sense-faculties) having particular contents provide a foundation for general conceptions. The criticism is that Aquinas fallaciously moves from content departicularization to ontological dematerialization, whereas there is nothing in the former that requires or supports the latter, and so far as abstractness of content is concerned this is compatible with it being carried by a material representation.

Acts of intellectual judgement may be accompanied by all sorts of conscious imagery or by none, but their intrinsic content is abstract. At one point Kenny writes, 'one of the differences between sensation and thought, as Aquinas himself is happy to point out in other places, is that there is not a medium of thought in the same way as there are media of vision or sound'.[31] Relatedly, while the conceptual contents of such acts may have empirical extensions they may also intend *abstracta* or *entia immaterialia*: as in a universally quantified mathematical formula, or in the judgement that every angel is a species unto itself. This allowed, the critic may reassert the distinction between acts and contents and insist that the absence of sensory accompaniments and the evident non-materiality of contents is compatible with the acts themselves being material.

In the case of sensory-experience Aquinas's account involves material causation and this may encourage the thought that presentational content per se is compatible with materiality. A consequent characterization of cognition in general might then take the form of distinguishing act and content and deploying this in the ways considered above. But there is another possibility compatible with the materiality of sensory cognition but which blocks the act/content distinction as formulated. Instead of distinguishing representations as vehicles of content from representational content as such, suppose we identify sensory acts with their sensuous contents, and intellectual acts with their conceptual contents, treating both as pure *Vorstellungen* or cognitive presentations. On that account the presentation of a material particular as the content of a sensory act is identical with a state of the sensory system of the subject, which state is itself a material particular. That is to say, the seeing of a patch of red just is an activation of the sensory system. Similarly the presentation of an abstract universal, being immaterial in content is thereby immaterial in substance. One may say it is an activation of the intellect but that is hardly likely to satisfy someone in search of an account of the phenomenology of intellectual acts. It is an implication of this position, however, that there is

[31] *Aquinas on Mind*, p. 133.

no such thing as the phenomenology of intellection. It may be the case that intellectual acts are accompanied by phenomenal features but these are not essential to them and do not provide their content. There is nothing 'it is like' to think that every triangle is a trilateral but utterances or other actions may be expressions of it.

This possibility explains the asymmetry between sense experience and intellectual cognition: in the former one is aware of a synthesis of received material form and sentient corporeality; in the latter there is nothing sensible of which to be aware. It also provides the basis for a re-examination of an argument that deserves close attention not only as key to an important theme in Aquinas's work but as a route into the issue of materialism and immaterialism which bypasses something of the blockage arising from the neo-Cartesian obsession with phenomenal consciousness.

7. Sympathy for the Soul

There is, however, more work to be done and I shall end simply by outlining some directions this might take. Earlier we saw Kenny speaking of the vehicle of a power being an 'abiding' and an 'underlying' actuality, but I speculated that once we set aside the empirical expectation of a supporting vehicle there may be a remaining philosophical motivation in seeking something actual besides the power itself, rooted in the general Aristotelian requirement that potentialities be keyed to actualities. The power of intellectual cognition is in fact keyed to two actualities: the intellectual agent, and the intellectual acts in which the power is exercised, and this dual tethering serves both to meet the actuality requirement and, together with the contents of acts, to provide interconnected individuation conditions: a given thought (a particular mental *act*) is the one it is in virtue of its being a thought of *A*, about *B* at *t*.

Two questions remain. First, and in distinction from the issue of whether a cognitive power needs an organic vehicle, do intellectual acts need to be connected to behavioural expressions and/or elements in phenomenal consciousness? It is no part of the argument for the immateriality of thought that they do not have such connections, nor that such connections might not be required for the mind to engage with the world of particulars. But are they essential per se? Here there is deep issue. In the case of perception and in imagination a sensuous or imagistic presentation is required both to provide the substance of the activity and to serve as an occasion for the exercise of concepts referred to the objects of such acts. This is not to say that any sensuous or quasi-sensuous occurrence is the object of perception or imagination, but it gives a medium through which that object is presented to the subject. What then of intellection? If this is immaterial, and if Aquinas and Kenny are right, as I believe they are, that the sensory is materially realized, then the sensuous cannot be even partly constitutive of intellection given that it deals with particulars while intellectual acts concern universals. But is there not a remaining need for something to provide an occasion and ground for the application of concepts in an intellectual judgement?[32]

This need is connected with the fact that mental acts must be performed. In the case of perception the occurrence of changes in the senses provides a sensuous presentation to the subject and relates the act to him as agent/owner. How can anything like this be effected in the absence of a medium of thought? And hence how can thoughts be assigned ownership? An answer I think may lie in the area of reflexivity. Second-order thoughts directed upon first-order ones have a place in the scheme of self-attribution but they cannot be its primary ground since logically such thoughts may also be directed upon the thoughts of others. The matter of 'ownership' will be secured, however, if some thoughts are self-reflexive; if their form is such as *(I am thinking) Fs are Gs*. The argument for this is not phenomenological but transcendental: unless it were so then the idea of first-person ownership would not be available, and practical reasoning-cum-intentional action would be impossible.[33]

If something of this sort is correct then the beginnings of an answer may be in view to another idea that causes Kenny queasiness: the notion that the agent of intellectual activity, the intellectual soul, being the cause of immaterial acts is itself immaterial and therefore may subsist actively in the absence of the body that it had previously animated. In ending on this note I am conscious that it is not at all what Tony Kenny had in mind when he wrote that 'If Wittgenstein was right, philosophy . . . should alter course in a way that would make it more sympathetic to medieval preoccupations', but I sense that even here his reluctance to follow Aquinas and the Thomists is more a matter of doubt than of outright rejection. At any rate that is my hope.

---

[32] For an interesting discussion related to these themes see D. W. Hamlyn, 'Thinking', in H. D. Lewis (ed.), *Contemporary British Philosophy* (London: Allen & Unwin, 1976).

[33] For further discussion of these difficult issues see John Haldane, '(I am) Thinking' *Ratio* 16 (2003).

7

'Whatever is Changing is Being Changed by Something Else': A Reappraisal of Premise One of the First Way

DAVID S. ODERBERG

1. Introduction

The publication in 1969 of Anthony Kenny's *The Five Ways*[1] was an important moment in contemporary philosophy of religion. In it, Kenny presented a detailed and systematic critique of the famous Five Ways of St Thomas Aquinas by which the existence of God could be proved using philosophical reasoning without any appeal to faith or revelation. The critical reception was somewhat mixed, provoking, unsurprisingly, a less sympathetic response from Peter Geach than from Antony Flew.[2] Speaking anecdotally, however, after many years of discussing philosophy of religion with both philosophers and theologians, and perusing some of the numerous standard undergraduate (and graduate) reading lists on proofs for the existence of God, I have formed the impression that Kenny's book has had a major and lasting influence on the consensus concerning the cogency of the Five Ways.

That consensus is assuredly negative. Aquinas's arguments are sometimes praised for their depth and ingenuity, but in general they are esteemed a failure, whether glorious or not. And Kenny's critique is one of the first works to

---

[1] A. Kenny, *The Five Ways: St. Thomas Aquinas' Proofs of God's Existence* (London: Routledge and Kegan Paul, 1969).

[2] P. T. Geach, review of *The Five Ways*, *Philosophical Quarterly* 20 (1970), pp. 311–12; Antony Flew, review of *The Five Ways*, *Philosophical Review* 80 (1971), pp. 411–15.

which any philosopher of religion would point his students or colleagues for a (probably the) *locus classicus* in which the debunking exercise is successfully carried out. Kenny accuses Aquinas of numerous logical fallacies, equivocations, irrelevancies, and—perhaps the most memorable accusation—of tying his arguments, especially the First and Second Ways, to an outdated and discredited Aristotelian/medieval cosmology.[3] There are those who treat the arguments more sympathetically, but they are in a decided minority and the conclusion, almost always, is that the arguments still fail.[4]

Moreover, it is clear that Kenny himself still stands by his decades-old critique of the Five Ways. Writing in 2004, he says:

By 1963 I had become too doubtful of several of the teachings of the Catholic Church to continue as a priest, and I returned to the life of a layman, becoming in 1964 a fellow of Balliol College and tutor in philosophy there. I continued to ponder the question whether it was possible to prove God's existence. The best place for an enquiry, I thought, would be the Five Ways of St Thomas Aquinas, the best-known and most revered of the proofs on offer. On careful examination I was unable to find that any of the arguments were successful; they depended more than met the eye on a background of outdated Aristotelian cosmology, and in places contained identifiable fallacies of argument. I published these negative results in a book *The Five Ways*.[5]

The First and Second Ways, I contend, have far more going for them than is commonly supposed. They are not tied to outdated cosmology, nor is Aquinas guilty of the fallacies Kenny levels at him. It is true that the arguments require the appreciation of certain metaphysical principles that are unfamiliar or seem archaic to the contemporary philosophical mind: it is for this reason that they have largely faded into obscurity, replaced in modern debate by,

---

[3] For the typical response to the first two Ways (both or one of the two), see for example: J. L. Mackie, *The Miracle of Theism: Arguments for and against the Existence of God* (Oxford: Clarendon Press, 1982), p. 87; G. H. Smith, *Atheism: The Case against God* (Buffalo, NY: Prometheus Books, 1979), p. 245; M. Martin, *Atheism: A Philosophical Justification* (Philadelphia: Temple University Press, 1990), pp. 98–9; R. Swinburne, *The Existence of God* (Oxford: Clarendon Press, 1991; rev. edn), p. 119.

[4] C. J. F. Martin, *Thomas Aquinas: God and Explanations* (Edinburgh: Edinburgh University Press, 1997) (the arguments succeed); W. L. Craig, *The Cosmological Argument from Plato to Leibniz* (Eugene, Ore.: Wipf and Stock, 1980), pp. 158–81 (mainly expository); N. Kretzmann, *The Metaphysics of Theism: Aquinas's Natural Theology in Summa Contra Gentiles I* (Oxford, Clarendon Press, 1997), ch. 2 (mainly analyses an argument from the *Summa Contra Gentiles* that closely parallels the First Way, though Kretzmann seeks to distinguish it from the latter; the argument ultimately fails); S. MacDonald, 'Aquinas's Parasitic Cosmological Argument', *Medieval Philosophy and Theology* 1 (1991), pp. 119–55 (the argument fails in its own right and (dubiously, in my view) needs supplementation by the Third Way); W. L. Rowe, *The Cosmological Argument* (Princeton: Princeton University Press, 1975), pp. 10–39 (the arguments ultimately fail since they rely on some or other version of the Principle of Sufficient Reason, none of which can be known to be true).

[5] A. Kenny, *The Unknown God* (London: Continuum, 2004), p. 2.

for instance, the Kalam Cosmological Argument.[6] In particular, the notion of causation employed by Aquinas in the arguments has a decidedly obscure ring to modern ears. Nevertheless, with some unpacking and an attempt at a sympathetic reading, we can see that the arguments are in fact strong ones, ripe for reinvestigation and reappraisal. In this paper I will focus solely on the First Way—moreover, only on its first premise, which is a key component of the Aristotelian/Thomistic metaphysic. I do not purport to establish in the following discussion that the premise is unassailable, only to defend it against the more common objections and to demonstrate its plausibility. In particular, as with the work of Aquinas in general it is important not to let the discussion of his ideas get mired in what can be interminable and often fruitless exegesis. If Aquinas is to have any currency for contemporary thought he needs as much as possible to be extracted from his historical context and evaluated, as all great philosophers should be, in terms of his timeless contributions to the search for truth. Hence, despite the inevitable excursuses into both interpretation and the secondary literature, I will consider premise 1 of the First Way in a mostly context-independent fashion, stipulating the interpretations I place on Aquinas's words. Having said that, I will also stay very close to Kenny's own evaluation, taking his objections one at a time.

2. The First Way

The First Way is sometimes known as the argument from change or motion.[7] The argument is presented in its most mature, albeit brief, form in the *Summa Theologiae*,[8] and in more detail in the *Summa Contra Gentiles*.[9] In truth, the final and arguably definitive statement is in the *Compendium Theologiae*,

---

[6] See Q. Smith and W. L. Craig, *Theism, Atheism, and Big Bang Cosmology* (Oxford: Clarendon Press, 1993), and the many writings of both Smith and Craig on this famous Islamic argument that also had the support of, among others, St Bonaventure (though rejected by Aquinas). For a summary, see my 'The Cosmological Argument', in C. Meister and P. Copan (eds), *The Routledge Companion to Philosophy of Religion* (London: Routledge, 2007), pp. 341–50.

[7] Where 'motion' (*motus*) means, for Aquinas, change in general, not just change of place (local motion).

[8] *Summa Theologiae* [1266–73] (hereafter '*ST*') Ia, qu. 2 art. 3. For a good translation, see *The 'Summa Theologica' of St. Thomas Aquinas, Literally Translated by the Fathers of the English Dominican Province*, vol. i (London: Burns Oates and Washbourne Ltd, 1920), pp. 24–5.

[9] *Summa Contra Gentiles* [1261–4] (hereafter '*ScG*') I.13. For a good translation, see A. C. Pegis (ed.), *On the Truth of the Catholic Faith (Summa Contra Gentiles)*, bk 1 (Garden City, NY: Image Books, 1955), pp. 85–90. For some of the exegetical issues surrounding the relation between the arguments of *ST* and those of *ScG*, see Kretzmann, *The Metaphysics of Theism*, ch. 2. I will occasionally draw on arguments from *ScG* in support of premise 1 of the First Way, but will not suppose that there are potential new 'ways' to be found outside *ST*.

composed a year or two before Aquinas's death. It is no more than a sketch, albeit very important, and differs little from the more detailed version in *ST*.[10] The argument itself is easily stated:

(1) Everything that is changing is being changed by something else;
(2) But the series of changers and things changing cannot be infinitely long; therefore
(3) There must be a first cause of all change, which we call God.[11]

Aquinas calls this the 'more manifest way'[12] of proving the existence of God. By this he means, as traditionally held, that the argument is itself the most obvious and clearly convincing of the Five Ways, and *not*, as sometimes held,[13] that the argument begins from the most evident empirical phenomena, namely cases of physical change. If he did not think this, it would be inexplicable why the First Way appears as the one and only proof of the existence of God in the *Compendium*. Moreover, the argument is supposed to be complete in itself, that is, to show the existence of an immovable first mover (changer) from which the other key properties of God, such as necessity and eternity, are inferred either directly or via supplementation by standard premises from natural theology. Again, this is evident from the *Compendium*.[14]

Hence the argument stands or falls on its own merits, and should not be taken as a jumping-off point for Aquinas's other arguments, a 'good enough' place to start if one wants to prove that God exists, an incomplete first attempt, or some such. Either the First Way is itself a proof of the existence of God or it is not. For Kenny, the argument fails on a number of fronts, leading him to add his voice to that of Suárez to the effect that the First Way is 'impotent' ('*inefficax*', according to Suárez) to prove the existence of a prime mover.[15] His objections are directed at both premises, as well as at the conclusion that the unmoved mover must be anything like the divine being of classical monotheism. Moreover, the objections focus both on apparent counterexamples to the premises and on the general reasoning, in particular

---

[10] *Compendium*, pt 1, ch. 3; C. Vollert (trans.), *Compendium of Theology by St. Thomas Aquinas* (St Louis, Mo.: B. Herder Book Co., 1947), p. 9. (References will be to this translation, given by page number, unless otherwise indicated.) In n. 67 I refer to one exception by which the version in the *Compendium* does differ somewhat from the other main versions.

[11] For some of the exegetical issues see Kenny's own discussion, as well as Craig, *The Cosmological Argument*, pp. 161–74 and MacDonald, 'Aquinas's Parasitic Cosmological Argument'. Rowe's discussion in *The Cosmological Argument*, pp. 10–39 also contains useful interpretive material.

[12] 'manifestior via'.   [13] For example, by MacDonald: 'Aquinas's Parasitic Argument', p. 155.

[14] *Compendium*: pt 1, chs 4–10, pp. 9–15. Again, this goes against the interpretation given by MacDonald in 'Aquinas's Parasitic Argument'; see esp. pp. 153–5.

[15] Kenny, *Five Ways*, p. 33.

concerning actuality and potentiality, to which Aquinas appeals in defence of his argument. I will now take his objections one by one.

3. Motion Per Se and Per Accidens

Kenny's first kind of alleged counterexample exploits the Aristotelian distinction between motion (or change) per se and motion (or change) per accidens.[16] If a is moving because it is located in b, then a is moving per accidens, for instance a sleeping man in a moving ship. The man moves per se when he stands up and walks. The per se movement of a red billiard ball struck by a cue involves the per accidens movement of the redness located in it (the sense of 'location' being analogous but not identical). If a is a part of b and b changes because a changes, then b changes per accidens. So if a person is struck on the hand then the *person* is struck. (Again, there is an analogous sense of 'location' involved here, so the three cases are arguably species of a common genus.)

Now Kenny takes the example of himself sitting at his keyboard.[17] He moves his fingers (per se), yet it seems his fingers move him (per accidens). The dilemma is as follows. If his fingers move him and he moves his fingers, the motion is circular: it 'cannot be an asymmetrical relation', which it needs to be for the infinite regress argument to work (via premise 2). Hence premise 1 is 'useless' for the First Way. Or else Kenny moves his fingers but his fingers do not move him; i.e., he is in motion *because* of the motion of his fingers, but is not moved *by* the motion of his fingers. In which case premise 1 has a counterexample. Either way, premise 1 is flawed.

Kenny, however, goes on to acknowledge that Aquinas believes animals (including human beings) are moved by their souls. (Note that the movement is not the pure efficient causation of one physical object moving another. The soul is the *form* of the body, and as such exercises a special kind of formal causation by which, as a part of the animal's essence, it *directs* the efficient causation of the animal's bodily constituents—neural parts, muscles, limbs, and so on.[18]) Hence, as he accepts, on this view his fingers are moved by his soul yet

[16] Kenny, *Five Ways*, pp. 13–14. See Aristotle, *Physics* 254b7, in W. D. Ross (ed.), *The Works of Aristotle Translated into English*, vol. ii (Oxford: Clarendon Press, 1930); Aquinas, *Commentary on Aristotle's Physics* VIII.1022, trans. R. J. Blackwell, R. J. Spath, and W. E. Thirlkel (London: Routledge and Kegan Paul, 1963), pp. 504–5. (Kenny, *Five Ways*, p. 13 has '102 ff.' for Aquinas, which is presumably a misprint.)

[17] Kenny, *Five Ways*, p. 14.

[18] The very idea of soul as cause will, of course, have an odd ring to contemporary ears. To say that the causation is *formal* rather than *efficient* might seem merely to enshrine the idea in equally odd

his soul is not moved by his fingers, and so the movement relationship is after all asymmetrical. The problem now, he concludes, is that '[t]he Aristotelian soul of any animal or plant will be an unmoved mover in the required sense'.[19] I will return to this last point soon. For the moment, this small retreat by Kenny needs to be enlarged somewhat. On the hylemorphic view of animals advocated by both Aquinas and Aristotle,[20] the soul of a living thing is what causes it to behave in the way that is natural for it. The soul directs the motion of organic parts, fingers included. It is consistent with the claim that souls move fingers, that human beings are moved by their fingers, where that motion is per accidens. So on hylemorphism, Kenny's fingers are moved (per se) by his soul. He, Kenny, not being identical with his soul, is moved (per accidens) by his fingers (since the fingers are part of the human). Whether, as Kenny questions, he is moved *by* his fingers or *because* of his fingers is superfluous to the argument. The movement relation is still asymmetrical, as Aquinas requires. On the other hand, if we reject the very idea that Kenny is moved either by or because of his fingers, i.e. that in no sense do his fingers move him,

---

terminology rather than to render it plausible. I do not in this paper argue for the existence of the soul (which I do in 'Hylemorphic Dualism', in E. F. Paul, F. D. Miller, and J. Paul (eds), *Personal Identity* (Cambridge: Cambridge University Press, 2005)). My point here is that if one assumes its existence along Aristotelian/Thomistic lines, one must ascribe causal powers to it as a real constituent of living substances. Yet it is not a constituent on an ontological par with body parts; rather, it is a fundamental constituent, along with matter, of the whole substance. In biological organisms its causal powers derive from the fact that, in union with matter, it is able to direct the organism's development and behaviour. The situation is to that extent no different from that obtaining with non-living substances, which—for the essentialist—have essences with causal powers. The causal powers of an object with mass, for instance, derive from what it is to *be* an object with mass, i.e. from the essence of such an object. To say that the object's *essence* has causal powers is simply to refer the object's causal powers back to the essence of the object. In hylemorphic terms, the *form* of the object provides (in union with matter) the causal powers that enable the object to behave in the way it characteristically does. This is what it means to say that the soul, through formal causation, directs the behaviour of the organism. One might, of course, want to reject this way of understanding things altogether, but to do so is *eo ipso* to reject hylemorphism. (I defend hylemorphism in my *Real Essentialism* (London: Routledge, 2007).)

[19] Kenny, *Five Ways*, p. 15.

[20] There is room for some debate as to whether Aristotle shared Aquinas's view that it is specifically the soul that moves the animal. Kenny says no, citing *Physics* 254b25ff. where Aristotle seems to hold that everything in motion is moved by something, not necessarily something *else*. Yet just after this, at 254b30, Aristotle is clear that in animals what suffers motion and what causes motion are distinct, from which it is evident that he, like Aquinas, thinks that whatever is in motion is caused to be in motion by something else, even in animals. Whether this something else was, for Aristotle, the soul or another part of the animal can be put to one side, but in any case he is clear that it is only 'in this sense' (*houtō*, 254b31) that the animal as a whole causes itself to move. Moreover, it is very clear in Aristotle's *On the Motion of Animals*, especially pt 10, that the soul moves the body: 'We have explained by what means the soul moves [*kinei*] the body [these two words implied by the context] when a part [of the body] is moved . . . [the soul] is in a kind of governing place/is a kind of governing principle of the body [*en tini archei*]'.

then there is *no* counterexample to premise 1. The dialectical position is not that since Kenny is changing and the only candidate changer is his fingers, yet the latter idea is unacceptable, his changing therefore has no changer—contra premise 1. Rather, the 'oddness' (to use Kenny's word) of positing such a causal relationship, if the oddness be accepted, is transmitted to the very *assumption* that when Kenny types he is in motion *in any other sense* than that he (or his soul, for that matter) moves his fingers. It is not as though he is in motion in some sense other than this but that his motion is not caused by anything, the only candidate being the unacceptably odd one of his fingers. We can now see more clearly why Kenny's dilemma fails on hylemorphism. Kenny is right, however, to raise the problem. For the hylemorphist cannot simply retreat to the position that formal causation by the soul is a 'special' kind of causation in order to avoid legitimate questions concerning the asymmetry or otherwise of the causal relationship between soul and body. Formal causation is strictly a kind of *causation*, and as such the issue of whether there is an unacceptable circularity in the causal relationship between soul and body is as relevant as for efficient causation between bodily parts. Still, for the hylemorphist there is no circularity.

On a purely materialist view, the dilemma disappears altogether. For in no way would Kenny's fingers cause him to move. His neural firings would be caused by external and internal material stimuli, and these would in turn cause the movement of his fingers. The causal chain would begin outside Kenny, and within him would involve neural activity causing muscle movement, terminating outside him in the motion of the keys on the keyboard. Again, there would be no circularity in the relevant causal processes and no lingering counterexample to premise 1. Kenny does not consider a materialist interpretation, focusing only on the hylemorphic view. We do well, however, to see to what extent Aquinas's argument carries weight independently of certain metaphysical presuppositions, in particular hylemorphism, that most philosophers currently reject. Moreover, if Aquinas is to be defended against endless ad hominem objections, it is worthwhile seeing whether his argument is detachable from other parts of his overall metaphysical outlook. We should not expect complete detachability, but the argument arguably fares even better when examined on assumptions more favourable to materialism than to hylemorphism, just as Aquinas, though he believed in the finitude of the past, was explicit that the First and Second Ways did not depend on this assumption.

4. The Soul as 'Mundane Primary Mover'

A mundane primary mover[21] is a natural unmoved mover, i.e., something that moves other things in the sense Aquinas intends—simultaneously, via one or more instrumental causes—but is not itself immovable or in any way a candidate for a divine being. In various places Kenny, among other critics, objects that premise 1 leads, at most, to mundane primary movers, not to God.[22] Kenny's opening shot is his charge that the idea of an unmoved mover 'will not lead us beyond a stationary billiard ball'.[23] The argument, in other words, does not take us to the *immovable* mover required for a proof of the existence of God.

I will come back to inorganic entities later, when discussing inertia, impetus, gravity, and related matters. For now I want to concentrate on the idea that premise 1, in the organic case, does not lead beyond mundane primary movers such as humans and other animals. The particular question of whether the argument as a whole takes us to an *immovable* first mover must await a separate treatment. According to Kenny, if we accept that animals are moved by their souls, then '[t]he Aristotelian soul of any animal . . . will be an unmoved mover in the required sense',[24] the required sense being that of the terminus of a chain of simultaneously acting causes. Kenny does not elaborate the objection, but the idea is that since on premise 1 whatever is changing is being changed by another, animal changes require distinct changers: digits and limbs are moved by muscles, which are moved by the nervous system, which is moved by the brain (simply put). On the hylemorphic view, it is the *soul* of the animal that will be the ulti-mate source of all these changes—even changes to the brain—as the animal's directive, essential principle imbued with causal powers. In a human the soul is immaterial; in a non-human animal it is material, that is, wholly dependent for its operation on the animal's material constitution.[25] In either case, there seems no reason to go beyond the soul as the primary mover of the animal.

Yet the soul itself undergoes changes. Animals undergo changes of desire and belief,[26] changes in their perceptions, changes of feeling, as do human

---

[21] The term comes from MacDonald, 'Aquinas's Parasitic Cosmological Argument'.

[22] MacDonald discusses mundane primary movers, ibid., pp. 146 ff.   [23] Kenny, *Five Ways*, p. 13.

[24] Ibid., p. 15. The ellipsis in the quotation replaces 'or plant'. I omit consideration of plants, since if the charge in respect of animals can be refuted, a fortiori it can be refuted for plants.

[25] For more on the materiality of animal souls and immateriality of human souls, see ch. 10 of my *Real Essentialism* and also 'Hylemorphic Dualism'.

[26] Whether animals have beliefs at all is debatable, but I will not canvass this issue.

beings. People change their minds, adopt new goals, acquire new thoughts. For a hylemorphist, these changes are not merely changes in a body but alterations to a soul. And the materialist, whilst eschewing talk of souls, readily accepts that humans and other animals undergo changes of mind/brain, and will seek to translate all talk of changes to a soul into talk of changes to minds/brains as well as bodies. More importantly, and of crucial relevance to the argument, an animal's soul undergoes changes *in the exercise* of its—the soul's—powers. When a dog starts towards the food bowl, its soul is not merely causing the dog to move, but is itself changing in the exercise of this causal activity: the dog gets hungrier, more excited, anticipates the delicious meal ahead, and so on. Again, soul-talk aside, the materialist will not demur. As the dog's brain causes the impulses that lead to canine locomotion, so that brain buzzes with activity. So much is commonplace, and for the purposes at hand human behaviour is no different. As Kenny moves his fingers on the keyboard, he thinks about what he has just written and what he is going to write next; perhaps he considers making a cup of tea or remembers something he needed to get from the shop. And so on. It is *in the exercise* of causal powers leading to bodily movement that the soul, and for the materialist the mind/brain, undergoes its own changes. And premise 1 says that whatever changes requires a changer. So the soul too needs a changer.

Yet what changes the soul? For Aquinas, there are many causes—for example bodily changes, objects of knowledge, and objects of perception. When it comes to human action, the main cause of change to the soul is the 'appetible object' (the object that is sought or desired).[27] There are two aspects to an appetible object—the mind-independent universal or particular to which the agent tends in its behaviour, and that universal or particular as conceived or thought about in the mind of the agent. So when Fred buys a pizza for dinner, the universal *pizza* is one aspect of the appetible object of his action: he is motivated by pizza, and pizzas are mind-independent. But he also has the concept *pizza* in his mind, and is motivated by this. The concept is a universal in the mind.[28] This does not imply overdetermination: the concept *pizza* in Fred's mind just is the universal *pizza*, but that universal enters the mind of anyone who grasps it and so acquires the concept of it. He is not motivated by two things—a concept and a universal. He is motivated by one thing doing double duty as an objective feature of the world and also as a literal part of Fred's mental inventory.

[27] 'appetitum alicuius appetibilis': *ScG* 1.13.28; Pegis trans., bk 1, p. 94.
[28] On concepts and universals, see my 'Concepts, Dualism, and the Human Intellect', in A. Antonietti, A. Corradini, and E. J. Lowe (eds), *Psycho-Physical Dualism Today: An Interdisciplinary Approach* (Lanham, Md: Lexington Books/Rowman and Littlefield, 2008).

The crucial point is that agents are motivated by things. In hylemorphic terms, Fred's soul, like Fido's soul, initiates certain kinds of behaviour in response to effects that things have upon it. For a materialist, external objects have effects upon the nervous systems of agents, and those nervous systems stimulate action. Yet it is evident that the external objects that move either souls or nervous systems are themselves changing. Pizzas are changing: what was the most common pizza to be found on menus ten years ago is not so now, for example. Individual pizzas change as well: the one Fred is looking at in the restaurant window is getting cooler and more stale as he looks. We can frame the whole issue in terms of particulars only, saying—as materialists of a nominalist persuasion would want to—that the particular things that motivate action are themselves subject to change. But since, on the Thomistic view, we must include universals as appetible objects, we must also say that the universals that motivate action also change. And universals change in virtue of the way they are instantiated. For example, if the proportion of pepperoni pizzas produced increases from 10 per cent to 90 per cent, the universal *pizza* changes by having a different kind of preponderant instance. In other words, the *way* the universal *pizza* is manifested in the world changes, and this is a change to the universal itself, which acquires a new accidental characteristic—being such that 90 per cent of its instances are now pepperoni.

It might be objected that even if the above is true, the chain of changers and changed things can only take us to the happiness of the agent as final appetible object, and not beyond this.[29] Whether the chain leads to God is not something I consider here. But the chain must reach beyond happiness since happiness, like other universals such as *pizza*, is also subject to change in terms of the way in which it is or might be instantiated. The essence of happiness might not change, but the way in which Fred chooses to instantiate it in his life will be not only changeable but actually changing over the course of his life. More generally, the earthly conditions in which happiness can be instantiated by human agents are continually changing. A rising or falling standard of living, for instance, will cause changes in the ways in which people can achieve happiness, say by limiting or enlarging their options. This will entail changes to the universal itself—changes to the accidental features by which happiness, qua universal, is instantiated or instantiable.

What I claim to have established, therefore, is that souls will not be mundane primary movers and so Kenny's objection fails. Souls will not be primary movers at all. That humans have free will does not salvage the objection. It is not, as far as I can tell, and in any case should not be implicit in premise 1 that

[29] MacDonald, 'Aquinas's Parasitic Cosmological Argument', p. 151.

whatever is changing is being *deterministically* changed by another. The soul of a free agent is changed by external objects, but it need not be deterministically changed by them. Objects and events that *influence* free will, and so contribute to its changing, do not ipso facto *destroy* free will. There is no need to fill the gap by saying that the soul also, to some extent, changes itself; all we need to say is that the soul has some kind of ill-understood spontaneity whereby, when it does change in response to objects, it does so non-deterministically. Perhaps there is not much further we can go in analysing what freedom amounts to, but for present purposes we need not try.[30]

5. Inertia

One of Kenny's key objections to premise 1 is that it rests on physical theory that has been superseded by Newton and/or Einstein. The case in point is local motion, which, to recall, is just one of the kinds of change subsumed under the premise. For Aristotle, the local motion of a body (I will for now use the term 'motion' to mean only local motion) is caused by the medium of the air surrounding the body. Aquinas concurs. On the impetus theory of Jean Buridan, there is a 'motive force' (*vis motiva, impetus*) impressed into the moving body by whatever initially moved it.[31] On either theory, the moving body has a mover. Kenny objects that for Aristotle, the air would be an unmoved mover, and Aristotle does seem to speak that way.[32] Given that the sense of motion in this context is *local*, we can accept with Aristotle that the air in no wise moves locally once, say, the thrower of a projectile, having released the object, ceases to disturb the air. But we can still hold that the air moves *qualitatively*, i.e., that it changes as it exercises its power of locally moving the projectile, and this change would require a changer. Again, on the impetus theory, we could hold that the motive power was impressed upon the parts of the moving body, and given that the parts are not identical to the whole, the local motion of the body would have, as premise 1 requires, a mover distinct from itself.

So much is mere speculation. Nor is it nearly as important as the issue of whether classical mechanics, via the law of inertia, has removed altogether

---

[30] I leave aside complex questions concerning Aquinas's own view of the role that God plays in influencing a free agent's choices. The issue has a vexed interpretive history.

[31] For Aristotle, see *Physics* 266b30; for Buridan, see extracts from his *Questions on the Eighth Book of the Physics*, in E. Grant, *A Sourcebook in Medieval Science* (Cambridge, Mass.: Harvard University Press, 1974), p. 275.

[32] *Physics* 267a5–7.

the need for a mover of that which moves locally. A quick and strategically effective approach by some philosophers such as Scott MacDonald has been simply to exclude inertial frames of reference, i.e. frames in which there is uniform velocity, from premise 1. The idea is that premise 1, as far as local motion is concerned, only applies to changes in rest or velocity, i.e. to non-inertial/accelerated motion.[33] A principled reason for making this exclusion would be that uniform local motion might be considered a merely relational or extrinsic property of things, whereas premise 1 should be restricted to intrinsic change only.[34] A basic metaphysical reason underlying this idea is that change involves a transition from potentiality to actuality, and such a transition must be intrinsic. If the uniform motion of a body is relational, then the transition will not be intrinsic to the moving body. If *all* uniform motion is relational, then there will be no such intrinsic transition, and we can leave uniform motion to one side as not involving genuine intrinsic alteration in anything. If uniform motion does, on the other hand, require some intrinsic alteration in something or other (absolute space, let us suppose), then we can instead look to the change in that thing as a phenomenon requiring a cause, and premise 1 will apply again. I will consider actuality and potentiality later, but for now we can consider an analogy with time. If uniform relative motion is metaphysically on a par with (hypothetically) the passage of an object through time without that object's undergoing any intrinsic change, we might be even more comfortable with excluding uniform motion from premise 1. We might, nevertheless, treat the temporal passage of an object without intrinsic change as relational to the intrinsic ageing of some other object. We could then apply premise 1 to the intrinsic change in the latter object. Or we might treat such a passage as relative to an intrinsic change in absolute time, in which case we would apply premise 1 to the change in absolute time. I do not suggest this analogy is mandatory, only that it is a plausible one that might be given in support of an exclusion of uniform motion from premise 1. Kenny quips[35] that such an exclusion in favour of applying premise 1 to *non*-inertial motion only, would give us an argument in favour of an 'unaccelerated accelerator' rather than an unmoved mover. The quip is no more than that, of course: remembering that local motion is but a species of change, the restriction of premise 1 to acceleration means merely that whatever changes from a state of rest or uniform motion requires something distinct to change it, just as the

[33] Kenny, *Five Ways*, p. 29; MacDonald, 'Aquinas's Parasitic Cosmological Argument', pp. 136–7; R. Garrigou-Lagrange, *God: His Existence and Nature*, vol. i, trans. B. Rose, OSB (St Louis, Mo.: B. Herder, 1949), pp. 272, 276 (citing Bulliot and Janet).
[34] MacDonald, 'Aquinas's Parasitic Cosmological Argument', pp. 136–7.
[35] Kenny, *Five Ways*, p. 29.

application of a coat of green paint to a red wall does not require us to postulate an unpainted painter.

Another approach, called by Kenny a 'counter-attack', is to insist on the requirement that uniform motion requires a cause. This is most famously embodied in Mach's Principle (so named by Einstein), which in its simplest form states that 'mass there influences inertia here'. More formally, it says that inertia is causally determined by the large-scale structure and distribution of matter in the universe.[36] The idea, reminiscent of the 'archaic cosmology' of Aristotle, is that even the distant stars have an effect on relatively small-scale local motions, both inertial and non-inertial. Einstein himself was at one time sympathetic to the principle, writing to Mach that '*inertia* has its origins in a kind of *interaction* of bodies', though he later rejected it.[37] Moreover, the Lense-Thirring Effect, derived from General Relativity, predicts that the rotation of an object would alter space-time, dragging a nearby object out of position compared to the predictions of Newtonian physics. This, if experimentally verified, would give support to Mach's Principle from within General Relativity, and whilst the existence of such verification is controversial, some physicists claim accurate measurement of the effect has been made using satellites.[38] The status of Mach's Principle is still a matter of debate (both its truth and its compatibility with General Relativity), and Kenny himself is not prepared to rule it out on experimental grounds as a plausible response to the criticism of premise 1 based on inertia. He does have a brief philosophical criticism, however, which is that the relation of change/motion required by the First Way is asymmetrical, whereas the gravitational attraction of bodies is symmetrical. Hence if Mach's Principle is invoked, 'the principle that whatever is in motion is moved by something else can be verified in a universe in which there are no unmoved movers, but only two bodies, each in motion and each moving the other'.[39]

The problem with this criticism, however, is whether the scenario sketched by Kenny is in fact compatible with both premises 1 and 2 of the First

---

[36] For readings on Mach's Principle, see J. Barbour and H. Pfister (eds), *Mach's Principle: From Newton's Bucket to Quantum Gravity* (vol. 6 of *Einstein Studies*) (Boston/Basel/Berlin: Birkhäuser, 1995).

[37] Einstein, letter to Ernst Mach, Zurich, 25 June 1913, cited in J. D. Norton, 'Mach's Principle before Einstein', in Barbour and Pfister (eds), *Mach's Principle*, pp. 9–57, at 24.

[38] I. Ciufolini, E. Pavlis, F. Chieppa, E. Fernandes-Vieira, and J. Pérez-Mercader, 'Test of General Relativity and Measurement of the Lense-Thirring Effect with Two Earth Satellites', *Science* 279 (1998), pp. 2100–3. For a prominent contemporary defence of Mach's Principle, see the work of the physicist Julian Barbour, at http://www.platonia.com/index.html [accessed 5 Sept. 2008]. For an opponent, see J. H. Higbie, 'Mach's Principle in General Relativity', *General Relativity and Gravitation* 3 (1972), pp. 101–9.

[39] Kenny, *Five Ways*, pp. 30–1.

Way. There is a dilemma. On the one hand, as Kenny himself acknowledges, premise 1 is that whatever is moving is being moved by something *distinct*. On the scenario he sketches, if the kind of causation invoked is transitive, it is *in principle impossible* to say whether either body is really being moved by something distinct. For at any stage in this simple causal loop, one will have to say either that body *a* is moved by body *b* or that *a* is moved by itself (since by transitivity if *a* is moved by *b* and *b* is moved by *a*, then *a* is moved by itself), and the converse. But it will not be possible to take any stage in the loop as privileged, so it will not be possible to say whether either body is being moved by something distinct from itself, whereas premise 1 *requires* a moving body to be moved by something distinct from itself. Premise 1, contrary to Kenny's assertion, will not be verified. On the other hand, if the causation involved is not transitive, then although at each stage in the loop either body will indeed be moved by something distinct from itself, thus verifying premise 1, the very *infinity* of the loop will still be incompatible with premise 2, and if the grounds for premise 2, which require separate treatment on another occasion, are good then Kenny's scenario is a non-starter. On either horn of the dilemma, the scenario will not succeed in undermining the First Way, assuming we have greater metaphysical grounds for believing both premises than for entertaining the possibility of the scenario. It is useless to appeal to physics, whether Newton, Mach, or Einstein, to defend the possibility of the causal loop sketched by Kenny if the *metaphysical* grounds for ruling it out are solid. Moreover, there is no way of verifying such a scenario empirically just as there is no way of verifying the law of inertia empirically: both are mere idealizations, the latter also a mere assumption.[40] Therefore, Kenny's two-body scenario is at the least not *obviously* possible, as he seems to think, and so not an obvious problem for the First Way.

6. Generators and Obstacle Removers

Kenny points out that Aristotle and Aquinas recognize two particular categories of moving agents among others: generators and obstacle removers.[41] They cite heavy and light things, which move naturally in virtue of whatever it was

---

[40] According to Henri Poincaré, the law of inertia is neither an a priori truth nor verifiable experimentally: see *Science and Hypothesis* (London: Walter Scott Publishing, 1905), pp. 91–3. Of course it may be a good assumption given the derivability of classical mechanics in part from it, but my point is simply that there is no way of verifying it empirically.

[41] Kenny, *Five Ways*, p. 17. See *Physics* 255b25–256a5; Aquinas, *Commentary* VIII.1035–6 (trans., pp. 511–12).

that generated their natures, that is, made them heavy or light. Such objects may also move in virtue of the removal of an obstacle. Kenny believes there are counterexamples to premise 1 among such movers: 'if someone pulls out a bathplug the water may continue to flow downwards long after he has gone away, and if we ask for the generating cause of the heaviness of a falling boulder we may not find one later than the cooling of the earth's crust'.[42]

Neither counterexample works. The person who removes the bathplug causes the water to *begin* to flow by removing an obstacle;[43] the *continued* motion, however, is caused by gravity. In the case of the falling boulder, heaviness is not a change but a quality, and so we are not interested in that. Rather, we are interested in the boulder's motion: what caused it to begin to move will be, say, a volcanic eruption or some other event. Its continued movement will be caused by gravity. Kenny goes on shortly afterward[44] to refer to the *tendency* of the boulder to fall, but then introduces irrelevant, occasionalist-tainted references by some supposed followers of Aquinas to the 'immediate action of the Creator' in actualizing such a tendency. This is no part of Aquinas's or of Aristotle's thinking. Instead, we must say that the falling of the boulder is caused by gravity. But does gravity itself need an explanation? In what sense is it changing?

Here we run up against our ignorance of the way the universe works. It is possible that gravitational attraction is produced by rotation—of a planet, stars, the sun, the galaxy, and for all we know the entire universe. (If the universe itself rotates, this looks like a violation of Mach's Principle, but discussion of this is highly speculative and can be left aside.[45]) Or perhaps gravity is produced by the action of real particles, the hypothetical gravitons. Perhaps motion of parts within an object contributes to gravitational effects. Or maybe all of gravity is explicable, via General Relativity, by changes in the structure of space-time. We do not know. But what seems clear enough is that the explanation of gravitational behaviour will have to invoke some kind or kinds of change in material objects. According to premise 1, these changes will themselves require a cause.

[42] Kenny, *Five Ways*, p. 17.
[43] We might even doubt whether obstacle removers are within the purview of genuine *causes of change* in the sense required for the argument (and the sense conceived by Aquinas). I am assuming they are for present purposes, given that Kenny makes use of them; but if they are not, so much the worse for Kenny's objection. Gravity, then, would be the cause of the water's motion from beginning to end, with the removal of the plug being something like the removal of a *condition* that prevents gravity from producing the water's motion. (I am indebted to Brian Davies for this point.)
[44] Ibid., p. 18.   [45] P. Birch, 'Is the Universe Rotating?', *Nature* 298 (1982), pp. 451–4.

7. Laws of Nature

This raises the general question of the laws of nature, of which the universal law of gravitation is an example (at least, as currently held, when supplemented in a more precise way by the equations of General Relativity). On a Humean view of laws, they are mere regularities derivable from the behaviour of objects. No explanation follows concerning the causes of the behaviour. Premise 1 requires that anything undergoing a process of change requires a cause of that change. The Humean cannot appeal to the laws themselves as an explanation, since these just are behavioural regularities, in other words regular changes in things. So although a Humean will not be able to explain regular behaviour by appealing to laws that in some sense cause behaviour, he will not escape the need to explain changes, at however basic a level, in terms of causes of change.[46]

An immanentist view of laws sees them as expressing the essential tendencies of objects to behave in certain ways. Objects obey laws because they obey their own natures.[47] The laws of nature, put simply, are the laws of *natures*. Objects have the tendencies they have because of their natures, whether it is the tendency of an object to attract another, to resist certain forces, to collapse under certain forces, or of a living thing to act in whatever way it needs to thrive or flourish. In general, things have what might be called *standing tendencies* to certain kinds of behaviour. A magnet has the standing tendency to pull iron particles towards it even if it is not doing so. A cat has the standing tendency to stalk smaller animals even if it is not doing so. Aristotle and Aquinas called such tendencies 'second potentialities'/'first actualities'.[48]

As noted above, objects change in the exercise of their causal powers. This does not mean that an object loses the nature or essence it possesses when, via that essence, it exercises its powers. Rather, the object itself undergoes changes, and the nature of the object changes in the same sense that a universal changes when its instances change, as discussed above. Rover does not cease to be a dog when he barks, but he acquires an accidental quality, that of barking,

---

[46] The Humean, of course, will himself deny the need to postulate a cause of every change, as he does not see the need to postulate a cause for every beginning of existence. My point, however, is simply that the Humean view of laws postulates the existence of changes no less than the immanentist view, and so posits a phenomenon that, according to premise 1, requires a cause.

[47] See my *Real Essentialism*, ch. 6; also B. Ellis, *Scientific Essentialism* (Cambridge: Cambridge University Press, 2001).

[48] See, for example: *ST* IaIIae, qu. 49, art. 3, ad 1 (Burns Oates edn, vol. vii (1927), p. 9); *De Anima*, bk 2: 412a6–11, in W. D. Ross (ed.) *The Works of Aristotle*, vol. iii (1931); Aquinas, *Commentary on Aristotle's De Anima*, trans. K. Foster and S. Humphries (Notre Dame, Ind.: Dumb Ox Books, 1994; orig. pub. 1951), sect. 216, p. 73.

which is a manifestation of his canine nature. The canine nature changes only inasmuch as its powers are exercised in a certain way: it is now the nature of a presently barking dog. The change to Rover requires a cause, such as the smell of food or the appearance of a cat in his field of vision. Laws of nature tie some accidents more than others to the natures of things; for laws of nature involve a special kind of accidents, what are traditionally called *properties* or *propria*, and sometimes in contemporary parlance *necessary* accidents.[49] Rover's being a mammal, for instance, is tied very closely[50] to mammalian properties such as having hair[51] and being a member of a kind whose females lactate. Biological laws concerning mammals invoke precisely the mammalian properties, and the same applies to all objects, living and non-living.[52] Hence the exercise of powers that come under the category of property in this strict Aristotelian sense necessarily involve changes to the nature of the object exercising the power. Again, the object does not cease to be what it is; rather, its exercise of natural powers, i.e. powers deriving from its nature, entails changes to the nature: the nature *expresses* itself in a certain way, and so becomes the nature of an object that is itself changing. This is why we should expect that the exercise of gravitational power by a material object should involve changes to the object: its nature, in this case to have mass, expresses itself in gravitational attraction. And this should involve changes to the object itself via the expression of its nature; and so we should expect gravitation to be caused by, say, interactions among the object's particles, or rotation, or some other change in the behaviour of the object *qua* possessor of mass. This is not to deny that there are such conditions as *states*. Solidity, fragility, being red, being at rest, and so on, are genuine states. My point is only that to be a genuine state is to be static at a certain level—relative to a certain observer or certain other objects, within a given margin of experimental accuracy, and the like. A solid object is indeed in a state of solidity, but we know that the maintenance of that solidity requires much molecular activity within the object's crystal structure, among other things. The same for fragility. Also, we know that being in the state of having a certain colour requires activities of reflection and absorption, or else (in the dark) activities that *dispose* the object to reflection and absorption when exposed to light. And so on.

[49] For more on *propria*, i.e. properties in the strict, traditional sense, see my *Real Essentialism*, ch. 7; also K. Fine, 'Sense of Essence', in W. Sinnott-Armstrong (ed.), *Modality, Morality, and Belief: Essays in Honor of Ruth Barcan Marcus* (Cambridge: Cambridge University Press, 1995); M. Gorman, 'The Essential and the Accidental', *Ratio* 18 (2005), pp. 276–89.

[50] In a way we do not fully understand and on which work needs to be done.

[51] Albeit minimal in the case of *Cetacea* (whales, dolphins, porpoises).

[52] The further question of whether every member of essential kind *K* must have all of the *K*-properties cannot be explored here. For further discussion see *Real Essentialism*, ch. 7.

The point of this small digression is to draw out the idea that premise 1 of the First Way cannot be impugned by appealing to laws of nature as 'mundane primary movers' with which the metaphysical buck stops, as it were. Nor can it be undermined by appealing to an infinite regress of laws. On the second point, Kenny says that there may be 'no theoretical end to the process' of asking why certain laws hold.[53] In other words, there may be no basic laws, where in this context a basic law is one that has no further explanation within the material universe. Let us call such laws *relatively* basic. I submit that it is a mistake to think there might be no such laws. If there were no end to the process of explanation within the material universe, this would imply an infinite level of complexity in objects. This point is not tied to the issue of reductionism. Of course, for a reductionist the infinite complexity would be microstructural; but one could equally well be a non-reductionist and hold to some other kind of infinite complexity, say in powers of behaviour, or perhaps in numbers of dimensions, whether spatio-temporal or otherwise, according to which behaviour can be measured. But why should we expect any such infinity of complexity? All objects (God or the Prime Mover aside) are finite, delimited entities with specific natures. Matter, as both Aristotle and Aquinas thought, might be infinitely divisible in potentiality—but this would not entail infinite complexity in kinds of behaviour. It might entail an infinite number of possible kinds of manifestation of a given power, but that is a different phenomenon. The kinds of power possessed by a thing would still be finite, given its finite nature.

If we accept that there are relatively basic laws, on the other hand, this does not require that we be reductionists either. A reductionist, typically, will posit basic physical or mathematical laws as being the ones in no need of further explanation. But one might be a non-reductionist and hold that there are basic laws in each of the special sciences, including perhaps the social sciences. Reductionist or not, the believer in relatively basic laws must posit the existence of relatively basic *changes* in objects that do not require further causal explanation within the material universe. But what premise 1 rules out is the possibility that such changes require *no causal explanation whatsoever*, i.e., that there might be basic laws in an *absolute* sense. If obedience to laws requires changes in objects via the expression of their natures, relatively basic laws require relatively basic changes. But all non-basic changes require causes according to premise 1, so why should relatively basic changes be any different? The phenomenon of change is the same whether it is relatively basic or non-basic. Merely to stipulate that there might be absolutely basic

53 Kenny, *Five Ways*, p. 31.

laws—laws requiring no causal explanation whatsoever—does not give us a reason why we should make an explanatory exception for relatively basic changes if it is true that all other changes require causes. And if we express the idea in Humean terms the point remains the same. Relatively basic laws will on the Humean view of laws require relatively basic regularities, and these will involve relatively basic changes. No mention need be made of natures, but the problem is identical. Kenny offers no argument for thinking that premise 1 can be undermined by positing relatively basic laws; he simply tells us that such laws might exist and so require no further explanation *at all*—in other words, that the relatively basic laws might also be absolutely basic. He goes on to say that the First Way does not seek to explain why the relatively basic laws hold.[54] The argument is not to an Author of Nature, he points out, but to 'the efficient cause of the actual motions of substances in the world'.[55] This claim is misleading, however, because of the intimate connection between being the Author of Nature and being the Author of Natures. The First Way argues to an uncaused cause of all change. Given that laws involve changes, the argument is ipso facto an argument to the cause of all laws. If there are absolutely basic laws, the argument is vitiated since not all changes will require a cause. But Kenny has given us no reason to think that there are any basic laws in this sense. If there is a cause of all changes, then there are no absolutely basic changes, and so no absolutely basic laws, if to be an absolutely basic change means to be uncaused. But the supporter of the First Way can still posit relatively basic changes—changes, and hence laws, that do not have a cause *within the material universe*. Perhaps, if the First Way is sound, this is as basic as we can hope to get.

8. Act and Potency

Aquinas's central argument for premise 1 is based on the distinction between actuality and potentiality. Change involves the becoming actual of some accident or feature that is merely potential.[56] The potentially ripe banana is

---

[54] Kenny, *Five Ways*, pp. 32–3.   [55] Ibid., p. 33.

[56] This way of putting it might sound as though the only sort of change involved in the argument is accidental or merely qualitative change, as opposed to substantial change. But substantial change also involves the coming into existence of actual qualities that, prior to the change, are merely potential. For example, when water is electrolysed into hydrogen and oxygen, not only does a substance cease to exist and another (two others) come into existence, but so do new qualities, i.e. the chemical properties of hydrogen and oxygen (e.g. boiling point) that are not present in water. Lest the reader object that this idea commits us to the Identity of Indiscernibles, which is contestable, we can add that substantial

actually unripe, and when it becomes ripe its potential ripeness becomes actual. Its actual unripeness disappears. All change is, as Aquinas puts it, the 'reduction of something from potentiality to actuality'.[57] But, as he goes on to argue, 'nothing can be reduced from potentiality to actuality, except by something in a state of actuality'.[58] Why? 'Now it is not possible that the same thing should be at once in actuality and potentiality in the same respect, but only in different respects. For what is actually hot cannot simultaneously be potentially hot; but it is simultaneously potentially cold. It is therefore impossible that in the same respect and in the same way a thing should be both mover and moved, *i.e.*, that it should move itself. Therefore, whatever is in motion must be put in motion by another.'[59]

Although this is Aquinas's main argument for premise 1, it is given short shrift by Kenny, as it has been by other commentators (due, evidently, to his influence).[60] The main objection he and they level at Aquinas is that he seems to rely on the proposition

> (A) Whatever actualizes the potentiality of another thing to have a certain feature F must already have F itself.

Hence Kenny's putative counterexamples: 'a kingmaker need not himself be king, and it is not dead men who commit murders.'[61] Again: 'A man who fattens oxen need not himself be fat.'[62] Moreover, if (A) is modified or supplemented in the following way to take account of predicates that are vague in the sense of being dimension-relative, such as 'hot', 'tall', and so on:

> (V) A can make B become F-er only if A is itself F-er than B.

we come up against counterexamples such as the production of heat by friction.[63] Furthermore, neither (A) nor (V) can be true of local motion. A

---

change without discernibility still requires the coming into existence of a new actuality consisting of the distinct individuality of the new yet indiscernible substance. Again, we do not need to be haecceitists to believe this. Aquinas's argument applies equally to such a case without commitment to haecceitism; all that is necessary is that there be a new actuality.

[57] *ST* Ia, qu. 2, art. 3: 'Movere enim nihil aliud est quam educere aliquid de potentia in actum' (Burns Oates trans., vol. i (1920), pp. 24–5).

[58] Ibid.: 'de potentia autem non potest aliquid reduci in actum, nisi per aliquod ens in actu'.

[59] Ibid.: 'Non autem est possibile ut idem sit simul in actu et potentia secundum idem, sed solum secundum diversa, quod enim est calidum in actu, non potest simul esse calidum in potentia, sed est simul frigidum in potentia. Impossibile est ergo quod, secundum idem et eodem modo, aliquid sit movens et motum, vel quod moveat seipsum. Omne ergo quod movetur, oportet ab alio moveri.'

[60] Kenny, *Five Ways*, pp. 20–3; Rowe, *Cosmological Argument*, p. 15; J. Hick, *Arguments for the Existence of God* (New York: Herder and Herder, 1971), pp. 40–1.

[61] Kenny, *Five Ways*, p. 21.   [62] Ibid., p. 22.

[63] Kenny makes a curious point about this at p. 22. He says that although (V) fits the production of heat by conduction—e.g. boiling a kettle—'unfortunately it will no longer be true that nothing is

thing does not need to be in place P when it moves another thing to that place. Nor need it be closer to P than another object as it causes that object to be closer to P than itself. (The latter might work for some cases of magnetic attraction but not for propulsion, for example.)

We have seen that MacDonald accepts Kenny's specific objection from local motion and excludes it, wrongly in my view, from the purview of premise 1. But he also takes on board Kenny's general objections to the actuality/potentiality argument for premise 1, trying to salvage the argument by appeal to a more complex set of criteria concerning what state of actuality an object must be in when it changes another. In brief, he says that Aquinas could be interpreted as holding that if A causes B to change to state S, then A must be either: (i) in S itself; (ii) in S to a degree greater than B; or (iii) in some state S′ that has 'greater actuality' than S.[64] The concept of greater actuality requires an understanding of Aquinas's theory of a hierarchy of perfection of natures, but MacDonald leaves this to one side and I do not propose to canvass it here. The idea, though, is that if we restrict ourselves to immediate causes (again, the idea is left vague by MacDonald), we can deny that the farmer who fattens oxen needs to be fat, that the murderer needs, absurdly, to be dead, and so on. All that is required is that the immediate cause of a thing's entering a certain state S be itself in a state of actuality with respect to S that is 'sufficient'[65] to bring about the change, and the sufficiency must be explained in terms of greater degree, greater perfection, or perhaps some allied notion.

It is difficult to deny that Aquinas believed in such an idea,[66] though to interpret it in a non-circular and non-question-begging yet contentful way is no small matter. In any case, MacDonald does not defend it, he merely seeks to present a version of what he calls Aquinas's weak 'principle of sufficient reason'

both moving and moved in the same respect. For the kettle may be getting hotter while making the water hotter.' How is this a counterexample? The kettle is actually getting hotter, so it is not potentially getting hotter. It is actually at, say, 78 degrees and actually moving to the potential temperature of 80 degrees, so it is not potentially 78 degrees nor potentially moving to the potential temperature of 80. Kenny seems to be doing exactly what he warns against at the very beginning, namely equivocating over transitive and intransitive senses of 'move'. The kettle is moving (transitively) the water at the same time as it is itself moving (intransitively). If the kettle is 78 degrees and moving towards 80, while the water is 76 degrees and moving towards 78, how is the kettle both moving and moved in the same respect? In what way is it both actual and potential in the same respect? I confess to finding it difficult to know exactly what Kenny is talking about, though it seems that whatever it is, it is due to an irrelevant reference to what the kettle is doing to the water, not what the kettle is undergoing itself.

[64] MacDonald, 'Aquinas's Parasitic Cosmological Argument', p. 134.   [65] Ibid., p.135.
[66] Following Aristotle: *Metaphysics* 1034a22, 1070b30, in W. D. Ross (ed.) *The Works of Aristotle*, vol. viii (1928); Aquinas, *Commentary on Aristotle's Metaphysics*, trans. J. P. Rowan (1961; Notre Dame, Ind.: Dumb Ox Books, 1995), pp. 482–3, 786–7.

that is not obviously vitiated by Kenny's objections and that plays a crucial role in the First Way. To this extent what he says is useful and interesting. But it is not, I submit, at all relevant, at least not to the presentation of the argument in either of the *Summas*.[67] All that Aquinas requires is that the change of anything from being potentially *F* to actually *F* requires *some distinct actuality* to bring about the change.[68] This is not to say that Aquinas escapes blame for the misinterpretation by commentators such as Kenny. For he uses the example of fire's being actually hot when it makes wood change from being potentially hot to being actually hot. So when he goes on to assert that nothing can be both mover and moved in the same respect and in the same way, in other words actually *F* and potentially *F*, it is natural to assume that he has in mind the idea that only something distinct which is actually *F* can make something change from being potentially *F* to actually *F*. Yet the assumption may be resisted. All that is required is the proposition that the transition from potentiality to actuality requires something actual to cause it to occur. But since the state of being potentially *F*, for some feature or accident *F*, contains no actuality, the state of being potentially *F* cannot actualize itself. Hence the state of being potentially *F* must be actualized (i.e., caused to change to the state of being actually *F*) by something *distinct* from the state of being potentially *F*. Now that distinct thing might itself be another feature *G*, or it might be a part of an object, or it might be the whole object—i.e., the object that possesses the state of being potentially *F*. So it is of no avail to the critic to claim that an object can change itself as long as the object as a whole, under no other causal influence outside the boundaries of the object, moves from being potentially *F* to being actually *F*. An unripe banana will at least begin to ripen in a dark room. But this is no counterexample to premise 1. For the banana will undergo the transition from being potentially ripe to being actually ripe (or semi-ripe) in virtue of causes distinct from the state of being potentially ripe: chemical constituents within the banana will initiate the transition. But the transition or process of change cannot initiate itself. Similarly, as we saw earlier, the loosely called self-movement of any living thing is not, for the purposes of the First Way, strict self-movement. One part of an animal will cause another part to undergo a transition from potentiality to actuality. But

---

[67] In the argument as briefly stated in the *Compendium* (see n. 10) Aquinas does refer to the 'lower' being moved by the 'higher': 'For we see that all things that move are moved by others, the lower indeed by the higher, as the elements are moved by the heavenly bodies' ('Videmus enim omnia quae moventur, ab aliis moveri: inferiora quidem per superiora, sicut elementa per corpora caelestia'). So I would not want to rule out the possibility of MacDonald's interpretation's being relevant to this way of putting the argument.

[68] For an admirable realization and defence of this point against Kenny, see Craig, *The Cosmological Argument*, pp. 172–3. See also Martin, *Thomas Aquinas*, ch. 9.

the transition will not cause itself. No process from potentiality to actuality is self-actualizing. As Christopher Martin puts it: 'Neither being non-F nor being capable of becoming F offer us any explanation of the fact which we have to explain, which is that it [some object] becomes F. If there is to be any explanation of its becoming F, it must be at the very least in virtue of some other aspect, given by some other true description: a description which is not purely negative, such as "−is not-F", nor purely potential, such as "−can become F".'[69]

Put this way, the argument from actuality and potentially is strong and appears immune to the sorts of counterexample Kenny raises. Dead men do not commit murders, but actual men do, just as actual farmers are needed to fatten oxen. The very idea that a mere potentiality—that which does not itself actually exist—could make the transition to actuality without the concurrent causal activity of something actual that is distinct from the potentiality should strike one as absurd, as it struck Aquinas and Aristotle. Only actualities make actualities out of potentialities.

One might wonder, though, whether one potentiality might not actualize another potentiality. It is one thing to say that something other than the potentiality must actualize it, and another to say that the distinct actualizer must itself be actual. Yet a moment's reflection shows the thought that one potentiality might actualize another to be bizarre. How can one mere potentiality actualize another? Could an unripe banana be made ripe by the banana's being potentially straight, or potentially warm, or potentially long? We can take the analysis to the micro-level but it makes no difference. No mere potential chemical reaction can actualize another potential reaction. Put in more contemporary terms, one power cannot cause another power to manifest itself or be exercised. Only if the first power is itself actualized in some way can it actualize the second. The power of thought does not cause one to exercise the power of speech; but actually *thinking* might cause one to speak.

If one is to grasp fully the truth of this idea, one must give up thinking of actualities solely in terms of substances. In the Aristotelian/Thomistic system, actualities include substances but also features or accidents (of which intrinsic qualities are a sub-category). Not only do substances have causal influences on other substances, but they do so on accidents: a person can turn an instance of red into an instance of black with a coat of paint.[70] Accidents have effects

---

[69] *Thomas Aquinas*, p. 137.
[70] This is a loose way of speaking. By replacing an instance of redness with an instance of blackness, the painter causes one quality instance to go out of existence and be replaced by another. But this too

on substances: being fat makes a person prone to illness. And accidents have effects on other accidents: pollution of the air causes foul smells. Once we realize that causal relations can occur between all kinds of actuality, we see that the kinds of causal process Aquinas has in mind in the First Way are very broad indeed. Yet his point is the same in all cases: whether the process of change involves substances, accidents, or some combination of both, it must always involve actualities' turning potentialities into other actualities. We can, however, say something more specific. For at any point in its existence, a material object will have only a finite number of qualities. So even a causal process involving only the qualities of a single substance would at some point, if traced through a large enough number of qualities, have to extend beyond the substance to *other* substances possessing other qualities. Causal processes involving qualities necessarily piggy-back on the substances having the qualities. If premise 1 is true *and* if we rule out infinite circular causal processes (whether because of the truth of premise 1 or of premise 2: see earlier), at some point in a process of changes within a substance we will have to step outside the boundaries of the substance and look for a cause of change in some other substance. Thus the chain of causes must be traced through distinct substances, not just distinct qualities and not just qualities within a single substance. And if premise 2 is correct, the chain cannot be infinite. If the conclusion follows from the premises, there must be a wholly immovable mover, a final terminus and cause of all change in the universe, yet not itself part of the universe.

9. Conclusion

Whether premise 2 is true and the conclusion follows from the premises are two large subjects I cannot tackle here. Kenny has many objections to both, and they deserve separate treatment. The present discussion, however, has concentrated only on his many objections to premise 1: whatever is changing is being changed by something else. It is a key element, not only of Aquinas's natural theology but of the whole metaphysic that underlies it. Hence it is worthy of lengthy consideration in its own right, not of the manifest neglect accorded it by contemporary philosophy. If I have not shown the proposition conclusively to be true, I hope at least to have shown it to be

---

is to cause a change, since to destroy a quality instance is to change it. The subject of change need not always survive a change, even though *something* must survive a change. For more, see *Real Essentialism*, ch. 4.

plausible, defensible, and immune to the many and by now famous criticisms fired at it by Kenny in his influential work. Kenny may be wrong about premise 1; but he is instructively wrong. Confronting his critique shows, I submit, that the First Way, long neglected by all but a few, is worthy of serious reappraisal.[71]

[71] I am grateful to Brian Davies for comments on a draft of this paper.

8

The Action of God

BRIAN DAVIES

To say that something acts is normally to say that it brings about an effect. And this is the sense of 'act' that I have in mind in what follows. Medieval authors often distinguish between 'transient' and 'immanent' action (*actio transiens* and *actio manens*) so as to allow for a difference between, say, Fred's cutting Bill's hair, and Fred's coming to admire him.[1] And there is a serious difference to be flagged here. A biography of Aquinas can be accurate (complete, indeed) without mentioning that Anthony Kenny came to admire him, albeit with reservations. It is not, however 'immanent' action with which I am here concerned. My focus is on action in the sense that Aquinas has in mind when he speaks of 'agent' (or 'efficient') causation. And, with an eye on this sense of 'action', I want briefly to report, and briefly to reflect, on what Aquinas says about God's action.

1. Agent Causes and Being

Writing with an obvious debt to Aristotle, Aquinas regularly says that agent causes are, for the most part, material individuals which bring about changes in other things.[2] According to him, paradigm examples of agent causation would be my roasting a chicken (effecting change of quality), chocolate bars increasing someone's weight (effecting change of quantity), and a boat taking someone from Dover to Calais (effecting change of place). Yet Aquinas goes beyond Aristotle in what he has to say about agent causation. For he asserts that

---

[1] Cf. Thomas Aquinas, *Summa Contra Gentiles* I.73; John Duns Scotus, *Ordinatio*, Bk 1, d. 3, pars 3, qu. 2, *Opinio Propria*.

[2] Cf. *Sententia super Metaphysicam* ('Commentary on Aristotle's *Metaphysics*') V.2 and V.3. For a recent defence of the same position, see P. M. S. Hacker, *Human Nature: The Categorial Framework* (Oxford: Blackwell Publishing, 2007), ch. 2.

God is an agent cause that does *not* change anything. According to Aquinas, God acts as an agent cause insofar as, and *only insofar as*, he creates, and, says Aquinas, for God to create something is not for him to bring about a change in it.[3] In Aquinas's view, for X to be changed by Y, X must pre-exist Y's act of changing or modifying[4], and, Aquinas reasons, nothing created by God can pre-exist God's act of creating it. So creation is not a change.[5] In Aquinas's terms, for God to create something (for God to act) is for God causally to account for something's having *esse*.

Is this a believable suggestion? The term *esse* can be rendered into English as 'being', or 'existence', so it might be thought that what Aquinas says about God as the cause of *esse* offends against the logic of existential statements when that is properly understood. The idea here would be that existence is not a property of objects or individuals, that '____ exist(s)' is not a first-level predicate, that sentences like 'Socrates exists' make no sense and are comparable to sentences like 'Socrates is numerous'.[6] Yet why should we accept any of that? An argument frequently given for doing so is that not to do so would lead us to self-contradiction. If '____ exists' serves to inform us about something, then what of '____ does not exist'? Should we not suppose that this expression is used to deny that a particular informative predicate (i.e., '____ exists') is truly applicable to something? In that case, however, how could it ever be true that, for example, critics of Aquinas do not exist? If it is true to say of such critics that they do not exist, must they not first exist for this to be true of them? So must not ascriptions of non-existence, if existence is a property, all be self-refuting?

As I say, this is an argument frequently offered. But it is a bad one. For we do not have to take negative existential propositions as presupposing the existence of their subjects and to be predicating/asserting something of them. We should take them to be denying that their subject terms have a referent or referents. 'Critics of Aquinas do not exist' should not be construed as telling us that existing critics of Aquinas lack a property that other things have. It should

[3] Aquinas is prepared to distinguish between God's creating and God's bringing about a change in something created. See, for example, *De Potentia* 3.7. In making this distinction, however, Aquinas is not denying that the existence of a thing in process of change is, as changing, being created. Nor is he asserting that God is doing something in addition to creating when accounting for something undergoing change. For Aquinas, for God to bring it about that something undergoes change is for God to bring it about that something changing is being created. Cf. *Summa Contra Gentiles* II.6.
[4] Cf. *De Potentia* 3.2 and *Summa Contra Gentiles* II.17.
[5] Cf. *Summa Contra Gentiles* II.17 and *Summa Theologiae* Ia, qu. 45, art. 3.
[6] For a strident, and, perhaps, the best available defence of this position, see C. J. F. Williams, *What Is Existence?* (Oxford: Clarendon Press, 1981). For Williams attacking Aquinas with an eye on it, see Philip L. Quinn and Charles Taliaferro (eds), *A Companion to the Philosophy of Religion* (Oxford: Blackwell, 1997), ch. 27 ('Being').

be understood as telling us that nothing that exists is a critic of Aquinas (or that '_____ is a critic of Aquinas' is not truly affirmable of anything). 'Critics of Aquinas do not exist' *could* be true, and it is *in fact* true that, for example, dinosaurs do not exist. To agree that this is so, however, is not automatically to presuppose that what 'Critics of Aquinas do not exist' or what 'Dinosaurs do not exist' assert is false. Statements like 'Dinosaurs do not exist' should not be thought of as purporting to tell us something about existing dinosaurs (and what 'properties' they have or lack). The same goes for statements like 'Socrates does not exist'. That is a true statement (said of the famous Greek philosopher), but it would be wrong to suggest that it is true only if it is false. On the assumption that existence can somehow be thought of as property of things, we do not contradict ourselves when making assertions like 'Critics of Aquinas do not exist'. We would only contradict ourselves if, absurdly, we were to assert that *not existing* is a property of existing things.[7]

It has been suggested, with a nod to Wittgenstein's *Philosophical Investigations*, that existence cannot be truly ascribed to individuals since, 'outside philosophy', we have no use for sentences like 'Socrates exists'.[8] And I have sympathy for this position. Coming out of the blue, sentences like 'Socrates exists' would baffle people. Do we tend to go around naming people and stating that they exist? No. Do we commonly say things like 'The largest city in Iowa exists' or 'The United States exists'? Of course not. And what would anybody, 'outside philosophy', be doing when saying, for example, 'I exist'? One might take the words to mean 'I am still alive', or 'I am not dead yet'. But would people who want to make it clear that they are still alive, or not dead yet, try to get their point over by saying 'I exist'? Hardly.

Yet it *does* make sense to say things like 'Socrates exists', even if we do not often make such assertions—and why *should* we unless we have special reason to do so? For, as Peter Geach and Anthony Kenny have observed, there is a sense of '_____ exist(s)' which signifies 'actual existence' (Geach) or 'individual existence' (Kenny).[9] To say that critics of Aquinas exist may

---

[7] What I am saying here would have been accepted by most medieval philosophers, who would typically have added that negative statements in general are true if their subject refers to nothing. They would have said, for example, that 'Santa Claus lives at the North Pole' is false, not because he lives somewhere else, but because he lives nowhere, and that 'Santa Claus does not live at the North Pole' ('It is not the case that Santa lives at the North Pole') is true for the same reason.

[8] Cf. Williams, *What Is Existence?*, p. 79: 'Outside philosophy we have no need of "Mr Bailey exists" or "*Je suis*". If someone wishes to persuade me that "_____ exist" can function as a first level-predicate, he will have to show me a sentence which I can recognize as usable outside philosophy and which is formed by wrapping "_____ exists" round a genuine proper name'.

[9] For Geach, see *God and the Soul* (London: Routledge & Kegan Paul, 1969), ch. 4. For Kenny, see *Aquinas on Being* (Oxford: Clarendon Press, 2002), ch. 2.

not be to tell anyone anything about a given individual, for one can know that there are critics of Aquinas without knowing that, for example, Anthony Kenny is a critic of Aquinas.[10] Consider, however, 'Mount Everest exists, but the World Trade Center does not'. I can see no reason to deny that this is a true proposition, one which we have many reasons for accepting. Here, though, we are surely predicating existence of something individual. 'Mount Everest exists' is an excellent example of a proposition which ascribes, and truly ascribes, existence to an individual (an individual mountain). And there are surely many other comparable propositions. I have a cat called Smokey. I used to have one called Tiddles. Smokey is still alive, but Tiddles is dead. Why can I not, therefore, say (and truly say) 'Smokey exists, but Tiddles does not'? Who, except, perhaps, a philosopher, would fail to understand me here? When my friends come to visit me at home, I do not, of course, point to Smokey and say 'He exists'. That would be an odd thing to do ordinarily (though not, perhaps, with an appropriate context provided)[11]. But it does not, therefore, follow that 'Smokey exists' is nonsense and cannot be thought of as truly telling us something when it comes to Smokey.[12]

2. Does 'Exists' Inform?

So we can, I think, resist the view that individuals cannot intelligibly be said to exist. Now, though, we need to see how this conclusion bears on what Aquinas (remember Aquinas?) has to say about God's action as the source of the *esse* of things. And something to recognize at the outset is that, in a serious sense, Aquinas agrees with the suggestion that to say that something exists is not to inform us about it.

[10] I do not, though, see why 'Critics of Aquinas exist' should not be thought of as telling us something about all (individual) critics of Aquinas. For familiar reasons, from what Frege and Russell have said, one may wish to analyse statements like 'Critics of Aquinas exist' along the lines '____ is a critic of Aquinas' is truly affirmable of something. This analysis works, I think, but is not forced on us. We could just as well take 'Critics of Aquinas' to refer to all the critics of Aquinas that there are, and to say that they exist could be taken to say something true of each of them (unless, of course, no individual can properly be said to exist).

[11] Let us suppose that my friends have been told that Smokey has died. Knowing that, I might, with an eye on the famous Monty Python parrot sketch, jubilantly point to him and declare: 'Not so! He has not joined the choir invisible! He is not demised! He has not passed on! He is not a stiff! He is not bereft of life! He has not ceased to be! He is not an ex-cat! He exists!'

[12] For a defence of this conclusion see Colin McGinn, *Logical Properties* (Oxford: Clarendon Press, 2000), ch. 2.

Kant famously asserted that we cannot put 'exists' into a description of what something is.[13] And it is not hard to see what he was seeking to note. We may say that Smokey is grey, and agile, and in my garden, but noting that he exists would not be to add to an account of what he is (to say that he is grey, and agile, and in my garden, would seem to presuppose that he exists to start with). To say what Smokey is would, first and foremost, be to say that he is a cat. As Aristotle would have observed, it would be to place him in the category of substance. There are things that Smokey can be said to be which take us beyond the fact of his being feline. He can be said to be grey, or agile, or in my garden. And to say such things of him would, in a perfectly ordinary sense, be to describe him (and, therefore, in one sense, to say what he is). Yet it would seem weird to suggest that we might significantly augment our description of Smokey by adding 'and he exists'. If I were to say 'I have two cats which are different since one of them exists and the other does not', most people would take me to be joking, and, I think, Aquinas would agree with them. We should, he thinks, accept that 'exists' can be predicated of an individual, as in 'Socrates is' (*Socrates est*).[14] He never suggests, however, that to say that something exists (that is has *esse*) is to distinguish it from other things in the way that we might distinguish between a cat and a dog, or between a cat that is grey and a cat that is white, or between a non-agile cat in a house and an agile cat in a garden. For Aquinas, *esse* is not a 'form'. In his view, to say that something has *esse* is not to say that it is a substance of a certain kind (that it is, for example, a cat and not a dog), or that it has a characteristic that other things lack (that, for example, it is bald and not hairy, or thin and not fat).[15] In terms of our normal use of the word 'description' (which I take us chiefly to employ with an eye on differences and similarities between existing things), Aquinas does not suppose that we are describing something when saying that it has *esse* (that it exists).

In that case, however, what *does* Aquinas mean when he says that things have *esse*? To understand him here it helps, to begin with, to recognize that, for him, we need to note differences between what we might casually refer to as 'things'.

[13] Immanuel Kant, *Critique of Pure Reason*, trans. Paul Guyer and Allen W. Wood (Cambridge: Cambridge University Press, 1997), A592–602/B620–630.
[14] Cf. *Expositio libri Perihermeneias* (Commentary on Aristotle's *On Interpretation*), bk 2, lecture 2. 'Hoc verbum *est* quandoque in enunciatione praedicatur secundum se; ut cum "Socrates est", per quod nihil aliud intendimus significare, quam quod Socrates sit in rerum natura'.
[15] Cf. *Summa Theologiae* Ia, qu. 76, art. 4 and *Summa Contra Gentiles* II.68.

3. Things and Things

For example, Aquinas thinks that we should distinguish between naturally occurring substances (naturally occurring individuals) and artefacts. According to Aquinas, a cat is a naturally occurring substance, a naturally occurring individual with a distinct nature, something in the world which can be compared and contrasted with other naturally occurring individuals. Yet Aquinas would deny that, say, a clock, or a car, or a house is any such thing. For him, an artefact is an *ens per accidens* (a being only by coincidence), not something in nature (not something naturally occurring), not, in Aquinas's language, an *ens per se*.[16] For Aquinas, an artefact is an *ens per accidens* since it is (coincidentally) made up of materials which, in nature, have an identity of their own.[17]

Another distinction that Aquinas makes when it comes to 'things' is one which we can appreciate by thinking of Anthony Kenny and noting that he is a philosopher. Tony does not have to be a philosopher in order to be what he is considered as the (adorable) naturally occurring substance that he is—i.e., a human being. Tony's being a philosopher depends on him being a human being to start with, and knowing that he is a human being does not involve knowing that he is a philosopher (or a farmer, or a postman). That Anthony Kenny is a philosopher, thinks Aquinas, is 'accidental' to him. It is not something we ought to mention in an account of what he is 'essentially' (i.e., human). For Aquinas, Tony *qua* philosopher is also an *ens per accidens*.[18]

Yet another distinction between 'things' that Aquinas makes is one which he expresses by suggesting that there can be a difference between a true statement and one which singles out a naturally occurring substance and tells us something about it.[19] 'Peter is blind' may be true, but does it follow that the blindness of Peter exists as Peter exists? Aquinas thinks not since to say that Peter is blind is only to say that he cannot see. For Aquinas, blindness is not a naturally occurring substance, anymore than an artefact or a postman is. There are, he agrees, people who are blind, just as there are artefacts and postmen. When concerned with what there is, though, he thinks that the primary things are naturally occurring substances.

[16] Cf. *Sententia super Metaphysicam* V.8.
[17] As I look at my computer I wonder which of its elements are things in nature with an identity of their own, and I am lost to provide an answer. However, as we know, people have to work with what they find in the world in order to fabricate artefacts. So I presume that some account can be given of what, in nature, has ended up to become my computer.
[18] Cf. *Sententia super Metaphysicam* V.9 and VII.3.   [19] Cf. *Sententia super Metaphysicam* V.9.

4. Questions to Ask and the Meanings of Words

Confronted by such a substance, one can, Aquinas holds, ask what it is essentially, what it takes for it to exist at all. What is Smokey? It would (believe me) be true to say that he is grey, that he sleeps on my bed, and that he has many admirers. First and foremost, though, he is a cat. That is the bottom line. How could anyone sensibly deny that this is so? And Aquinas thinks (a) that we can ask what Smokey is just insofar as he is a cat, and (b) that for Smokey to be is for him to be a cat. Yet Aquinas does not also believe that a true answer to the question 'What is a cat?' would simply tell us what the word 'cat' means. Of course, we can ask what something is, be given a 'nominal definition', and then be perfectly happy. What is a unicorn? A unicorn is a horse-like creature with a horn on its forehead. No problem here. That is what a unicorn is (check the dictionaries). When talking about what things are essentially, however, Aquinas is not concerned with nominal definitions. He is concerned with true accounts of what there is in the physical universe. There is, he thinks, a difference to be noted between the questions *an est* ('Is it?') and *quid est* ('What is it?').

Suppose we wonder whether there are any unicorns. We shall, Aquinas reasons, have to start with some understanding of the word 'unicorn'. And we shall then have to see whether anything matches this meaning—whether anything can truly be said to be what people have in mind by the word 'unicorn'. Suppose we discover that some things *are* horse-like creatures with horns on their foreheads. Then, so Aquinas might say, the answer to the question 'Are there any unicorns?' is 'Yes'. He would not, however, add that we, therefore, know what a unicorn is. We could, he would say, only come to know what a unicorn is by examining unicorns, by noting how they resemble other things, and how they differ from them, by noting how they typically behave, and so on (i.e., by developing a scientific understanding of unicorns). Knowing what something is essentially is, for Aquinas, not a matter of being able to provide an account of what a word means. It is a matter of knowing that particular (existing) substances really are thus and so. As Aquinas says when commenting on Aristotle's *Posterior Analytics*, 'If there is nothing to have its essence signified by a definition, then the definition is no different from the explanation of the meaning of a term'.[20]

---

[20] *Expositio libri Posteriorum Analyticorum* ('Commentary on Aristotle's *Posterior Analytics*'), bk 2, lecture 6. The Latin reads: 'Si non sit aliqua res cuius essentiam definitio significet nihil differt definitio a ratione exponente significationem alicuius nominis'.

This is partly (and here I stress 'partly') what Aquinas has in mind when he speaks of things having *esse*. His view is that something has *esse* if it actually exists, if it is there so that we can truly say what it actually is considered as the substance that it is (so that we can provide a 'real' as opposed to a 'nominal' definition of it). Artefacts, postmen, and blindness are not, in his view substances, so they do not have *esse*.[21] Cats, by contrast, are, for Aquinas, substances, so they do have *esse*. As is not the case when it comes to unicorns (and admitting that we can give an account of what 'unicorn' means), we can, thinks Aquinas, lay hold of cats and truly say what they actually are, what they are simply considered as cats. One might reject what Aquinas says here by suggesting that we should never take ourselves to have uttered the last word when it comes to what any naturally occurring substance is. But Aquinas would not disagree with this suggestion. He speaks at one point about the difficulty of knowing the essence even of a fly.[22] Not having some complete and incorrigible account of what something actually is, however, is not the same as not being able to know what some naturally occurring substance has to be in order to exist at all. 'Smokey is a cat', and I defy anyone to deny this.[23] But am I now, therefore, committed to insisting that what scientific students of cats tell us about them admits of no addition? Hardly. This fact, however, does not entail that talk about the essence of a cat is out of place. Given what we know of cats, we are certainly entitled to say that no cat is a reptile, that no cat can explain why water boils at 100 degrees centigrade, that no cat is triangular, or omnipresent, or timeless, or inanimate. We are equally entitled to say that all cats are carnivorous mammals, that they have similar (specifiable) bone structures, that they have hearts, lungs, brains, and teeth (distinguishable from those of some other animals), and so on. Check with the zoologists. And to say all of this is not just to note the meaning of the word 'cat'. It is to say that certain things can truly be said of actual cats. In Aquinas's language, it would be to say that cats have both *essentia* (essence) and *esse* (existence/being).

---

[21] As I say below, Aquinas does not mean that these things do not exist (period). His point is that artefacts and postmen only exist since certain substances happen (coincidentally) to come together. As for blindness, Aquinas does not deny that blind people exist, but he denies that blindness, which he takes to be a lack of being, has any substantial identity of its own.

[22] *Collationes Credo in Deum* ('Conferences on the Apostles Creed'), 1. Cf. *Summa Contra Gentiles* I.3.

[23] It might be suggested that what I call 'Smokey' is actually a mechanical artefact, with an appearance that disguises the fact—an artefact, perhaps, beamed down by aliens. Should that prove to be true, then Smokey, obviously, would not be a cat. But a cat is what he actually is (check him out).

5. Artefacts, Other Things, and Existing

In opposition to Aquinas, one might challenge his distinction between artefacts, postmen, blindness, and things having *esse*. These, one might say, are really indistinguishable since they can all be thought of as things that exist. Yet Aquinas can happily take this suggestion on board (should he find himself forced to dialogue in contemporary English). Nothing that he says implies that we cannot truly reply 'Yes' to questions like 'Is there a computer on the table?', 'Is there a postman approaching?', or 'Is it true that blindness is real, and not an illusion?'. But he would want to note that an artefact (by definition the work of a human artisan) only comes to be as we produce it for purposes of our own using materials available to us, as is not the case with, say, a cat. He would also want to say that nothing is naturally a postman, that a postman is just someone who happens (accidentally, or coincidentally, and not necessarily), to be both a man and someone employed in a certain way, and that blindness is no nameable individual or property (or predicate or attribute) able to exist on its own.[24] And Aquinas is, surely, right in all of this. Artefacts are nothing but human products. Postmen are nothing but people who happen to be doing a certain sort of job at a particular time in their lives. Blindness is real only in the sense that some people cannot see. Prior to the 'being' of artefacts, postmen, blindness, and the like, come existing substances, natural units. How, I am inclined to ask, can anyone sensibly deny this?

Can we, however, give some precise content to the notion of things simply existing? We can sharply distinguish between something's being a cat and something's being a dog. Can we in the same way distinguish between something's existing and something's not existing? Aquinas, as I have noted, seems to think not since he maintains that existence as ascribable to individuals is not what we might naturally think of as a distinguishing property of any kind. His notion of *esse* has been attacked by noting the absurdity of suggesting that we might, for example, check a collection of buttercups so as to see which ones exist and which ones do not.[25] Yet Aquinas does not think that something that has *esse* is descriptively different (let alone empirically descriptively different) from anything else that has *esse*, or from anything else without *esse* either. For him, it would be equally true to say that Smokey, the angel Gabriel, and,

[24] Cf. *Sententia super Metaphysicam* IV.1, IV.2, and VII.1.
[25] Cf. C. J. F. Williams, *Being, Identity, and Truth* (Oxford: Clarendon Press, 1992), ch. 1.

happily, Anthony Kenny all exist. In that case, however, ought he not to conclude that we cannot be attributing anything significant to any individual when saying that it exists (has *esse*)?

Having asserted 'I think an almost unbelievable amount of false philosophy has arisen through not realizing what "existence" means', Bertrand Russell went on to say 'It is perfectly clear that, if there were such a thing as this existence of individuals that we talk of, it would be absolutely impossible for it not to apply, and that is the characteristic of a mistake'.[26] And if Russell is right, then Aquinas and I are wrong. But it is, surely, Russell who is wrong here. He presumably means that if existence is truly attributable to individuals, then there is some necessity about it being so attributable, that, for example, if it is true that Smokey exists, then it is necessarily true that he exists. But why should we suppose that if Smokey exists, he exists necessarily? Russell may have been thinking that, if it is true that existing is truly attributable to individuals, then to deny that something or other exists is to utter a contradiction, or say something meaningless. As I argued above, however, negative existential assertions do not need to be construed as denying existence to what exists. 'Smokey does not exist' is not equivalent to 'It is the case that Smokey, this individual that I am pointing to, is non-existent'. And even if existence is attributable to an individual, it does not follow that the individual has to exist anymore than it follows from 'Smokey is feline' that 'Smokey is feline' is true of necessity. If there were no Smokey (if Smokey did not exist), he would not be there to be either feline or non-feline.

Again, though, can we give some sharp account of what it is for something to exist, for something, as Aquinas would say, to have *esse*? Not, I think, in the sense in which we can give an account of what it is for something to belong to a particular natural kind, or to have properties or attributes that other things lack.[27] If Aquinas is right to ascribe existence to individuals, then existence (*esse*) is ascribable to things regardless of the categories to which they belong. Existence, we might say, is indefinable; there are no simpler notions which we can bring together in order to get someone to see what it is for something simply to exist.[28] Yet it does not, therefore, follow that we cannot intelligibly and truly speak of different things existing (having *esse*), or not existing, or that

---

[26] *Logic and Knowledge* (London: George Allen and Unwin, 1956), p. 241.

[27] You might say that the Cheshire Cat lacks the property or attribute of existing that I have. But can we say that the (non-existing) Cheshire Cat is *different* from anything that exists? I am inclined to think not. For some discussion of this issue, see A. N. Prior, *Objects of Thought* (Oxford: Clarendon Press, 1971), ch. 8.

[28] In 'How Real is Substantial Change?' (*The Monist*, July 2006) E. J. Lowe suggests that the concept of existence is a 'primitive' and, thus, an indefinable one. I think that Lowe is right to say this, and, indeed, right in pretty much everything he says in his excellent paper.

we cannot get people to see what we mean when doing so. 'Socrates does not exist, but Smokey does'. That, I claim, is both meaningful and true (at the time at which I write). Can I unpack it somewhat? Clearly I can. I can say 'Socrates is dead, but Smokey is alive'. So, when it comes to living things, to exist is to be alive (as Aquinas frequently says, *vivere viventibus est esse*). And what about non-living things? My desk exists, but it is not alive. So, for example, 'My desk exists, but the World Trade Center does not' cannot be construed as saying that my desk is alive while the World Trade Center is dead. But it can be similarly (we might say 'analogically') construed. Like the World Trade Center, my desk has not existed always. Both came to exist when they were built. My desk sits solidly in my living room. Unlike the World Trade Center, it has not been destroyed. It could be destroyed and would then not exist, just like the World Trade Center.

In general, so it seems to me, we can indeed understand what it is for something to exist (learn what 'exists' means as it is truly ascribable to individuals, whether naturally occurring substances or *entia per accidens*) by noting that it makes sense to say of various things that they did not exist, that they came to exist, that they continue to exist, and that they no longer exist. Understanding what it is for something particular to exist will depend on knowing what the thing in question is. So we do not know what it is for a living thing to exist just by knowing about inanimate objects. But we can certainly get a handle on existence as ascribable to living things even from a knowledge of inanimate ones. And this is something that is well understood even 'outside philosophy'. '＿＿ exist(s)', considered as applicable to individuals, has a robust life in day-to-day discourse. My friends might think me ailing should I start declaiming 'I exist' or 'Paris exists'. They would, however, have no problem understanding me should I say that all the people in the world exist, but won't exist when a hundred or so years have passed, or that lots of things exist now which did not exist in the past. They would have no problem understanding me should I say that the earth did not always exist, and that it will probably not exist when the sun becomes a red giant. Scientists sometimes speak about the 'life cycle' of stars. What do they mean by doing so? I presume that they mean that some stars came to be, continue to be, and shall cease to be.

6. Existence as Caused By God

Aquinas, however, does not just say that existence can be ascribed to individuals. As I have noted, he also claims that it is efficiently caused by God, that God brings about everything's having *esse*, that God acts by being the source of the *esse* of things. So what shall we make of this further claim? What, indeed, does Aquinas intend by making it?

He does not mean that God causally accounts for everything that can be said to be. He does not hold that God causally accounts for every statement of the form 'X exists' being true. He does not, for example, think that God causally accounts for it being true that God exists (*Deus est*). And, though he agrees that we can, for example, truly say that blindness exists, and though he thinks that there would be no blindness were it not for God, he does not, in a serious sense, take God to be causally responsible for blindness.[29] As I have noted, blindness (and comparable privations) do not, for Aquinas, have *esse*. They are not existing subjects in their own right. Their 'existence', is, so to speak, parasitic. They exist, thinks Aquinas, only insofar as something (having *esse*) is lacking or deprived in some way.[30]

When speaking of something as having *esse* Aquinas is squarely focusing on the existence of naturally occurring substances, the fact that there are, for example, cats (some of which lack sight). He is also focusing on certain things that can be affirmed about such substances without saying what they are essentially. He would say that Smokey is essentially a cat, and that feline properties or attributes can, therefore, be ascribed to him. Yet he would also agree that Smokey has a certain weight, colour, degree of agility, and so on. According to Aquinas, these aspects of Smokey, which Aquinas would call 'accidental forms', certainly exist. For him, the weight, colour, and agility of Smokey are as real as Smokey, even though they are not a discrete set of objects distinct from him (as Aquinas would say, they have *inesse*—being-in [a subject] rather than *esse* [being]). Not so, however, when it comes to what Smokey lacks. Not so, also, when it comes to what might be said of Smokey, not because of what he actually is, but because of how something else is. Suppose that Smokey is blind. Aquinas would say that to note this fact is only to assert that Smokey cannot see, that he lacks the power of sight, and who could sensibly contradict him? So Aquinas, rightly, it seems to me, would have to deny that the blindness of Smokey is something's having *esse*. Again, suppose that Smokey comes to be adored by my neighbour. Aquinas would not suppose that being adored by my neighbour is any actual form ascribable to Smokey, something that constitutes what it is for him to exist at any given time.[31] And rightly so again. Bertrand Russell once praised a robust sense of

---

[29] For more on this see my *The Reality of Evil and the Problem of Evil* (London and New York: Continuum, 2006).

[30] *Summa Contra Gentiles* III.9.   [31] Cf. *Summa Theologiae* Ia, qu. 28, art. 1.

reality.[32] Aquinas, we might say, has just such a sense. In spite of what we might call the 'surface grammar' of much that we say, we should not, he thinks, suppose that, in a list of what there is, we should include what something lacks (e.g., the ability to see) or what something might be said to be only because of what is going on in something else (e.g., admiration). In Aquinas's view, everything that has *esse* is either a naturally occurring substance or a genuinely inhering positive feature of such a substance.[33] It is with respect to these, so he thinks, that we are confronted by the action of God.

Why so? Not because he holds, as the famous Jesuit philosopher Francisco Suárez (1548–1617) seems to have done, that such things might not exist (are 'contingent') and, therefore, depend for their existence on what cannot be thought of as not existing and is, therefore 'necessary'.[34] For Aquinas, the distinction between what is contingent (able to be or not to be) and necessary (not able not to be) is a distinction to be made *within* the world of things having *esse*. In his view, various things (open to our inspection) come into being and pass away (so they are contingent, and may exist or not exist), and the fact that this is so is explicable in scientific terms. Yet Aquinas also believes that there are things which are necessary, things in the created order which do not spring up and pass away as, for example, cats do. So Aquinas does not think that the existence of Smokey, considered as something in the universe that might not have existed, can only be accounted for with reference to God. Thinking of Smokey, Aquinas would not say that his existence depends on God just because he is contingent (the contingency of Smokey would lead Aquinas to ask about the causes in the created world that gave rise to him). He would say that Smokey, together with all 'necessary beings' created by God (i.e., things not generated or able to perish) depend on God since *what* he is can be distinguished from the fact *that* he is (a distinction of *esse* and *essentia*).[35]

Again (and, perhaps, contrary to what some readers may have taken me to be saying above when talking of God as Creator), Aquinas does not think that the *esse* of things implies the existence of God since the universe must have had a beginning and since God has to be invoked to account for this fact. Aquinas holds that there is no way of proving that the universe had a beginning.[36] He takes it to be a theological truth that the universe did, indeed, begin to be. Speaking philosophically, however, he only claims that what we might call the 'sheer existence' of things requires an agent (divine) cause. As he puts it in one place: 'Among all effects, the most universal is being itself. Hence, it must be the proper effect of the first and most universal cause, which is God'.[37] And why should 'universal being' need a cause? Aquinas's answer is that all substances, and their inhering accidental forms (i.e., whatever we might seek to account for scientifically, and whatever we might take to be matters for scientific explanation), are *not to be expected*, given *what* they are, *to exist*, and, therefore, raise a causal question. It is no matter for surprise that people get drunk when consuming a lot of whisky. Yet we might be surprised to find an inebriated pope on the steps of St Peter's basilica. Our lack of surprise in the first case derives from what we know about the natures of people and alcohol, which leads us to expect a certain result when people drink whisky in certain quantities. Our surprise in the second case derives from it being no part of our understanding of 'pope' that a pope should be drunk anywhere close to Vatican City. And, with this thought (or thoughts like it) in mind, Aquinas suggests that we should be surprised that (wonder about the fact that, seek causally to account for the fact that) substances exist at all. For, he reasons, existence (having *esse*) does not belong to any of them given what they are. Given what they are, it is *not to be expected* that they exist. They could not be what they are if they did not exist. But how come they exist?[38]

Aquinas has sometimes been interpreted as here saying that we can understand what a noun means without knowing that there is anything to be named by it, that we can know, say, what 'unicorn' means without knowing that there are any unicorns.[39] And Aquinas does, indeed, believe that this is so, as

---

[36] Cf. *De Aeternitate Mundi* ('On the Eternity of the World'), in which Aquinas argues that, from the viewpoint of philosophy, it cannot be established either that the universe had a beginning or that it did not.

[37] *Summa Theologiae* Ia, qu. 45, art. 5. Aquinas's Latin reads: 'Inter omnes autem effectus universalissimum est ipsum esse. Unde oportet quod sit proprius effectus primae et universalissimae causae, quae est Deus'.

[38] Given what we know about the universe and what is in it, we might, of course, naturally expect certain things to come to exist. We might, for example, naturally expect conception to occur, and for someone to come to exist, when people have had sex (at a certain time, and without the use of contraceptives). But Aquinas is not denying this (obvious) point. He is saying that nothing that exists in the universe is to be expected to exist given its nature as documented in text books on biology, astronomy, physics, and so on.

[39] Cf. Anthony Kenny, *Aquinas on Being*, ch. 2. I discuss Kenny's reading at some length in 'Kenny on Aquinas on Being', *The Modern Schoolman* 82 (2005). For a comparable, and, I think, excellent, discussion

you can see from the fact that he rejects a version of the so-called Ontological Argument by observing: 'If we do not grant that something in fact exists than which nothing greater can be thought (and nobody denying the existence of God would grant this), the conclusion that God in fact exists does not follow'.[40] Aquinas's basic point here is that, no matter what meaning/sense/definition one invokes when it comes to the word 'God', it does not follow that God exists. Yet this conclusion is not what Aquinas is pressing when saying that *esse* does not belong to substances by nature. That teaching is asserting that knowing what *actually* existing things are by nature does not involve knowing that any one of them (to be singled out individually) exists. Speaking at one level, Aquinas maintains that everything has to exist, for he does not believe in what we might call non-existing essences (or properties considered as 'abstract objects', or 'possible worlds' in which non-existing things somehow manage to exist). To have an essence is, for Aquinas, to have *esse*. And, in his book, all essences are actual. He thinks that, if something ceases to exist, we are not left with an essence lacking existence; we are left with a meaningful noun which is not the name of anything. But Aquinas does not take this to entail that, given what we know of its essence, any individual to which an essence can be truly ascribed simply has to exist. He does not take it to mean that it is *natural* (only to be expected) for any given substance to have *esse*.[41] I can know what Smokey (an existing cat) is by nature. Yet my knowledge of what Smokey is by nature (this, of course, being something ascribable to all actual cats) does not come with an inbuilt knowledge that *he* exists. So how come Smokey? And how come any other individual substances you care to mention? Questions like these would not arise with respect to what *naturally* exists, with respect to what is such that *it is only to be expected* that it exists. But, thinks Aquinas, they arise if we are concerned with that which does not have 'existence' built into what it is by nature (so to speak).

Here, it seems to me, Aquinas is correct. So I think that the existence of substances, and their inhering properties (as opposed to 'properties' like 'being admired by X') does raise a causal question that is not settled by noting that they exist and by noting what they are (or by noting what in the universe

---

of Kenny, see Gyula Klima, 'On Kenny on Aquinas on Being', *International Philosophical Quarterly* 44 (2004). See also Lawrence Dewan, 'On Anthony Kenny's *Aquinas on Being*', *Nova et Vetera* 3/2 (2005), pp. 350 ff.

[40] *Summa Theologiae* Ia, qu. 2, art. 1. I quote from Brian Davies and Brian Leftow (eds), *Thomas Aquinas, Summa Theologiae, 'Questions on God'* (Cambridge: Cambridge University Press, 2006), p. 22.

[41] In one sense, of course, he does, for he thinks that all existing substances have *esse* and that there cannot be any which lack it. My point is that Aquinas does not believe that knowing what an existing substance is by nature is to know that it cannot fail to exist.

gave/gives rise to them). Given what we know of cats and various other things, it is *only to be expected* that cats (and other things) behave thus and so in certain circumstances. Given what we know of human beings and antibiotics, it is *only to be expected* that, all things being equal, people with chest infections get better when taking antibiotics. And so on. Yet to know what something (actual) is by nature (Smokey, for example) is not to know that it is *only to be expected* that the thing exists—unless we know that it is something the nature of which is to be (that it is something which cannot not exist, as, of course, Aquinas takes God to be). Aquinas, correctly again in my view, says that we do not know that existing belongs by nature to anything we have in mind when we single out things in the universe, or when we note what, in the universe, accounts for them coming to be or continuing to be. You may reply that existing cats, dogs, planets, galaxies, or whatever, exist since they cannot not exist. But if they were things that cannot not exist, then each and every one of them would always have to exist (i.e., Smokey could never die, and could not have been born either), which is patently false.

It has been said that we should seek to account for what we encounter in the world (existing individuals or real processes) in terms of what is part of the world. And I do not wish to deny this. I think, as Aquinas seemed to, that for any existing thing or process you care to specify, we should expect there to be what we would normally call a scientific explanation. Faced by Smokey, I assume that his being there is explicable without recourse to theological assertions. He is there because of his parent cats. And cats are there because of whatever it is in the world that gave rise to and continues to support the existence of cats. And that, too, is there because of something or other in the world. We can move from biological explanations to explanations in terms of physics, and then to what we might call 'the basic truths about the universe and its ways of working'. But how come all of *this*? Can we not push our causal questions to the point where they take us beyond scientific explanations? I see no reason why we should not do so. We could say that the universe is *just there* and refuse to ask what accounts for it being there. To do so, however, would be to issue a fiat rather than to offer an argument. It would also be to take leave of our natural inclination to ask what accounts for what does not have to be so.

In other words, I think that Aquinas is right to say that the existence of what makes up what we tend to call 'the universe' raises the (causal) question 'Why is there something rather than nothing?' Most philosophers would associate that question with Leibniz, whose thinking contrasts strongly with that of Aquinas, and is, in the end, incompatible with it. But 'Why is there something rather than nothing?' does well enough as a way of drawing attention to what

Aquinas has in mind when he says that God acts insofar as he brings it about that things have *esse*. For, in his view, God's causing of the being of creatures is a matter of his making to be anything that we might sensibly think of as a part of the universe. In this sense, it is a matter of God making the difference between there being something rather than nothing. And Aquinas, I think, can be defended for thinking of God as making this difference. It would, of course, be wrong to suggest that there might be something called 'Nothing' which could sensibly be thought of as existing. 'Nothing' is not the name of anything that exists or that might exist. 'There is nothing in the box' does not mean that there is something that is the nothing in the box. Aquinas is not arguing otherwise, however. He is not claiming that we can imagine or describe absolute nothingness. Nor is he thinking of nothingness as a space into which existing things can be placed. He is saying that, if everything is such that what it is (its essence) does not guarantee that it is (its *esse*), then nothing has to be, which seems to me correct, and which naturally leads to the question 'Then how come anything is?'—a question which (unless we take ourselves to be talking of what exists by nature) evidently looks for a cause making it to be that anything exists, a cause acting so to bring about the existence of everything we might intelligibly think of as part of the universe.

7. Action and Change

Does it, however, make sense to suppose that something acts without producing a change? As I have noted, (a) Aquinas thinks that God can be said to act insofar as he creates (insofar as he accounts for the *esse* of what does not exist by nature), and (b) Aquinas does not think of God's action here as the bringing about of a change. And, so I ought now to add, Aquinas does not think that God himself changes when he acts. God, for Aquinas, is immutable.[42] Yet should we not say that the notion of agent causation is inextricably bound up with the notion of change taking place? Is not agent causing always a matter of something's doing something to something (modifying it somehow)? And must not a cause of change always itself undergo change? Is it not true that, as Bede Rundle puts it, we 'can get no grip on the idea of an agent *doing* something where the doing, the bringing about, is not an episode in time, something involving a changing agent and a change induced through its actions'?[43]

---

[42] Cf. *Summa Theologiae* Ia, qu. 9, art. 1.
[43] Bede Rundle, *Why there is Something rather than Nothing* (Oxford: Clarendon Press, 2004), p. 77.

Actually, it is not too hard to think of non-theological examples of action which does not result in change. Consider keeping a large book in place by holding it in one's palm for a while. If that is not action, then, surely, nothing is. But the action is not making a change. Rather, it is preventing a change from happening which would otherwise happen by nature. And, so Aquinas might add, God's action consists in preventing the things he is continuously creating from falling into nothing, which otherwise would have to occur by their nature, which is not the same as their being. In general, of course, agent causes *do* bring it about that things change. But why should we suppose that they *always*, or *must*, do this? As we have seen, it is not part of the concept of agent causation that an agent cause produces change. And, so we might add, if, in Aquinas's sense, we have reason for believing that the *esse* of something *can* be caused since it *is* caused, we have other grounds for supposing that not all agent causation is the producing of a change in something.

One might reply 'Yet all agent causes must undergo change as they bring about their effects'. This does not seem to me conceptually necessary, however. There is a seductive and influential picture of agent causation (famously to be found in the writings of David Hume) according to which one should sharply distinguish between a cause and its effect.[44] Yet this is not how Aquinas views agent causation, and with good reason, for the effect of an agent cause is just *the cause in action*. Suppose that I clean a plate. This would seem to be a clear instance of agent causality. The plate becomes clean *because* of me. Yet my causing, my acting, here cannot be thought of apart from the 'coming to be clean' on the part of the plate. It is not as though *first* I do such and such and, *then*, have an effect. I clean the plate *only* as the plate *comes to be* clean. Again (an example favoured by both Aristotle and Aquinas), suppose that I succeed in teaching someone. Do I do so by going through processes distinguishable from the occurrence of learning? No. Teaching occurs *only* as learning occurs.[45] I succeed in teaching people only as they come to learn by virtue of me (what I do while *trying* to teach is not teaching). And so on in general. Agent causation is not a matter of action plus, or followed by, effect. As Aquinas puts it: 'Action and passion are not two changes but one and the same change, called action in so far as it is caused by an agent, and passion in so far as it takes place in a patient'.[46]

---

[44] Cf. David Hume, *An Inquiry Concerning Human Understanding* IV.1, and *A Treatise of Human Nature* I.3.3.

[45] Happily for people earning their living as teachers, most educational establishments are blissfully ignorant of this fact.

[46] *In Libros Physicorum* ('Commentary on Aristotle's *Physics*') 3.5. 'Actio et passio non sunt duo motus, sed unus et idem motus: secundum enim quod est ab agente dicitur actio, secundum autem quod est in patiente dicitur passio'. Cf. *Summa Contra Gentiles* II.16.

We begin, thinks Aquinas, by seeing cause and effect as separate, but our aim is to reinterpret the effect as nothing but the active presence of the cause.[47] In that case, however, it seems far from obvious that only what is part of a changing world can act so as bring about an effect. I can only wash plates or teach people by changing in various ways. If, though, it makes sense to suppose that there is an agent which accounts for the existence of what does not exist by nature, the existence of anything we might regard as a spatio-temporal individual, then it would be true to say that there can be agent causation which does not involve a cause undergoing any change.

One might try to turn this argument back on me by suggesting that because agent causation always involves change it follows that there is no agent which accounts for the existence of what does not exist by nature, that there is no non-spatio-temporal agent cause. As I have said, though, I do not see that it is part of the concept of agent cause that such a cause has itself to undergo change. As I have also said, the existence of what does not exist by nature raises a causal question which leads naturally to the notion of there being agent causation which is not the causation of an agent undergoing change.

That there is such causation is part and parcel of Aquinas's account of God's action, and the claim that it *could* occur is defended by him as he argues that it *has* occurred (and that it continues to occur). Aquinas is aware that agent causation is regularly a matter of changeable agents bringing change about in particular contexts. This, as I have noted, is the notion of agent causation from which he starts, one which does not presume any truths about God. Unlike some thinkers, however, Aquinas also holds that there are questions to which the answer is God—one being 'How come any universe at all?', a question which, if admitted as legitimate, cannot be answered by appealing to any spatio-temporal individual. Thinking along these lines, Aquinas holds that we just *do* have reason for extending our usual understanding of the expression 'efficient or agent cause'.

8. Conclusion

Aquinas, of course, does not think that this is all that needs to be said about God's action. He asks, for example, 'What account of God's nature should we give on the assumption that for God to act is for God to create?'[48] He also asks

---

[47] Cf. Herbert McCabe, *Faith Within Reason* (London and New York: Continuum, 2007), p. 55.

[48] Cf. *Summa Theologiae* Ia, qu. 3–26.

whether God's creative action is compatible with human freedom.[49] And he asks questions like 'How can we sensibly attribute to God what we attribute to creatures?' He asks, and tries to answer, a huge number of questions similar to these ones. In his view, though, to ask such questions seriously, and in hope of a true answer (philosophically speaking, anyway), is first of all to recognize how it is that for God to act (*actio transiens*) is, first and foremost, for God to create. I have tried to give some account of what he means by saying so, and how he might be defended.[50]

---

[49] Cf. *In Aristotelis Librum Peri Hermeneias*, 1.14.

[50] For comments on previous versions of the above I am very grateful to Christopher Arroyo, David Braine, John Cottingham, Bryan Frances, Peter Hacker, Gyula Klima, Anthony Lisska, Timothy McDermott, David Oderberg, and Giorgio Pini.

Part III

Descartes

9

The Physics and Metaphysics of the Mind: Descartes and Regius

DESMOND M. CLARKE

> Dualism is the idea that there are two worlds. There is the physical world which contains matter...[and] there is another psychical world; mental events and states belong to a private world...According to dualism the two separate realms of mental and physical realities interact, if at all, only in a mysterious manner...
>
> Anthony Kenny[1]

1. Introduction

There can be little doubt that Descartes is a dualist of some kind. There is also no doubt that Descartes's account of mind and body is usually understood as Kenny describes dualism above, as a theory about two radically different kinds of reality, which are both present in human nature and interact in a manner that cannot be understood in terms of the kinds of causal interaction that occur in the material world.

This reading assumes that Descartes combined metaphysical and experiential knowledge-claims—the former, that the created world divides into two basic, non-overlapping types of entity (the material and the immaterial), the latter that mind and body interact[2]—and that he confidently asserted this

---

[1] Anthony Kenny, *The Metaphysics of Mind* (Oxford: Clarendon Press, 1989), p. 1.

[2] Descartes to Elizabeth, 28 June 1643: 'people who never philosophize and use only their senses have no doubt that the soul moves the body and that the body acts on the soul' (AT III 692: CSMK 227). See also Descartes to Arnauld, 29 July 1648 (AT V 222: CSMK 358).

188 DESMOND M. CLARKE

twofold claim while acknowledging the inexplicability of how mind–body interaction could take place. On this account, the privileged status of onto-logical claims is immunized against epistemological doubts. That seems a strange position to attribute to Descartes, unless the texts make it unavoidable. It assumes certainty, not just about the content of one's ideas, but about the realities that correspond to them. However, Cartesian knowledge-claims about physical phenomena, and especially about their explanations, were acknowledged to fall far short of certainty, because they rely unavoidably on hypotheses. Since claims about the 'immaterial' presuppose knowledge of the limits of the material, any uncertainty about the latter renders equally uncertain claims about the respective boundaries between the material and the immaterial.

As these concerns are developed in the following discussion, they open up the possibility of interpreting Descartes in another way, in which dualism characterizes primarily our *knowledge* rather than the realities that we claim to know. On this interpretation, dualism enters Descartes's discussion of the mental at a point where it prevents him—or should prevent him—from mak-ing the ontological claims that would be required for substance dualism. This introduces a considerable gap between (i) the conclusion that his arguments are capable of supporting, and (ii) the conclusion that Descartes sets out to establish in the *Meditations*, concerning the 'the distinction between the human soul and the body' (AT VII: CSM II 12).[3] Instead of showing that mind and matter are two kinds of substance that we know are really distinct, it merely introduces enough ignorance or uncertainty into our knowledge of mental realities to make it reasonable to refrain from claiming that they are physical or material. When understood in that way, Cartesian dualism makes a much weaker than expected contribution to the apologetic enterprise that was inaugurated by Pope Leo X in response to supporters of Averroism,[4] and it supports the

---

[3] Descartes gave different accounts of his objectives in the subtitle of the first two editions of the *Meditations*. The first edition (1641) mentioned demonstrating 'the immortality of the soul'. The second edition (1642) reduced the author's ambition to establishing the 'distinction' of body and soul, and he accepted Mersenne's comment that he 'had not said one word about the immortality of the soul' in it (AT III 265: CSMK 163). However, it is clear that Descartes had in mind what he called a 'real' distinction between the human mind and the body, rather than a modal (otherwise formal) or conceptual (*sola ratione*) distinction. 'Two substances are said to be *really distinct* when each of them can exist apart from the other' (AT VII 162: CSM II 114). Since 'the mind and the body are substances . . . which can exist apart from each other' (AT VII 170: CSM II 120), they are really distinct.

[4] 'In its eighth session the Lateran Council held under Leo X condemned those to take this position [i.e. of holding that the soul dies with the body, or that there is only one soul for all of humanity], and expressly enjoined Christian philosophers to refute their arguments and use all their powers to establish the truth; so I have not hesitated to attempt this task as well' (AT VII 3: CSM II 4).

sympathetic criticisms offered by his erstwhile supporter at Utrecht University, Henricus Regius.[5]

2. Physics and Metaphysics

Descartes consistently distinguishes two (and only two) kinds of finite substance, the physical and the mental. This is most evident in the *Principia*, where he claims in Part I, art. 54 that 'we can easily have two clear and distinct notions or ideas, one of created thinking substance, and the other of corporeal substance' (AT VIIIA 25: CSM I 211). This distinction is initially conceptual, i.e. between two notions or ideas. Having two such concepts is evidently not sufficient for Descartes to conclude that there exist two kinds of finite substance which correspond to the concepts of mind and matter. In parallel with the conceptual distinction, Descartes is usually assumed to rely on another distinction between sensory thought and so-called 'pure perception', and to apply the former to knowledge of material realities and the latter to knowledge of the immaterial. Thirdly, although the precise extension of the term 'metaphysics' when used by Descartes is open to discussion, it seems to be beyond doubt that he classified discussions of the immaterial world (including the human soul and God) within the scope of metaphysics.[6] On a first reading, then, one might be tempted to conclude that there are two types of Cartesian understanding or perception, that these are applied to two kinds of substance, and that the 'pure' perception of immaterial realities is assigned to a discipline called metaphysics. For example, Descartes wrote to Princess Elizabeth that 'metaphysical thoughts, which exercise the pure intellect, help to familiarize us with the notion of the soul' (AT III 692: CSMK III 227). Such a system of interrelated dualisms, however, depends on the validity of the Cartesian inference from so-called clear and distinct ideas to claims about the realities that they denote.

Somewhat baffled readers of Descartes have been familiar, since 1641, with the considerations on which he apparently relies in the *Meditations* to show that the human mind is really distinct from matter. In the 'Preface to the Reader'

[5] For the context in which Descartes published the *Meditations* and the subsequent controversies it provoked, see D. Clarke, *Descartes: A Biography* (Cambridge: Cambridge University Press, 2006), chs. 7, 8, and 11. I also borrow from my *Descartes's Theory of Mind* (Oxford: Oxford University Press, 2003) for Descartes's critique of substantial forms as explanations of natural phenomena.

[6] According to the Preface to the French edition of the *Principia*, metaphysics contains 'the principles of knowledge, including the explanation of the principal attributes of God, the non-material nature of our souls and all the clear and distinct notions which are in us' (AT IX–1 14: CSM I 186). In contemporary philosophy, metaphysics is obviously not limited to discussions of the immaterial, and it is not necessary here to decide whether it was so limited in Descartes's usage.

he acknowledged that readers of the *Discourse on Method* (1637) had submitted objections, as he had requested, and that there had been only two objections worth mentioning as relevant to his subsequent discussion of the human soul and God in the *Meditations*. The first objection was as follows:

From the fact that the human mind, when directed towards itself, does not perceive itself to be anything other than a thinking thing, it does not follow that its nature or essence consists only in its being a thinking thing, where the word 'only' excludes everything else that could be said to belong to the nature of the soul. My answer . . . is that, in that passage, it was not my intention to make those exclusions in an order corresponding to the actual truth of the matter . . . but merely in an order corresponding to my own perception.   (AT VII 7–8: CSM II 7)

He subsequently claimed to have shown, in the Sixth Meditation, how to make the transition validly from what he perceived to what is the case. However, none of Descartes's contemporaries found his argument[s] persuasive, and all six sets of objections raised the same objection in various forms. Mersenne summarized one version of that general response, when he gathered comments from different readers and submitted them collectively as the Sixth Objections:

. . . when you say you are thinking and that you exist, someone might maintain that you . . . are merely in motion, and that you are nothing else but corporeal motion. For no one has yet been able to grasp that demonstration of yours by which you think you have proved that what you call thought cannot be a kind of corporeal motion . . . Can you therefore show us (for we will give [it] our closest attention and our powers of perception are, we think, reasonably keen) that it is self-contradictory [*repugnare*] that our thoughts should be reducible to these corporeal motions?   (AT VII 413: CSM II 278)

Descartes had already answered a similar objection from Gassendi, in the Fifth Replies. He argued there that he should not be required to demonstrate that every claim that he refused to make was false: 'in order to philosophize correctly, there is no need for us to prove the falsity of everything which we do not admit because we do not know whether or not it is true. We simply have to take great care not to admit anything as true when we cannot prove it to be so' (AT VII 354: CSM II 245). In other words, one begins from what one knows, and one draws valid inferences from that whenever possible. If that cannot be done, no further argument is required or should be expected to prove the falsity of some conclusion that is not supported by a valid inference. One simply refrains from making such claims.

That suggests the question: how can Descartes establish the negative thesis that the human soul is not material, rather than admit simply that we do not know whether it is material or otherwise, and that we should therefore refrain from making either claim? If one knew (a) all and only the properties of matter, and if one knew (b) that there is at least one property in the mind which falls outside the scope of (a), one could conclude that the mind is non-material. Without knowing (a), however, Descartes is in danger of committing the mistake of which Bourdin teasingly accused him. Bourdin argued that if a peasant had seen only a limited number of animals, he might conclude that a novel creature is not an animal because it is not like anything he had seen before; with similarly poor logic, Descartes was accused of concluding that thought is not an activity of a physical system because it does not resemble familiar physical bodies. Bourdin warned that such an argument includes an unjustified 'concealed premise', namely, that 'nothing belongs to the body apart from what I formerly understood to belong to it' (AT VII 497: CSM II 337).[7]

Before writing the *Meditations*, Descartes had available the means to avoid making that mistake. He had embarked on a very ambitious explanatory project when he began work on what developed into *Le Monde*. He made clear the type of explanation in natural philosophy that he rejected (what might be called, for the sake of brevity, scholastic circular explanations), and the kind that he accepted. He hoped, improbably, to explain all natural phenomena, such as those that fell within the scope of astronomy, magnetism, anatomy, and physiology, including sense perception in animals.[8] The methods required to implement this project implied a radical change in the kind of certainty that one could justifiably claim for one's conclusions and, consequently, a redefinition of what is meant by 'knowledge' of natural phenomena. While it is not necessary here to review the details of Cartesian natural philosophy—the methods it used, and the results it achieved—Descartes's unrelenting commitment throughout his whole career to the investigation of a wide range of natural phenomena suggests that he hoped to produce a new natural philosophy that would replace that which had been traditionally taught in colleges in Europe.

It is also clear that, from the beginning of his research, Descartes assumed some distinction between physics and metaphysics and that he included in the latter discussions of God and the soul. This provided a provisional line

[7] Descartes seems to accept this point later, in the *Conversation with Burman*, trans. J. Cottingham (Oxford: Clarendon Press, 1976), p. 11, when he conceded that none of his concepts was adequate to the reality of which it was a concept: 'The same can be said with regard to the body, and its extension, and everything else. As for the author, he has never attributed to himself adequate knowledge of anything whatsoever' (AT V 152).

[8] The ambitious scope of the plan is evident in the *Treatise on Man* (AT XI, 200–2: CSM I 107–8). He planned to explain 'all the phenomena of nature' (to Mersenne, 13 November 1629: AT I 70: CSMK 7) and 'all the principal human functions' (to Mersenne, January 1630: AT I 109).

of demarcation that allowed him to deny that he was publishing anything about metaphysics 'before I have seen how my treatise on physics is received' (AT I 144: CSMK 22). At this point in time, he was not claiming to have a method by which to decide the appropriate ontological category for every phenomenon that falls within our experience; he was merely attempting to avoid getting into discussions that could provoke theological objections.

The main reason for not claiming to have a method for discriminating between physical and metaphysical realities was that there could be a significant difference, in any phenomenon, between appearance and reality. Even in the case of thinking, although the mere belief that one is thinking is sufficient to guarantee the fact that one is thinking, there is no corresponding guarantee that the nature of human thought is as it appears to the thinking subject. The recognition of this fact was one of the most fundamental innovations of Descartes's philosophy, and it preceded methodologically and chronologically the acceptance of any traditional classification of phenomena into distinct ontological classes.

3. Appearance and Reality

Descartes argued, from the first lines of Le Monde, that there may be a significant difference between a sensory experience that we have and the reality that is being experienced. 'There may be a difference between the sensation we have of light...and what it is in the objects that produces this sensation within us' (AT XI 3: CSM I 81). This crucial insight, admittedly first articulated by Galileo, opened up a chasm between (i) the initial descriptions we give of our subjective experiences, and (ii) the descriptions that may be justified, in the light of the best theories available, of the realities of which we are having an experience.[9] Descartes never gives any indication, throughout his career, of resiling from this insight. He reminds readers, at the beginning of the Fourth Meditation, 'of the fact that there is very little about corporeal things that is truly perceived' (AT VII 52–3: CSM II 37). That must mean, not only that sensory perceptions provide unreliable evidence about the nature of physical phenomena, but equally that we cannot rely on our sensory perceptions to make claims about what corporeal objects are incapable of doing. This is repeated in the Principles, where he reminds readers that we may report

---

[9] Galileo introduces this distinction in The Assayer (1623), in Stillman Drake (ed.), Discoveries and Opinions of Galileo (New York: Doubleday, 1957), pp. 274–7.

with confidence the experiences that we have in sensations and emotions, but we must be very careful when making judgements about what is actually taking place during their occurrence: 'There remain sensations, emotions and appetites. These may be clearly perceived provided we take great care in our judgements concerning them to include no more than what is strictly contained in our perception . . .' (AT VIIIA 32: CSM I 216).

I wish to argue that this distinction between appearance and reality, which was applied initially to the way in which the objects of sensory perception are conceived as a result of sensation, should apply generally to the objects of all kinds of thinking.[10] Accordingly, when we reflect on our thinking and self-consciously focus on what it is like to think, it would be a mistake to assume that the inner experience or awareness of thinking validates either the conceptual description of it that we provide, or, even less plausibly, any explanation of thinking that specifies the kinds of entities which are allegedly involved in the activity of thinking. Descartes is less explicit about the first of these conclusions than the second. While the textual evidence is less than compelling, I shall argue that a consistent reading of Descartes requires the application to thinking, in general, of the claim that he had first made explicitly and narrowly about sensation.

Descartes always classified sensation or sensory awareness as a form of thinking. In the Second Meditation, he included 'a thing that . . . has sensory perceptions' in the scope of 'a thing that thinks' (AT VII 28: CSM II 19). One of the objectives of the *Meditations* seems to have been to train readers in where to look (inwardly) for instances of 'thinking' and thereby to facilitate their acquisition of an appropriate idea of what thought is and, by analogy or otherwise, an idea of God.[11] If readers reflected, as proposed, on their awareness of thinking, the first challenge was to describe their experience in terms that did not beg the question about the nature of the reality that was being experienced. Descartes is conscious of this issue in the Second Meditation, when he attempts to describe thought without assuming dualism.

---

[10] The alternative reading is that Descartes applies the distinction only to thoughts that originate in sensations, and that he relies on a form of intellectual perception to which the distinction between appearance and reality is inapplicable when he makes claims about pure thought. I argue against the viability of this alternative interpretation of Descartes below, as did Regius.

[11] Descartes was sensitive to objections, familiar to scholastic philosophers, that it is impossible for a finite human mind to comprehend an infinite God (AT VII 368: CSM II 253). He was equally convinced that we could not acquire even an inadequate idea of God by inspecting material things, including pictures or representations of God. His suggestion, in the *Meditations*, was that we should begin with 'the form or idea of understanding; and by indefinitely extending this . . . form the idea of God's understanding . . . a similar procedure applies to the other attributes of God' (AT VII 188: CSM II 132). See also AT VII 137: CSM II 98.

He had assumed that he had no body, no senses, etc., and yet he was still aware of the fact that he was thinking. That did not imply that it was impossible that his thinking was taking place in a body.

> May it not perhaps be the case that these very things which I am supposing to be nothing, because they are unknown to me, are in reality identical with the 'I' of which I am aware? I do not know, and for the moment I shall not argue the point, since I can make judgements only about things which are known to me.   (AT VII 27: CSM II 18)[12]

Descartes had no reason to conclude, at this point in the argument, that his thinking was some kind of immaterial activity. He conceded as much in reply to an objection from Gassendi:

> I said in one place that while the soul is in doubt about the existence of all material things, it knows itself *praecise tantum*—'in the strict sense only'—as an immaterial substance; and seven or eight lines further down I showed that by the words 'in the strict sense only' I do not at all mean an entire exclusion or negation, but only an abstraction from material things; for I said that in spite of this we are not sure that there is nothing corporeal in the soul, even though we do not recognize anything corporeal in it.   (AT IX–1, 215: CSM II 276)

The mention of 'an immaterial substance' here might suggest that Descartes had skipped a few steps in the argument and had decided prematurely that the 'I' who was the subject of thinking was an immaterial substance. When Hobbes objected to that apparent move, Descartes's reply reflected the provisional character of his interim description of thinking.

> We do not come to know a substance immediately, through being aware of the substance itself; we come to know it only through its being the subject of certain acts. Hence it is perfectly reasonable, and indeed sanctioned by usage, for us to use different names for substances which we recognize as being the subject of quite different acts or accidents. And it is reasonable for us to leave until later the examination of whether these different names signify different things or one and the same thing.   (AT VII 176: CSM II 124)[13]

Descartes should not therefore be understood as claiming, in the Second Meditation, to know that he is (or is partly) an immaterial substance. He

---

[12] The same caution is mentioned in the Fourth Meditation: 'I happen to be in doubt as to whether the thinking nature which is in me, or rather which I am, is distinct from this corporeal nature or identical with it...my intellect has not yet come upon any persuasive reason in favour of one alternative rather than the other' (AT VII 59: CSM II 41).

[13] There is a similar clarification in Descartes to Reneri for Pollot, April/May 1638: 'Of course one may wonder whether the nature which thinks may perhaps be the same as the nature which occupies space, so that there is one nature which is both intellectual and corporeal; but by the method which I suggested, it is known only as intellectual' (AT II 38: CSMK 98).

merely has an experience of the activity of thinking taking place within him, and he needs a description of that activity which does not beg any questions about the realities that explain the experience. If understood in that way, it is reasonable for Descartes to refrain from describing thinking as an act of a physical system, because we do not experience thinking subjectively as something material, such as the movement of corpuscles. But the logic of the argument demands that he must also refrain from deciding that it is something immaterial. To do so would be to anticipate the mistake one finds in Berkeley (see below), that the very experience of sensation somehow validates the concepts used to describe the experience.

Once this step is taken in the *Meditations*, Descartes should be aware that his thinking may in fact be some form of bodily activity of which he is unaware in the course of thinking. It is not possible to resolve that issue by simply looking more carefully—a kind of focused inward staring—at the experience of thinking. The only possible way to move from (1) the experience of thinking, to (2) claims about the nature of what is occurring while one is thinking, is to *speculate* about the most satisfactory explanation of our thinking experiences, just as Descartes had speculated in *Le Monde* about the explanation of feeling pain. There were various options available for this speculative effort, some of which are sufficiently familiar to require only a brief mention.

The most obvious option was to use the scholastic framework of substantial forms to explain how thinking occurs.[14] Descartes had argued consistently since 1630 that substantial forms were non-explanatory in principle, and it would have been inconsistent to invoke them in the early 1640s as a way of explaining human thought. The implausibility of such a move was not lost on Regius, who is discussed below, and it must have been even more obvious to its original author.

At the other end of the spectrum, Descartes could have suggested that all human thinking occurs as a result of the interaction of small parts of

[14] Without claiming improbably that all scholastics endorsed the same understanding of substantial forms, Descartes summarized the focus of his objections as follows, in a letter to Regius (January 1642): 'when we deny substantial forms, we mean by the expression a certain substance joined to matter, making up with it a merely corporeal whole, and which, no less than matter and even more than matter—since it is called an actuality and matter only a potentiality—is a true substance, or self-subsistent thing. Such a substance, or substantial form, present in purely corporeal things but distinct from matter...' (AT III 502: CSMK III 207). Since Descartes claimed that neither he nor his scholastic predecessors understood what is meant by a scholastic form, it would have been self-defeating on his part to provide an intelligible definition. The term 'scholastic form' seemed to imply that what is merely a feature of something, such as the ability to think, is also capable of independent existence like a thing or substance.

matter in motion, which is the kind of explanation he had proposed for the physiological activities associated with sensation and the passions. Hobbes adopted that solution, but it was so speculative and so unsupported by the evidence then available that it could not have been justified, in 1641, as an *explanation* of human thinking. In fact, there were no remotely plausible hypotheses available, at that time, which would link small parts of matter in motion with our experience of thinking, and if Descartes had adopted that hypothesis it would have been as non-explanatory as reverting to substantial forms.

Descartes chose instead, quite reasonably, to leave undecided temporarily the question of whether thinking and physical activities are sufficiently similar to be attributable to a single subject, or are such that they cannot be explained as attributes of the same subject. Pending further argument in the Sixth Meditation, he assigned thinking and walking to subjects that are described in radically different ways, and he left open the possibility that these conceptually distinct subjects may, in reality, turn out to be identical.

However, Descartes subsequently claims to conclude, in the Sixth Meditation, from his conception of the mind as a something that thinks that the mind is 'distinct' from anything that is material. 'The fact that I can clearly and distinctly understand one thing [*rem*] apart from another is enough to make me certain that the two things are distinct [*diversa*]' (AT VII 78: CSM II 54). One of the considerations on which he relied here was that material things are necessarily divisible, whereas 'the mind is utterly indivisible' (AT VII 86: CSM II 59). However, Descartes still stops short of claiming explicitly that the human mind is an *immaterial substance* in the text of the six Meditations. The clarifications offered in the Replies to Objections review this inference a number of times and go beyond the claims made in the *Meditations*. In reply to Hobbes, he wrote: 'Once we have formed two distinct concepts of these two substances, it is easy, on the basis of what is said in the Sixth Meditation, to establish whether they are one and the same or different [*diversae*]' (AT VII 176: CSM II 124). It may have seemed easy to Descartes, but one would like to have seen the argument being made more explicitly. Thus the full text published in 1641, which includes six sets of objections and replies as an integral part of the work, avoided being explicit about the argument while simultaneously implying a form of dualism that has since provided almost unlimited scope for scholarly interpretation.

It is difficult to avoid the conclusion that Descartes's contemporaries, even those such as Arnauld who were sympathetic to his objectives, were unconvinced by the 'considerations' presented in the Sixth Meditation. Those who were unsympathetic, such as Martin Schoock—Voetius' spokesman, and the author of *Admiranda methodus*—claimed that the obvious weakness of the arguments used by Descartes to demonstrate the spirituality of the soul and the existence of God showed that his real objective was to undermine those Christian beliefs. One of those who was initially sympathetic, and yet came to the same conclusion as Schoock, was the Cartesian natural philosopher Henricus Regius.[15]

4. Regius and the Physics of the Mind

Regius seems genuinely to have believed, on the basis of what the Scriptures teach, that the human soul is an immaterial and immortal substance. Although he had been accused of doubting this religious belief early in his career while teaching at Naarden, there is no evidence of any discrepancy between his religious beliefs and what he wrote about the spirituality of the soul in various editions of his main work, *Fundamenta physices*. There he claimed that 'it is most clearly revealed to us, in Holy Scripture, that the mind is really nothing other than a substance, or something that is really distinct from the body and that, of itself, it can subsist apart'.[16] Nonetheless, Regius rejected Cartesian arguments in support of that claim and, over time, he gradually became an open critic of Cartesian metaphysics in general.

Both philosophers agreed about how to proceed in natural philosophy and this sustained their correspondence between 1638 until 1641, when it was proposed, in one of the university disputations over which Regius presided (December 1641), that the human soul and body are two distinct substances that are united accidentally. Descartes was very concerned by this turn of events, because he was afraid of sharing responsibility for a position that he claimed was heretical for a Roman Catholic author. It is easy to see, in retrospect, how Regius came to this conclusion. He had been convinced by Descartes's critique of substantial forms, as it applies to natural philosophy, and he was particularly influenced by reading a manuscript draft of *Le Monde*. He learned from Descartes that one explains nothing about the functioning of the heart if one says that it has a 'pulsific faculty'; likewise, it explains nothing about human thinking to say that we have a 'thinking faculty'. He therefore could not accept that it *explained* anything to describe the mind as the substantial form of the body and yet his religious belief, mentioned above,

---

[15] See the entry on Regius in the *Stanford Encyclopedia of Philosophy* (http://plato.stanford.edu/contents/html).

[16] *Fundamenta physices* (Amsterdam: Louis Elsevier, 1646), p. 246.

implied that human souls are substances insofar as they survive the death of the body.

However, Regius' differences with Descartes ran much deeper than this issue about the link between the human mind and the body, even though he initially made every effort to be conciliatory towards the French philosopher and to minimize explicit differences of opinion. Regius approached questions about the human mind and its explanation with a different epistemology from that apparently adopted by Descartes. This reflected his training in medicine and his preference for empirical evidence to support claims made even about the mind. For example, Regius argued that there was no reason to postulate innate ideas, as Descartes seemed to understand that term, because all our ideas can be explained as originating in sensation.

The mind, in order to think, does not seem to need innate ideas, images, notions or axioms; rather, its innate faculty of thinking is sufficient on its own in order for it to complete all its thinking activities. This is evident in the perception of pain, colour, taste, and other similar perceptions, which are genuinely perceived by the mind, although none of those ideas is innate. Nor is there any reason why some ideas rather than others should be innate by their very nature.[17]

Regius applied this denial of innateness even to the idea of God, which Descartes had described as innate in the *Meditations*. 'Even the idea of God...does not seem to be innate in us, but is produced in us initially by observing things or is passed on to us by others.'[18] Under pressure in 1647, Descartes eventually accepted the same position in the *Notae*, when he conceded that his disagreement with Regius was merely verbal: 'I have never written or taken the view that the mind requires innate ideas which are something distinct from its own faculty of thinking' (AT VIIIB 357: CSM I 303). Regius went even further and denied that there is any such faculty as 'pure understanding' if that means that the human mind thinks about some realities without using the body. Instead, he claimed that the mind is 'organically' united with the body and that all its thinking depends on the appropriate functioning of the brain.

The underlying differences between these two philosophers, who had formerly defended the same 'new philosophy', became increasingly evident following publication of the *Meditations*, and they appeared to be irreconcilable when Descartes read an advance draft of the *Fundamenta physices* in 1645. The Utrecht philosopher believed that he had understood Descartes correctly—he had studied the unpublished *Le Monde*, he had corresponded with Descartes frequently about the emptiness of scholastic explanations of natural phenomena

---

[17] *Fundamenta physices*, p. 251.   [18] Ibid., p. 252.

and, as a result, he had not expected his mentor to publish a tract on metaphysics that was written in a patently scholastic idiom. However, he was reluctant to express his reservations about the *Meditations* and he seemed content to develop the natural philosophy that he shared with Descartes.

In contrast, Descartes did not hesitate to express his grave misgivings when he read the lengthy discussion of human nature in chapter XII (entitled *De Homine*) of Regius' book.

When I came to the chapter on man, and saw there what you hold concerning the human mind and God . . . I was completely astounded and saddened . . . I beg you to forgive me if I open my heart to you as freely as if you were my brother . . . I find it necessary to declare once and for all that I differ from you on metaphysical questions as much as I possibly could, and I shall even put this declaration into print if your book should see the light of day.   (AT IV 249–50: CSMK 254–5)

This threat to go 'into print' was implemented as soon as Regius published his book in 1646; the following year, Descartes disowned his former acolyte in the Preface to the French edition of the *Principia* (AT IXB 19–20: CSM I 189). For his part, Regius had come to the same conclusion as Descartes—that there was an irreconcilable discrepancy between himself and Descartes in metaphysics.

However, Regius thought that the discrepancy was also *within* Descartes's own philosophy, and that the claims made about the human mind and God in the *Meditations* did not reflect what its author genuinely believed about those questions. He was bold enough to express this view in a letter to Descartes in July 1645, which helped to precipitate the sudden end to their correspondence and the subsequent bitter dispute between them.

You will not be surprised at my conduct when I tell you that many honourable and intelligent people have often told me that they think too highly of your intelligence not to believe that, in the depths of your soul, you hold opinions that are the opposite of those that appear publicly under your name. And to avoid misleading you about anything, many of them here [in Utrecht] are convinced that you have discredited your philosophy very much by publishing your metaphysics. You promised nothing that was not clear, certain and evident; however, if one were to judge by these beginnings [of your metaphysics], these people claim that they include nothing that is not obscure and uncertain, and that the disputes you had with competent people on the occasion of this publication serve only to multiply the doubts and uncertainties. It is useless to reply to them that your arguments are indeed such as you had promised. They will reply that there is no enthusiast, impious person, or fool who cannot say the same about their extravagancies and their follies.   (AT IV 255)

This suggestion of intellectual dishonesty on Descartes's part had the effect that one would expect on someone who was so sensitive to criticism. Descartes found it particularly objectionable because it coincided with the objections that had been published since 1643 by Calvinist critics in Utrecht, especially in the *Admiranda methodus*—to the effect that Descartes was a cryptic atheist, and that he did not really believe his own metaphysics.

From Regius' point of view, however, there was a genuine problem in reconciling two different strands in Descartes's philosophy.[19] He was also convinced that the arguments used in the *Meditations*, both for the distinctness of the mind and body and for the existence of God, were invalid. One of the arguments used by Descartes to support a real distinction (in the Cartesian sense) between mind and body was that one can doubt or even deny the existence of the body although one cannot, while doing so, doubt the existence of one's own thought. Regius commented on that argument in the second edition of his book, which was retitled as *Philosophia naturalis*:

The fact that we can doubt the body but cannot possibly doubt the mind does not prevent the mind from being a mode of the body. That merely proves that, while we are doubting the body, we cannot say with certainty that the mind is its mode. In the mean time, since the body about which we doubt may nevertheless subsist and since there is no reason why it may not be modified by the mind—which is evident from what has been said earlier—this is enough to show that the mind of which we are certain may be a mode of that doubtful body.[20]

This was also the position that Regius had proposed in the heat of controversy in 1647, in *A Brief Explanation of the Human Mind or Rational Soul*:

So far as the nature of things is concerned, the possibility seems to be open that the mind can be either a substance or a mode of a corporeal substance. Or, if we are to follow some philosophers, who hold that extension and thought are attributes which are present in certain substances, as in subjects, then since these attributes are not opposites but merely different, there is no reason why the mind should not be a sort of attribute co-existing with extension in the same subject, though the one attribute is not included in the concept of the other. For whatever we can conceive of can exist. Now, it is conceivable that the mind is some such item; for none of these implies a contradiction.   (AT VIIIB 342–3: CSM I 294–5)

This is a Cartesian-style argument used against Descartes. The concept of 'thought' refers to an attribute of some kind. However, although that concept and the concepts in terms of which we usually think of bodies have nothing in

---

[19] The apparent discontinuity in Descartes's philosophy was also discussed in Catherine Wilson, 'Descartes and the Corporeal Mind: Some Implications of the Regius Affair', Stephen Gaukroger et al. (eds.), *Descartes' Natural Philosophy* (London and New York, 2000), pp. 659–79.

[20] *Philosophia naturalis* (Amsterdam: L. Elsevier, 1654), p. 338.

common, they are not incompatible.[21] In fact, if they were such, it would not be possible for the corresponding attributes to be predicated simultaneously of human agents. It is therefore not impossible for these attributes to coexist in the same subject. Since, by Descartes's principles, whatever we can conceive of is capable of being realized, at least by God, it is impossible to decide simply by an examination of the concepts of thought and extension whether or not the corresponding attributes may belong to one and the same subject. Regius concluded that these attributes 'may both be present in the same simple subject'.[22] By making this argument, Regius anticipated by almost fifty years the argument later made famous by Locke, in the *Essay*, that we have no reason to think that God could not superadd thinking to a material subject.[23]

Regius also objected to the argument used by Descartes, in the Fifth Meditation, to prove the existence of God. Descartes had argued, from the concept of God who exists necessarily, if at all, to the conclusion that it is necessarily true that God exists. Regius accepted that the 'actual and necessary existence of God is comprehended in the idea or concept of God'. However, it does not follow from that concept that God exists actually and necessarily. 'It merely follows that, if he existed anywhere, he would exist necessarily rather than contingently or that, in that case, he would not be capable of not existing.'[24]

In summary, Regius was no more convinced by Descartes's arguments for a real distinction between mind and matter than many of his other readers in the 1640s. At the same time, he was very conscious of Descartes's critique of substantial forms as non-explanatory, and of the implied need to explain the mental—if that were possible—by reference to realities that are described in terms other than those by which the subjective experience of thinking is described. Although Regius does not say so, the only plausible conclusion of his various claims was that (according to philosophical arguments) God could have created human beings so that their thinking emerged from complex activities in the body, but that (according to the Scriptures) God freely chose to locate human thinking as an activity in a distinct, immaterial substance.

5. Descartes's Dualism

Descartes is often interpreted as if he led his readers into a philosophical cul-de-sac. According to this interpretation, the *Meditations* proposes and defends,

---

[21] I use the term 'incompatible' here to describe concepts which, when applied to a single subject, give rise to logically inconsistent claims about it.

[22] *Philosophia naturalis*, p. 337.

[23] John Locke, *An Essay concerning Human Understanding* [1690], Bk IV, ch. 3, §6.

[24] *Philosophia naturalis*, p. 357.

as a theory of mental activities, the view that the mind is an immaterial substance that interacts with the human body (which is described as a material substance) in a manner that is not understood. It is difficult, despite its popularity, to reconcile this interpretation with the texts, for the following reasons.

Descartes argued throughout his philosophical career against what he described pejoratively as the 'philosophical entities' that were used in the scholastic tradition, and he classified substantial forms and real qualities among such entities.[25] He also argued, consistently, that one could never explain any observed phenomenon by attributing to it a faculty or power that is defined exclusively in terms of the phenomenon to be explained. 'Dormitive power' cannot explain how sleeping powder works if it means nothing more than 'whatever it is, in sleeping powder, that causes one to fall asleep'. Likewise, one cannot explain how human beings succeed in thinking by attributing to them a capacity for thinking.

Although Descartes rejected substantial forms for many reasons, it is equally obvious that he resorted to the scholastic language of substances to denote the subjects of properties. However, he also denied that we have any knowledge of substances, understood in this sense, apart from knowledge of their properties. This precluded any misinformed attempt to explain the properties of something by reference to the subject of which they are predicated, as if we had independent knowledge of the so-called substance. Our knowledge is acquired in the opposite direction: we discover [some of] the properties of something, and we then claim to know that thing only as the subject of those properties. More importantly, we know nothing more about it apart from our knowledge of its properties. Descartes clarified that point in reply to Arnauld:

We do not have immediate knowledge of substances, as I have noted elsewhere. We know them only by perceiving certain forms or attributes [*formas sive attributa*] which must inhere in something if they are to exist; and we call the thing in which they inhere a 'substance'. But if we subsequently wanted to strip the substance of the attributes through which we know it, we would be destroying our entire knowledge

---

[25] Descartes applied the term 'real qualities' to qualities that were apparently conceived by others as if they were substances. He denied that he was capable of understanding such a self-contradictory entity. 'My principal reason for rejecting these real qualities is that I do not see that the human mind has any notion, or particular idea, to conceive them by.' Descartes to Mersenne, 26 April 1643 (AT III 649: CSMK III 216). See also Sixth Replies to Objections (AT VII 441: CSM II 297). See n. 14 above for 'substantial forms', which Descartes often linked with real qualities as objectionable for the same reasons, i.e. that they were conceived of as (in his phrase) 'little souls' in purely material things.

of it. We might be able to apply various words to it, but we could not have a clear and distinct perception of what we meant by these words.   (AT VII 222: CSM II 156)

Thus there is no added explanatory value in talking about the substance of some phenomenon that requires an explanation, because nothing is known of the substance apart from the fact that it is the subject of the properties that require an explanation.

These objections to the apparent explanatory role of substantial forms and substances do not presuppose, on Descartes's part, that he is committed to some particular kind of explanation, such as mechanistic explanations, or that he wished to reduce all theories to the kind of corpuscular theory advanced in *Le Monde*. They derive, rather, from his theory of explanation,[26] and from his understanding of what was meant in scholastic philosophy by the term 'substance'.

The texts in which Descartes, according to Regius, strayed into metaphysical claims that were inconsistent with the central, novel features of his philosophy, can therefore be read charitably along the following lines. In the *Meditations*, Descartes described certain phenomena that are accessible to our awareness when we reflect on our own thinking. These included all the phenomena that are manifest in a 'thinking thing' [*res cogitans*] (AT VII 28: CSM II 19), such as willing, remembering, imagining, doubting, affirming or denying, or having sensory perceptions. The starting point for any subsequent ontological claim, then, is a description of those phenomena. Evidently, any description involves the use of language and this may provide the first occasion on which mistaken assumptions are made.

Descartes must be granted discretion to apply words, as names, to the features of human thinking that he claims to recognize by reflection. If he performs this task carefully, e.g. by using the kind of naming system proposed by Kripke, he can attach whatever linguistic labels he wishes to the features that he distinguishes.[27] However, this naming exercise is constantly in danger of sliding into descriptions and of anticipating the explanatory stage of the enterprise; it should not, therefore, classify some features as material and others as immaterial, unless these terms are used in a conditional manner. For example, Descartes could define the term 'material' as denoting those

---

[26] See Descartes to Mersenne, April 1646 (AT IV 398).

[27] Saul A. Kripke, *Naming and Necessity* (Oxford: Blackwell, 1982), argued that names should be understood as rigid designators that remain indissolubly connected with their referents in all possible worlds. In contrast, descriptions (even definite descriptions) have variable referents in different possible worlds.

204 DESMOND M. CLARKE

features that typically cluster in familiar phenomena in our environment, such as stones, houses, stars, etc. However, for the reasons given by Bourdin, that definition could never justify a conclusion that some novel attribute (for example, of our mental experience) is 'non-material', except in the trivial sense that it does not usually occur in familiar material objects. In that sense, one's initial description is conditional on what may be learned from subsequent experiences.

The crucial step towards dualism, which was identified in various ways by all the readers who were invited to respond to the *Meditations*, was the inference from (i) a description of how thinking is experienced by the subject who is thinking, to (ii) the claim made by Descartes about its ontological status. The extreme ambiguity of Descartes's use of the term 'idea', in Latin or French, may have facilitated the obscurity of this inference.[28] Descartes defines 'idea' in the Second Replies as follows: 'I understand this term [idea] to mean the form of any thought, immediate perception of which makes me aware of the thought' (AT VII 160: CSM II 113). However, since he had defined thoughts immediately before this sentence as 'anything that is within us in such a way that we are immediately aware of it', his definition of 'idea'—when combined with that provided for ideas in a strict sense in the Third Meditation—should be understood as follows. When we reflect on our thinking, we find that some of our thoughts are such that they enable us to think about something else. In the words of the Third Meditation, these thoughts 'are as it were the images of things, and it is only in these cases that the term "idea" is strictly appropriate' (AT VII 37: CSM II 25). However, we are also aware of all [many of?] our thoughts, and in this sense the very activity of thinking functions as an 'idea' of the activity itself, and our reflective awareness of thinking thus provides us with an idea of thought.

Descartes had effectively undermined the assumption of similarity between our ideas and the realities that correspond to them in the case of pain. In the sensation of pain, despite the clarity of the experience, one cannot assume that what is taking place during that experience has any features that resemble the experience itself. One might object that pains are caused by bodily states, and that such states give rise to notoriously 'unclear' or 'indistinct' ideas in the subject's mind, whereas the clarity and distinctiveness of our idea of a thought is not compromised by a similar corporeal origin. However, that response

---

[28] A. Kenny, *Descartes: A Study of his Philosophy* (New York: Random House, 1968), pp. 96–125, reviews some of this ambiguity. For the use of the term *idée* to denote brain-states, see Clarke, *Descartes's Theory of Mind*, pp. 54–5.

begs the question at issue, of whether thoughts are actually caused by bodily states and are therefore subject to the same caution as sensation when making inferences from the experience of thinking to the reality of what occurs during thinking. Thus, if Descartes observes his own caution about the validity of inferences from ideas to their corresponding realities, he cannot conclude immediately from the reflective awareness of what it is like to think to any conclusion about what thinking actually is. Just as 'there may be a difference between the sensation we have of light . . . and what it is in the objects that produces this sensation within us' (AT XI 3: CSM I 81), there may be a significant difference between our experience of thinking and what is actually taking place in us while we think.

A minor detour in the direction of Berkeley may clarify this further. Berkeley took it for granted, without argument, that ideas or perceptions are 'immaterial' in some sense. He defines ideas, in the *Principles of Human Knowledge*, as 'inert, fleeting, dependent beings, which subsist not by themselves, but are supported by or exist in minds or spiritual substances'.[29] However, there is nothing in the experience of perceiving or having ideas that validates the conceptual description of it that Berkeley adopts. By 'conceptual' here is meant a description that goes beyond merely attaching a linguistic label, and which locates the reality in question in relation to, and in contrast with, other realities to which related terms are applied.

Whether Descartes made the same mistake or not depends on the degree of charity that one applies when reading the texts. He had at least implicitly acknowledged the means to avoid doing so when he endorsed Galileo's distinction between our sensations or perceptions and the realities that cause them. The logic of his innovations in natural philosophy implies that the only way to make knowledge-claims about what is taking place in sensation and, in general, in thinking is by inference to the best explanation. Such an inference to the best explanation, in 1641, left unresolved the underlying nature of the entities or processes responsible for thinking. As a result, Descartes was justified in claiming with confidence only that he could not explain the processes involved in thinking.

This would leave Descartes with the following conclusion. The features of thinking (in the wide sense in which he used that term, to include sensation, remembering, etc.) that are revealed by introspection of our subjective experience do not coincide with the familiar features by which we recognize

---

[29] George Berkeley, *A Treatise Concerning the Principles of Human Knowledge* (Dublin, 1710), Pt I, sect. 89.

physical or material phenomena. It is not true that they have no features in common; for example, they both take place in time. The most likely explanation of all physical phenomena, in 1641, was (Descartes thought) that they are or result from small particles of matter in motion. The subsequent history of the sciences has shown how inadequate that assumption was. However, it would be a strange complaint to make against Descartes that he did not anticipate developments in the sciences that occurred centuries after his death. The significant disparity in the observed features of thinking and of physical bodies suggested a provisional property dualism. However, as Regius (and later Locke) argued, that does not justify the conclusion that such disparate but not incompatible properties are incapable of coexisting in a single subject. To reach that conclusion, it would require a new argument to the effect that the properties in question are logically inconsistent or, more plausibly, are 'naturally' incompatible. Descartes did not present any arguments to show the latter. In fact he acknowledged, especially in the Sixth Meditation, that many sensations such as 'hunger, thirst, pain, and so on are nothing but confused modes of thinking which arise from the union and, as it were, intermingling [*ab unione & quasi permixtione*] of the mind with the body' (AT VII 81: CSM II 56). In that sense, at least, our experience confirms that thinking and the familiar attributes of bodies are sufficiently compatible to occur in the same subject.

One way of reading Descartes's dualism, then, is to see it as an impasse in his efforts to construct a meaningful explanation of the experience of thinking. His dominant objective, in writing the *Meditations*, was to contribute to the apologetic enterprise that had been endorsed by the Council of Trent. This involved providing philosophical arguments to support or explain some of the central religious beliefs of the Roman Catholic Church, such as the immortality of the human soul, the existence of God, the presence of Christ in the Eucharist, etc. While Descartes explicitly distanced himself from the scholastic account of transubstantiation and offered an alternative philosophical account of the underlying religious belief, he wrote the *Meditations* with the intention of providing persuasive arguments for the real distinction of the mind from the body and for the existence of God. The latter presupposed the former, because the idea of God on which he relied was constructed by extrapolating features of the idea of a thinking self.

His efforts, however, were spectacularly unsuccessful. As Regius reported, somewhat reluctantly, the controversies that followed publication of the two editions of the *Meditations*, in 1641 and 1642, showed that none of the readers who submitted objections or published responses was persuaded by his arguments, including those who were Catholic priests or theologians and others who, as Calvinists, were equally dependent on the philosophical resources of the Aristotelian tradition. Cartesian dualism is not, then, a theory of human nature, but an epistemological indicator of the point at which attempts to construct a coherent explanation of human thought reached an impasse in the early seventeenth century, and thereby provided a temporary foothold that could be exploited in support of Descartes's apologetic enterprise.

10

Cartesian Autonomy

JOHN COTTINGHAM

1. Introduction

In contrast to those many philosophers writing today who ignore or downplay philosophy's relationship to its past, Anthony Kenny has chosen to concentrate much of his work over the past forty years on a number of key figures in the history of philosophy. 'Reaching up to the mind of some great philosopher of the past', Kenny has himself observed, is one very effective way of achieving philosophical insight.[1] History of philosophy, as practised by Kenny, so far from being a merely antiquarian or instrumental discipline, often turns out to be in itself a very fruitful way of philosophizing. For philosophy is not a matter of acquiring new knowledge but (as Kenny has put it) 'a matter of understanding, that is to say, of organizing what is known'.[2] In carefully examining the organizational structures produced by the great minds of the past, we can gain a vivid sense of the philosophical problems they grappled with, which are often surprisingly close to those that occupy the 'cutting-edge' practitioners of today, sometimes prefiguring their mistakes, and frequently anticipating the solutions triumphantly produced as 'new research' by those who disdain to consult anything not published in the last ten years. In describing his own philosophical career, Kenny has been very modest in explaining the rationale for his decision to concentrate on the history of philosophy.[3] But to read his extraordinarily incisive work on the canonical philosophers, meticulously accurate in its textual scholarship, yet always expressed, as he puts

---

[1] A. Kenny, *What I Believe* (London: Continuum, 2006), p. 14.   [2] Ibid.
[3] 'In my first years as a professional philosopher, I attempted to make original discoveries in . . . areas such as . . . the theory of action . . . After I had written a few books in this area, however, I realised that I was not able enough to compete with the best of my philosophical colleagues. I came to see that the best contribution I could make to the subject was to provide introductions, in contemporary terms, to the great philosophers of the past.' Ibid.

it, 'in contemporary terms',[4] with an eye to illuminating matters of enduring philosophical importance, is to be left in no doubt that it constitutes, in its own right, a philosophical achievement of a very high order.

René Descartes, one of the major figures whom Kenny has written about, and whom he describes as among those he most admires and from whom he has learnt most,[5] is a particularly fascinating subject for those concerned with philosophy's relationship to its history. Descartes stands at the threshold of modernity, personifying the brave attempt of modern man to strike out alone, unhampered by the dead weight of past authority, and consulting only 'good sense' or reason, that 'best distributed thing in the world'.[6] Yet, as is necessarily the case with all of us, Descartes's ways of thinking, even when he seemed to himself to be consulting nothing but his own inner 'good sense', were significantly influenced by the intellectual culture in which he grew up. Although he was a genuine innovator—one of the chief inaugurators of a new phase in our understanding of the physical world, who helped to shape the very idea of 'science' as we now use that term—his metaphysics was in many respects a much more traditional affair. 'Too often,' as Kenny dryly observes, 'when Descartes tells us that something is taught by the natural light in our souls, he produces a doctrine taught by the Jesuits at La Flèche.'[7] Armed with a formidable knowledge of the strands in classical and medieval thought out of which the backcloth to Cartesian thought was woven, Kenny has been able to reveal many of the hidden assumptions that continued to inform Descartes's thought, despite the vaunted Cartesian programme of sweeping everything away and 'starting afresh right from the foundations'.[8]

The tension between the new and the old is strikingly apparent in Descartes's account of human freedom, one of the most problematic, and still relatively understudied aspects of his thought. On the one hand, the whole Cartesian project for founding a new system of knowledge seems to emphasize the epistemic and volitional independence of the researcher. In his intellectual autobiography, in the *Discourse on the Method*, Descartes describes himself, once having 'emerged from the control of his teachers', as deciding to 'abandon book learning entirely' and seek knowledge 'within myself or the great book of the world'.[9] Later, in his metaphysical masterpiece, the *Meditations*, he presents himself as operating 'quite alone', as a kind of autonomous rational

[4] Ibid.   [5] Ibid., p. 15.

[6] *Discourse on the Method* [*Discours de la méthode*, 1637], Part One (AT VI 1: CSM I 111).

[7] A. Kenny, *Descartes* (New York: Random House, 1968), pp. 61–2.

[8] *Meditations on First Philosophy* [*Meditationes de prima philosophia*, 1641], First Meditation (AT VII 17: CSM II 12).

[9] *Discourse*, Part One (AT VI 9: CSM I 115).

inquirer, actively exercising his will to discard the baggage of preconceived opinion,[10] and pushing doubt to its limits in order to uncover a solid basis for knowledge. All this appears to suggest a distinctly 'modern' vision of the free and independent thinker, launching himself on his philosophical inquiries by the self-determining power of the will, which, as Descartes put it in his last published work, is essentially active,[11] and 'by its nature so free that it can never be constrained'.[12] On the other hand, we find at the heart of Descartes's metaphysics much that seems to suggest a very different view of the human mind, as utterly dependent and subordinate, capable of finding enlightenment only through humble contemplation of the 'immense light' of its creator.[13] Our will, on this much less modern-looking picture, is operating properly in so far as it passively and indeed automatically acquiesces in what is irresistibly delivered by the light of truth.[14]

This paper will start by looking at the two, seemingly incompatible, accounts of human freedom that Descartes provides in the Fourth Meditation, taking as its starting point Anthony Kenny's highly influential analysis of the relevant text. I shall suggest that Kenny's analysis is essentially correct, but that it leaves some interesting questions unanswered about the place of activity and passivity in the Cartesian account of our pursuit of truth and goodness. An exploration of these matters will lead us into Descartes's account of the role of the will in the sphere of morality and the good life, and, finally, to the question of the respective roles of faith and reason in the Cartesian system.

2. Two-Way Power or Spontaneous Acquiescence?

In ways which are perhaps hard for many philosophers working today to appreciate, Descartes approaches the human predicament from a deeply ingrained sense of our human creatureliness. The reasoning in the Third Meditation,

---

[10] In rejecting preconceived opinions, the meditator decides to 'turn his will wholly in the contrary direction [*voluntate plane in contrarium versa*]': First Meditation (AT VII 22: CSM II 15).

[11] 'Celles que je nomme [les] actions [de l'âme] sont toutes nos volontés, à cause que nous expérimentons qu'elles viennent directement de notre âme, et semblent ne dépendre que d'elle' *Passions of the Soul* [*Les Passions de l'âme*, 1649], art. 17 (AT XII 342: CSM I 335).

[12] *Passions*, art. 41 (AT XI 359: CSM I 343).

[13] Third Meditation, final paragraph (AT VII 52: CSM II 35–6).

[14] The minds of all of us are so moulded by nature that 'whenever we perceive something clearly we spontaneously assent to it and are quite unable to doubt its truth' ('omnium animis a natura impressa est ut quoties aliquid clare percipimus, ei sponte assentiamur, et nullo modo possimus dubitare quin sit verum'). *Principles of Philosophy* [*Principia philosophiae*, 1644], Pt I, art. 43 (AT VIII 21: CSM II 207).

which leads the meditator to awareness of God by reflecting on how his own finite mind could not have produced the idea of an infinite being, is in some ways as Anselmian in its character as the later Fifth Meditation argument, which is in part influenced by Anselm's famous 'ontological' argument.[15] Just as this latter argument, as originally presented by Anselm, depends on God's exceeding our power to grasp him (he is greater than anything that can be conceived),[16] so Descartes's argument in the Third Meditation hinges on the inability of a being that is essentially lacking or deficient[17] to produce the idea of God from its own resources. In both writers there is a sense of dependency, as the mind of 'wretched man' is 'stirred up to the contemplation of a God' whose 'lofty heights it cannot reach'(Anselm),[18] or as the meditator endeavours to 'gaze upon, wonder at and adore' the immense light 'in so far as the eye of the darkened intellect can bear it' (Descartes).[19]

Whether the devout and submissive tone found in these texts is compatible with the proper goals of philosophical inquiry is a fascinating question which there is no space to explore here.[20] For our present purposes, the focus on 'creatureliness' sets the scene for a proper understanding of the Cartesian approach to human freedom. Having established his divine authorship,

---

[15] Descartes argues that a supremely perfect being cannot lack the perfection of existence (AT VII 66: CSM II 46), while Anselm argues that something than which nothing greater can be conceived cannot exist merely in the understanding (*Proslogion* [1077–8], ch. 2). These formulations are, of course, very far from identical. Nevertheless, despite Descartes's efforts to assert the originality of his own approach, the discussion in the First Replies shows that he was fully familiar with the original Anselmian formulation, and Thomas's criticism of it, so the general influence of Anselm's reasoning is hard to deny. See First Replies, AT VII 115 ff.: CSM II 82 ff., and Aquinas, *Summa Theologiae* [1266–73], Ia. qu. 2, art. 1.

[16] 'id quo nihil maius cogitari potest'; *Proslogion*, ch. 2.

[17] 'How could I understand that I doubted or desired—that is lacked something—and that I was not wholly perfect, unless there were in me some idea of a more perfect being which enabled me to recognize my own defects by comparison?' Third Meditation, AT VII 46: CSM II 31.

[18] Anselm's 'excitatio mentis ad contemplandum Deum' is addressed to 'wretched' or 'insignificant' man (*homuncio*), and ends with the humble disclaimer: 'Non tento, Domine, penetrare altitudinem tuam, quia nullatenus comparo illi intellectum meum.' *Proslogion*, ch. 1.

[19] 'immensi hujus luminis pulchritudinem, quantum caligantis ingenii mei acies ferre poterit, intueri, admirari, adorare.' Third Meditation (AT VII 52: CSM II 36). The element of 'devoutness' manifested here and elsewhere in Descartes's philosophy is something that many modern anglophone commentators systematically ignore. For more on this, see J. Cottingham, 'The Desecularization of Descartes', forthcoming in N. Jacobs and C. Firestone (eds), *Rethinking the Enlightenment* (Notre Dame, Ind.: University of Notre Dame Press, 2010).

[20] Some may be tempted to answer 'Of course it isn't!', but the issue is more complex. Granted, philosophy, the 'love of wisdom', is essentially connected to the pursuit of truth; but it is not clear that all truth is necessarily such as to require detached and dispassionate scrutiny for its proper apprehension. See further J. Cottingham, *The Spiritual Dimension* (Cambridge: Cambridge University Press, 2005), ch. 1, §3.

the meditator immediately affirms that this supports the (traditional Judaeo-Christian) conception that we are made in the 'image and likeness' of God.[21] One might expect the Cartesian 'rationalist' to identify the key similarity here as residing in our power of reason—the 'natural light' in each soul that somehow derives from the 'immense light' of the Deity. But Descartes in fact goes on to insist that it is 'above all in virtue of the *will* that I bear the image and likeness of God'. Descartes explains that God's will, though infinitely more efficacious, more informed, and ranging over vastly more objects, nevertheless 'does not seem any greater than mine when considered in the essential and strict sense'.[22] This a direct reprise of a thesis of Anselm, who argues in his *De Libero Arbitrio* that although a vast distance separates the free will of humans from that of God, 'yet the definition of freedom expressed in the word ought to be identical'.[23] Divine freedom and human freedom are, as far as their essential nature goes, the same.

If humans are in some sense 'divinely' free, one might expect this sense to be explicated in terms of the unrestricted *power* of the will—especially since in discussing God's freedom in other texts Descartes lays great emphasis on the power of his will.[24] But in his conception of freedom Descartes was also influenced by a long tradition which had linked freedom not so much to power as to moral *perfection* or rectitude. Anselm is again a key figure here, for whom the definition of freedom does not include the power of sinning—or else, he argues, we should have to say that the good angels and God have no freedom, 'which it is impious to say'.[25] Thomas Aquinas takes a similar line when he argues that the redeemed in heaven, though wholly free, no longer have the ability to will evil: 'Where there is no defect in apprehending there can be no volition for evil.'[26] And in general, the standard line in Aquinas is that

[21] 'The mere fact that God created me is a very strong basis for believing that I am made in his image and likeness.' Third Meditation (AT VII 51: CSM II 35). The notion goes back to Genesis 1:26–7. For the distinction between the terms 'image' and 'likeness', see Aquinas, *Summa Theologiae* Ia, qu. 93, esp. arts. 1 and 9.

[22] 'in se formaliter & praecise spectata'; Fourth Meditation, AT VII 57: CSM II 40.

[23] 'Quamvis differat liberum arbitrium hominum a libero arbitrio Dei...definitio tamen hujus libertatis in utriusque, secundum hoc nomen, eadem debet esse.' Anselm, *De Libero Arbitrio* [c.1084], ch. 1.

[24] In God there is 'no difference between essence and power'. Letter to More of 15 April 1649 (AT V 343: CSMK 373). See also letter to Mersenne of 27 May 1630 (AT I 152: CSM 25), and *Conversation with Burman* [1648] (AT V 160: CSMK 343).

[25] *De Libero Arbitrio*, ch 1. Sophie Berman, in an illuminating discussion of this passage, comments: 'the capacity to sin, when added to the will, diminishes freedom, and the lack of the capacity augments it, so that nothing is freer than a will which cannot fall from rectitude into sin'. 'Human Free Will in Anselm and Descartes', *Saint Anselm Journal* 2/1 (Fall 2004), §I.

[26] *Quaestiones disputatae de veritate* [1256–9], 22, 6. See further E. Stump, *Aquinas* (London: Routledge, 2003), ch. 9, p. 299.

freedom does not require alternative possibilities (the ability to do otherwise). Freedom, he argues, 'is opposed to the necessity of coercion, but not to the necessity of natural inclination'.[27]

It is with this background in mind that we must read the crucial text in the Fourth Meditation where Descartes explicates his conception of human freedom.

For the will simply consists in our ability to do or not do something (that is, to affirm or deny, to pursue or avoid); or rather, it consists simply in the fact that when the intellect puts something forward, we are moved to affirm or deny or to pursue or avoid it in such a way that we do not feel ourselves to be determined by any external force. For in order to be free, there is no need for me to be capable of going in each of two directions; on the contrary, the more I incline in one direction—either because I clearly understand that reasons of truth and goodness point that way, or because of a divinely produced disposition of my inmost thought—the freer is my choice. Neither divine grace nor natural knowledge ever diminishes freedom; on the contrary, they increase and strengthen it.[28]

The passage has puzzled commentators, because it seems to start by defining freedom as a two-way power (to x or not to x), and then immediately appears to contradict that by saying that 'there is no need' for such a two-way power, but on the contrary all that is necessary is a spontaneous and unconstrained movement of the will[29] following on clear apprehension of 'reasons of truth and goodness' (what the schoolmen had called 'freedom of spontaneity').

In Kenny's masterly discussion of this passage, he notes the tension and interprets Descartes as saying (i) that freewill *often* (when we do *not* have clear and distinct perception) consists in the two-way power to assent or

---

[27] Ibid. Compare *Summa Theologiae* Ia, qu. 82: 'Natural necessity does not take away the freedom of the will.'

[28] 'quia tantum in eo consistit, quod idem vel facere vel non facere (hoc est affirmare vel negare, prosequi vel fugere) possumus, vel potius in eo tantum, quod ad id quod nobis ab intellectu proponitur affirmandum vel negandum, sive prosequendum vel fugiendum, ita feramur, ut a nulla vi externa nos ad id determinari sentiamus. Neque enim opus est me in utramque partem ferri posse, ut sim liber, sed contra, quo magis in unam propendeo, sive quia rationem veri & boni in ea evidenter intelligo, sive quia Deus intima cogitationis meae ita disponit, tanto liberius illam eligo; nec sane divine gratia, nec naturalis cognitio unquam imminuunt libertatem, sed potius augent & corroborant.' AT VII 57–8: CSM II 40. The translation is from my revised one-volume edition of Descartes' *Meditations*, Cambridge, 1996.

[29] I am inclined to agree with Michelle Beyssade (contra Kenny) that the Latin phrase 'ita feramur' in the passage just quoted 'is not here used in a passive sense, but is employed in a manner corresponding to the middle voice in Greek: 'middle', because, despite its grammatically passive form, it has an active sense, which corresponds to the reflexive form in French [so that] the correct French rendering would be *se porter* as distinct from *être porté*. M. Beyssade, 'Descartes's Doctrine of Freedom', in J. Cottingham (ed.), *Reason, Will and Sensation* (Oxford: Oxford University Press, 1994), ch. 10, pp. 177–206, at p. 194. It is significant that in the 1647 French translation of the *Meditations, feramur* is rendered by the active expression, *nous agissons* (AT IX 46).

not, but *sometimes* (when we *do* perceive clearly) consists only in liberty of spontaneity; and further (ii) that the latter is all that is essential to it.[30] As we shall see in the next section, part (ii) of this requires some qualification (since a full account of how Cartesian freedom operates needs to introduce a further dimension to our freewill). As for part (i) of Kenny's interpretation, this seems to me entirely correct, though to explain why Descartes expressed himself in the somewhat curious way he did, we need to place the quotation in its exact context. As we have just seen, the whole passage is supposed to be an explication of the sense in which human freewill, considered in its essential nature, is identical with God's (the conjunction 'for', Latin *quia*, which opens the passage, makes it unavoidable that what follows is supposed to be an elucidation of the 'divine' aspect of human freedom just referred to in the previous sentence). Descartes's train of thought, I suggest, leads him naturally to start by interpreting this 'divine' aspect in terms of an unlimited power—the power to *x* or not to *x* (and we know from other texts that he does indeed attribute such an unlimited power to God).[31] But he then checks or corrects himself, with the 'Or rather' (Latin *vel potius*) that introduces a revised definition, which moves the emphasis away from power and focuses instead on the Anselmian consideration of the moral perfection or rectitude of the will.[32] Its perfection is that it operates spontaneously, in perfect harmony with the deliverances of the intellect concerning truth and goodness. To assent, automatically and spontaneously, to clearly and distinctly perceived truth is no diminution of freedom, Descartes insists, but an 'increase and strengthening' of it. As he puts it a paragraph later, recounting his reasoning in the Cogito, 'I *could not but judge* that something I understood so clearly was true, but this was not because I was compelled to judge by some external force, but because a great light in the intellect was accompanied by a great inclination in the will.'[33]

Comparisons between divine and human attributes are always problematic, for many reasons, but especially because of the traditional doctrine of the divine simplicity and unity, which Descartes accepted. For God, intellect and will are one and the same, and (says Descartes) 'He always understands and wills all

---

[30] A. Kenny, 'Descartes on the Will', in R. J. Butler (ed.), *Cartesian Studies* (Oxford: Blackwell, 1972), ch. 1, pp. 1–31, at p. 18.

[31] See especially *Meditations*, Sixth Replies, AT VII 432: CSM II 291, to be discussed later.

[32] 'The liberty of the will is the capacity of preserving rectitude of the will for the sake of rectitude itself.' Anselm, *De Libero Arbitrio*, ch. 3.

[33] 'ex magna luce in intellectu magna consequuta est propensio in voluntate'; AT VII 59: CSM II 41.

things by means of a single identical and perfectly simple act.'[34] We humans cannot of course aspire to anything like this (perhaps we cannot even grasp what it would be like for a being to enjoy such unity and simplicity);[35] but in the case of clearly and distinctly perceived truths, there can at least be, even in the human case, a kind of perfect harmony between intellect and will. When I apprehend such propositions as 'Cogito ergo sum', or 'two plus three equals five',[36] my perception of the truths in question is accompanied by an automatic and unavoidable assent or affirmation.[37] There is no greater perfection that can be imagined than to have one's voluntary assent inextricably linked to fully clear and adequate intellectual perception in this way; and it makes perfect sense, in Descartes's terms, to see this as the kind of freedom that discloses our human nature as bearing the image and likeness of God, in whom intellect and will are united.

Humans are, however, unlike God in that there are many things they do *not* perceive clearly and distinctly. Here there is a two-way power, to 'plump', indifferently, for one or another of two alternatives (for example, I may say: 'yes, the universe had a beginning in time'; or 'no, it did not'). Is this a quasi-divine power? Clearly not, for many reasons. In the first place, there is a risk of plumping for the wrong answer; and even should my choice happen to be correct, it will be a matter of luck.[38] So what is involved in my power of choice in such cases can hardly be a perfection, but rather, as Descartes puts it 'a defect in knowledge or a kind of negation'.[39] The very fact that the will in such cases is operating 'on its own', as it were, instead of in tandem with the perceptions of the intellect, is a sign of its outreaching its proper function—something Descartes identifies as the very cause of error and sin. So

[34] *Principles*, Pt I, art. 23.

[35] The simplicity of God, whereby he understands and wills by a single act, is among those truths about God that Descartes says we can understand (*intelligere*) but not grasp (*comprehendere*) or conceive (*concipere*). See *Conversation with Burman*, AT V 165: CSMK 347, and (for discussion of the distinction between understanding and grasping) J. Cottingham (ed.), *Descartes' Conversation with Burman* (Oxford: Clarendon, 1976), p. 76.

[36] The arithmetical proposition is the other example Descartes gives as ranking equally with the Cogito in the Third Meditation (AT VII 36: CSM II 25).

[37] So much so that Spinoza makes a plausible case for saying that intellect and will are really one and the same. Benedict Spinoza, *Ethics* [*Ethica more geometrico demonstrata*, c.1665], Pt II, prop. 49 Cor. See further J. Cottingham, 'The Intellect, the Will and the Passions: Spinoza's Critique of Descartes', *Journal of the History of Philosophy* 26/2 (April 1988), pp. 239–57, reprinted in Cottingham, *Cartesian Reflections* (Oxford: Oxford University Press, 2008), ch. 10.

[38] 'If I go for the alternative that is false, then obviously I shall be in error; if I take the other side, then it is by pure chance that I arrive at the truth, and I shall still be at fault [since my determination of the truth is not based on intellectual perception].' Fourth Meditation, AT VII 60: CSM II 41.

[39] 'defectus sive negatio quaedam'; AT VII 58: CSM II 40.

to be 'indifferent' between two alternatives (i.e. to be in a state where I can see no clear reason that would generate unavoidable assent to one rather than the other) is, as Descartes puts it, the very 'lowest grade of freedom'.[40]

The upshot of all this is that our will sometimes has, like God's, the power of unrestricted self-determination; but since, when we are deciding what to affirm or to pursue, this power arises only in cases where we are ignorant of the relevant reasons or their relative strength, it turns out to be, in the human case, not a power to rejoice in, but simply a recipe for error. But our will also has the natural disposition to work in total harmony with the clear perceptions of the intellect, and here it approaches the unity and simplicity of the divine mind, in such a way as to qualify as a genuine perfection.

Nevertheless, if this is Descartes's meaning, one wonders if he is not glossing over a radical gulf between what constitutes the perfection of the will in the divine and the human cases. Although I have described the will working 'in harmony' with the intellect when we are assenting to clear and distinct perceptions, phenomenologically speaking what happens may seem more like passivity than activity. The assent of the will 'follows' (*consequitur*) the perception of the intellect, but it does so irresistibly and automatically, without, it seems, the agent having any sense of being in control of events. It is true that the assent is 'spontaneous'—a kind of free-flowing outward movement of approval which is not constrained or 'determined by any external force'. But we do not seem to have a picture of an active, self-determining agent so much as that of an agent who is *responsive* to reasons of truth and goodness that have to be acknowledged whether we like it or not.

To be sure, being naturally responsive to the right reasons (of truth and goodness) is no bad thing. And the 'spontaneity' involved serves to mark out a genuine and important difference from those cases where we are externally constrained (for example by drugs, or hypnotism) to choose a given alternative irrespective of its merit. So 'freedom of enlightenment' (*liberté éclairée*)[41] is a freedom worth having. But the worry about passivity still remains. We may be uncomfortable about thinking of ourselves as 'epistemic robots', programmed to assent to certain truths (or to judge certain goods worthy of pursuit). And indeed Descartes himself seems to acknowledge this elsewhere, when he links freedom to responsibility, and refers to that 'supreme perfection' in humans,

---

[40] 'infimus gradus libertatis'; ibid. As many commentators have noted, Descartes's use of the term 'indifference' in discussing the will can give rise to confusion; I shall return to this point later.

[41] This is the apt label of the great French Cartesian scholar Ferdinand Alquié. See F. Alquié (ed.), *Descartes, Œuvres philosophiques* (Paris: Garnier, 1963–73), vol. ii, p. 461.

whereby they are 'the authors of their actions and deserving of praise for what they do'. He goes on:

We do not praise automatons for accurately producing all the movements they were designed to perform, because the production of these movements occurs necessarily...By the same principle, when we embrace the truth, our doing so voluntarily is *much more to our credit than would be the case if we could not do otherwise*.[42]

The upshot is that Descartes himself seems to hanker for a more active, more autonomous conception of human freedom than his exposition in the Fourth Meditation apparently allows for. To see how he provides the resources for this stronger conception of human freedom (strong enough to support epistemic and moral responsibility), we need to look elsewhere.

3. A Real and Positive Power of the Will: 'Executive Freedom'

Early critics of the *Meditations* were worried by the 'spontaneity' approach in the Fourth Meditation, because it detached freedom from the absolute two-way power which seemed to them essential, at least for divine freedom. The concept of *indifference*, they pointed out, which Descartes had described as not belonging to the perfection of the will but only to its imperfection (namely, when we are ignorant of the reasons favouring one choice over another), had traditionally been associated with the absolute power of God, who was standardly considered to be entirely free or 'indifferent'—for example in deciding either to create or not create the world. But his choice was clearly not an arbitrary plumping in the absence of reasons. 'Who doubts', asked these critics, 'that God has always perceived with the clearest vision what he should do or refrain from doing?' So surely, they insisted, clear and distinct perception should not be thought to remove indifference of choice.[43]

On the terminological point, concerning 'indifference', Descartes readily admitted, in his reply to these critics and elsewhere, that his own usage might have been somewhat confusing. If indifference (as per the Fourth Meditation) means wavering through ignorance and then arbitrarily plumping for one alternative over the other, this is indeed the lowest grade of freedom, greatly

---

[42] *Principles*, Pt I, art. 37 (AT VIII 18−19: CSM I 205); emphasis supplied.
[43] *Meditations*, Sixth Objections, AT VII 416−17: CSM II 280−1.

surpassed by the spontaneous assent to truth where ignorance disappears and one alternative is clearly seen as correct. But the 'indifference' found in God's will is a different matter—it is a kind of supreme and unrestricted power of the will. Since God is pure activity, nothing is really prior to his will: it makes no sense to speak of anything being 'thought of in the divine intellect as true or good prior to his will to make it so'. And hence

the supreme indifference found in God is the supreme indication of his omnipotence. But as for humans, we find that the nature of all goodness and truth is already determined by God, and our will cannot tend towards anything else . . . We are never indifferent except when we do not know which of the two alternatives is the better or truer . . . Hence the indifference which belongs to human freedom is very different from that which belong to divine freedom.[44]

This clears up the terminological point, but it does, once more, place a radical gulf between human and divine freedom. If goodness and truth is already, as it were, laid out for us, waiting for us to respond to it, by accurate intellectual perception and the automatic assent that follows, then is Descartes saying we have to give up any aspiration to 'freedom of indifference' in the stronger, positive sense in which it is ascribed to God?

Some might be inclined to respond by saying that if we are being urged to give up this 'stronger', more divine kind of freedom, so much the better, since it does not make much sense anyway. The ideal of active self-determination ascribed to God, which we humans fall short of, is not easy to understand, because we cannot really grasp what it could mean for a mind to will and to understand by means of a single simple act. In the case of the truths of logic (which Descartes regarded as decreed by God's will),[45] it is not easy to see how something that is created by an act of will could also be a *truth* for its creator in any recognizable sense. In the ethical as opposed to the logical sphere, where we are considering the eternal moral truths such as that cruelty is wrong, things hardly seem easier. Perhaps what is envisaged is something along the lines of what Kant meant when he spoke of the autonomy of a 'rational nature', as that aspect of the will whereby it must be considered as *selbstgesetzgebend* ('giving the law to itself').[46] But even if such a notion is intelligible, there can clearly be no question of such autonomy in the human case. Human beings cannot

---

[44] *Meditations*, Sixth Replies, AT VII 432–3: CSM II 292.

[45] 'From all eternity He willed and understood them to be, and by that very fact he created them.' Letter to Mersenne of 27 May 1630 (AT I 152: CSMK 25).

[46] *Groundwork for the Metaphysic of Morals* [*Grundlegung zur Metaphysik der Sitten*, 1785], ch. 2; Akademie edn (Berlin: Reimer/De Gruyter, 1900–), vol. iv, pp. 436, 431; trans. T. E. Hill Jr and A. Zweig (Oxford: Oxford University Press, 2003), pp. 236, 232.

(despite the later confused fantasy of Nietzsche)[47] create value by an act of will, as if something could be made to be good or bad merely by a decision to pursue or avoid it. For all his talk of the 'divine' nature of human freedom, would it not be far clearer and more coherent for Descartes to abandon this notion, and rest content, as indeed he appears to be doing in this passage from the Sixth Replies, with the more modest conception of 'freedom of enlightenment', where the fantasy of self-determination gives way to rational acquiescence or allegiance to the reasons of truth and goodness that constrain our assent once we grasp them properly?

Certainly, freedom of enlightenment is, and remains, a central (and sound) plank in Descartes's account of human freedom. But he did also insist that the human will possesses what he called, in a letter to the Jesuit Denis Mesland, a 'real and positive power of self-determination' (une puissance réelle et positive de se déterminer).[48] As Kenny has elegantly shown in his analysis of this letter, this does not contradict the earlier account of spontaneous and automatic assent to clearly and distinctly perceived truths. It emerges from the letter that we do enjoy a two-way power to determine whether we assent or not, but that the only way this can be done is by failing to attend to the relevant reasons. 'As soon as our attention turns from the reasons that show us that the thing is good for us . . . we can call up before our mind some other reason to make us doubt it, and so suspend our judgement.'[49]

Focusing on the notion of attention seems to me to provide Descartes with a convincing way of vindicating the kind of 'active' freedom necessary for human epistemic and moral responsibility, without forcing him into a doubtfully coherent model of quasi-divine 'creative liberty'. The importance of attention in Descartes's analysis of the workings of the mind can scarcely be exaggerated. Right from the construction of the foundations of his system, when considering how far doubt can be pushed (might I not go wrong even in the simplest matters—even adding two and three or counting the sides of

[47] Nietzsche envisages a 'new philosopher' with a spirit 'strong enough to revalue and invert eternal values'. Friedrich Nietzsche, Beyond Good and Evil [Jenseits von Gut und Böse, 1886], trans. W. Kaufmann (New York: Random House, 1966), §203. Some of the relevant considerations against the Nietzschean position are raised in my The Spiritual Dimension (Cambridge: Cambridge University Press, 2005), ch. 3, esp. §2. See also sect. 2 of my 'Impartiality and Ethical Formation', forthcoming in B. Feltham and J. Cottingham (eds), Partiality and Impartiality (Oxford: Oxford University Press).

[48] Letter to Mesland of 2 May 1644 (AT IV 116: CSMK 234).

[49] Ibid. See also Kenny, 'Descartes on the Will', pp. 23–4. Kenny goes on to argue, very convincingly to my mind, that a later letter (supposedly to Mesland) of 9 February 1645, arguing that 'it is always open to us to hold back from pursuing a clearly known good' (AT IV 173: CSMK 245), contains nothing that cannot be reconciled with the position taken in the earlier letter, namely that the only way to avoid assenting to a clearly perceived truth is by failure of attention.

a square?), Descartes makes a crucial distinction between what can happen at one remove, as it were, and what can happen *'whenever I turn to the truths themselves'*.[50] I may entertain radical doubts about my ability to apprehend mathematical truths, but when I actually focus on 'two plus three equals five', then the natural (divinely created) propensity of the mind to assent to clear and distinct truths kicks in, and I cannot but spontaneously and immediately accept the truth of the proposition. The time-dimension is crucial: just as the certainty of the Cogito in the Second Meditation lasts only 'as long as it is put forward by me and conceived in my mind' (*quoties profertur vel mente concipitur*),[51] so the determination of the will to assent to the clear deliverances of the intellect lasts only so long as I am focused on the relevant propositions (*quoties ad ipsas res ... me converto*).[52] Now the crucial point is that this focusing is a positive act of the will, within our direct voluntary control. This helps to explain how, for Descartes, human beings are more than doxastic robots, obeying the programs of their divinely designed minds. They are truly in control of the circumstances of their search for the truth, since the irresistibility of the natural light will always be contingent on their own free choice as to how far they keep the light focused.[53]

So the power to attend, or to relax or divert our attention, is a basic power of the will that turns out to be crucial for the exercise of some of our most important human intellectual capacities. Shifting the focus to this basic power takes us to a more fundamental level of freedom than both kinds of freedom hitherto discussed: on the one hand, the freedom to choose between alternatives (or to accept the truth of this proposition rather than that); and on the other hand the 'freedom of spontaneity' which is manifest in the easy flow of a straightforward judgement guided by reason and free from external interference. Instead it takes us to the kind of very simple power that we exercise when someone says 'Consider this piece of news!', or 'Picture an orange cut in half!', or 'Think of a number less than five!' If one wants a label to distinguish this kind of freedom from both freedom of spontaneity and freedom of 'indifference', one might decide to call it *executive freedom*.[54] Notice, moreover, that when I exercise such a power, I am aware of being its

---

[50] AT VII 36: CSM II 25.   [51] AT VII 25: CSM II 17.
[52] Third Meditation, AT VII 36: CSM II 25.
[53] For further discussion of the notion of 'doxastic responsibility' in Descartes, see my 'Descartes and the Voluntariness of Belief', in *The Monist* 85/3 (October 2002), pp. 343–60, repr. in Cottingham, *Cartesian Reflections*, ch. 11.
[54] Executive freedom does, to be sure, have the kind of spontaneous and unconstrained 'flow' associated with freedom of spontaneity, and may also be linked to the ability to decide otherwise associated with freedom of indifference, but unlike both the former and the latter it is not concerned with the making of judgements.

'author' in a direct and immediate way that seems to allow no room for doubt or quibble. 'Concentrate on this right-angled triangle.' Unless I am exhausted or drugged or otherwise incapacitated, I am simply free to do it (or refuse to do it), 'just like that'.[55]

I suggest, then, that underpinning all Descartes's discussions of the various types and degrees of freedom so far examined is a more basic notion, that of 'executive freedom', which he took to be something absolutely simple and self-evident. This is consistent with many of his remarks about the axiomatic nature of our freedom—remarks that cannot without strain be applied to the other kinds of freedom so far discussed. Our freewill, he said, was *per se nota* (or, in French, *se connaît sans preuve*); it is 'one of the first and most common notions that are innate in us'.[56] Moreover, it has the kind of self-evidence that is directly attested by our inner experience: We just have to 'go down deep into ourselves', and we will simply see that the our will is 'absolute and perfect'.[57] Or again, 'we have inner awareness of our freedom'.[58] It is a freedom, furthermore, that is manifested both in simple 'mentalistic' cases, like attending to a mathematical proposition, and also in the performance (again, barring incapacitating circumstances) of simple bodily actions ('look over here!'). There is for Descartes not quite the same immediacy in the case of bodily movements, since the efficacy of our volitions (unlike what happens in the purely mental case) has to be mediated by physiological events (in the brain and nervous system); but he is quite comfortable about citing physical actions as equally good illustrations of the self-evident freedom of the will, which is 'by its nature so free that it cannot be constrained'.[59]

Once the importance of this basic executive freedom has been grasped, it becomes easy to see how Descartes was so confident about our having the kind of authorship of our actions that legitimates responsibility, praise, and

[55] As Descartes sometimes puts it, such volitions are acts which proceed 'directly from the soul'; or as we might say, they come directly from me, so that I am their author in an immediate and straightforward sense. See *Passions of the Soul*, art. 17 (AT XII 342: CSM I 335).

[56] *Principles*, Pt I, art. 39.

[57] 'descendat modo unusquisque in sepetipsum et experiatur annon perfectam et absolutam habeat voluntatem'; *Conversation with Burman*, AT V 159: CSMK 342.

[58] 'intime conscii sumus nostrae libertatis'; ibid. See also Cottingham (ed.), *Descartes' Conversation with Burman*, pp. xxxvi ff. Compare Third Replies: 'I have made no assumptions about freedom beyond what all of us experience within ourselves' (AT VII 191: CSM II 134).

[59] *Passions of the Soul*, art. 41. According to Descartes's somewhat bizarre theory of psycho-physical interaction, the soul has the direct power 'simply by willing' to bring about movements in the pineal gland, just as, in the purely mental case, it has the power to, for example, attend to a given mathematical truth. For an illuminating discussion of Descartes's views on the functioning of the will in relation to the body, see D. Clarke, *Descartes's Theory of the Mind* (Oxford: Clarendon Press, 2003), pp. 151 ff.

blame. Because our divinely bestowed propensity to assent to clearly perceived truth is dependent on exercising our freedom to attend or otherwise to the relevant propositions, humans enjoy a genuine responsibility for their beliefs. They retain the status of autonomous and active agents, who can be praised for opening themselves to the truth, or blamed for failing to keep focused on it. This autonomy, of course, has a darker side. Since the infallibly truth-obedient propensity of the mind depends on the capriciously attentive power of the will, the freedom which God or Nature[60] gave us was bestowed at a price—the price of allowing the possibility of evil, whether epistemic error or moral transgression, into the world. The former, and the strategies for avoiding it, are of course the main theme of the Fourth Meditation, while the latter and how to guard against it are a principal theme of Descartes's last work, *The Passions of the Soul*. It is to the role of the will in the moral sphere that we shall now turn, in the final section of this exploration of Descartes's account of freedom.

4. Freedom, Moral Goodness, and Faith

Men preferred the darkness to the light, says the Fourth Evangelist,[61] implying what is glaringly and sadly obvious, that humans always have the ability to turn away from the good and the true. As we have seen, what Descartes adds to this ancient theme is that this can happen with regard to clearly perceived truths only, as it were, when we fail to attend, or relax the attention, letting the relevant propositions slip out of focus. But how can we prevent things going awry in the practical sphere of moral action and the conduct of life?

In the case of theoretical reason, Descartes offers a very simple recipe for the avoidance of error: 'remember to withhold judgement when the truth is not clearly perceived'.[62] In the practical sphere, this will evidently not work, as he had noted as early as the *Discourse*. The exigencies of ordinary human life, and the need to make prompt decisions to cope with everyday contingencies, would mean we should be paralysed, or starve, if we made decisions based only on clear and adequate intellectual perception.[63] (As David Hume aptly observed, there is no guarantee—at least not one that the mind can obtain

---

[60] The Spinozistic sounding phrase 'God or Nature' is in fact Cartesian: see *Principles of Philosophy*, Pt I, art. 28. See further J. Cottingham, *The Rationalists* (Oxford: Oxford University Press, 1988), pp. 92 ff.

[61] 'êgapêsan hoi anthrôpoi mallon to skotos ê to phôs'; John 3:19.

[62] Fourth Meditation (AT VII 61–2: CSM II 43).

[63] 'In everyday life we must often act without delay ... when it is not in our power to discern the truest opinions.' *Discourse*, Part Three, AT VI 25: CSM I 123.

by carefully focusing on the relevant propositions—that the bread I ate at lunchtime will not poison me at supper.[64]) Provisionally then, until we have worked out a moral system based on clear and distinct perceptions of the good, we may have to rely on conventional moral codes and probabilistic rules of thumb in working out how best to live.

Nevertheless, eventually we should, in Descartes's view, be able to work out a rational blueprint for the good life.[65] As we have seen, Descartes maintained in the Fourth Meditation that the intellect had the power to clearly and distinctly perceive 'reasons of goodness' no less than 'reasons of truth' (and that once clearly perceived, these truths irresistibly generate the assent of the will). So for Descartes, there is at least the possibility of our being able to have access to a complete science of morals, an integrated structure of principles for the conduct of life, just as much as is the case with the other branches of the Cartesian tree of knowledge, which grow organically out of the same metaphysical roots.[66] And those who are careful and attentive enough can take advantage of that knowledge by carefully focusing on the relevant principles in their day-to-day lives.

There is, however, a special problem about the practical implementation of this programme. As noted already, the irresistibility of the natural light is in place only so long as the will employs its 'executive' power of remaining focused on the relevant truths. So the key to the moral life is a 'firm and constant resolution to use our freedom well'.[67] It is good, as Descartes wrote to Mesland, 'to pay attention and thus ensure that our will follows so promptly the light of our understanding that it is in no way indifferent'.[68] But remaining so focused is particularly hard in the domain of ordinary life and action, because of the operation of the *passions*—the emotions and feelings arising from our embodied nature as human beings[69]—which may exert a distracting influence. So although the intellect may clearly perceive that x is a better course of action than y, the lesser good involved in y may be represented (as a result of lust, or ambition, or greed, for example) in an alluring light which diverts our concentration:

Often passion makes us believe certain things to be much better and more desirable than they are; then, when we have taken much trouble to acquire them, and in the

[64] David Hume, *An Enquiry concerning Human Understanding* [1748], Sect. IV, pt 2.
[65] As he resoundingly declared in the preface to the French edition of his magnum opus, the *Principles of Philosophy*, the construction of a perfect moral system—*la plus parfaite morale*—was to be the crowning aim of his philosophy. Preface to the 1647 French translation of the *Principles of Philosophy* (AT IXB 14–15: CSM I 186).
[66] Ibid.   [67] *Passions of the Soul*, art. 153, speaking of the master virtue of 'generosity'.
[68] Letter of 2 May 1644 (AT IV 117: CSMK 234).   [69] *Passions of the Soul*, arts. 27–34.

process lost the chance of possessing other more genuine goods, possession of them brings home to us their defects; and thence arise dissatisfaction, regret and remorse.[70]

To counteract the potentially damaging effects of the passions, Descartes (as I have explored at length elsewhere)[71] devised an elaborate strategy for reprogramming them, with the aid of scientific knowledge of their physiological basis. With sufficient ingenuity, he envisaged that the passions could be trained and guided so as to subserve the clear perceptions of the intellect about what is truly valuable, rather than, as so often happens, pulling us off course.[72] This is, in effect, the old Platonic and Stoic dream of the mastery of the more recalcitrant parts of the soul, but in Descartes's vision this goal is realized through drawing on our scientific knowledge of the workings of the nervous system and how those workings are correlated with the operation of the emotions.

The resulting picture appears in many respects to put human beings very much in charge of the pursuit of the good life. Cartesian man seems to emerge as a relatively autonomous being, making use of scientific knowledge to control and channel the emotions, and exercising an unconstrained executive liberty in focusing on the truths disclosed by reason. It is true that all the faculties involved here are seen by Descartes as ultimately bestowed on us by the creator, but the programme for the conduct of life seems to fall almost entirely within the domain of natural reason, in the widest sense of that term, rather than drawing on revelation, or positing any need for religious belief as a key ingredient of a worthwhile human existence. This accords with the undoubted fact that Descartes was a thinker who constructed his philosophy as far as possible without reference to revealed theology, or matters of faith.[73] Nevertheless, I should like to conclude this paper by suggesting that the notion of faith does in fact occupy a legitimate and coherent place within his overall conception of the best life for human beings.

In the Dedicatory Letter prefaced to the first edition of the *Meditations*, Descartes deploys a fairly standard argument that religious faith is an auxiliary

---

[70] Letter to Elizabeth of 1 September 1645 (AT IV 284: CSMK 263–4). Descartes goes on to say that the passions often 'represent the goods to which they tend with greater splendour than they deserve and they make us imagine pleasure to be much greater before we possess them than our subsequent experiences show them to be'.

[71] See J. Cottingham, *Philosophy and the Good Life: Reason and the Passions in Greek, Cartesian and Psychoanalytic Ethics* (Cambridge: Cambridge University Press, 1998), ch. 3.

[72] See for example *Passions of the Soul*, art. 50.

[73] 'I wanted as far as possible to avoid all theological controversies and stay within the limits of natural philosophy.' To Mesland of 2 May 1644 (AT IV 117: CSMK 234). For a general discussion of Descartes's attitude to theology and theologians, see Cottingham, *Descartes' Conversation with Burman*, pp. 115 ff.

to moral virtue because it offers to those struggling to be virtuous the rewards of the afterlife.[74] In view of his subsequent acknowledgement of the difficulties we face in remaining focused on the good, the argument has a clear relevance to his conception of the human moral predicament, and hence may be more than merely a conventional piece of deference to the theologians to whom the letter was addressed. However that may be, there is a more extended, indeed philosophically crucial, discussion of faith, in the second of the sets of Replies published with the *Meditations*, where it emerges as one of the sources of illumination alongside the natural light of reason. Descartes declares that there is for the human mind a 'double source' of clarity or transparency (*duplex claritas sive perspicuitas*), one coming from the natural light, the other from divine grace.[75] The latter, the *lumen supernaturale*,[76] gives rise, no less than the natural light, to the irresistible assent of the intellect. Indeed, the phrasing in the key passage from the Fourth Meditation which we quoted earlier can now be understood better: irresistible assent can be produced *either* by 'clearly perceived reasons of truth and goodness' (the natural light) *or* by a 'divinely produced disposition of my thought' (the supernatural light).[77]

Being open to divine grace, then, can yield illumination which is as valid as the illumination produced by rational cognition of clear and distinctly perceived truths. Yet there is clearly a problem which Descartes needs to face here. The foundation stone of his entire philosophical method is that we should not give our assent to matters that are not clear. Yet the truths of faith (for example the doctrines of the Trinity and the Incarnation) evidently do not come anywhere near the kind of perspicuous self-evidence that applies to the Cogito, say, or the proposition that two plus three makes five. The most Descartes was himself prepared to say about the concept of the Trinity, for example, was that it contained *elements* that were clear (for example, the number three!).[78] So despite the talk of 'illumination', one may complain that Descartes is violating his own fundamental philosophical principles by defending assent to a class of revealed truths. There may, of course, be many motives for religious allegiance to articles of faith, but (so runs the complaint) such allegiance can hardly be presented as virtuous from an epistemic point of view.

A similarly negative view of the epistemic and ethical status of faith has been strongly advanced by Anthony Kenny (not in connection with Descartes, but as a general aspect of his own philosophical outlook, though it has obvious

---

[74] Dedicatory Letter to the Dean and Doctors of the Faculty of Theology at Paris, AT VII 2: CSM II 3.

[75] AT VII 147–8: CSM II 105.   [76] Second Replies, AT VII 148, line 27: CSM II 106.

[77] AT VII 58 lines 1–2: CSM II 40.   [78] *Conversation with Burman*, AT V 165: CSMK 347.

relevance to our present discussion of Descartes). 'In my view,' Kenny argues, 'faith is not a virtue, but a vice, unless certain conditions are fulfilled.' The conditions, he goes on to explain include 'that the existence of God can be rationally established without appeal to faith', and that 'the historical events that are claimed to constitute the divine revelation must be independently established as historically certain—as having the same certainty, say, as that Charles I was beheaded in London, or that Cicero was once consul in Rome'.[79] As far as the first condition goes, Descartes would presumably have claimed to have met it in his proofs in the Third and Fifth Meditations, though it is (to say the least) a debatable question whether they are successful. What of the second condition, and in general of his attitude to the evidence for revealed truths, which cannot by their nature aspire to demonstrative certainty?

Descartes never discusses the historical probabilities of the central events of the Christian faith to which he himself subscribed, but his remarks on the nature of revealed truths suggest he might well have been happy to concede that the evidence for the Resurrection, for example, does not come near to meeting the standards of historical certainty proposed by Kenny. In fact, Descartes was prepared to concede that many revealed truths were not just inadequately evidenced but positively obscure in their content. 'No one has ever denied that the subject matter [of many articles of faith] may be obscure—indeed obscurity itself.' But, he continued, we may still have a 'formal reason', as opposed to a reason based on the clarity of the subject matter, for accepting them:

This formal reason consists in a certain inner light which comes from God, and when we are supernaturally illumined by it we are confident that what is put forward for us to believe has been revealed by God himself. And it is quite impossible for him to lie; this is more certain than any natural light, and is often even more evident because of the light of grace.[80]

If the 'reason' invoked here is supposed to be of the kind which might survive dispassionate and impartial scrutiny by any rational inquirer, then the prospects do not look good. The believer may be subjectively 'confident' that a given article of faith is one which God himself has inclined him, by grace, to accept; but that plainly does not constitute independent rational support for its truth.

In his subsequent comments on the status of faith, and the other 'matters which should be embraced by the will', in the paragraph following that just quoted, Descartes goes on to refer to a distinction he frequently makes

[79] Kenny, *What I Believe*, pp. 59–60.   [80] Second Replies, AT VII 148: CSM II 105.

elsewhere between 'the conduct of life, and the contemplation of the truth'. In the former sphere, he remarks, 'I am very far from believing that we should assent only to what is clearly perceived.'[81] Stephen Menn, in a sensitive interpretation of Descartes's position in this passage, has commented that 'the confidence in revealed truths is analogous to confidence in the other sorts of truth we need for living as happily as possible; just as belief in the nutritive value of food is necessary for my physical health, so belief in the saving value of grace is necessary for my spiritual health, for my general well-being in this world and the next'.[82]

Unfortunately, the analogy on which this implicit defence of Descartes is founded seems not a particularly satisfying one. In the conduct of life, my confidence in certain courses of action, for example eating certain types of food, though not based on 'clear and distinct perception', is at least based on good probabilistic evidence. But in the religious case, we seem to lack anything like similar evidence that assent to the articles of faith is necessary for morally and spiritually healthy life. We have ample grounds for thinking that people who do not eat properly have wretched lives. But (unless we make the question-begging manoeuvre of allowing only a religious life to count as 'spiritually healthy'), religious faith, to judge from ordinary observation, appears to be neither a necessary nor a sufficient condition for a morally and spiritually healthy life. There are many non-believers who lead morally healthy and harmonious lives, and, conversely, many believers who lead disordered and morally dubious lives.

A more plausible defence of the epistemic respectability of faith can be drawn from materials provided by Descartes's contemporary, Blaise Pascal. Pascal, like Kenny, took a dim view of purported logical demonstrations of God, and he would (one may reasonably infer) have taken an equally dim view of basing the claims of faith on historical evidence. We are just not in a position, Pascal argued, to establish any conclusions about the existence and nature of God using the impartial tools of reason.[83] But he maintained that a volitional act of commitment (for example starting to engage in practices of worship) would in due course generate valid faith.[84] On a plausible interpretation of this proposal, what Pascal is suggesting is a deliberate act of opening oneself to

---

[81] AT VII 149: CSM II 106.

[82] S. Menn, *Descartes and Augustine* (Cambridge: Cambridge University Press, 1998), p. 332.

[83] Blaise Pascal, *Pensées* ('Thoughts') [1670], ed. L. Lafuma (Paris: Seuil, 1962), no. 418.

[84] 'You want to cure yourself of unbelief, and you ask for remedies: learn from those who were hampered like you and who now wager all they possess. These are people who know the road you would like to follow; they are cured of the malady for which you seek a cure; so follow them and begin as they did—*by acting as if they believed*, by taking holy water, having masses said, and so on. In the natural course of events this in itself will make you believe, this will train you.' *Pensées*, no 418.

the possibility of receiving divine grace. But this is not a completely irrational 'leap of faith' of a Kierkegaardian kind,[85] since the idea is that the subject *starts engaging in worship from an agnostic perspective* (that such a thing is possible is, interestingly, something that Kenny himself has eloquently argued for in his later work).[86] Such an individual, Pascal argues, may in due course *become* a believer, in virtue of subsequent internal changes that have put him in a position to receive evidence which will be retrospective confirmation that the initial decision to engage in religious praxis was a good one.[87] Although his initial stance may have been neutral or sceptical, further down the line after making the commitment the 'light of grace' or *lumen gratiae* (to use the Cartesian phrase)[88] will disclose evidence that simply was not available before the commitment was made.[89]

So although the Pascalian recommendation to act 'as if you believe' may seem like a piece of irrationality, it is not. There are many other cases where a prior practical commitment has to be made in order to open the subject to the possibility of receiving evidence that may retrospectively confirm the validity of that commitment. The kind of commitment involved in a close personal relationship such as marriage provides one such example: the evidence which will emerge, if all goes well, to establish that the choice was the right one is simply not available 'from the outside', from the standpoint of one coldly requiring prior demonstrative or probabilistic warrant before embarking on the journey.[90] Whether Descartes would have been sympathetic to this Pascalian approach we cannot know. But it is consistent with his assertion of a supernatural light that operates via grace to produce a 'disposition of my inmost

[85] Kierkegaard talks in very different terms from Pascal's, of an existential, and perhaps even contra-rational struggle to maintain a willed act of faith, 'out on the deep, over seventy thousand fathoms of water'. Søren Kierkegaard, *Concluding Unscientific Postscript* [*Afsluttende Uvidenskabelig Efterskrift*, 1846], trans. D. F. Swenson (Princeton: Princeton University Press, 1941), p. 182.

[86] See his account of his 'devout agnosticism' in A. Kenny, 'Worshipping an Unknown God', *Ratio* 19/4 (December 2006), pp. 441–53, repr. in J. Cottingham (ed.), *The Meaning of Theism* (Oxford: Blackwell, 2007), ch. 4.

[87] For this interpretation of Pascal, see Ward Jones, 'Religious Conversion, Self-Deception and Pascal's Wager', *Journal of the History of Philosophy* 36/2 (April 1998), p. 172.

[88] AT VII 148, line 12: CSM II 105.

[89] Such evidence, it should be stressed, is not simply a matter of subjective feeling or conviction. It may, for example, involve glimpsing the presence of God in the sacraments, or in the beauty of the natural world; for more about the status of such intimations, see Alvin Plantinga, 'Religion and Epistemology', in E. Craig (ed.) *Routledge Encyclopedia of Philosophy* (London: Routledge, 1998), vol. viii, p. 214. The facts so accessed are, the believer would say, perfectly objective ones, even though the conditions for accessing them may involve an internal change in the subject. For more on objective truth and subjective accessibility conditions, see J. Cottingham, 'What Difference does it Make? The Nature and Significance of Religious Belief', in *Ratio* 19/4 (December 2006), pp. 401–20, repr. in Cottingham (ed.), *The Meaning of Theism*, ch. 2.

[90] See further Cottingham, *The Spiritual Dimension*, ch. 1, §3.

thoughts' to assent to matters where dispassionate rational scrutiny alone could not reveal the truth.

What, in conclusion, becomes of the 'modern' Cartesian man, striking out independently to establish the truth? The actual Descartes, as we know, retained his religious faith throughout his life, and there is no reason to doubt the genuineness of his convictions. His metaphysical inquiries, as we have seen, though premised on the need for critical rational scrutiny of every stage of the reasoning, nevertheless express a strong sense of the human meditator's dependency on the divine source of truth and goodness whose contemplation 'enables us to know the greatest joy of which we are capable in this life'.[91] In his account of our freedom, he laid emphasis on our spontaneous and irresistible assent generated by the 'reasons of truth and goodness' that proceed from that source, while at the same time preserving our human responsibility by making that assent dependent on the individual's power to attend to the light, or turn away from it. The overall picture of our human freedom is an attractive and coherent one,[92] which is all of a piece with its author's theistic worldview. And if the wholehearted adoption of that worldview required him to take on board truths of faith which could not be validated by detached rational scrutiny, such commitment can, if the argument of this closing section has been right, be defended as consistent with the demands of philosophical integrity. For Cartesian autonomy, in the end, is the autonomy of a being who recognizes its own limitations; it lies in the proper exercise of reason and will by dependent subjects whose ultimate welfare depends on orienting ourselves towards a truth and goodness we did not create.

---

[91] Third Meditation, final sentence.

[92] Notwithstanding some confusions and unclarities in some of his formulations; see, for example, those exposed by Kenny in 'Descartes on the Will', p. 31.

11

Descartes's Theory of Perceptual Cognition and the Question of Moral Sensibility

STEPHEN GAUKROGER

1. Introduction

It is appropriate that a collection celebrating the work of Anthony Kenny should be entitled 'Mind, Method, and Morality', and I would like to bring out the connections between these three aspects of themes in Descartes, by focusing on his account of perceptual cognition. That the first two themes should be at issue is to be expected; but there is a degree of integration in Descartes's thought which has been generally neglected, and which, I shall argue, enables us to move from cognitive to affective states, and thereby to questions of morality.

It is important to remind ourselves at the outset that, in the eighteenth and nineteenth centuries, Descartes was often treated as a dangerous materialist, largely because, in the wake of La Mettrie's *L'Homme Machine*, there was a widespread perception that his mechanistic account of the psycho-physiology of animals might be applied to human beings, as La Mettrie had urged.[1] Descartes was not an advocate of a materialist theory of mind,[2] but he did have a materialist and mechanist theory of animal cognition, which also covered that range of psycho-physiological functions that humans share with animals, and which, I shall argue, shaped his account of distinctively human perceptual knowledge.

---

[1] See the Introduction to S. Gaukroger, *Descartes, An Intellectual Biography* (Oxford: Clarendon Press, 1995), and, for more detail, L. Cohen Rosenfield, *From Beast-Machine to Man-Machine* (New York: Octagon, 1968) and A. Vartanian, *La Mettrie's L'Homme Machine* (Princeton: Princeton University Press, 1960).

[2] Contrary to H. Caton, *The Origin of Subjectivity* (New Haven: Yale University Press, 1973) and R. B. Carter, *Descartes's Medical Philosophy* (Baltimore: Johns Hopkins University Press, 1983).

We can distinguish four types of (putative) cognitive operations/states in Descartes's general treatment of cognition: reflex behaviour, animal perceptual cognition, perceptual cognition by an embodied mind, and intellectual cognition. The third of these has occasionally been confused with the fourth, as in occasionalist doctrines in the seventeenth century,[3] and in the twentieth century in Ryle's famous doctrine of 'the ghost in the machine'.[4] These both tend to treat cognition by an embodied mind in terms of a mind which has the typical characteristics of a disembodied mind but which interacts with a body to which it is somehow mysteriously connected.[5] There is also a much more widespread conflation of animal cognition with reflex behaviour, with the result that the former is implicitly or explicitly treated as consisting solely in reflex response.

I suggest that we shall get a better understanding of Descartes's account of perceptual cognition if we pay close attention to two things.[6] First, reflex behaviour and intellectual cognition are of marginal interest as far as perceptual cognition is concerned, as we shall see: the former because it is barely a case of cognition at all, and the latter because intellectual cognition and perceptual cognition are distinct and separate kinds of operation in Descartes. So our focus must be on the second and third cases: animal cognition and embodied cognition. Second, instead of taking human cognition as the reference case and extrapolating to animal cognition, I propose we start with animal cognition, which is literally mindless on Descartes's account, and explore just what types of perceptual cognitive state are possible at this mindless level, and then ask what changes the addition of a mind brings about: and in the process learn a little more about just how Descartes conceives of a mind in this context.

Mind/body dualism, a doctrine to which Descartes is committed, treats the mind and the body as two completely separate substances, which do not admit of degrees. Many of Descartes's predecessors and contemporaries believed that they were able to capture the differences between, say, inanimate things, plants, animals, and human beings, by postulating various degrees

---

[3] The *locus classicus* is Book I of Malebranche's *Search after Truth*.

[4] See G. Ryle, *The Concept of Mind* (London: Hutchinson, 1949).

[5] J. Cottingham, 'Descartes's Trialism', *Mind* 93 (1985), pp. 218–30, brings out just how different embodied and disembodied minds are. See also A. Rorty, 'Descartes on Thinking with the Body', in J. Cottingham (ed.), *The Cambridge Companion to Descartes* (Cambridge: Cambridge University Press, 1992).

[6] I shall argue in terms of perceptual cognition, rather than knowledge, because I am not concerned at all with the sceptically driven epistemology that philosophers since the end of the nineteenth century have seen as constitutive of Descartes's project. Sceptically driven epistemology is just one stream in a far more complex programme which, on balance, is far more naturalistic that has commonly been recognized. Talking in terms of cognition rather than knowledge helps in preventing the assumption that what is at issue is sceptically driven epistemology.

of 'soul'—vegetative, sensible, and rational—which often blended into one another. Descartes, by contrast, because he admitted as separate (finite) substances only matter and the human rational soul, or mind, was left with a sharp divide between those entities which have minds—namely human beings—and those which did not: inanimate things, plants, animals. The question is whether this prevented him from ascribing cognitive states to animals. If we start with human cognition, we may be tempted, first, to associate mind with cognition and assume that anything without mind is without cognition, and second, to put inanimate things, plants, and animals on a par, as far as cognition is concerned. But if we start from Descartes's detailed accounts of cognitive processes in mindless animals, we shall instead be forced to ask just how it is possible for animals to have such cognitive states if they are literally mindless, and if we discover—as I hope to show we shall—that good sense can be made out of this approach in Descartes, then rather than simply assuming that a mind is necessary for perceptual cognition, we can ask just what having a mind adds to perceptual cognition, how it enhances it.

2. Non-Representational Cognition

Neither reflex response nor intellectual cognition are representational on Descartes's account, the first because it is in the nature of the reflex arc that it not be representational, the second because the kind of grasp afforded by intellectual cognition is direct, as opposed to representational. Representation seems peculiar to the case of perceptual cognition in Descartes, and it will help us understand how it functions if we distinguish it clearly from those cases in which representation is not involved.

Descartes is often credited with the discovery of the reflex arc, and in *L'Homme* he sets out an account whereby the proximity of one's foot to a flame causes the pores in the foot to open, as a result of which 'animal spirits from cavity F enter and are carried through it, some to the muscles that serve to pull the foot away from the fire, and some to the muscles that make the hands move and the whole body turn in order to protect itself' (AT X 142: CSM I 102). What is referred to here as 'cavity F' is often mistaken for the pineal gland, despite the fact that Descartes consistently labelled the pineal gland H in *L'Homme*, and never refers to the pineal gland as a cavity. F is almost certainly one of the cerebral ventricles.[7] It is important that, in this account of

---

[7] See J. Sutton, *Philosophy and Memory Traces* (Cambridge: Cambridge University Press, 1998), pp. 77–9. Descartes's labelling, which at first appears eccentric since he does not use the letters of

simple stimulus-response, the pineal gland is not involved. Descartes's account of the anatomy of perception is in many respects little more than a reworking of medieval faculty psychology: the five external senses, when stimulated, produce excitations which are transmitted to the *sensus communis*, where they are unified into a single perceptual item, and then processed through the memory and the imagination, to produce a single unified cognition, which in Descartes's account takes the form of a representation on the surface of the pineal gland (AT X 179–89). In other words, there is a distinction between those forms of animal response to sensory stimulation that do not involve the pineal gland, and those which do. The former involve no representation of the stimulus: their function is exclusively to preserve the body from harm, and so they must act in the fastest possible way, one which directly engages the muscles: indeed, Descartes's view is that this is an instantaneous process (AT X 142–3). To interpose a cognitive representation of the stimulus in this operation would delay it without benefit.

To what extent such a process can be regarded as cognitive is largely a semantic question, but it will be helpful for our purposes to confine the use of the term 'cognitive' to perceptual processes that involve some form of cognitive representation. The reason for this is that there is a question as to whether animals, on the Cartesian account, exhibit a genuine form of cognition. The answer that has usually been given—implicitly or explicitly—is that they are capable only of a reflex action, and it has been assumed that this is not a genuine form of cognition. I want to make the case that Cartesian automata are capable of a form of genuine cognition, which is quite different from reflex response because it involves cognitive representation; but, as we shall see, it lacks an element of perceptual judgement that characterizes what Descartes treats as typically human perceptual cognition.

At the other extreme from reflex response is intellectual cognition. This effectively comes in two varieties. Intellectual cognition is the characteristic activity of a disembodied mind, but there is also a form of intellectual cognition in embodied minds. Information on the cognitive states of a disembodied mind is very scant in Descartes, and puzzling when it is provided. A disembodied mind has no sensory input either from perception, because it has no external sense organs (the organs of the five senses) and no internal sense organs (such as that in which the *sensus communis* is located), or from memory or

the alphabet systematically, derives from the C. Bauhin, *Théâtre anatomique* (Paris, 1620–1), which Descartes—who had not been successful in identifying the pineal gland in the human brain, even though he had found it without difficulty in the heads of cattle and sheep—uses as his standard source: on this, see the notes and introduction to A. Bitbol-Hespériès, *Le Monde, L'Homme* (Paris: Seuil, 1996).

imagination, both of which require corporeal organs on his account. It seems that all that the disembodied mind can do is contemplate without perceptions or memories. Descartes does invoke something which he calls 'intellectual memory' on a number of occasions. Such intellectual memory might seem to be a distinctive feature of the cognition of the disembodied mind, along with the contemplation of universals, but his brief remarks on it are not consistent with one another. In a letter of condolence to Constantijn Huygens on the death of his wife, he tells Huygens that we shall recognize our loved ones in the afterlife 'for I believe we have an intellectual memory which is certainly independent of the body' (AT III 580). This seems clear-cut, but two other mentions of such intellectual memory indicate that it is not a form of memory at all. In the first place, Descartes tells Burman that 'intellectual memory has universals rather than particulars as its objects' (AT V 150). Second, these universals are not related in a temporal sequence in intellectual memory, for, he writes, 'where purely intellectual things are concerned, memory in the strict sense is not involved; they are thought of just as readily irrespective of whether it is the first or the second time they come to mind—unless, as often happens, they are associated with particular names, in which case, since the latter are corporeal, we do indeed remember them' (AT III 425: CSMK 190).

So the content of an intellectual memory is a synchronic relation between universals, not, as with corporeal memory, a diachronic relation between particulars. The former is surely just what would otherwise, and more helpfully, be described as contemplation of universals. The fact that universals are grasped, and that they are grasped non-temporally, suggests that in such thought we are not representing universals to ourselves, in the way in which we would represent sensible particulars to ourselves, for on Descartes's view—and indeed in the view of all philosophers in the seventeenth century[8]—we cannot grasp particulars directly, but only by means of perceptual representations, whereas there is no reason why we should not grasp universals directly. This holds not just for disembodied cognition, where the objects of contemplation appear to be *sui generis*, but also for that intellectual cognition where the objects of contemplation can be abstracted from sense perception. Intellectual cognition in the embodied case occurs when the intellect abstracts from perceptual representations in the imagination (i.e. the pineal gland) and contemplates them as abstracted universals or some other form of abstraction such as the abstraction of numbers. Although this process plays a role in perceptual

---

[8] See J. Yolton, *Perceptual Acquaintance* (Oxford: Blackwell, 1984).

cognition, it is explicitly not tantamount to perceptual cognition, which is representational.

Descartes rarely invokes intellectual cognition, and opportunities for confusing it with perceptual cognition are rare, although this has not stopped generations of philosophers effectively making this their life's work.[9] One such occasion is in the *Meditations*, where we get a strong form of dualism which seems to be leading one towards the idea that thought in human beings is intellectual cognition *per se*, but after apparently beginning to lead us down this path,[10] Descartes suddenly pulls back, issuing an explicit denial, at the beginning of Meditation 6, telling us that the soul is not 'like a sailor in a ship', and using the phenomenon of pain to show that the mind does not simply inspect bodily states but rather that mind and body participate as a 'union' in these cognitive states. More generally, whenever he offers an extended description of cognitive and affective states, it is in a straightforwardly naturalistic context, as in the *Regulae*, Rules 12 to 14, and in Part V of *L'Homme* (AT X 142–69) or in the context of what he later called the 'intimate union of mind and body', as in *Les Passions de l'âme*.[11] Moreover, his criticisms of alternative theories of cognition indicates that the point of dualism, in the context of cognition, is not to give us two things—mind and body—where we might have been satisfied with one, but to show that there are only two things, not the four postulated by his Aristotelian contemporaries—body, vegetative soul, sensitive soul, rational soul.

3. Representational Cognition in Automata

Descartes postulated a single kind of matter in the universe and this matter is inert, homogeneous, and qualitatively undifferentiated. The boundaries of bodies are determined by motion relative to surrounding matter and any variation in properties is a function of the size, speed, and direction of the matter. It is with this notion of matter that Descartes attempts to

---

[9] The tradition starts with Malebranche. Leibniz and (to a lesser extent) Locke read Descartes through Malebranche, and Berkeley and Hume were much more concerned with Malebranche than with Descartes: see C. J. McCracken, *Malebranche and British Philosophy* (Oxford: Clarendon Press, 1983).

[10] I say 'apparently' because it is open to dispute whether this is in fact the direction in which Descartes is heading up to this point. See G. P. Baker and K. J. Morris, *Descartes's Dualism* (London: Routledge, 1996).

[11] The treatment of the passions up to section 146 is naturalistic: from section 146 onwards moral psychology takes over.

account for all functions and behaviour of animals, including such apparently goal-directed functions as the development of the foetus and perceptual cognition.

There are three kinds of approach to which his mechanist account can be seen as an alternative. These attempt to provide an account of physiology that aims to explain various functional differences between organs either, first, in terms of qualitatively different kinds of matter, or, second, in terms of some non-material principle guiding those functions, or, third, in goal-directed terms which cannot be captured mechanistically.

In the first case, what was usually invoked was the traditional doctrine of the four elements—earth, air, fire, and water. However, already in *Le Monde*, Descartes had questioned both the basis for this doctrine and whether the accounts it produced could have any explanatory value or informative content. Instead he had offered his own accounts of phenomena such as burning, and of the different physical properties of solids and fluids in terms of his much more economical single matter theory (AT X 7–32). At a general level, the argument is that invoking the traditional theory of the elements explains nothing, and the cases they are invoked to explain in physical theory can actually be accounted for fully in terms of a single type of matter: all there is for Descartes is material extension. When we turn to physiology, the same considerations apply. Why try to account for differences in physiological function in terms of a theory of matter which would not explain anything anyway, and which can be replaced by something much more economical?

In the second case, a parallel set of considerations holds. Instead of a theory of elements, what are invoked are various classes of 'soul': vegetative, sensitive, and rational souls. These classes of soul carry different powers, and were supposed to capture various qualitative differences that emerge as we ascend the chain of being from inanimate matter, to vegetable life, to animal life, to human beings; or alternatively, as we ascend from those functions we share with plants, to those we share with animals, to those that are distinctively human. Descartes certainly thinks that distinctively human capacities require the postulation of a separate soul, but the postulation of a hierarchy of souls—and more specifically, the postulation of a 'sensitive soul' to account for animal sentience—is a different matter. First, it is unnecessary, since one can, Descartes believes, explain vegetable and animal capacities simply in terms of matter. Secondly, the postulation of a hierarchy of souls does not actually explain anything: it does nothing more than label the stages at which various differences are considered to emerge, while giving the impression that the cause of the difference has been identified. Thirdly, a hierarchy of souls obscures the all-important distinction between the soul and the body, suggesting that the differences may be ones of degree, something that Descartes singles out for criticism in his theory of the passions.[12]

The third case, that of the apparent goal-directedness of certain physiological processes, is the most serious challenge to a mechanist physiology, and while his account of perceptual cognition is reductionist, in that nothing other than mechanical processes are involved, it is not eliminativist, in that what he tries to show is that these mechanical processes have a level of structuring imposed upon them that allows for recognitional capacities, something which he indicates, at least at an elementary level, not to be beyond the capabilities of a mechanist theory: the aim is to show how function can be generated purely within the resources of mechanism.

It is important, in considering these matters, to understand what the novelty of Descartes's attempt to mechanize physiology lay in. It did not lie in construing psycho-physiological functions corporeally. Many psycho-physiological functions had been construed corporeally before Descartes by writers on physiology, and indeed there had been an extensive concern from Galen onwards with the localization of particular faculties in the cerebral ventricles. There was even an orthodox tradition, dating back to the Church Fathers, of construing thought in corporeal terms, a tradition which the 'theologians and philosophers' who compiled the sixth set of objections to Descartes's *Meditationes* describe explicitly and approvingly as the 'soul thinking by means of corporeal motions' (AT VII 413–14: CSM II 279). Descartes's aim was to show that a number of psycho-physiological functions that had traditionally been recognized as being corporeal could be accounted for without rendering matter sentient. That is the novel part of the programme. What is original about Descartes's project is not that it construes the faculties in corporeal terms, but his attempt to show that construing them in corporeal terms did not contradict the central tenet of mechanism that matter was inert. It should also be noted that the difference between an animal as traditionally conceived and a Cartesian automaton is not a difference between soft, fleshy organic entities and clockwork robots, but a conceptual difference between how physiological processes are to be understood.[13] Descartes's conception of

---

[12] See the discussion in Gaukroger, *Descartes*, pp. 394–405.

[13] Descartes speaks of animals as 'automata', a term that also covers human bodies when not considered as animated by a soul. The terminology is misleading, however, for as John Cottingham points out, in the seventeenth century it meant little more than a 'self-moving thing' and Leibniz, defending his claim that we possess 'freedom of spontaneity', speaks of the human soul as a 'kind of spiritual automaton', meaning no more than that its action-generating impulses arise solely *ad interno*, and produce effects without the intervention of any external cause: J. Cottingham, 'A Brute to the Brutes?', *Philosophy* 53 (1978), pp. 551–9: 553, repr. in J. Cottingham, *Cartesian Reflections* (Oxford: Oxford University Press, 2008), ch. 8.

animal capacities and behaviour is in essence no different from that of most of his contemporaries, and he attributes not just cognitive but also affective states to them.[14] What is novel about his treatment is the way he accounts for these states.

Descartes has a particular quarrel with the attempt to treat perception as a goal-directed process: it is not just that thinking of goals gets us nowhere. Rather, trying to think through perception in terms of its goals points us in a direction that is demonstrably wrong. Aristotle had maintained that we have the sense organs we do because they naturally display to us the nature of the world, and his account of the optics and physiology of perception hinged on what he took its function to be. Among other things, the optics and physiology had to be construed in such a way as to yield perceptual images that resembled what was perceived. However, as Descartes knew, the optics and physiology that Aristotle's account yielded turned out to be completely wrong and Descartes's own account of perception, in the *Regulae* for example, starts from a new understanding of the optics and physiology of vision and uses this understanding to explore what form visual cognition might take.

Visual cognition involves cognitive response. This isn't a problem for an account that construes the sense organs primarily in terms of their function, that subordinates structure to function, as Aristotle's account did. Descartes wants to subordinate function to structure: he wants there to be nothing more to function than what an examination of structure reveals. The problem in perceptual cognition is to recognize the goal-directedness of perceptual cognition—the goal is cognition, the means perception—without rendering this a teleological process. It is basically the problem of capturing the idea of realizing a function without the Aristotelian/scholastic notion of intrinsic final ends.

The faculties involved in perceptual cognition—the 'external' sense organs, the common sense, the memory, and the imagination—had traditionally been construed in corporeal terms, with a good deal of attention having been given to localization of faculties in the cerebral ventricles by physiologists. But the construal of some level of cognitive functioning in corporeal terms had been associated with various attempts to render matter itself sentient, by invoking the functional idea of a 'sensitive soul' regulating the corporeal processes from

---

[14] He writes to the Marquis of Newcastle (AT IV 574: CSMK 303) that magpies have passions, and ascribes joy, hope, and fear to dogs, horses, and monkeys. The idea that different species of animals manifested particular passions and or virtues goes back at least to the Patristic writers, and supplied a staple diet of iconography for medieval and Renaissance writers and painters. Early modern writers go along with this story: see P. Harrison, 'Reading the Passions: the Fall, the Passions, and Dominion over nature', in S. Gaukroger (ed.), *The Soft Underbelly of Reason* (London: Routledge, 1998).

inside. To the extent that he is concerned to show that organic processes, including some cognitive operations, can be construed wholly mechanistically, Descartes has to make sure that his account is compatible with the inertness of matter. His aim is to show that the structure and behaviour of bodies are to be explained in the same way that we explain the structure and behaviour of machines, and in doing this he wants to show how a form of genuine cognition occurs in animals and that this can be captured in mechanistic terms. He does not want to show that cognition does not occur at all, that *instead of* a cognitive process we have a merely mechanical one. The aim is to explain animal cognition, not explain it away.

Take the case of visual cognition. We can distinguish between mere response to a visual stimulus, in which the parts of the automaton simply react in a fixed way; visual awareness, in which the perceiver has a mental representation of the object or state of affairs that caused the visual stimulus in the first place; and perceptual judgement, the power to reflect on and make a judgement about (e.g. a judgement as to the veridicality of) this representation. Descartes clearly restricts the last to human beings—it requires the possession of a mind/rational soul. Which of the first two are we to attribute to animals on Descartes's account? The automaton could react directly to the corpuscular action that makes up light without actually *seeing* anything, as a genuine machine might, but this is not how Descartes describes the visual process in automata in *L'Homme*. He tells us, for example, that the 'figures traced in the spirits on the [pineal] gland, where the seat of imagination and common sense is, should be taken to be ideas, that is, to be the forms or images that the rational soul will consider directly when, being united to this machine, it will imagine or will sense any object' (AT X 176–7: CSM I 106). This indicates that there are representations on the pineal gland of the automaton. It is in fact difficult to see how they could not have representations of the world if we are to talk about visual cognition. And it makes no sense to talk about them having representations but not being aware of the content of these representations. Moreover, Descartes certainly does not deny states such as memory to animals, and, if one thinks of memory in terms of a cognitive operation, remembering something is just about the paradigm case of grasping the content of a representation.

The problem is that, while Descartes can allow that automata have representations, it is not immediately clear how he can allow that they grasp the content of these representations if they are not aware of them as representations: if, unlike human beings, they cannot make judgements about them as representations, e.g. about their veridicality.

In what sense can automata be aware of the content of representations without being able to respond to them as representations? Descartes's problem might be put in these terms. The behaviour of automata is such that they must be construed as responding to perceptual and other cognitive stimuli in a genuinely cognitive way, that is, in a way that goes beyond a stimulus-response arc. In other words, their behaviour indicates that they are sentient. But they are not conscious: that is, they have no awareness of their own cognitive states as such and so cannot make judgements as to their content. Consequently, Descartes has to account for the behaviour of sentient but non-conscious automata. Because automata are literally 'mindless', this can only be done in terms of a mechanistic physiology.

In general terms, what we need to do is to capture the difference between sentient and non-sentient behaviour, and set out how this is reflected in differences at the level of a mechanistic physiology. On the first question, the difference between sentience and non-sentience, this is of course a grey area, but one crucial difference that we might point to is that there is a sense in which sentient beings are able to process information: that is, they are able to interpret stimuli, and this interpretation determines their response. Descartes gives us some hints as to how this difference might be manifested in chapter 1 of Le Monde, for not only is it established there that there is a certain level of processing of visual information that requires nothing over and above corporeal organs, but we are also given some account of what such processing would consist in.

In chapter 1 of Le Monde, Descartes looks at the relation between the physical agitation of matter that results in a stimulation of the eye, and the visual cognition that we have as a result of this. Previously, his account had focused on getting the 'perceptual' part of perceptual cognition right, whereas here he concentrates on the 'cognition' side of the question. By contrast with the Regulae, for example, in Le Monde perceptual cognition is not thought of in causal terms, and it is not thought of as a multi-stage process. Rather, the treatment focuses on two questions: the form of the representation, and the question of how we are able to respond to certain properties or events as information.

On the first question, Descartes rejects a resemblance theory of perception of the kind that Aristotle and his followers had assumed must hold if perception is to be veridical. He argues that in order to represent the world, the perceptual image need not resemble it (AT XI 3–6; CSM I 81–2). Indeed, many features of our perceptual image of the world—colours, sounds, odours, etc.—are not features of the world at all. In L'Homme he goes on to apply the representation account to another cognitive operation, namely memory, with very significant consequences. Because his contemporaries had assumed that mnemonic representations, or memory traces, must resemble the original perceptual source, since that is what we recall, their attention was devoted to how such a huge amount of detail could possibly be stored, and they proposed various accounts of storage, many of which focussed on the large surface area provided by the crinkled surface of the brain.[15] Descartes's approach is completely different to this. Pineal patterns do not have to be stored separately and faithfully: they do not have to be kept in the same form between experiencing and remembering. His account suggests a dispositional model in which storage may be implicit rather than explicit: a memory may be generated from stored items without itself being a stored item. In this connection, we should recall that Descartes offers an associative account of memory in which brain filaments are bent and rearranged in particular ways depending on the regularity of particular operations. In this way, partial input can result in total recall, so that 'if I see two eyes with a nose, I at once imagine a forehead and a mouth and all the other parts of the face' (AT XI 179).

On the second question, what Descartes effectively proposes is that we conceive of visual cognition, not in terms of the mechanical-causal process involved in perception, but in terms of a single unified act of comprehension. He spells this out in terms of a new linguistic model of perception:

As you know, the fact that words bear no resemblance to the things they signify does not prevent them from causing us to conceive of those things, often without our paying attention to the sounds of the words or to their syllables. Thus it can turn out that, having heard something and understood its meaning perfectly well, we might not be able to say in what language it was uttered. Now if words, which signify something only through human convention, are sufficient to make us think of things to which they bear no resemblance, why should not nature also have established some sign which would make us have a sensation of light, even if that sign had in it nothing that resembled this sensation. And is it not thus that nature has established laughter and tears, to make us read joy and sorrow on the face of men?   (AT XI 4: CSM I 81)

If we distinguish between the question of how perceptual information is conveyed, and the question of how perceptual information is represented, then we can see that Descartes is retaining a causal-mechanical model for the first, and advocating a linguistic model for the second. On the linguistic model, we grasp an idea in virtue of a sign which represents that idea to us. So, in the case of a conventional linguistic sign, when we know English, the word 'dog' conveys to us the idea of a dog. And just as conventional signs do not resemble what they signify, so too natural signs do not resemble what they signify either.

---

[15] See the discussion in Sutton, *Philosophy and Memory Traces*.

Descartes tells us that there is in nature a sign which is responsible for our sensation of light, but which is not itself light, and which does not resemble light. All there is in nature is motion. In the case of a natural sign like motion, provided we have the ability to recognize and interpret it, when we sense a particular motion what it will convey to us is light. Light is what we will experience when we respond in the appropriate way to the sign. As examples of natural signs, Descartes tells us that tears are a natural sign of sadness and laughter a natural sign of joy. One of the things that distinguishes signs from causes is that whether a sign signifies something to us—that is, whether we can call it a sign in the first place—depends on our ability to recognize and interpret the sign, and it is this ability on our part that makes the signs what they are. Causation is clearly different from this, for causes do not depend in any way upon our ability to recognize them. The question is what makes natural signs *signs*. It cannot be, or cannot merely be, something in nature, for something cannot be a sign for us unless we can recognize it, so it must be something in us that makes tears, or laughter, or a particular kind of motion, signs. This something in us must be an acquired or an innate capacity; and Descartes's view is that it is an innate capacity which, it will turn out, God has provided us with. There would be no natural signs unless we had the capacity to recognize them as such.

Here, I suggest we have the two key pieces in the account of sentience. Sentient responses are different from non-sentient responses in that, in the latter case, we can give a full account merely by showing the causal-mechanical processes involved. In the case of sentient responses, this will not tell us everything we need to know, and we need to supplement it with a different kind of account. There is an element of reciprocity in perceptual cognition as linguistically modelled that we do not find in the causal-mechanical account. The linguistic model enables us to grasp what perceptual understanding consists in, whereas the causal-mechanical account describes what physical-cum-physiological processes must occur if this understanding is to take place. This is a core difference between sentience and non-sentience. The next question is whether such a form of interpretation modelled on language is realizable in a mechanistic physiology alone. What is needed over and above the causal-mechanical account that we provide of non-sentient responses? Above all, what we need is some means of forming representations in response to perceptual stimuli, and we need some means of storing and recalling these representations. In one sense, many automata—those to which we are inclined to ascribe some kind of sophistication in perceptual cognition, such as higher mammals—clearly have the physiological means to do this: they have pineal glands, which is where perceptual representations are formed, and they have memories, i.e. corporeal means of storage of representations.

But Descartes needs to say more than this, and it is in his tantalizingly brief account of light in the first chapter of *Le Monde* that he gives his indication of what this 'more' might be. Remember that we are told that light is not the stimulus but the response to the stimulus. The stimulus is a particular kind of motion in the smallest kind of matter which is transmitted via the second matter. Now note also that in order to respond to this particular kind of motion by perceiving light, we have to be able to respond in the right way (this is what makes this a significatory event as well as a causal one). To be able to respond in the right way, we need some kind of innate or built-in capacity. Here the question arises whether such innate capacities are part of our corporeal organs or our minds. One only has to note the fact that automata are able to see, that is, perceive light, whereas disembodied minds are not, to recognize that the capacity to grasp various kinds of translational and rotary motion as light must naturally reside in corporeal organs. Descartes never suggests that automata cannot respond to natural signs; indeed, such functions as nutrition in higher animals, where the appropriate kind of food has to be sought out visually or olfactorily, clearly require such recognitional capacities. Indeed, more generally, it is difficult to explain how animal instincts are to be accounted for if not in terms of some innate capacity.

In more modern terms, what we need is 'hard wiring'. The brain needs to be fitted out so as to respond in the appropriate way. The hard wiring makes sure you get the right kind of representations: that you see light, that is, have a visual image which displays shapes and colours, when stimulated in the requisite way. It is not something in nature that causes us to have visual images, it is a combination of a stimulation produced by nature and certain features of an animal's physiology which result in a particular kind of representation, a visual perception.

It is important to realize here that, in the case of perceptual cognition in automata, Descartes's aim is not to deny that there is a functional story to be told, but rather to indicate how the functional story can be translated into the terms of a mechanistic physiology without losing the key insight that perception of x by y involves x *meaning something to* y, so that, for example, y perceives x as a lion. What is needed is the capacity to translate the visual stimulation, which might be characterized as agitation of the corpuscles making up the retina, into the requisite perceptual representation, that is, one that conveys the idea of a lion. This can be achieved by the requisite corporeal organs in the brain.

In particular, along with memory, there are a number of very sophisticated cognitive operations that we can attribute to animals on Descartes's account. One of these is distance perception. Distance perception involves calculation on Descartes's account because what makes contact with the eye from the observed object—rays made up of streams of light corpuscles[16]—does not and cannot convey information about the distance of its source. Since Descartes restricts causal processes to those involving contact action, the perceiver has to be able to gauge the distance of any source purely from information given within the visual process itself; that is, distance is not 'immediately perceived', as Berkeley was later to put it. How distance is perceived is set out, in Discourse 6 of the *Dioptrique*, in terms of an unconscious natural geometry, whereby we calculate distance from the angles at which the light rays strike the eye: knowing this, and knowing the distance between the eyes, we know the base angles and base length of a triangle, the height of which can be calculated from this information. We are not aware of any such calculation, of course, and Descartes describes the process as being 'ordained by nature' (AT X 134–5), which indicates it comes under psycho-physiology rather than mental activity proper: in particular, it is not a matter of intellectual judgement. It might be asked how an inferential process like calculation, unconscious or otherwise, could be ascribed to a mindless animal. But in Rule 2 of the *Regulae*, Descartes tells us that 'none of the errors to which men—men, I say, not brute animals—are liable is ever due to faulty inference' (AT X 365: CSM I 12) because our inference is always guided by the natural light of reason, which is infallible. In other words, brute animals make inferences, but, since they lack the natural light of reason, these are at least occasionally faulty: Descartes is prepared to construe inference, at least at some level, as a psycho-physiological process. Moreover, as we shall see below, there is a clear difference, at the level of the faculties involved, between distance perception and forms of quantitative cognition of the world involving the intellect, even though these are both forms of perceptual cognition and both take place in the imagination.

A second sophisticated cognitive operation which is a matter of pure psycho-physiology, and hence available to mindless animals, is colour perception, which involves enhancement of visual information on the Cartesian account. This is a capacity which, like distance perception, involves no conscious intellectual activity on our part, and seems similarly ordained by nature, but it requires

---

[16] Strictly speaking what we have here is a transverse motion of the fine matter packing the interstices between the corpuscles making up the medium, whose action is transmitted instantaneously in a straight line: see ch. 14 of *Le Monde*: AT X 97–103.

significant cognitive processing. On Descartes's account of colour, the natural world is colourless, but when the fine corpuscles making up light rays are reflected off surfaces having particular structural features they are given a spin, which results in a rotation of the rays. What we experience when our eyes are stimulated by this rotation is colour, because of an innate faculty that we have to respond in this way (see, e.g., AT VIIIA 359: CSM I 304). Now we perceive colours as if they were in world, so it might seem that God has given us deceptive faculties in this respect. Descartes denies this, arguing that sensory perception has been given to us by God for the preservation of our bodies: as he puts it in Meditation 6, 'the proper purpose of sensory perceptions given me by nature is simply to inform the mind of what is beneficial or harmful for the mind/body composite' (AT VII 83: CSM II 57). This is one of the few doctrines on which all Cartesians in the seventeenth century were agreed, even Malebranche and Arnauld, who agreed on little else. Arnauld gives the best statement of the doctrine:

It must not be imagined that there is nothing in [a body] which causes it to appear to me to be of one colour rather than another. This is surely due to a different arrangement of the small parts of their surface, which is responsible for the corpuscles which are reflected from the [body] towards our eyes stimulating the fibres of the optic nerve in different ways. But because our soul would find it too difficult to discern the difference in these stimulations, which is only one of degree, God has decided in this respect to give us the means to discern them more easily by those sensations of different colours, which he has willed be caused in our soul on the occasion of these various stimulations of the optic nerve, just as tapestry workers have a pattern, which they call a 'rough pattern', where the various shades of the same colour are indicated by completely different colours, so that they are less liable to mistake them.[17]

Arnauld talks of the 'soul' here, because he is concerned with human visual cognition, but there is no conscious interpretation on our part, and nothing in principle to prevent the same capacity in animals: and we must remember here no one in the seventeenth century even raised the question of whether animals might not see the world as coloured. Indeed, colour enhancement in visual cognition is a paradigm psycho-physiological operation.

4. The 'Self' and Morality

What is at stake in Descartes's account of representational cognition in automata is the construal of all cognitive functions in terms of corporeal processes which

[17] A. Arnauld, *On True and False Ideas*, ed. and trans. S. Gaukroger (Manchester: Manchester University Press, 1990), pp. 131–2.

involve only inert matter. It might be thought that this rids cognition of goal-directedness. If it did, if animal cognition were not to be construed in terms of cognitive goals, then surely this would be tantamount to eliminativism. But in fact Descartes does not deny cognitive goals in animal cognition any more than he denies developmental goals in his embryology. In his account of the development of the foetus,[18] he does not deny that there is question as to why constituent matter of the foetus behaves in such a way that the foetus develops into an adult of a particular species: a camel foetus develops into a camel, a horse foetus into a horse, and so on. But it develops into an animal of a particular species not because the foetal matter in camels and horses is different: Descartes's notion of material extension does not allow of different kinds of matter. Nor is it because there is some soul or spirit in the foetus which guides it in different ways. Finally, nor is there some internally goal-directed process at work here: to admit that would be to admit that matter could harbour goals. What he is saying is that the explanation for foetal development is not something *internal* to the development of the foetus, but something *external* to it. God made it so, that is, he structured the animal's womb in such a way so that foetal matter contained in it developed in one way rather than another. God's causality here is restricted to that of final cause. And God is an external cause, whereas what Descartes is concerned with are internal causes. The same holds for his account of perceptual cognition. Descartes does not deny that God has given automata the sense organs they have, along with various cognitive abilities such as distance estimation and colour enhancement, so that they might sustain themselves in the world. It is just that the question of *how* the sense organs operate, which is what he is concerned with, is different from *why* they operate in that way: indeed, on Descartes's account, these are *completely* different questions.

However, when the body is considered, no longer as the body of an animal or an *homme machine*, but as part of what Descartes refers to as 'the substantial union of mind and body' then intrinsic goals re-enter the picture. Human beings are able to reflect upon and make judgements about the content of their perceptual representations—they are able to make judgements as to their veridicality, for example—and the nature of perception is transformed as a result. Unlike the perceptual cognition of an automaton, which has no intrinsic goals, human perception must be considered in terms of a goal, the goal of understanding the world, and it can be criticized, for example, to the extent to which it fails to achieve that goal. Intrinsic goals enter the picture because

---

[18] Part I of *Description du corps humain*, AT XI 252–86, translated in S. Gaukroger, *Descartes: The World and Other Writings* (Cambridge: Cambridge University Press, 1998), pp. 186–205.

of the presence of a conscious intelligence, and that, on Descartes's account, is their proper place.

If, on the Cartesian account, what marks out animals from human beings at the level of the range of cognitive operations is less significant than it has often been taken to be, it is nevertheless significant. But there is no question that Descartes took these differences as being the core difference between human beings and animals. The cognitive operations we have discussed are relatively discrete operations: they are, in modern terminology, modular. One of the reasons that Descartes, in the *Passions of the Soul*, rejects accounts of our psychology that break up the mind into higher and lower functions, as the Scholastic accounts did, is because he fears the fragmentation of the mind that results from such a conception. Indeed, the unity of subjectivity comes into its own in Descartes's criticisms of the habit of scholastic psychology of breaking up the mind into higher and lower faculties (AT XI 364: CSM I 345–6). What he fears is fragmentation of the soul: how can we hold ourselves responsible if there is not something that lies behind our cognitive and affective states? Unity of subjectivity is, however, not in fact something that comes naturally, and it is rarely achieved fully. Indeed, a good deal of Cartesian moral philosophy consists in advice on how to shape oneself into a unified self, so that one can take control of one's passions, use them fruitfully, and thereby form oneself as a fully morally responsible agent. The transcendence of modularity, the forging of a mental unity, is above all the shaping of a moral *persona*: the shaping of something that is capable of a moral life.

The difference between human beings and animals, on Descartes's account, lies not so much in the nature of the cognitive states available to human beings and animals (although there are some differences, as we have seen) but in the fact that cognitive and affective states in animals are fragmented and dispersed, or modularized, whereas human beings have a 'self', something that holds together these cognitive and affective states, this being a necessary condition of our ability to question whether these cognitive states are veridical (e.g. to ask whether the world is really coloured, as it appears to be), or whether particular affective states which we experience are the appropriate ones. This 'self' is what exercises acts of will, and it gives human beings a unified mental life lacking in automata, which is why, cognitively sophisticated as these automata may be, we do not treat them as being able to reflect epistemologically on the nature of their cognitive states, why we do not hold them morally responsible, and why they are not capable of language (AT VI 65–7: CSM I 139–40). A unified mental life is indispensable for these functions, and full modularity, of the kind Descartes effectively postulates in automata, is incompatible with everything from language to moral responsibility.

5. The Reception of the Cartesian Theory of Moral Sensibility

Once we ask what unity of subjectivity amounts to in Descartes, it soon becomes clear that we are dealing with questions of the unity of the person, and the issues are not restricted to cognitive states but essentially include affective states and questions of morality. It is in these terms that the problem of Cartesian 'rationalism' was posed in the eighteenth century. What was at issue was not an epistemological doctrine, but the theory of affective states and moral psychology that I have just outlined, and the criticism came primarily from French Lockeans such as Condillac and Diderot. For both Locke and Descartes, our standing as human—and above all moral—agents depends on our ability to rise above cognitive modularity, but the way in which they try to establish this differs radically: whereas for Descartes, as we have seen, it is a question of unity of subjectivity, for Locke and the French Lockeans it is a matter of unity of sensibility.[19] This is not the place to enter in discussion of what the unity of sensibility consists in for Locke,[20] or how this doctrine is modified in the hands of French Lockeans. Rather, I want simply to draw attention to the moral dimension of the criticism of the Cartesian doctrine, and the best example here is Diderot.

In his *Letter on The Blind*,[21] Diderot focused on the question of how the 'mentality' of a blind person, not just his perceptual states, differs from that of a sighted person, and what this tells us about sensibility in general. His interest focused on the case of Nicholas Saunderson, the blind Lucasian Professor of Mathematics at Cambridge and author of a large posthumously published two-volume *Elements of Algebra*. In effect, what Diderot does is to use the case of Saunderson to pit unity of sensibility against a Cartesian unity of subjectivity, arguing that the unity of sensibility, properly construed, is essentially something socially responsible that encourages a well-formed *persona*, whereas the Cartesian is insensible to the world and works merely in abstractions. It is Saunderson's very blindness that in effect denies him a fully developed unity of sensibility. A deficient sensibility is primarily a question

[19] See S. Gaukroger, '"Home Alone": Cognitive Solipsism in the Early-Modern Era', *Proceedings and Addresses of the American Philosophical Association* 80/2 (2006), pp. 63–78.

[20] For the details of how the doctrine emerges in Locke see S. Gaukroger, 'The Role of Natural Philosophy in the Development of Locke's Empiricism', *British Journal for the History of Philosophy* (17 (2009), pp. 57–86).

[21] *Lettre sur les aveugles*, in Denis Diderot, *Œuvres philosophiques*, ed. P. Vernière (Paris: Garnier, 1961), pp. 81–146.

of an emotional, aesthetic, and moral challenge for Diderot. Because of their impoverished sensibilities, the blind turn their minds inwards and are drawn to thinking in terms of abstractions. Jessica Riskin puts the point well, noting that 'this made them natural mathematicians and rationalists: in a word, Cartesians. Conversely, Cartesians' abstract, inward focus made them insensible to the world outside their minds: philosophically blind.' This leads Diderot to suggest that both the blind and Cartesians, because of their solipsistic cast of mind, were inhumane.[22] The blind offer a crucial case study for Diderot because he believes that their abstract manner of experiencing pain in others weakens their sense of sympathy for the suffering of others.[23] The situation is in effect the analogue of what in the Cartesian case would be someone—lacking the ability to unify their mental life (perhaps because of melancholia or what we would now think of as various forms of neuroses), and thereby failing to shape them satisfactorily into a moral *persona*—whose moral agency, and humanity, would be deficient in comparison with someone (an *honnête homme*) who had achieved this.

In his treatment of blindness, Diderot attempted to connect lack of sensation and lack of sensibility in a very literal way, but we do not need to follow him in this regard to appreciate the force of the general question of where the ideas that regulate our lives—our moral, emotional, social, political, and intellectual lives—come from. The consequences for language, culture, and history of the Lockean claim that all knowledge derives from sense perception had been drawn in detail by Condillac and his approach is developed in Diderot, in a distinctive effort to separate morality completely from religion and to rebuild it on a sensationalist basis. It is axiomatic to the sensationalist project that one begins life with a *tabula rasa*, and the question is not just how one develops a cognitive, affective, and moral life on this basis, but also to discover whether there are any guidelines that we can follow in cultivating responsible citizens. What is ultimately at stake for Diderot is the sensory basis of civic life, where the contrast is between sensibility and what he considers solipsistic rationalism. Diderot is asking far more work of Descartes's account of cognition here than the kind of sceptically driven epistemology that has dominated consideration of Descartes since the end of the nineteenth century could possibly do. But what he is asking would not have been alien to the Cartesian project: quite the contrary, it helps us recognize a dimension of the problem that an exclusive focus on sceptically driven epistemology has wholly obscured.

[22] Jessica Riskin, *Science in the Age of Sensibility* (Chicago: University of Chicago Press, 2002), p. 21.
[23] See, for example, Diderot, *Œuvres philosophiques*, pp. 92–3, where he suggests that the reaction to a man urinating and spurting blood is effectively on a par in the blind.

6. Conclusion

Jonathan Barnes once wrote that 'by contrast with Aristotle, Descartes's philosophical range was limited'.[24] Ignoring Descartes's work in natural philosophy, mathematics, physiology, and anatomy, Barnes confines Descartes's contribution to epistemology, and it is perhaps not surprising that, working with this caricature, he comes to the conclusion that he does. But missing the moral dimension in Descartes's work, while certainly more excusable, is in the long run no less serious.

In exploring the role that mind plays in perceptual cognition for Descartes, I have argued that it is not a question of establishing cognitive contact with the physical world, for the corporeal cognitive processes are sufficient for that, as is clear from his account of cognition in automata, but rather that of providing a means of making perceptual judgements. The uniquely mental procedures by which this is effected, by which perceptions are connected so that they become perceptions of a unified locus of subjectivity, enabling us to 'stand back' as it were from our representations of the world and make judgements about them, are also those that provide one with what Descartes considers to be the necessary conditions for free will and responsibility, and ultimately for moral agency. In other words, we are not dealing with a purely epistemological subject, but a subject which has a psychological, affective, and moral dimension as well. Descartes's critics such as Diderot believed that he was profoundly mistaken in the way in which he established moral agency, and Diderot tried to show that what he regarded as Descartes's purely intellectual reading of the constitution of the subject resulted in a morally stunted, solipsistic creature that inhabited a realm of its own rather than the real moral world. But, in broad terms, Diderot saw himself as engaged in the same kind of project, with the same aims, if pursuing a wholly different path to them.

Once we appreciate this dimension of the situation, we can see that the route I have followed to Descartes's moral theory is not as indirect as it might at first seem.[25] It is common in general histories of ethics to encounter a lacuna in the seventeenth century, as if epistemological questions had displaced moral ones completely. It is not that moral philosophy disappears in this period, however, but rather that it takes a form very different from that which we find in Plato, Aristotle, Kant, or Mill, for example. It is closer to Seneca and Stoic

---

[24] J. Barnes, 'Introduction', in J. Barnes (ed.), *The Cambridge Companion to Aristotle* (Cambridge: Cambridge University Press, 1995), p. xv.

[25] See also S. Gaukroger, *Descartes's System of Natural Philosophy* (Cambridge: Cambridge University Press, 2002), ch. 8.

models, which are more concerned about the shaping of the moral *persona* than they are about identifying virtues and prescribing conduct, for example. In short, it is not that moral philosophy is absent, just harder to find, given the models with which we are most familiar. Once we uncover it, however, what emerges is a rich vein, and the thought of Descartes can be displayed in a fuller way, offering a degree of comprehensiveness on a par with those two other philosophers whom Kenny has investigated so fruitfully, Aristotle and Aquinas.

12

Descartes and the Immortality of the Soul

MARLEEN ROZEMOND

1. Introduction

In the history of philosophy there is a long tradition of deriving the soul's immortality from its simplicity, a tradition that goes as far back as Plato's *Phaedo*. Something that is simple, according to this line of thinking, cannot go out of existence by natural processes because natural ceasing-to-be always happens as a result of decomposition. Consequently, if one can establish the simplicity of the human soul, one can be confident of its incorruptibility, as the Aristotelian scholastics often put the point, or natural immortality: God, of course, can cause its demise by withdrawing his concurrence, which during the early modern period and before was widely deemed necessary for the existence of creatures. Matter, on the other hand, was widely regarded as inherently composite and so divisible and corruptible, and of course, our natural death involves the demise of the human body. Consequently, there is a rich tradition of arguments for the simplicity of the human soul, and from there on to its immateriality and incorruptibility.

The argument from simplicity has its roots in Plato, who argued in the *Phaedo* that the soul is immortal because simple. Later philosophers employed an argument for the soul's simplicity from the claim that the subject of the mental must be simple because the unity of consciousness requires this. This argument suggested that in a composite subject the contents of our mental states would be distributed over the parts of the subject in a way that is incompatible with the fact that we connect contents in our thinking in various ways. Its best-known presentation occurs in Kant's Second Paralogism. Kant rejected the argument while expressing respect for it—he gave it the honorific title of 'the Achilles of all dialectical inferences in the pure doctrine of the soul'.[1] I will follow Kant's terminology and speak of the 'Achilles Argument'. During the early modern period this argument enjoyed considerable popularity. It was often offered in terms of consciousness, but other terms for mental phenomena were used and a range of mental phenomena was cited to support the argument.[2] The argument tends to appear in the writings of philosophers with a Platonist bent, or so it seems to me. Within Aristotelian scholasticism, to my knowledge, the argument does not appear.

Descartes did not use the Achilles Argument, but he did hold that the human soul is simple. Indeed, his treatment of the simplicity of the soul occupies a rather different place in his thinking than it did in the Achilles Argument. In this paper I aim to sort out just how the simplicity of the soul figures in Descartes's treatment of the mind. First, Descartes's main argument for dualism did not focus on the simplicity of the soul to establish its immateriality. That argument derives dualism from the clear and distinct perceptions of mind as thinking and unextended, body as extended and non-thinking.[3] Descartes does also argue for dualism from the claim that the mind is indivisible, body divisible, but this is a subsidiary argument. Furthermore, when Descartes focuses on the simplicity of the mind, he is generally concerned with the interaction and union of mind and body rather than the intrinsic nature of the soul or mind and its difference from the body. Second, the Achilles Argument derives the immortality of the soul from the simplicity that distinguishes it from body. Descartes did not claim to establish that the soul or mind is immortal (although he had claimed he did in the subtitle of the first edition of the *Meditations*), but in the Synopsis to the *Meditations* he does offer a sketch of how he would establish the immortality of the soul. It is tempting to see this sketch as an

---

[1] For Kant's statement of the argument, see *Critique of Pure Reason* A 352. For discussion of the history of this argument see Ben Lazare Mijuscovic, *The Achilles of Rational Arguments* (The Hague: Martinus Nijhoff, 1974), and for more detailed discussion of its occurrence in various philosophers, see Tom Lennon and Robert Stainton (eds), *The Achilles of Rationalist Psychology* (Dordrecht: Springer Verlag, 2008). The argument can be found as early as Plotinus (See *Enneads IV.7*, trans. A. H. Armstrong, Loeb Classics, Cambridge, Mass.: Harvard University Press, 1967). For discussion see Devin Henry, 'The Neoplatonic Achilles', in *The Achilles of Rationalist Psychology*.

[2] For instance, Leibniz thought the subject of *perception* must be simple and Leibniz did not think that all perceptions are conscious. Leibniz was remarkably quiet about why he thought perceptions must belong to simple subjects. For an argument see his early *The Confession of Nature against Atheists* of 1669, in Leroy E. Loemker (ed.), *Leibniz, Philosophical Papers and Letters* (Dordrecht: Reidel, 1969), p. 113; and in C. I. Gerhardt (ed.), *Die Philosophischen Schriften von Gottfried Wilhelm Leibniz* (7 vols, Berlin: Wiedmann, 1875–90; repr. Hildesheim: Georg Olms, 1978), vol. iv, pp. 109–10. Bayle argued that the subject of sense perception must be simple. For Bayle, see *Historical and Critical Dictionary: Selections*, trans. Richard H. Popkin (Indianapolis: Hackett, 1991), article 'Leucippus', p. 130.

[3] Yet another defence can be found in the well-known discussion of the difference of humans from animals and machines in the *Discourse on the Method* (AT VI 55–60: CSM I 139–41).

argument from the soul's indivisibility, which distinguishes it from matter, but things are more complicated. The argument begins with a consideration of the nature of substance, then it turns to the simplicity that distinguishes the soul from the body.[4] Furthermore, understanding of this line of argument benefits more from examination of its relationship to an approach to the immortality of the soul common in the Aristotelian scholastic tradition than by relating it to the Platonist argument from the simplicity of the soul. A result of my discussion will be that on several accounts Descartes's treatment of the soul's simplicity betrays his intense engagement with Aristotelian scholasticism. I choose the term 'engagement' deliberately: I will discuss how in some ways his statements of its simplicity are aimed to express disagreements with the scholastics, but other statements are expressions of agreement.

Scholastic Aristotelian conceptions of the human soul are characterized by an attempt to combine two rather different ideas. One of these is the conception of the soul as a spiritual substance that can exist without the body, and so is capable of an afterlife. On the other hand the scholastics accepted Aristotelian hylomorphism, and saw human beings as composites of matter and form. They referred to such forms as substantial forms, the kinds of forms that with prime matter constitute substances. They saw such forms as substances by contrast with accidents, but incomplete substances. Their ontology also contained accidental forms, forms like whiteness, which constitute accidents that belong to substances as opposed to being entities that constitute substances.

Descartes scholarship has often examined his thought in isolation from his historical background. Much good work has been done in this vein. At the same time, in recent decades serious attempts have been made to understand Descartes's thought in relation to its historical context. Aristotelian scholasticism is an important and prominent part of this background, but not all historians of philosophy relish venturing into its vast and complex expanses. Anthony Kenny is a rare scholar who has for a long time combined interest in Descartes with extensive and profound knowledge of Aristotelian scholasticism, in particular Aquinas. He has made important contributions both to Descartes scholarship and to the understanding of medieval philosophy. So it is with great pleasure that I contribute to this volume the following attempt to understand Descartes's tangling with immortality, simplicity, and Aristotelianism. I will

---

[4] For the view that Descartes relies on the notion of substance, see Matthew Stuart, *Descartes's Extended Substances*, in Rocco J. Gennaro and Charles Huenemann (eds), *New Essays on the Rationalists* (New York and Oxford: Oxford University Press, 1999); Dan Kaufman, 'Cartesian Substances, Individual Bodies, and Corruptibility', unpublished manuscript. Other interpreters have held that Descartes argues that immortality derives from indivisibility. My interpretation will argue that both views contain an element of truth.

relate Descartes's views both to Aquinas, who was prominent in the teachings of the Jesuit who taught Descartes at La Flèche, and to Francisco Suárez. It is hard to know how much Suárez Descartes knew, but he was enormously influential in the period. His views reflected the developments in scholasticism since Aquinas and his temporal proximity to Descartes, as well as his tendency to offer extensive overviews of the state of opinions on any matter at hand, makes him an enormously useful source of getting a sense of the scholastic views that were around in Descartes's time.[5]

2. The Divisibility Argument in the Sixth Meditation

Descartes states the argument as follows:

(1) For when I consider [the mind], or myself in so far as I am merely a thinking thing, I am unable to distinguish any parts within myself; I understand myself to be something quite single and whole [*integram*]. (2) Although the whole mind seems to be united to the whole body, I recognize that if a foot or arm or any other part of the body is cut off, nothing has thereby been taken away from the mind. (3) As for the faculties of willing, understanding, of sense perception and so on, these cannot be called parts of the mind, since it is one and the same mind that wills, and understands and has sensory perceptions.   (AT VII 86: CSM II 59)[6]

Our first order of business is to address a terminological point the significance of which is not clear to me: when Descartes addresses what looks like the issue of the simplicity of the soul, he does not use the term 'simplicity', rather he speaks of its 'indivisibility'. This is true, for instance, in the discussion of the divisibility argument for dualism both in the Sixth Meditation and in the Synopsis to the *Meditations*. Why doesn't Descartes use the term 'simple' and cognates?

One possible reason worth considering is that he wished to reserve the term simplicity for God. Philosophers before Descartes sometimes displayed reluctance to call the human soul simple by contrast with God. For instance, Suárez claimed that unlike God, the human soul is not simple. He held that the faculties of the soul are really distinct from the soul. One of the arguments he offered for this view was that the human soul is too imperfect to do everything itself; only God can carry out his operations without faculties distinct from

---

[5] I will use Suárez's *Disputationes Metaphysicae* (*Opera omnia*, Paris: Vivès, 26 vols, vol. 25–6), which were published in 1596, as well as his *De anima* (*Opera omnia*, Paris: Vivès, 26 vols, vol. 3) which was published posthumously in 1621, and edited by P. Alvarez, 1856.

[6] I use the translations from CSM with occasional changes.

himself. Suárez took himself to be in agreement on the real distinction of the faculties of the soul from the soul with a number of philosophers, including Aquinas and the Thomists generally, Cajetan, Giles of Rome, and Ficino (*De anima* II.i.2). Aquinas had argued that the soul's powers are not identical with its essence; ' "to be" and "to act" are the same in God alone'.[7] Suárez went so far as to say that the human soul, taken together with its faculties, is an aggregate, *unum per aggregationem*, thus seeming to depart starkly from a major tradition committed to its simplicity (*De anima* II.iii.10).[8] Much earlier, Augustine had held that the soul is simple compared to bodies, but not, or less so, compared with God.[9]

But Descartes does not even use the term 'simplicity' for God when he discusses the same absence of composition in God. He argues that God does not consist of parts because being composed of parts is an imperfection (*Discourse*, AT VI 35: CSM I 128), since it is evidence of dependence, dependence of God on his parts.[10] And so, he concludes, God is indivisible and undivided (AT VII 138: CSM II 99) and consequently not material.

Descartes does use the term 'simple' in a different type of context: he sometimes states that God's *nature* is simple, and what he means there that it is not a collection of attributes: 'the unity, simplicity or [*sive*] indivisibility of all the things that are in God is one of the main perfections that we understand to be in him' (AT VII 50: CSM II 34, see also AT VII 137: CSM II 98: 'we understand in God the immensity, unity, simplicity that comprehends all other attributes'). The use of the term 'simple' in this sense is not confined to God: in a discussion of dualism in *Comments on a Certain Broadsheet* Descartes calls mind and body simple as opposed to composite beings (*entia*). The mind–body whole is a composite subject (AT VIIIB 350: CSM I 299). It is striking that he calls *both* mind and body simple beings, and so the sense of simplicity at issue is clearly different from the type of simplicity or indivisibility that distinguishes minds and God from bodies. The relevant difference is that a simple being only has one principal attribute, while a composite being, like the human

---

[7] *Questions on the Soul*, qu. 12 (James Robb, trans. Marquette University Press, 1984), p. 156. See also *Summa Theologiae*, I, qu. 77, art. 1.

[8] Suárez's claim is at first sight puzzling: it seems more intuitive to express the view that the soul's faculties are really distinct from it by saying that while the soul in itself is simple, its faculties are accidents really distinct from it. But the context of Suárez's statement is the question whether producing the soul's powers takes an action over and above producing the soul itself. There is another sense in which for Suárez the soul, taken by itself, is simple. See the discussion of 'holenmerism' below.

[9] For a discussion of the simplicity of the soul in medieval philosophy, see Henrik Lagerlund, 'The Unity of the Soul and Contrary Appetites in Medieval Philosophy', in Lennon and Stainton (eds), *The Achilles of Rationalist Psychology*, pp. 75–91. For discussion of Augustine on this issue see pp. 76–8.

[10] For discussion of this idea in the scholastic tradition, see Marilyn Adams, *Ockham* (Notre Dame: University of Notre Dame Press, 1987), ch. 21.

being, has more than one. What these contexts of the simplicity terminology seem to have in common is that they concern some sort of *qualitative* lack of composition. (And of course, Descartes frequently spoke of 'simple natures'.) Following Descartes, from now on, I will speak of the indivisibility rather than the simplicity of the soul or mind when concerned with its nature as distinct from that of body.

Let us return now to the Divisibility Argument in the Sixth Meditation. It contains essentially 3 claims:

(1) The meditator cannot distinguish any parts in herself or her mind: she considers herself to be something 'single and whole—*integram*'.[11]

(2) Although the whole mind is united to the whole body, if a limb were to be cut off from the body, 'nothing would thereby be taken away from the mind'.

(3) The faculties of the mind—will, intellect, sense perception—are not parts of the mind, because it is one and the same mind that wants, understands and senses—*una et eadem mens*. The French, it is worth noting, is more emphatic: *car le meme esprit s'emploie tout entier...* (AT IX 68).

I will consider (1) and (3) together. How should we understand Descartes's denial that the mind has any parts? In his initial statement he offers no argument or clarification. The next two claims consider illustrations of the point, specific ways in which the soul or mind cannot be said to have parts.

It should be clear that Descartes's denial that the mind has parts is meant as a denial that it has really distinct parts. He allowed for three types of distinctions: In decreasing order of strength, the mind could in principle be subject to a *real*, a *modal*, or a *rational* distinction.[12] The idea that the mind is indivisible most naturally suggests an absence of really distinct parts. Descartes held that modal distinctions do apply to the mind: thoughts are modes of the mind, and earlier in the Sixth Meditation he describes its faculties of sensation and imagination

---

[11] CSM translate *integram* as 'complete', but I find that translation misleading given Descartes's technical use of the term 'complete'. See in particular his Fourth Replies, AT VII 222–7: CSM II 156–9).

[12] For Descartes's theory of distinctions, see *Principles* I.60–2. For a rudimentary understanding of the theory the following will do for our purposes. When a and b can exist without one another, they are really distinct. For Descartes a real distinction only obtains between different substances. When a and b are modally distinct, one can exist without the other, but not vice versa. A rational distinction obtains between a and b when neither can exist without the other, and they are merely conceptually distinct. This account is rough and ready, because I do not think that questions about separability are constitutive of the different types of distinction, rather they are signs of the particular types of distinction. For discussion, see my *Descartes's Dualism* (Cambridge, Mass.: Harvard University Press, 1998), pp. 3–12.

as modes of the mind (AT VII 78: CSM II 54). Since the modal distinction is stronger than the distinction of reason, we can ignore the relevance of the latter here. So Descartes must be denying that the mind has really distinct parts, and in this regard for him the mind is different in nature from the body; in his explanation of the notion of real distinction at *Principles* I.60 Descartes illustrates that distinction with the claim that any body has really distinct parts.

The faculties of the mind are an obvious candidate for a source of real distinctions within the mind, given that a number of scholastics held that they are really distinct from the mind. So Descartes makes a point of denying that they are such a source 'since it is one and the same mind that wills, senses, and understands'. The claim echoes his claim in the Second Meditation where he wrote that 'It is the same "I" who doubts, understands, affirms, denies, is willing, is unwilling, and also imagines and has sensory perceptions' (AT VII 28: CSM II 19).

Descartes's denial that the faculties of the mind are parts of it surely is meant to address the Aristotelian scholastics. But it would not be accurate to see it simply as an expression of disagreement with the scholastics in general, since among them there was debate about the nature of the distinction between the soul and its faculties. We saw that Suárez thought they are really distinct from the soul, and that he took himself to be agreeing with Aquinas and various Thomistae on this point, but he cites four different opinions on the matter (*De anima* II.i.2). Besides the view that the powers of the soul are really distinct from it, he cites the view that they are in no way distinct from the soul, which he attributes to Ockham; Scotus' view that they are formally distinct from the soul; the view that some powers are (sensitive and intellectual powers), others (vegetative powers) are not distinct from the soul, which Suárez attributes to Bonaventure and Durandus of St Pourçain.[13] So Descartes's rejection of the idea that the faculties of the soul are parts of it really means that he rejects the view held by some scholastics that they are really distinct from the soul.[14] He is taking a stance within a scholastic debate.

[13] This last view may seem particularly surprising. When Suárez introduces it he explains with the following reasoning: vegetative powers produce substances and an accidental power can't do that.

[14] At the same time there was a tendency among scholastics to think that there is a real distinction at work in the relations among the faculties at least when we experience conflicts between will and sensible appetite. This type of conflict was used as a ground for arguing that there must be two really distinct souls in humans, a rational and a sensitive soul, a view proposed, for instance, by Ockham, or else that even if there is just one soul in a human being the faculties of sensitive and rational appetite are really distinct, a view favoured by Suárez. Descartes's view is that the conflict in question is a conflict between body and soul rather than different souls or really distinct powers of the soul (*Passions* I.47).

(2) Let us now turn to Descartes's claim that although the soul is united to the whole body, cutting off a limb won't result in the separation of a soul-part. We find this claim again in the *Passions of the Soul*:

But in order to understand all these things more perfectly, it is necessary to know that the soul is really joined to the whole body, and that we cannot properly say that it is in one of its parts to the exclusion of the others, because [the body] is one and in a sense indivisible, because of the disposition of its organs that relate to each other in such a way that when one of them is removed, it renders the entire body defective. And because [the soul] is of a nature that has no relation to extension or to dimensions or other properties of the matter of which the body is composed, but only to the entire organization [*assemblage*] of its organs. This is clear from the fact that we cannot at all conceive of half or a third of a soul or of the extension that it occupies, and that it does not become smaller when a part of the body is cut off, but it separates off entirely when the organization of its organs is dissolved.   (*Passions* I.30)

Descartes here repeats the claim of the Sixth Meditation that cutting off a part of the body will not result in the loss of a part of the soul. He now uses this claim to argue that the soul is united to the whole body, which is in a sense indivisible. This notion of the whole body was absent from the Sixth Meditation. But in both texts Descartes supports the indivisibility of the mind by stating that cutting off a part of the body does not result in the loss of a part of the soul and that we cannot conceive of parts of the soul or mind. And so in both texts he is addressing the relation of the soul to the body in light of its indivisibility.

The claim that cutting off a limb won't result in the loss of a part of the soul can also be found in Suárez. The point of the claim is not to address the intrinsic nature of the soul, but rather to relate its nature to the body. Descartes's claim here is what he and many others often expressed by saying that 'the whole soul is whole in the whole body and whole in the parts'—*tota in tota et tota in qualibet parte* (see, for instance, Suárez, *De anima* I.xiv.9; Aquinas, *Summa Theologiae* I, qu. 76, art. 8; *Questions on the Soul*, qu. 10; Descartes, Sixth Replies, AT VII 442: CSM II 298; letter to Elizabeth of 21 May 1643, AT III 667: CSMK 219; and letter to Arnauld of 29 July 1648, AT V 222–3: CSMK 358). This is a notoriously enigmatic claim, which was labelled 'holenmerism' by Henry More.[15] I won't offer a full discussion of this idea here,[16] but the important points of the claim for our purposes are these.

---

[15] Henry More, *Manual of Metaphysics* (*Studien und Materialen zur Geschichte der Philosophie*, trans. Alexander Jacob, Hildesheim: Georg Olms Verlag, 1995), p. 98. This is a translation of More's *Enchiridion metaphysicum*.

[16] For extensive discussion, see Ed Grant, *Much Ado about Nothing: Theories of Space and Vacuum from the Middle Ages to the Scientific Revolution* (Cambridge: Cambridge University Press, 1981), and my 'Descartes, Mind–Body Union, and Holenmerism', *Philosophical Topics* 31 (2003), pp. 343–68.

Holenmerism was an attempt to analyse the relationship of a spiritual substance to body while preserving the simplicity and indivisibility of the spiritual substance. It was widely used in Aristotelian scholasticism, although it was not unique to that context; it was used previously by, for instance, Augustine. In scholasticism it was used in two contexts: (1) The action of a spiritual substance on the extended world—in particular the action of God on the material world. (2) The union of soul and body in a human being, which in Aristotelian scholasticism was understood as a hylomorphic substance, a composite of matter and form. In both cases the difficulty was to reconcile the presence of a spiritual substance in an extended body with the idea that the spiritual substance is not itself extended, in the sense in which matter was extended.

God can act anywhere in the physical world. According to many (but not all, for instance not Scotus), his doing so presupposes his presence in the location where he acts. But one would not want to say that God is present in virtue of one part of him being present in one part of the world, another part in another part of the world. If the spiritual substance were present in this way, as whole in whole and part in part, it would itself be extended and composite. But God cannot be composite; he has no parts and is absolutely simple. Whence the claim that it is not the case that God is present in each part of the material world in virtue of a part of him being present in a part of the material entity. Instead he is present in each part in his entirety: so he is whole in the whole and whole in the parts. And in this sense all spiritual substances are simple: God, angels, human souls.

The view that the human soul is whole in the whole body and whole in its parts was widespread. In scholastic Aristotelianism in the context of the union of body and soul the issue was how the soul as substantial form is present in the body: the issue here is not the action of the soul on the body, as Aquinas put it, its being the mover of the body, but its informing the body. Aquinas sharply distinguished the two: 'If the soul were united to the body only as its mover, then one could say that it does not exist in each part of the body, only in one part and that through this part it moves the other parts' (*Summa Theologiae* I, qu. 76, art. 8, see also *Questions on the Soul*, qu. 10).

Descartes's claim that when one cuts off a limb, one does not thereby remove a part of the soul suggests that context rather than the issue of mind–body interaction.[17] In arguing that the human rational soul is whole in the whole and whole in the parts, Suárez illustrates the point by claiming that when

---

[17] The scholastics used holenmerism for two purposes, but holenmerism was one idea for them. So Suárez offered an argument for holenmerism for God (when addressing God's action on the physical

an arm is cut off the soul remains in the rest of the body in the same way, while it ceases to inform the part that is cut off. (*De anima* I.xiv.9, 10). Furthermore, the context of Descartes's claim suggests that holenmerism is here not meant to explain interaction. Right after the divisibility argument Descartes turns to interaction, and he claims it occurs only in one place in the body:

I notice that my mind is not affected immediately by all the parts of the body, but only by the brain, or perhaps even by only one very small part of it, that is, by that part where it is said the common sense is located.   (AT VII 86: CSM II 59)

Indeed, Descartes uses the idea that the mind is indivisible to support this point about the location of interaction and he presents it as the reason he introduced the divisibility argument. And in the *Passions* we find the same: right after article 30, where he had expressed holenmerism, at the beginning of article 31 Descartes turns to his view that interaction takes place in a particular location: 'We need to know also that although the soul is joined to the whole body, nevertheless there is a certain part of the body where it exercises its functions more particularly than in all others'. He now identifies this part as 'a certain very small gland [*une certaine glande fort petite*]'. Here the soul exercises its functions 'immediately' from where it 'radiates [*rayonne*] throughout the rest of the body by means of the spirits, nerves and even the blood, which, participating in the impressions of the spirits, can carry them to all the other members' (*Passions* I.31, 34).

Holenmerism is certainly a very puzzling view, but it helps to see its point if we consider the contrast between the human soul and other types of forms, which are not present in bodies in that same way. Suárez argued that the soul of a worm or of a plant is in its body whole in the whole and part in the parts, and such souls are divisible. Their divisibility is evident from the fact that if we cut up a worm, both parts continue to wriggle. Similarly, when we cut off a branch from a plant, we may be able to graft it onto another one, or stick it into water to grow roots. These examples show that in some cases life continues in both parts of a substance that has been cut up, and so the soul is present in both (see Suárez, *De anima*, I.xiii.2, 3). But Suárez takes this to mean that the soul in these organisms has parts which informed the parts of the organisms and which now explain why the separated parts of the organism continue to live.[18]

---

world) on the basis that holenmerism applies to the human soul, where it was defended on the ground of its status as substantial form of the body (*Disputationes Metaphysicae* XXX.vii.44).

[18] For discussion see Dennis Des Chene, *Life's Form: Late Aristotelian Conceptions of the Soul* (Ithaca, NY: Cornell University Press, 2000), ch. 9.

While Descartes does not use holenmerism to address mind–body interaction in the Sixth Meditation, he does do so elsewhere, in particular in discussions of the action of mind on the body with which it is united so as to make a human being. The clearest text is the Sixth Replies, where he argues that a certain notion of heaviness derives from the notion of the soul:

I also saw that while heaviness remains extended throughout the heavy body, it could exercise its whole force in any part of it; for if the body were hung from a rope attached to any of its parts, it would pull the rope down with all its heaviness, just as if this heaviness was only in the part touching the rope instead of also being spread through the other parts. This is exactly the way in which I now understand the mind to be co-extended with the body: whole in the whole, and whole in any of its parts.   (AT VII 441–2: CSM II 297–8, see also the letter to Elizabeth of 21 May 1643, AT III 667: CSMK 219 and a letter to Arnauld of 29 July 1648, AT V 222–3: CSMK 358)

This use of holenmerism is not obviously consistent with Descartes's repeated claim that interaction occurs in one part of the body, the pineal gland. It would take us too far afield to address this issue here, however.[19] What is noteworthy for our purposes is that this is another context in which Descartes addresses, albeit not in those terms, the indivisibility and simplicity of the human soul, and he does so when concerned with its relationship to the body.

Descartes may seem to be implying agreement with the hylomorphism of the scholastics in suggesting that the human soul or mind is whole in the whole and whole in the parts of the human body. But Descartes was a dualist, not a hylomorphist. Of course, some disagree with the denial of hylomorphism on Descartes's behalf, most notably Paul Hoffman.[20] But it is important to note that holenmerism was not unique to Aristotelian scholasticism: it was used by Augustine and Plotinus, and Suárez and Aquinas both cite Augustine as holding the view: in his *sed contra* Aquinas wrote: 'But on the other hand, Augustine said in *De Trinitate* VI, that the soul is in any body both whole in the whole and whole in any of its parts'.[21] So its appearance in Descartes does not necessarily indicate acceptance of hylomorphism. Furthermore, when addressing the union of soul and body, holenmerism was employed by the Aristotelian scholastics to address precisely that feature of the human soul that

[19] But see my 'Descartes, Mind–Body Union, and Holenmerism'.
[20] See in particular his 'The Union of Descartes's Man', *Philosophical Review* (1986), pp. 356–8, but also 'Cartesian Composites', *Journal of the History of Philosophy* 37/2 (1999), pp. 251–70. 'Descartes's Theory of Distinction', *Philosophy and Phenomenological Research* 44/1 (2002), pp. 57–78. 'Descartes's Watch Analogy', *British Journal for the History of Philosophy* 15/3 (2007), pp. 561–7.
[21] Aquinas, *Summa Theologiae* I, qu. 77, art. 8. See Augustine, *De Trinitate* VI.8, 210–11.

strains against its status as a substantial form, namely its character as a spiritual substance.[22]

(3) It is noteworthy that Descartes's divisibility argument is dominated by concerns about the mind's relation to the body. First, the context of the argument in the Sixth Meditation is Descartes's discussion of the interaction of mind and body in view of his explanation for why the body sometimes sends the wrong signal to the mind about goings on internal to it. Descartes's explanation appeals to the fact that the soul is simple and so united to the body only in one place, receiving information from the rest of the body indirectly. So the reason Descartes gives for offering the divisibility argument is not in the first place a desire to establish its immateriality.[23] Second, the point of holenmerism here as elsewhere is to address the union with the body: cutting off a limb won't remove a part of the soul. So the passage is striking for its focus on the relationship of the mind to the body. And Descartes's use of holenmerism in the context of the action of mind on body elsewhere is another instance of his addressing the issues of the indivisibility of the soul in the context of its relationship to the body.

3. The Immortality of the Soul

The Synopsis to the *Meditations* is one of the most prominent texts about the immortality of the soul in Descartes. His treatment of the issue there displays a striking contrast to the Platonistic history of arguing for the immortality of the soul from its simplicity. First, Descartes presents both of his arguments for dualism from the Sixth Meditation and writes that he does not establish the soul's immortality in the *Meditations*—although, as is well known, the title of the first edition of the *Meditations* claimed the work does accomplish this. The arguments for dualism, he explains, only give us *hope* of an afterlife: their conclusion ensures that the demise of the body does not entail the demise of the mind or soul. So at this point he pointedly refuses to derive the soul's (natural) immortality from the indivisibility that distinguishes it from body. Then he says that he does not offer an argument for immortality in the *Meditations*, because 'the premises from which the very immortality of the soul can be derived

---

[22] For more discussion, see Kenny, *Aquinas on Mind* (London and New York: Routledge, 1993), chs 11 and 12, and my *Descartes's Dualism*, ch. 5.

[23] This strikes me as somewhat puzzling, and it is not clear what to think of Descartes's attitude to the argument. He does claim that it is sufficient by itself to establish that conclusion, and moreover, in the Synopsis he notes that it establishes that the natures of mind and body are not merely different, but opposite.

depend on an explanation of the whole of physics' (AT VII 13–14: CSM II 10). This is an extraordinary claim: why would establishing the immortality of the soul require a discussion of physics? Why couldn't one simply focus on the nature of the soul? In particular, given that this pronouncement immediately follows his claim that the real distinction is confirmed by the argument that mind is indivisible, body is divisible, one would expect him to do exactly this by focusing on the mind's indivisibility. But he does not do so. Here is what he says instead:

... [T]he premises that lead to the conclusion that the soul is immortal depend on an account of the whole of physics. This is required for two reasons. First, we need to know that absolutely all substances, or [*sive*] things that must be created by God in order to exist, are by their nature incorruptible and cannot ever cease to exist unless they are reduced to nothingness by God's denying his concurrence to them. Secondly, we need to recognize that body, taken in general, is a substance, so that it too never perishes. But the human body in so far as it differs from other bodies, is simply made up of a certain configuration of limbs and other accidents of this sort, whereas the human mind is not made up of any accidents in this way, but is a pure substance ... (AT VII 13–14: CSM II 10)

So we find ourselves with two very remarkable results:

(1) Rather than deriving the immortality of the soul from its indivisibility, Descartes seems to derive it from the fact that it is a pure substance. Pure substances only go out of existence as a result of God withdrawing his concurrence. And this is not peculiar to mental substances: body in general is also pure substance and so similarly does not go out of existence except as a result of God withdrawing his concurrence. By contrast, the tradition of the Achilles Argument does not derive immortality from the soul's status as substance; rather it contends that mind or soul is simple and so incorruptible, and this distinguishes it from body. At the same time Descartes suggests that there is a notion of the human body, as a type of body that is corruptible, while there is no corresponding sense in which a mind can be said to be corruptible. I will set this last idea aside for now, but will return to it at the end of the present section.

(2) In order to establish the conclusion that the soul is immortal Descartes thinks he needs all of physics. The reasons he offers are that the argument requires that: (a) all (pure) substances are by their nature incorruptible; (b) we need to understand that body in general is pure substance and so also does not cease to exist, while the human body is a configuration of modes, and easily goes out of existence. But there is no corresponding sense of the human mind as made up of modes.

These two reasons call for an explanation. I wish to pursue the following line of thought.[24] The reason Descartes thought he needed all of physics was that he thought he needed to show he could do physics without substantial forms and that getting rid of substantial forms paves the way for recognizing the immortality of the soul. Here is how that is relevant.

A kindred line of thought can be found in the *Discourse on the Method*. Descartes there argued that it is easier to see that the human soul is immortal if we recognize that animals are just machines. The reason is that on that view there are no souls in animals, and that removes one obstacle to recognizing human immortality: the obstacle that arises from the difficulty of establishing that human souls are different enough from animal souls so that we can see that human souls are, but animal souls are not immortal. So here Descartes indicates that his commitment to the very wide scope of mechanistic explanation helps support the immortality of the human soul.

Descartes makes a similar connection between immortality of the human soul and the rejection of substantial forms in a letter to Regius:

[F]rom the opinion that affirms substantial forms it is very easy to slip into the opinion of those who say that the human soul is corporeal and mortal; when it is acknowledged that [the human soul] alone is a substantial form, and that the others consists of the configuration and motion of parts, this very privileged status it has over the others shows that it differs from them in nature, and this difference in nature opens a very easy road to showing its immateriality and immortality, as can be seen in the recently published *Meditations on First Philosophy*.   (AT III 503: CSMK 207–8)

So Descartes claims that a rejection of substantial forms (except for the case of the human soul) generates support for the immateriality and immortality of the human soul. Substantial forms generally must be supplanted by configurations of modes. This is what in fact Descartes proposes for the human body in the Synopsis: it is a configuration of limbs and other modes rather than a composite of matter and form—although what specifically is at stake in this passage in terms of the function of the modes is different from what is at stake in the letter to Regius, as we will see in a moment.[25]

So we can see that Descartes thought there was a connection between rejecting substantial forms and supporting the immortality of the human soul.

---

[24] This line of thought springs from a suggestion made to me by Jeff McDonough. Jeff suggested that Descartes thought he needed to do all of physics because he thought he needed to show that he could deal with life without substantial forms. I am broadening the point to the idea that Descartes thought he could do all of natural philosophy without substantial forms.

[25] I discuss Descartes's rejection of substantial forms more fully in my *Descartes's Dualism*, ch. 4. For more discussion of this letter to Regius see in particular pp. 123–33.

Furthermore, he writes in this letter that there are two main arguments against them, and they connect directly to his discussion in the Synopsis:

The arguments or physical proofs, which we think would force a truth-loving mind to abandon substantial forms, are mainly the following *a priori* or metaphysical ones. It is contradictory [*repugnet*] that a substance should come into existence without being created from nothing by God; but we see that every day many so-called substantial forms come into existence from nothing; and yet the people who think they are substances do not believe that they are created by God; therefore their view is mistaken. This is confirmed by the example of the soul, which is the true substantial form of the human being. For the soul is thought to be immediately created by God for no other reason than that it is a substance. Furthermore, since other substantial forms are not thought to be created in this way, but as only educed from the potency of matter, they should not be regarded as substances. It is clear from this also that it is not those who deny substantial forms, but those who affirm them who 'can be driven by solid arguments to become beasts or atheists'.   (AT III 505: CSMK 208)

So in this letter Descartes offers a view of substance—which is the conception of pure substance of the Synopsis—according to which a substance is created *de novo* by God. He directs this view as a 'metaphysical or theological' argument against substantial forms: substantial forms are thought to be substances but they are not regarded as created by God, and this is inconsistent, on the conception of substance Descartes favours.

But a rejection of substantial forms also undermines the Aristotelian conception of hylomorphic substances which do not come to be as a result of creation, but which are composites that come to be as a result of substantial forms coming to be through natural processes (they are 'educed from matter') and which can cease to be through natural processes. While Descartes's explicit target in this 'theological' argument is the existence of such forms, it also undermines the hylomorphic composites they help constitute, and that is what is relevant to his discussion of immortality in the Synopsis, as we shall see in a moment.

Now why would this involve doing all of physics? In the same letter to Regius Descartes offers a second argument against substantial forms that answers this question:

The second proof is taken from the end or use of substantial forms; for they were introduced by the philosophers for no other reason than that through them they could account for the proper actions of natural things, of which this form is the principle and root, as we said in a previous thesis. But it is not possible to give an account of any natural action through these forms, because those who affirm them believe that they are obscure and that they do not understand them.   (AT III 506: CSMK 208)

Descartes is referring to a central argument for substantial forms found among the scholastics. This argument contends that there must be substantial forms in natural substances because they are needed to explain the characteristic behaviour of particular types of substances. For instance, Suárez wrote:

The second principal argument for the existence of substantial form is gathered from various indications arising from accidents and operations of natural beings, which indicate that a substantial form underlies them. . . . For if water, for example, is heated, and later the external cause of the heat is removed, the water returns to its original coldness because of an intrinsic force, as experience attests.   (Suárez, *Disputationes Metaphysicae* XV.i.8)

Descartes proposes that substantial forms cannot do this job, that his mechanistic modes can do it, so these forms are superfluous. But consequently his view of (pure) substance can be supported by showing that he could do physics just in terms of extension and its modes, without substantial forms. Doing so would support his abandonment of substantial forms and consequently of hylomorphic composite substances in favour of his simplified ontology of pure substances and modes.

There is no explicit mention of substantial forms in the Synopsis, but Descartes's explanation of how he would support the immortality of the soul bears the marks of their elimination. Recall that he offers two reasons why doing all of physics is required. One of these reasons lies in his conception of pure substance, the other is the distinction between body in general, which is pure substance, and the human body, and his claim that this distinction does not apply to the soul or mind. The ontology he proposes here contains souls on one hand, and on the other hand (1) extended stuff as material substance, (2) configurations of modes that generate individual bodies like the human body.[26] Extended stuff does not go out of existence during natural processes of change any more than the human soul does: it merely undergoes changes in modes. And when certain changes in configurations of modes occur in the human body, changes that are deadly, the human body ceases to be.

From an Aristotelian scholastic point of view both notions of body that Descartes proposes here are completely alien. First, the scholastics did not have a notion of body as pure substance in Descartes's sense. The only pure substances they recognized in this sense were spiritual substances—God, angels,

---

[26] Descartes's claim that modes generate the human body should be handled gingerly. The Latin is *conflatum*: the best translation here is something like: 'brought about by combining'. The precise role of the modes deserves attention on account of the objection that modes are posterior to substances, and so cannot individuate them. It is only once a substance is constituted that it can have modes. Scotus and Spinoza are among those who would raise this objection. I am grateful to John Carriero for noting the relevance of this point.

and human souls—although the status of the human soul as spiritual substance as well as substantial form is complicated. For the scholastics, bodies, including human bodies, are composites of matter and form, and the separation of these two is what constitutes corruption and the natural ceasing-to-be of bodies. For the scholastics there also was no notion of the human body as a configuration of accidents: accidents inhere in a body, for instance the human body, that is a metaphysically prior composite of form and matter. In sum, Descartes expresses here in the Synopsis a view of body that is radically different from the Aristotelian scholastic view, and the crucial difference is his abandonment of substantial forms.[27]

So I wish to propose that in the Synopsis Descartes says that doing all of physics supports the immortality of the soul because it results in an elimination of substantial forms, and this elimination makes it easier to recognize the immortality of the soul. The letter to Regius makes explicit that Descartes sees a connection between the elimination of substantial forms and the immortality of the soul, but the line of argument in the Synopsis is different from the letter to Regius in the following respect. In the letter Descartes had argued against substantial forms on two grounds: on the basis of a conception of substance as something that is created *de novo*, and on the ground that they are superfluous. Behind his cryptic remarks in the Synopsis, I suggest, is the following idea: Descartes is thinking that this conception of substance emerges from the elimination of substantial forms by doing physics, an enterprise that renders them superfluous. And the elimination of substantial forms supports the immortality of the human soul because this elimination removes the presence of entities that are confusing with regard to the question of ceasing-to-be: substantial forms were thought of as substances and yet able to cease to be through natural processes. That idea was present in the letter to Regius. Furthermore, as I noted before, while the letter to Regius is focused on rejecting substantial forms, the Synopsis really focuses on a different issue: the resulting rejection of hylomorphic substances. Consequently, Descartes rejects the possibility that a substance can go out of existence as a result of a separation

---

[27] AT VII 356: CSM II 246; AT III 503, 505: CSM III 207–8; and AT IV 346: CSM III 279. Obviously, this discussion touches on controversial issues about the status of individual material substances in Descartes. I can't enter into that discussion here. Unlike some interpreters, I do not think that there is only one material substance for Descartes, this strikes me as a misreading of the phrase 'matter in general'. His point about its incorruptibility, in my view, is that 'matter in general', that is, matter as such, can't decompose in the way a hylomorphic substance can. Like Locke later, Descartes distinguishes between a human body and the chunk of matter with which it coincides (although Locke's and Descartes's notions of the human body differ in important ways). For Descartes, the human body can cease to be since its identity depends on its modes.

of matter and form, which was the Aristotelian conception of the corruption, the natural ceasing-to-be, of substances.

Getting rid of substantial forms, for Descartes, means that we are left with just pure substances, which cannot cease to be by natural processes; all that is left is changes in configuration of modes. Even bodies cannot be corrupted in the Aristotelian sense any more, since they are no longer composites of matter and form. And in this sense 'matter in general' is pure substance and incorruptible.[28]

So it should now be clear how Descartes's argument for immortality derives support from doing physics, and also why he focuses on the notion of pure substance. At this point, I wish to return to the connection with questions about indivisibility. First, as I noted, it is very striking that while Descartes does argue that the human soul is indivisible as opposed to the body, he does not rely on this sense of indivisibility in his sketch of an argument for its immortality, and instead employs his conception of pure substance. But there is a sense in which he does invoke a type of indivisibility, an Aristotelian type: pure substances are not composites of matter and form, they are created by God *de novo*. And this type of non-composition was important in Scholastic arguments for immortality. For instance, while in his argument for the incorruptibility of the human soul Aquinas did not focus on this idea, it did play a role in his argumentation. He argued that the human soul is incorruptible because it is a subsisting form and part of his reasoning is that it is not a composite of matter and form:

Corruption is entirely impossible not only for the [human soul] but for anything subsisting that is only a form. For it is manifest that whatever belongs to something intrinsically [*secundum se*] is inseparable from it. Being, however, belongs *per se* to form, which is act. Hence matter acquires actual being insofar as it acquires form. And this is how corruption happens to it, by form being separated from it. It is impossible, however, that form is separated from itself. Hence it is impossible that a subsisting form ceases to be.   (*Summa Theologiae* I, qu. 75, art. 6)

This is a difficult and very compressed argument, and I will not attempt a full explanation.[29] But the following ideas are central: first, the argument relies on the idea that being belongs to form (rather than matter). Second, the human soul is a subsisting form, that is, a form that has existence in and of itself and

---

[28] I do not think this means for Descartes that there is only one material substance. Rather his point is that matter in general cannot be corrupted in this sense. Any part of matter is incorruptible and pure substance in this sense, even though its configuration of modes may change, parts of matter are really distinct (see *Principles* I.60), and may be separated from each other in space.

[29] For discussion, see Anthony Kenny, *Aquinas on Mind*, esp. p. 142.

its existence does not depend on being a constituent of a composite substance or in virtue of being joined to something else. Third, the argument relies on the idea that the soul is not a composite of form and matter, but is just a form, and in that sense simple. Aquinas thinks he can use these ideas to argue that being is inseparable from the human soul. Suárez finds this argument obscure. He proposes that rather than focusing on the inseparability of being from a subsisting form it is better to focus on the simplicity of a subsisting form (*De anima*, I.x.23). So in this sense simplicity or indivisibility is important in this Aristotelian argument for the incorruptibility of the human soul, and that sense of indivisibility, we have seen, plays a role in Descartes's argument in the Synopsis.

Finally, let me return to the sense in which the soul is indivisible but the body is not that is at stake in the Divisibility Argument of the Sixth Meditation. This sense of indivisibility does play a role in Descartes's reasoning about immortality, albeit in perhaps a subsidiary way. Recall that he concludes his sketch of an argument for immortality as follows:

> But the human body in so far as it differs from other bodies, is simply made up of a certain configuration of limbs and other accidents of this sort, whereas the human mind is not made up of any accidents in this way, but is a pure substance . . . From this it follows that the body perishes easily, but the mind is immortal by its very nature.

So while body and mind both as pure substances are incorruptible, there is a sense of body, the human body, that is corruptible, because it ceases to be when certain changes in modes occur. But there is no sense in which a human mind is individuated in virtue of a configuration of modes, so no corresponding ceasing-to-be of minds exists. But surely that difference results from the fact that body is divisible, but mind is not: as the argument in the Sixth Meditation explains, we can distinguish really distinct parts of bodies in virtue of their modes, but we cannot distinguish really distinct parts for minds.

4. Conclusion

There are several reasons why Descartes stands out with respect to a long tradition of thinking about the human soul as simple. While he addresses its simplicity, or as he preferred to say, its indivisibility on a variety of occasions, his focus is not on its intrinsic nature, or on the distinction with body, rather he raises the issue when concerned with the positive side of the relationship with body, its union and interaction with the human body. His main argument for dualism does not focus on its simplicity. He does offer an argument for dualism on the ground that the mind is indivisible, the body is divisible. But he introduces this argument ostensibly in order to address concerns about interaction. Furthermore, in the tradition of the Achilles Argument, the immortality of the human soul was derived directly from its simplicity. Descartes's sketch of an argument for immortality takes a different route. His remarks in the Synopsis are cryptic, in particular, his comment that the argument requires doing all of physics. I have argued that behind this remark lies his rejection of substantial forms and I have offered an explanation for why this rejection supports immortality in the way suggested by the remarks in the Synopsis. Descartes's suggestion for an argument for dualism, then, does not focus in the first instance on the indivisibility of the soul that distinguishes it from body. It begins with the rejection of hylomorphism, and a focus on a conception of pure substance as incorruptible. Both mind and 'matter in general' are such substances. But in the end, the argument does use a difference between mind and body with respect to indivisibility, a difference that is at the heart of the divisibility argument.

Part IV

Wittgenstein

13

The Development of Wittgenstein's Philosophy of Psychology

PETER HACKER

Anthony Kenny has, over the last half a century, been one of the leading Wittgenstein scholars in the world, and one of the pioneers in applying Wittgenstein's ideas and methods to novel domains and problems. I was fortunate to have met Tony when I was a Junior Research Fellow at Balliol more than forty years ago. The depth of his thought, the breadth of his knowledge, the clarity and incisiveness of his writings have inspired me throughout my professional life. In his paper 'Wittgenstein's Early Philosophy of Mind', Tony was the first to delve beneath the surface of the *Tractatus* to disclose the hidden philosophico-psychological presuppositions of the book.[1] The following essay, a small token of gratitude for all that I have learnt from Tony, begins from the same point and tells the subsequent tale of the development of Wittgenstein's philosophy of psychology.

1. Prolegomenon

An overview of Wittgenstein's engagement with problems in the philosophy of psychology must start with the very beginning of his philosophical career, not because we can find there early reflections on the subject, but rather because we find there an array of relatively unreflective presuppositions. These are of interest for two reasons. First, they form the well-concealed

---

[1] A. J. P. Kenny, 'Wittgenstein's Early Philosophy of Mind', repr. in his *The Legacy of Wittgenstein* (Oxford: Blackwell, 1984), pp. 1–9.

psychological hinterland of the logic and metaphysics of symbolism of the *Tractatus*. So they shed light on the book. Secondly, these presuppositions were largely misconceived and became the target of Wittgenstein's critical investigations in the 1930s. The themes—meaning something, wanting, intending, understanding, explaining the meaning of an expression, knowing what an expression means, believing things to be so—in effect provided Wittgenstein's gateway to investigations into the philosophy of psychology.

When Wittgenstein returned to philosophy in 1929, the psychological presuppositions that characterized his early work only gradually came under scrutiny. That is not surprising. Locating the roots of one's thought and then pulling them up is no easy matter. *The Big Typescript* was an early attempt to weld his new philosophy into a unified whole that would both confront the errors and misconceptions of the *Tractatus* and elaborate his new ideas on the nature of language and linguistic representation. These attempts continued throughout the 1930s and 1940s with the *Umarbeitung*, the *Zweite Umarbeitung, Eine Philosophische Betrachtung*, and the four different drafts of the *Philosophical Investigations* that preoccupied him until 1946/7. Here, in his second masterwork, we find a sustained engagement with the subjects of understanding, privacy of experience, the impossibility of a private language the nominata of which are supposedly 'private' experiences, expressions ('Äusserungen') of the 'inner', thinking, imagination and mental images, mind and behaviour, the first-person pronoun, consciousness, intentionality, memory and recognition, the will and voluntary action, intention, and meaning something. Most of these have a direct bearing on the central themes of the book. But with regard to others, such as the nature of psychological investigation, of mental states, recognition, voluntariness and the will, and the nature of intention (the remarks on which were all added only in the final draft), Wittgenstein's interest was caught by these topics in their own right.

In 1946 Wittgenstein turned explicitly to investigations in philosophy of psychology. The last lecture courses he gave as professor at Cambridge in 1946–7 were on the philosophy of psychology, and from April 1946 until March 1949, he bent his efforts to explorations in this domain. The results were the MSS volumes 130–8, comprising some 1,900 pages of notes. A selection from these, completed in October 1947, was dictated to form TS 229, since published as *Remarks on the Philosophy of Psychology*, volume 1. A further selection was dictated to form TS 232, completed in October 1948, and since published as *Remarks on the Philosophy of Psychology*, volume 2. These selections are not reordered or arranged—they are merely a sifting of material in chronological order.[2] The second half of MS 137 and the whole of MS 138, written between October 1948 and March 1949, and now published as *Last Writings on the Philosophy of Psychology*, volume 1, were not made into a typescript. But in the spring of 1949 Wittgenstein made a handwritten selection of remarks—the loose-leaf folder MS 144—which formed the basis for the lost typescript (TS 234) of what was published in 1953 as Part 2 of the *Investigations*. This contains 374 remarks, the large majority from MSS 137–8. It is doubtful whether this compilation was meant to be a part of the *Investigations*, and more probable that it was intended as a preliminary stage of a larger volume on the philosophy of psychology. Wittgenstein may have made the selection and dictated the typescript primarily to take it with him to America in the summer of 1949 in order to show his recent work to Norman Malcolm.[3]

The 1,900 pages of notes on the philosophy of psychology to some extent form a new departure for Wittgenstein, at least in the following sense. The *Investigations* is a Janus-faced book. On the one hand, it looks back critically to the *Tractatus* and the philosophical tradition of which Wittgenstein conceived it to be the culmination and termination. On the other hand, it goes over similar ground in a wholly novel way, advancing very different solutions to a wide range of problems concerning the nature of language, meaning, and linguistic representation. The subsequent writings on philosophical psychology do not have this counterpoint. Moreover, the style of the remarks is much less dialogical than in the *Investigations*. The author is no longer talking to an imaginary interlocutor, but, if to anyone at all, then to himself. The therapeutic note is much muted; and conceptual geography is everywhere evident. There is no systematic confrontation with his earlier self or with a

---

[2] He did, however, cut up one copy of TSS 229 and 232 into slips, and preserved 369 of them for future use. This collection of cuttings, together with cuttings from other typescripts, has been published as *Zettel*.

[3] Von Wright ('The Troubled History of Part II of the *Investigations*', *Grazer Philosophische Studien* 42 (1992), pp. 181–92) relates that on 18 February 1949 Wittgenstein wrote to Malcolm that he was planning to dictate materials that he had been working on since the autumn of 1948 and would send Malcolm a copy. In March Malcolm invited Wittgenstein to visit him in Cornell. Wittgenstein accepted the invitation. So he never sent Malcolm a typescript, but brought with him the typescript made in early July 1949 from MS 144 in order to show Malcolm later that month (see N. Malcolm, *Ludwig Wittgenstein—A Memoir*, 2nd edn (Oxford, Oxford University Press, 1984), p. 66). It is noteworthy that the discussion in which Wittgenstein told Rhees and Anscombe that he intended to suppress a good deal of the last 30 pages of the *Investigations* and to work 'what is in Part II, with further material, into its place' (PI, Editors' note) took place in Dublin in December 1948, *before* he had written MS 144, and six months before he had dictated it. It is, therefore, impossible to ascertain what he may have had in mind. The hypothesis that his writings were intended as preliminary work for a projected volume on the philosophy of psychology is, of course, perfectly compatible with the idea of modifying and adding *some* of the new material to the discussions of PI §§571–693 on expectation, belief, recognition, voluntariness, intention, and meaning something.

great tradition in the manner in which Augustine's picture of language provides the *mise en scène*, and the Augustinian conception of language a muted leitmotif, for the *Investigations*. The *Tractatus* is barely mentioned, and there are but few references, explicit or implicit, to his previous views. Few other writers are alluded to, although James is often used as a stalking horse, and Köhler and Gestalt psychology are subjected to criticism. Rather, what we find is a painstaking *exploration* of language games with psychological concepts. Many different concepts are investigated, patterns of similarity and difference are painstakingly teased out, and conceptual connections described. The tone is tentative. We see Wittgenstein applying the methods of philosophical analysis that he had developed over the previous sixteen years. Direct remarks on philosophy in general—so common in his earlier notes—are rare. That seems to be a subject that has now been settled and about which he has no further qualms. But there are numerous reflections on methodology in philosophical psychology as Wittgenstein struggles to determine his goal and to find his way. Although these writings are incomplete and unpolished, we can learn much about how he thought problems in philosophical psychology should be handled. That in turn sheds light on his general conception of philosophy and philosophical method.

In the following I shall survey the evolution of Wittgenstein's engagement with philosophy of psychology, and essay an overview of his conception of the subject.

2. The Psychological Hinterland of Wittgenstein's Early Philosophy

Anti-psychologism was increasingly common in Germany (e.g. Lotze) and Britain (e.g. the Absolute Idealists) towards the end of the nineteenth century. Wittgenstein inherited this methodological commitment from both Frege and Russell. As he put it bluntly, 'psychology is no more closely related to philosophy than any other natural science' (TLP 4.121), and he noted that his study of sign-language corresponds to the study of thought processes which philosophers used to consider essential for the philosophy of logic, and that he must take care not to get entangled in inessential psychological investigations.[4] The central subject of the *Tractatus*—the nature of the proposition and the

---

[4] Presumably he meant the investigation of the psychological nature of judgement, the difference between entertaining a proposition and believing it to be true, the nature of ideas and the differences between affirming and denying one idea or another, and so forth.

logico-metaphysical consequences that flow from its essential nature[5]—can and should be handled without reference to psychological considerations. For something *is* a proposition only insofar as it is meant and understood. So since, from a logical point of view, propositions are given, then meaning and understanding, qua psychological acts or processes, drop out of any *logical* considerations. Consequently, the psychological presuppositions of the book are largely tacit, and are made clear only by Wittgenstein's notebooks and correspondence. The following five points can be gleaned from these:

1. Excluding psychological considerations seemed to license avoiding reflection on psychological *concepts*. That meant taking for granted a range of unexamined preconceptions concerning meaning something, understanding, and thinking. These were anything but trivial or innocuous. Hence Wittgenstein's later remark in the *Investigations* §81, 'All this, however, can only appear in the right light when one has attained greater clarity about the concepts of understanding, meaning [*meinen*], and thinking. For it will then also become clear what can lead us (and did lead me [in MS 142, §78, he added here 'Log. Phil. Abh.']) to think that if anyone utters a sentence and *means* or *understands* it, he is operating a calculus according to definite rules.'

2. In 1915, Wittgenstein wrote: 'Names are necessary for an assertion that *this* thing possesses *that* property and so on. They link the propositional form with quite definite objects. And if the general description of the world is like a stencil of the world, the names pin it to the world so that the world is wholly covered by it' (NB 53). *How* are names connected to their meanings? The correlation of a name and its meaning, he had claimed in his 'Notes on Logic' in 1913, is *psychological* (NB 104). In 1915, he averred that it is *the speaker* who correlates the components of the picture with objects (NB 33f.) How then did Wittgenstein conceive of the mechanism of correlation effected by the user of a name?

3. Names have a meaning only in the context of a proposition, just as the toy cars and figures in the Paris lawcourt stand for specific cars and people only when they are arranged in a representation of the traffic accident under consideration, and not when the little cars and figures are put back in their boxes. One projects a state of affairs into a representing fact, and the elements of the representing fact stand for the elements of the state of affairs represented. The method of projection is 'to think the sense of the proposition' (TLP 3.11; or 'thinking the sense of the propositional sign' PTLP 3.12–3.13). The sense of a proposition is (roughly) the (possible) state of affairs it represents,[6] and

---

[5] An early title Wittgenstein proposed for the book was *Der Satz*.
[6] Strictly speaking it is the agreement and disagreement of the proposition with the obtaining and non-obtaining of the state of affairs it represents (cf. TLP 4.2).

thinking the sense of a proposition is, I suggest, *intending* or *meaning* BY the proposition (the sentence in use) *that* state of affairs. In so doing, one *means* by the constituent names of the proposition the constituent objects of the state of affairs meant. So it is the speaker's meaning (*meinen*) that correlates names with objects that are their meanings (*Bedeutungen*). (A corollary of this conception, not mentioned in the *Tractatus*, is that all understanding of the discourse of others is interpreting.)

This account of Wittgenstein's ideas has been challenged on the grounds that it takes for granted that 'thinking the sense of a proposition' is a 'mental proceeding' that constitutes the method of projection.[7] This is mistaken. It does not take any such thing for granted. It relies on Wittgenstein's assertion that the correlation of a name and its meaning is psychological (NB 104), that names link the propositional form with quite definite objects (NB 53), and that it is 'By my correlating the components of the picture with objects, [that] it comes to represent a situation and to be right or wrong' (NB 33 f.). The interpretation is strengthened by the fourth general point:

4. Explicitly in the *Notebooks* and implicitly in the *Tractatus*, Wittgenstein argued that propositions that appear to be vague in their surface grammar are actually determinate, or at least determinately indeterminate, in their depth grammar. A proposition like 'The book is lying on the table' appears vague, since it appears indeterminate what exactly counts as 'lying on', and hence the proposition might seem to lack any determinate truth value. However, the speaker means *something* by the sentence, 'and as much as we *certainly* mean, must surely be clear' (NB 67). What the speaker means may be a disjunction of possibilities, but each of the disjuncts must be sharp. So all indeterminacy is determinately indeterminate. Indeed, the speaker is at least sometimes in a position to assert 'I *know* what I mean; I mean just THIS (pointing to the appropriate complex with my finger)' (NB 70).

The interpretation is clinched by the fact that when Wittgenstein returned to philosophy in 1929, he continued for a while to conceive of intending or meaning (*meinen*) as the method of projection whereby a state of affairs is projected into a proposition. In MS 108, 218 f. he wrote:

... can the intention be an external relation?

Because the intention brings it about that this process is a picture which gets confirmed or disconfirmed and because this constitutes the real essence of intention, therefore the intention can be no [external] relation of the picture to something else. I see before me

---

[7] See Cora Diamond, 'Peter Winch on the *Tractatus* and the Unity of Wittgenstein's Philosophy', in A. Pichler and S. Säätelä (eds), *Wittgenstein: The Philosopher and his Work* (Bergen: Wittgenstein Archives at the University of Bergen, 2005), p. 147.

how the thought—the meant sentence [*gemeinte Satz*]—reaches right up to reality, i.e. already models its form in advance. As does the ruler, or perhaps just two gradation marks on it, with which reality is now especially compared?

One could say that the intention is the method of projection.

The picture (in the narrower sense) does not suffice because how it is to be compared with reality is not given with it. Together with it must be the method of projection; but then the picture indeed reaches right into the place where the object [*Gegenstand*][8] of the picture is.

It is the intention that determines what is *meant* and that transforms a mere sign into a representation of a possibility that may or may not be actualized. In MS 109, 218, he wrote 'An intention sets a standard against which the fact can be judged', so it is by meaning or intending the sign to represent a certain state of affairs that the sign becomes a true-or-false picture. In his lectures in Lent Term 1930, he remarked: 'The proposition is a picture', but not a picture by resemblance, like a portrait, but rather 'something which is *intended* to be a picture of another [*sic*] without resembling it . . . That it is a picture consists in the intention' (LWL 4). In MS 145, 49 f. (written in 1933) he discusses the manner in which we are prone to think of intention as giving life to the sign. It is, I think, plausible to view this as being also an articulation of how he himself had once thought:

By 'intention' I here mean what thinks the sign, what directs the sign, what gives it meaning,[9] what makes the sign fulfil its function, what uses the sign in thought. Intention seems to interpret, to give the final interpretation.

5. The last commitment to which I want to draw attention is patent in the letter to Russell of 19 August 1919. In response to Russell's question about what the constituents of a thought are and what their relation is to the components of the pictured fact, Wittgenstein replies 'I don't know *what* the constituents of the thought are but I know *that* it must have such constituents which correspond to the words of Language.[10] Again, the kind of relation of the constituents of thought and of the pictured fact is irrelevant. It would be

[8] 'Gegenstand' here could be translated either as 'subject' or 'object', and which of them one opts for affects the sense of the passage. I believe that what Wittgenstein had in mind was the state of affairs (the possibility) of which the thought is a picture. Whether that 'logical place' is 'occupied', i.e. whether the state of affairs obtains or not, determines whether the thought is true or false.

[9] 'Meinung', rather than 'Bedeutung'. It is used here in an Anglicism that is common in Wittgenstein's later writings, to signify meaning something. What he has in mind in this remark is: that in virtue of which something is meant by the sign.

[10] It is *this* kind of anankastic pronouncement that Wittgenstein later meant when he castigated himself for 'dogmatism' in the *Tractatus* (WWK 182 ff.), and not, as has recently been suggested, remarks about how words are used, or grammatical statements of rules for the use of words.

a matter of psychology to find out.' Further, to Russell's query of whether a Gedanke consists of words, Wittgenstein responds: 'No! But of psychical constituents that have the same sort of relation to reality as words. What those constituents are I don't know' (CL 69).

This expresses a highly problematic idea of a 'language of thought', which Wittgenstein was later to assail. It also poses a destructive dilemma: if thought constituents stand to the constituents of depicted facts in the same relation as words, then they are not 'intrinsically representational', and a further explanation—an interpretation—is required to link them to their meanings. Words, as we have just seen, are conceived to be linked to their meanings by *thinking*, namely: by thinking the sense of the sentence that expresses the thought, i.e. meaning by the sentence the state of affairs it represents, and hence meaning by the names the constituents of the state of affairs represented. But thoughts cannot be linked to what they are thoughts of by further acts of thinking, for then thought would not be 'the last interpretation', which it must be. On the other hand, if they are 'intrinsically representational', then they do not stand to their meanings in the same relation as words. Moreover, their supposedly intrinsic representational character would still need elucidating.[11]

There is a further conflict lurking in the background. On the one hand, the concepts of meaning, intending, understanding, interpreting, and thinking have to be, as Wittgenstein later put it, *metalogical*. Otherwise they would merely signify phenomena. But they cannot signify mere phenomena, since what they signify must contain *a picture* of what is meant or intended, of what is understood or thought—and no mere phenomenon can do that. Phenomena are not intentional; they may have a 'natural meaning', but not a 'non-natural' one. However, if they do not signify psychological phenomena, they cannot belong to the subject matter of psychology. So the only sense in which psychology could find out, for example, what the constituents of thoughts are would be that it could investigate thoughts 'from the outside'—for example, as cortical phenomena (MS 145, 48 f.). But that would be of no interest to philosophy.

---

[11] The resolution to this destructive dilemma is, of course, that thoughts are not representations at all. Any representation must have a medium of representation that has non-representational qualities (e.g. the colour of the ink, the timbre of the voice). But thoughts are, as Marshall McLuhan might have put it, all message and no medium. It is unfortunate that contemporary proponents of the LOT (language of thought) hypothesis are apparently unaware of this decisive objection to their misconceived hypothesis.

3. The 1930s and the *Investigations*

The early and mid-1930s were spent on two great tasks. The first consisted of attempting to articulate a new philosophy on the themes of the nature of language and linguistic representation, of thought and intentionality, of meaning and understanding, of the nature of mathematics and of philosophy itself. The second consisted of dismantling the philosophy of the *Tractatus*, identifying its errors and their sources. The destructive work went remarkably smoothly. Once Wittgenstein had rejected the independence postulate for elementary propositions and allocated the role of sempiternal objects to samples that belong to the means of representation, the whole structure of the *Tractatus* collapsed. But it took much longer to arrive at the alternative he presented in the *Investigations*.

A glance at the table of contents for *The Big Typescript* suggests extensive engagement with themes in philosophy of psychology. The section headings herald discussions of understanding, meaning (*meinen*), interpreting, thought and thinking; expectation, wish and their fulfilment; current experience, pain, and idealism; and so forth. However, this is misleading, since his engagement with all these themes is geared primarily to issues pertaining to his early philosophy and its demolition, on the one hand, and to the effort to find new solutions to much the same problems, on the other. The only question we need address for present purposes is what the achievements of *The Big Typescript* and its revisions were in respect of psychological concepts, on the one hand, and the psychological presuppositions that had arguably characterized his early philosophy, on the other.

First, he came to realize that thinking, understanding, and meaning are not metalogical concepts, but humdrum concepts like others. Wittgenstein used the term 'metalogical' to indicate a purported attribute of a fundamental concept (or of what is signified by such a concept) which was conceived to signify (or to be) what links the domain of logic, i.e. propositions, thoughts, representations of how things are, with reality. He had long been tempted to believe that 'understanding' is a metalogical word (MS 116, 16), the idea being that understanding is a metalogical process that gets one from the bare sign to its verifying fact (MS 110, 193). Similarly, one readily thinks of meaning something (*meinen*) as a metalogical act, and of *agreement with reality* as a metalogical concept that signifies the relation between picture and what is pictured. But this whole conception of a 'connection between language and reality' is misguided. 'Just as there is no metaphysics', he wrote on the opening page of *The Big Typescript* (BT 1), 'there is no metalogic; and the word "understanding", the expression "understanding a proposition", aren't metalogical. They are expressions of language like all others'. 'The proposition "I mean something..." is not metalogical' (Vol. XIV, Um. 27). 'Depicting' is no metalogical concept (BT 285ᵛ), and neither is 'agreement with reality' (MS 113, 49v; MS 115, 85). What a sentence means is said by *an explanation*, i.e. by *another sentence* (MS 116, 3)—so the very idea that processes of meaning and understanding are metalogical, foundational (MS 110, 160), necessary to link language to reality, or to bridge the apparent gap between an order and its execution (MS 110, 191; MS 116, 22) is chimerical. In the end, he came to realize that the very idea that thinking is something unique and mysterious is itself an illusion (cf. PI §§95, 97, 110).

Second, the supposition that language has, as it were, an inorganic and an organic part—a system of signs, and underlying psychological processes that infuse signs with life by thinking them, meaning such-and-such by them, understanding them as representing such-and-such—has to be abandoned (BT 283–7; cf. BB 3). The meaning of an expression is its use, and it is its use that gives it life.

Third, he accordingly reiterates his anti-psychologism. Psychological *phenomena* are of no concern to his logico-linguistic investigations (BT 284). The temptation to explain symbolic processes by reference to psychological ones, must be resisted (BT 283). It can never be essential to his investigation that a phenomenon of symbolizing takes place in the mind and not on paper (BT 284). So too, the psychological *process* of understanding is of no interest to him (BT 330). Indeed, one must beware of constructing a mythology of psychological processes (MS 114, 35), as he had done in the presuppositions underlying the *Tractatus*. But the *concepts* of understanding, meaning, knowing, interpreting, thinking, need elucidation (and subsequent elucidation was to show that understanding is not a process at all).

Over the next decade, as his reflections on these concepts evolved, he shifted from the formal or realist anti-psychologism that he had taken over from Frege to a form of philosophical anthropology in which full justice was done to these psychological concepts and their roles in the web of concepts surrounding the notions of linguistic representation, without lapsing into psychologism.

Fourth, the puzzlement about the pictoriality (intentionality) of the proposition, about how it is possible to think something that is not the case, about the possibility of a proposition's being false but nevertheless meaningful, dissolves. The *Tractatus* had tried to solve the problem by means of the picture theory of the proposition and its attendant modal realism (realism about objective metaphysical possibilities). The harmony between language and reality was orchestrated metalogically. Now Wittgenstein realized that '*It is in language that it is all done*' (PG 143). The discussions of expectation and wish are focused upon their 'business part', i.e. upon their pictoriality (how they 'reach right up to reality' and seemingly 'foreshadow the facts'), not upon those aspects of expectation that might concern the philosophy of psychology. It was confused to suppose that the expectation that *p* contains a picture of what is expected, and to construe that in terms of metalogical relations of words or thought-constituents to world. Rather, it is a simple rule of grammar that the expectation that *p* is the expectation that is fulfilled by its coming about that *p* (PG 161 f.). The patent internal relation between the expectation that *p* and the event that *p* is merely a shadow of a grammatical substitution-rule. The picture theory was a metaphysical mountain postulated to solve a puzzle that is dissolved by the description of a grammatical molehill.

Fifth, just as the relationship between a proposition and the fact that makes it true is not a relationship between thought and world, but an intra-grammatical one, so too 'The assignment of a name to an object is nothing other than that produced by the words "That is . . ." or by a table, etc. It is part of the symbolism. Therefore it's incorrect to say [as he once had] that the relationship between a name and an object is psychological' (BT 174).

It is clear that the metaphysics and modal realism of the *Tractatus* has been eliminated, the picture theory has collapsed and with it the whole idea of word-world semantic correlations. This has been replaced by an intra-grammatical resolution of the problems of the intentionality of the proposition. The thought that certain psychological acts and processes must be metalogical has been swept aside, but the insistence that psychology—the study of psychological *phenomena*—is irrelevant to logical investigations is retained. However, only a little progress has yet been made towards elucidation of the concepts of meaning something, thinking, understanding, and interpreting.

Throughout the 1930s and 1940s Wittgenstein laboured prodigiously. He clarified his ideas on metaphysics—a non-subject that rests on a confusion and conflation of empirical and conceptual questions. He elucidated the use of the first-person pronoun, and its misuse that informs both dualism and solipsism, and disentangled the knotted threads that lead to solipsism. These epistemological and metaphysical themes, though they touch questions in philosophy of psychology, are tangential and need not concern us. He also elucidated the concept of understanding—an ability, rather than a state or process; the concept of meaning something—neither a process nor an act of any kind; of interpreting—not an act or process that always accompanies understanding. He gave a detailed overview of the concepts of thinking and of imagining, where they bear on the overall theme of the *Investigations*. By and large, his engagement with specific psychological concepts is subordinate to more general concerns in philosophy. It is in the course of these clarifications that he laid the foundations for his subsequent engagement with philosophy of psychology. So before turning to the latter, I shall survey the former.

1. Wittgenstein clarified his position with regard to behaviourism. He agreed with logical behaviourists that behaviour is internally related to the mental, and with behaviourists in general that language learning is founded on brute training, that it presupposes natural behaviour and behavioural reaction, and that avowals of experience are themselves a form of behaviour. Unlike the behaviourists, however, he denied that the mental is a fiction (as Watson had insisted), or that the mental is reducible to behaviour (as logical behaviourists such as Carnap in the early 1930s and Hempel in the 1940s had suggested). Above all, he denied that behaviour is 'bare bodily movement'—a residual half of a false Cartesian duality. On the contrary, human behaviour is grasped as *animate*—as the behaviour of a living animal. It is perceived as *a manifestation* or *expression* of cognitive, cogitative, affective, and volitional powers, and is so described.

2. He clarified his position with regard to dualism and its conception of inner and outer as externally related domains. The dualist (and 'mentalist' or idealist) conception of the inner as ethereal (or 'pneumatic'—animated by psychic pneuma), as being privately owned, as a domain to which the subject has privileged access by introspection, and as the object of indubitable first-person knowledge is misconceived. The corresponding conception of the outer as 'mere bodily behaviour' is equally misguided. And the conception of the relationship between the inner and outer as *external* and *causal* is likewise flawed. Consciousness is no 'inner searchlight'; the ability to say how things are with one is not the result of a kind of 'inner perception'; self-consciousness is not a matter of an 'I think' being able to accompany all my representations; and experiences are not *this*-es and *thus*-es (qualia, as current jargon would have it) revealed to consciousness by introspection.

3. Stimulated by his reading of Köhler, Wittgenstein disagreed with the received conception of the distinction between psychology and the natural sciences. Psychology does not treat of processes in the mental sphere as the physicist does in the physical sphere (PI §571). That idea is rooted in dualist conceptions of mind and body and attendant misunderstandings of the relationships between the mental and its behavioural manifestations. But mental 'objects' (such as sensations), events, and processes, are not just like physical objects, events, and processes, only immaterial. The psychologist observes the behaviour of human beings (which is not 'bare bodily movement') and draws

conclusions about their minds, but not on the model of the physicist drawing inferences from the observed to the unobserved—as if the mental were hidden 'behind' the observable behaviour and as if the procedure were a kind of analogical or inductive inference, or an inference to the best explanation. The behaviour the psychologist observes is an *expression* of the mental. The pain, joy, depression, thought, intention, etc. are not hidden *behind* the painful movement, joyful smile, depressed mien and tone, expression of thought, intentional action, etc. The psychologist does not observe them 'indirectly', and the subject does not observe them 'directly'—since he does not observe them at all.

4. Wittgenstein paid more attention than any other philosopher to the asymmetry between first- and third-person present tense psychological propositions.[12] The asymmetry consists in the fact that predicating psychological attributes of others is warranted by what they do and say. By contrast, one's use of such sentences in the first-person present tense does not rest on one's observation of one's own behaviour. According to tradition, the asymmetry is a reflection of *epistemic* differences, explicable by reference to the essential (metaphysical) privacy of experience. Wittgenstein denied this. The asymmetry is an aspect of *grammatical* differences between first- and third-person utterances reflecting their different roles in our language-games. The first-person utterance is not, in the primal case, a *description* of anything (in particular, not of anything observed *in foro interno*) but rather an *expression*. But that does not preclude reports and descriptions of the inner (which remain unlike reports and descriptions of the outer). To be sure, not all expressions of the inner are extensions of primitive behaviour, but even when they are not (e.g. expressions of belief or intention), grammatical asymmetries persist.

5. For an important subclass of psychological verbs, it makes no (epistemic) sense to ascribe to oneself knowledge, belief, doubt, or certainty in the present tense. 'I know that I am in pain' may indeed have various uses, but no *epistemic* use.[13] Doubt and ignorance are excluded by grammar, and by the same token so are certainty and knowledge. Avowals of thought and experience do not rest on introspection (indeed, the very idea that they do depends on a misconception of introspection). They rest on nothing at all.

---

[12] For detailed discussion and defence of this point, see P. M. S. Hacker, 'Of Knowledge and of Knowing that One is in Pain', in Pichler and Säätelä (eds), *Wittgenstein: The Philosopher and his Works*, pp. 203–35.

[13] There is nothing contradictory about this. When one *forgets* one's troubles in the company of a cheerful friend, this is not a cognitive, mnemonic defect, but a matter of distraction of attention. So it is a non-epistemic use of 'to forget'. So too 'I know I am in pain' may be an emphatic or concessive, non-epistemic use of 'I know', altogether unlike 'I know he is in pain'.

6. In third-person cases, psychological attributes are predicated of agents on the basis of what they do and say (including their avowals of thought and experience) but this is not inductive evidence for the inner, it is *logically* good evidence or 'criteria'. The inner stands in need of outer criteria. Such evidence is circumstance-dependent and defeasible. But if not defeated it typically suffices for certainty.

7. The subject of psychological attributes is not the ego, the mind, or the body a sentient being may have, but the animal as a whole.[14]

8. The conception of experience as *privately owned*, such that different people cannot have the same experiences, but only similar ones, i.e. ones that are numerically distinct but qualitatively identical (different tokens of the same type, as some contemporary philosophers misguidedly put it) is mistaken. Insofar as it makes sense for two people to have the same experience, then, to be sure, it is perfectly common for different people to have the same experience.[15]

9. Concepts of experience are not acquired by means of association or by a private analogue of ostensive definition. There *is no such thing as* private ostensive definition, that is: the phrase 'a private ostensive definition' is excluded from the language, just as is the phrase 'checkmate in draughts' (Z §134). Similarly, there is no such thing as a memory of an experience fulfilling the function of a defining sample.

10. The limits of thought are the limits of the behavioural expression of thought. It is perfectly possible, in certain circumstances, for an animal to think and not show it. But it makes sense to ascribe thinking to an animal only insofar as the animal's behavioural repertoire includes such behaviour as *would* express what the animal is said to think. Consequently, the capacity to think in anything other than the most primitive manner is parasitic on the ability to speak. For all but the most primitive thinking can be expressed only in forms of linguistic or symbolic behaviour. Speech is not a translation from language-independent thoughts into words, and thinking is not normally an *accompaniment* of thoughtful speech.

[14] With the exception of verbs of sensation, such as 'to hurt', 'to itch', 'to tickle', which can be ascribed to the body and its parts.

[15] Why 'insofar as it makes sense'? It makes sense to say that you have the same headache as I if one has reason to believe that your headache, like mine, is dull, throbbing, and in the left temples. But it makes no sense to suppose that we *share* the same pain, as we might share the same house. And for us to have the same pain does not mean that you have my pain, as you might have my keys. *I* can't significantly be said have *my* pain either (since 'my pain' = 'the pain I have', and 'I have the pain I have' says nothing). 'N's pain' neither specifies a pain nor a relation of possession. So 'I have your pain' makes sense only if it has been specified *what* pain you have, and even then it is merely a clumsy way of saying that I have the same pain as you.

These controversial, indeed revolutionary, conceptual commitments are prominent in the *Investigations*. They are all grammatical clarifications supported by reasoned argument. Their denial leads to incoherence. And they provide a very substantial grammatical framework for more detailed investigations of the large network of psychological concepts that inform the lives of language-using creatures like us. It was to such investigations that Wittgenstein turned in 1946.

4. Remarks on the Philosophy of Psychology: Finding his Way

Wittgenstein's investigations into the nature of language, linguistic meaning, and representation led him, after 1944, deeper and deeper into philosophical questions concerning psychological concepts and psychological phenomena. He moved on three related fronts: the classification of psychological phenomena and the categories under which they are to be subsumed; the connective analysis of psychological concepts and the description of the language-games in which they are at home; and the connections between psychological concepts and certain very general facts of nature concerning ourselves and the world in which we live, which in an important sense condition our concepts. The latter strand in his reflections explains the (non-Humean) sense in which he can be said to have *naturalized* philosophy in general and philosophy of psychology in particular—but not by assimilating it to an 'armchair science' or by cleaving to a form of scientism.

These explorations, especially those into wanting, intending, and meaning something, proved to be fruitful—finding new pathways through old jungles. It was altogether natural that, with the completion of the final draft of the *Investigations*, Wittgenstein should turn to concentrated work on the philosophy of psychology. It is clear that he found the themes that he was working on of interest in their own right. When he was struggling with the similarities and differences between seeing something and imagining it, he remarked 'The problem with which I am basically concerned here is really much more wonderful than will perhaps appear to someone who reads these lines. For it is a very general conceptual problem. (Comparable, I believe, to a *great* problem in mathematics.)' (MS 136, 7a). He himself raised the question of the point of his investigations into philosophy of psychology:

Is it right to say that *my* investigations are characterized by a certain kind of purposelessness?—I don't mean that they are useless, but that they are not explicitly conducted with a view to a purpose. Is it then a case of 'l'art pour l'art'? I would *not* want to say that. That sounds too arty [*spielerisch*], and as if one wanted to say 'I do it because it is beautiful' or something like that.—But I could surely say: must everything we do be done with a clear purpose? And if not—is it therefore without any connection with the rest of life? Does it therefore have no consequences; or bad ones?   (MS 134, 154)

A couple of pages later, he responds further to his worries. The point of his classifications and comparisons of psychological phenomena is that they can answer a whole array of philosophical problems. It is a *method* (although, to be sure, not a mechanical one) of getting clear about conceptual difficulties (MS 134, 156). In some cases, e.g. Moore's paradox of belief or the paradox of puzzle pictures, Wittgenstein did tackle a philosophical conundrum directly. And here his investigations bring us to realize conceptual affinities and differences of which we were previously unaware. But for the most part, his concern was with plotting the conceptual terrain—what Ryle was later to call 'logical geography'.[16] For, as Wittgenstein put it, 'The philosopher wants to master the geography of concepts; to see every locality in its proximate and also in its most distant surroundings' (MS 137, 63a). Indeed,

In order to know your way about an environment, you don't merely need to be acquainted with the right path from one district to another; you need also to know where you'd get to if you took the wrong turning. This shows how similar our considerations are to travelling in a landscape with a view to constructing a map. And it is not impossible that such a map will sometime get constructed for the regions we are moving in.   (MS 131, 121 = RPP I, §303)

He himself is not so much engaged with constructing a detailed map as with preparing a preliminary survey, as it were, something that will enable people to orient themselves. He aimed not at exactness, but at surveyability (MS 134, 83), not at completeness, but at putting his reader in a position to shift for himself when he encounters conceptual difficulties (LW I, §686).[17]

He was, he wrote apropos his lectures, showing his pupils a segment of a vast landscape in which it is impossible that they should know their way around by themselves (MS 133, 44r).

The difficulty is to know one's way about among concepts of 'psychological phenomena'. To move about among them without repeatedly running up against an obstacle. That is to say: one has got to *master* the kinships and differences of concepts. As

[16] It is impossible to know whether Ryle got the analogy from Wittgenstein or hit upon it independently. What is clear, however, is that Wittgenstein was already using the geographical analogy in 1933/4 (see AWL 43; cp. LFM 44).

[17] He repeatedly castigates himself in 1948 for going into more detail than is necessary (MS 134, 98; 135, 186), remarking that 'It seems to me that I am still a long way from understanding these things, namely from the point where I know what I needn't talk about. I still get myself entangled in details, without knowing even whether I should talk about these things' (MS 136, 37a).

someone is master of the transition from any key to any other one, modulates from one to the other.   (MS 135, 73 = RPP I, §1054)

Of course, everyone has mastered the *use* of these commonplace psychological concepts—we are as familiar as can be with the language-games in which they are at home. But we lack an overview of the field of psychological concepts. This is emphatically *not* a matter of having an ability, but lacking a theoretic representation of that ability, or of knowing the meanings of psychological expressions but lacking a theory of their meaning.[18] The last thing we want, Wittgenstein averred, is a philosophical *theory* (MS 130, 218) that misguidedly tries to ape theories in the sciences. The aim is to produce surveyable representations or presentations ('Darstellungen') of segments of the domain of psychological language. The method is *descriptive*. But we are not accustomed to *comparing* the various concepts, whose use we have mastered, with each other. We are not used to *juxtaposing* different concepts in order to note similarities and differences. And that is just what we have to do in order to attain an overview of our psychological language. But when we try to describe these conceptual similarities and differences, sentences whose use we cannot survey constantly intrude themselves (MS 130, 220), leading to bafflement, distortion, and misrepresentation of the conceptual terrain.

In 1948, after he had been working on themes in the philosophy of psychology for almost two years, experimenting with different ways of classifying and ordering psychological concepts and phenomena, Wittgenstein remarked 'I am the inventor of certain discussion-clarifying devices; like someone who invented novel, more surveyable, ways of book-keeping' (MS 135, 146).[19] For part of his struggle throughout this period was to find a fruitful and illuminating method of *classifying*, or of *ordering*, the problematic concepts with which he was concerned. The result of a philosophical investigation, he remarked early in the course of his enquiries, is sometimes *a new filing system* (MS 130, 82). What did he have in mind? At one stage he suggested that maybe what is needed is 'a new nomenclature' for psychological categories.[20] What he meant is not so much a new terminology as a new *classification*. It is not that new *words* are needed—as if the trouble with psychology were an impoverished language. Nothing could be more wrong than supposing, as James often did, that mistakes and confusions in psychology could be remedied by introducing

---

[18] An idea that was the drive-shaft of M. A. E. Dummett's researches into theories of meaning for a natural language.

[19] A metaphor strikingly related to his much earlier remark 'Grammar is the account books of language' (PG 87).

[20] He notes parenthetically that this is a step that is only rarely to be recommended in philosophy.

new *names* (MS 134, 108).[21] What is needed is 'a profound change in our thought; for example, in what we are looking for and in what we stop looking for. Such changes, to be sure, often get expressed in a changed terminology' (ibid.). What did Wittgenstein have in mind here? I suspect that the *kind* of thing that he meant is that, for example, once we have cleared the ground of the houses of cards built out of misapprehensions of the concept of consciousness, the search for so-called neural correlates of consciousness will be abandoned, at least in its present form,[22] and be replaced by better questions which neuroscience *can* handle. Once we clarify what it is to possess a concept, we shall cease to search for a concept module in the brain where concepts are stored and correlated with words.[23] Once we have disentangled confusions about the concept of vision, we shall cease looking for the part of the brain that 'puts together the information' from the sense organs to form a 'picture' of 'the external world' around us,[24] and investigate the vehicle of our visual powers without the incumbrance of unintelligible questions.

So, what is needed, it seemed, was a new array of psychological categories in terms of which to *order* psychological concepts. What did he conceive to be the existing categories, and what was wrong with them? Arguably they were such general categories as *mental state, mental process, mental event, mental act,* and *experience.* Philosophers, psychologists, and cognitive neuroscientists are prone to rely on these very general terms in specifying their subject matter. So, we are often told at the beginning of an epistemological investigation, that

---

[21] This Jamesian misunderstanding continues. Colin Blakemore, for example, has recently suggested that some of the conceptual difficulties in cognitive neuroscience are due not to conceptual confusion but to 'inadequacy of vocabulary [of everyday language] and notation' ('Understanding Images in the Brain', in H. Barlow, C. Blakemore, and M. Weston-Smith (eds), *Images and Understanding* (Cambridge: Cambridge University Press, 1990), p. 283).

[22] Christhof Koch (like his late colleague, Francis Crick) aims to discover the neural correlates of consciousness. He suggests that 'Whenever information is represented in the NCC you are conscious of it. The goal is to discover *the minimal set of neuronal events and mechanisms jointly sufficient for a specific conscious percept.*' *The Quest for Consciousness* (Englewood, Colo.: Roberts and Company Publishers, 2004), p. 16.

[23] See, for example, W. J. M. Levelt, 'Accessing Words in Speech Production', *Cognition* 42 (1992), pp. 1–22. For critical discussion of the idea that there could be a 'concept module' in the brain that stores concepts, see M. R. Bennett and P. M. S. Hacker, 'Language and Cortical Function: Conceptual Developments', *Progress in Neurobiology* 80 (2006), pp. 20–52.

[24] For example, contemporary neuroscientists' formulation of what they call 'the binding problem': 'How is information carried by separate pathways brought together into a coherent visual image? . . . How does the brain construct a perceived world from sensory information and how does it bring it into consciousness? . . . what the visual system really does [is] to create a three-dimensional perception of the world which is different from the two dimensional image projected onto the retina' (E. R. Kandel and R. Wurtz, 'Constructing the Visual Image', in E. R. Kandel, J. H. Schwartz and T. M. Jessell (eds), *Principles of Neuroscience and Behaviour* (Stamford, Conn.: Apple and Lange, 1995), p. 492). For critical discussion of the binding problem, see M. R. Bennett and P. M. S. Hacker, *Philosophical Foundations of Neuroscience* (Oxford: Blackwell, 2003), pp. 137–43.

knowing is a mental state, just as being in pain is.[25] Similarly, it is a widespread view that believing is a mental state.[26] Philosophers and linguists alike conceive of understanding the speech of another as a process—of interpretation, or of deriving the truth-conditions of the heard sentence (which are conceived to constitute the meaning of the utterance) from the meanings of the individual words and their mode of combination.[27]

Wittgenstein held that these terms, far from signifying sharp and clear-cut categories, are exceedingly imprecise:

The concept of experience: like that of event, of process, of state, of something, of fact, of description and of statement. Here we think that we are standing on the hard bedrock, deeper than any special methods and language-games. But these extremely general terms have an extremely blurred meaning. They relate in practice to innumerable special cases, but that does not make them any *solider*; no, rather it makes them more fluid.   (RPP I §648)

In our superficial classifications, we go wrong before our enquiries have even properly commenced. He had already remarked on this in the *Investigations*:

How does the philosophical problem about mental processes and states and about behaviourism arise?—The first step is the one that altogether escapes notice. We talk

---

[25] See, for example, T. Williamson, *Knowledge and its Limits* (Oxford: Oxford University Press, 2000), p. 21, who claims that knowing *p* is a 'state of mind', that a state of mind is a mental state, and that the mental state that constitutes knowing *p* is an attitude towards a proposition. But a mental state is not the same as a state of mind. Knowing, lacking 'genuine duration', is not a mental state, let alone a state of mind. And, unlike 'ridicule', 'contradict', 'endorse', or 'approve', which *can* signify attitudes towards something propositional, such as rumours, stories, claims, declarations, statements, and indeed propositions, 'know' takes 'that-clauses', which such verbs do not (one cannot endorse that *p*). To know that *p*, unlike endorsing *the proposition* that *p*, is not to have any attitude to anything. (See B. Rundle, *Mind in Action* (Oxford: Clarendon Press, 1997), p. 62.)

[26] D. Davidson held that beliefs are correctly called 'states of mind' ('The Myth of the Subjective', repr. in his *Subjective, Intersubjective, Objective* (Oxford: Clarendon Press, 2001), p. 40), and that 'having a belief is . . . being in a state' ('Indeterminism and Antirealism', repr. in *Subjective, Intersubjective, Objective* p. 74). J. R. Searle holds that beliefs are 'intentional mental states' (*Intentionality* (Cambridge: Cambridge University Press, 1983), pp. 1–4), and T. Williamson (*Knowledge and its Limits*, p. 21) writes of believing that *p* as 'the paradigmatic mental state'. For ten reasons why it is mistaken to classify belief as a mental state, see P. M. S. Hacker, 'Of the Ontology of Belief', in Mark Siebel and Mark Textor (eds), *Semantik und Ontologie* (Frankfurt: Ontos Verlag, 2004), pp. 185–222. For a discussion of Wittgenstein's equivocal views, see P. M. S. Hacker, *Wittgenstein: Mind and Will* (Oxford: Blackwell, 1996), Exg. §§572–5.

[27] See, for example, M. A. E. Dummett, who claims that it is 'an undoubted fact that a process of derivation of some kind is involved in the understanding of a sentence' ('What Is a Theory of Meaning?', in S. Guttenplan (ed.), *Mind and Language* (Oxford: Clarendon Press, 1975), p. 112; see also his 'What Is a Theory of Meaning II?', in G. Evans and J. McDowell (eds), *Truth and Meaning: Essays in Semantics* (Oxford: Clarendon Press, 1976), pp. 69 f.; cf. N. Chomsky, *Reflections on Language* (London: Fontana, 1976), pp. 32 f.) and J. Fodor and J. J. Katz, 'What's Wrong with the Philosophy of Language?', in C. Lyas (ed.), *Philosophy and Linguistics* (London: Macmillan and St Martin's Press, 1971), p. 282.

of processes and states and leave their nature undecided. Sometime perhaps we shall know more about them—we think. But that is just what commits us to a particular way of looking at the matter. For we have a certain conception of what it means to learn to know a process better. (The decisive move in the conjuring trick has been made, and it was the very one that seemed to us quite innocent.)   (PI §308)

It seems utterly innocuous to classify knowledge or belief as mental states (after all, they are neither mental events, nor mental processes). What exactly these mental states are, we think, remains to be seen. And we proceed to speculate that they must surely be identical with brain states. But not only is it mistaken to take them to be mental states (*inter alia* because they lack 'genuine duration'), it is further evident that we have no conception whatsoever what might count as a brain state and what the criteria of identity for such brain states are. 'Thinking', we innocently proclaim, 'is a mysterious process, and we are a long way from fully understanding it'—and so we start *experimenting*—apparently without being aware *what* mystifies us (MS 135, 113), and without pausing to examine whether thinking is a *process* at all, and what differences there are even between those kinds of thinking that *do* approximate processes and incontrovertible processes.

We unthinkingly assume that mental states and processes are just like physical states and processes, only mental, that mental states are a species of state, another species of which is physical states. But that is precisely what we have no title to do. (Chess moves, Wittgenstein remarked, are not kinds of movements.) We think that mental processes are comparable to physical processes like digestion or breathing. But, Wittgenstein stresses, these are *incomparable*. If one wanted to find bodily conditions that *are* comparable to mental processes and states, they would be such things as the *quickness* of breath, the *irregularity* of the heartbeat, the *soundness* of digestion, and suchlike—all of which characterize corporeal behaviour (cf. RPP I §661).

Wittgenstein struggled to find a fruitful system of classification—initially, a *genealogy* of psychological concepts (MS 133, 73r = RPP I §722), or phenomena (MS 134, 83), and of experiences (MS 134, 124). (Whether he thought of these as the same investigation, or as different ones is unclear.) What did he mean by 'a genealogy'? This too is unclear, although some light is shed on the matter by the fact that he raises the question of whether what he is hunting for is something akin to the genealogy of different number concepts (such as natural numbers, signed integers, rationals, reals, etc.)—i.e. a kind of *logical* (non-historical) genealogy. Perhaps he meant such things as the reciprocal dependency of cognition and volition; the priority (contrary to the Cartesian and empiricist tradition) of observation statements (e.g. 'The chair is red') over perceptual statements, and of perceptual statements (e.g. 'I see . . .')

over sense-datum statements (e.g. 'It visually seems to me just as if...'); the dependence of the intelligibility of doubt upon the possibility of certainty; the presupposition of the possession of a tensed language for the possibility of regret or remorse; and so on. But I find it impossible to be sure, since it is far from evident whether Wittgenstein actually thought of himself as having even begun to carry out the project.

What does seem clear is that the idea of a systematic genealogy foundered. Wittgenstein then attempted to construct *a systematic scheme of hierarchical classification* based on the thought that the field of the psychological can be deemed to be that of *experiences*, subclasses of which are undergoings (subsuming both images and impressions), emotions (directed and undirected), and forms of conviction (e.g. belief, certainty and doubt) (MS 134, 42f. = RPP I §836–7; on 18 March 1947). For various reasons, this too proved fruitless.[28] Nevertheless, Wittgenstein persisted with two guidelines. First, that his task was to impose *an order* upon psychological concepts. Secondly, that this itself would involve *new* categorial concepts. He noted that Weierstrass had introduced a whole series of new concepts to impose an order upon thought about the differential calculus. 'In just that way it seems to me, I shall have to impose an order upon psychological thought by means of *new* concepts' (MS 135, 115; 30 July 1947). Strikingly, he invoked Goethe's idea of ordering botanical classification by reference to the organizing principle that the organs of the plant should be seen as transformations of a leaf. The affinity between his task in philosophy and Goethe's botanical project had occurred to Wittgenstein in the early 1930s, in connection with the idea of a surveyable representation ('Darstellung') of a domain of grammar.[29] Now he wrote:

What does a conceptual investigation do? Is it the natural history of human concepts?—Well, natural history describes, say, plants and animals. But could it not be that plants have been described in all their detail, and then someone turns up and notices analogies in their structure that nobody had noticed before? So he imposes an order on these descriptions. He says, e.g. 'Don't compare this part with that; rather, with this other one!' (Goethe wanted to do some such thing.) And in so doing, he is not necessarily speaking of descent [i.e. actual genealogy], but nevertheless the new way of arrangement might also give scientific investigation a new direction. He says 'Look

---

[28] See J. Schulte, *Experience and Expression* (Oxford: Clarendon Press, 1993), ch. 3 for a very helpful discussion of the matter.

[29] For detailed discussion see J. Schulte, 'Chor und Gesetz: Zur "morphologischen Methode" bei Goethe und Wittgenstein', repr. in *Chor und Gesetz* (Frankfurt am Main: Suhrkamp, 1990), and G. P. Baker and P. M. S. Hacker, 'Surveyability and Surveyable Representations', in *Wittgenstein: Understanding and Meaning*, vol. 1 of an *Analytical Commentary on the Philosophical Investigations*, 2nd edn, extensively revised by P. M. S. Hacker (Oxford, Blackwell, 2005), pt 1—*The Essays*.

at it in *this* way!'—and this may have advantages and consequences of different kinds. (MS 134, 153 = RPP I §950)

On 14 December 1947, he noted that where he had previously spoken of a genealogical tree, he could just as well have spoken of an *order* in which one should discuss psychological concepts and explain their connections. But, he remarked, he was not clear about this order, especially about its beginning (MS 135, 184 f.).

By 1948, however, Wittgenstein had apparently abandoned the idea of finding a specific sequential order in which one should discuss psychological concepts. (To suppose that there is would perhaps be akin to supposing that there is a specific sequential order in which one should describe a landscape.) There are *various* ways in which these concepts can be ordered for philosophical discussion, and which is most appropriate depends on one's purposes and interests. He had also abandoned the idea, never really executed, of introducing new classificatory concepts. He had introduced the novel concept of *genuine duration*—a very fruitful and illuminating one—but it was the only new concept for which he had found a need.[30] However, he did not abandon the idea of *imposing an order* upon our psychological concepts for purposes of surveyability.

We must always remember that we aren't trying to explain one psychological phenomenon in terms of another; rather, [taking them] as we find them, we should arrange them in an order. So we don't want to say that *this* is really *that*, but only, insofar as we can, to point to similarities and dissimilarities.   (MS 137, 9b; 6 February 1948)

This conception accords with something that he had written right at the beginning of his investigations into the philosophy of psychology:

Don't forget that we don't have to *explain* a phenomenon, but only to describe! What we are not looking for is a 'philosophical theory'.

A completely unordered description is of no value for us. But to see a relevant order is difficult, because it is concealed by the net of grammar.   (MS 130, 218 f.; 28 July 1946)

The purpose is a survey of the terrain of psychological concepts that will enable one to find one's way around. Indeed, he noted in January 1948, the importance of his treatment of the phenomena of mental life is not because he is keen on completeness, but because *each one casts light on the treatment of all*

---

[30] The only other novel concept mentioned is that of a 'germ'(MS 133, 87ᵛ), presumably like the experience of being about to do something—but, Wittgenstein immediately notes, this could be misleading (as James was misled into talking of experiencing a tendency), and he makes no use of the idea.

(MS 136, 129 = RPP II §311 (Z §465)). Each of his peregrinations displays the investigative methods and techniques of elucidation appropriate for plotting the terrain anywhere else in the landscape.

At the end of 1947 (MS 136, 3a–4a = RPP II §63; 18 December 1947), Wittgenstein drew up a plan for the treatment of psychological concepts without any genealogy, and without any hierarchical classification. He emphasized the first-third-person asymmetry characteristic of many psychological verbs and the associated distinction between expression and description. He distinguished sensations from kinaesthetic awareness, on the one hand, and from sense perception, on the other.[31] He began to sketch out differences between sense perceptions and visual and auditory mental images—a task he subsequently took up and treated in refined detail. Six days later, he limned the contours of the concept of emotion and of the related concepts of mood and attitude (MS 136, 27b = RPP II §148). For much of the remainder of his notes on the philosophy of psychology, he pursued the objective of comparing and contrasting psychological concepts. He often could not resist darting down side-streets from time to time to examine a little known but fascinating locality off the High Street (LFM 44), so we find long digressions and subsidiary investigations. Nevertheless, the objective and the methods had become reasonably clear. He was no longer hoping to introduce a new nomenclature, or new categories. He did not aim at a systematic genealogy of psychological concepts or phenomena, or at an order of introduction. So what exactly was he doing?

5. The Project

Wittgenstein came to see his goal as that of ordering psychological concepts in surveyable representations. Far from eschewing existing categories, he was perfectly willing to make use of them, with five provisos.

First, that it be clear that these categorial concepts are vague and elastic, hence not *very* useful in mapping the contours of psychological concepts. 'They relate in practice to innumerable special cases' (RPP I §648). With regard to expecting, Wittgenstein noted 'If one asks: is this a mental state—one sees that

---

[31] Sensations, e.g. pain, have genuine duration, degrees (from scarcely noticeable to unendurable), and qualitative mixtures. They have *a bodily location* (unlike seeing and hearing, but like feeling pressure, warmth or even taste). One knows, i.e. one can say, *where* a pain is. There is a distinctive reaction to touching *the place* of a pain. But the sensation of pain does not have a place-indicative component (just as there is no temporal sign to a memory image). Pain is differentiated from other sense experiences by its characteristic expression, which makes it akin to joy, which is not a sense experience at all (RPP II §63).

neither the answer "Yes" nor the answer "No" helps. There are too many (psychological) categories all of which could be called "mental states". The classification no longer helps here. One must distinguish the concepts from one another individually' (MS 167, 6). This is of capital importance—it rules out mechanical pigeon-holing.

Secondly, we must constantly bear in mind that these vague categorials, applied to the domain of the mental, are not species of a genus, of which the co-ordinate species are physical. The striking differences between, for example, a mental state (e.g. feeling excited) and a physical state (e.g. being in a filthy state), or between a mental act (e.g. deciding) and a physical act (e.g. shutting the door) need to be clarified and emphasized. Above all, we must beware of classifying something as a mental state (for example, knowledge or belief), or as a mental activity (for example, thinking), and cautiously leaving its nature undecided—thinking that sooner or later science will reveal the nature of this peculiar mental state or that strange mental process. But this apparent caution is in fact a form of negligence—and the decisive move in the conjuring trick has been executed without our even noticing it (PI §308).

Thirdly, there should be no presumption that a problematic concept (or phenomenon) is subsumable under *any* useful or illuminating existing category (belief, for example, is not). This should not be surprising—these very general terms were not introduced into our language to serve the special classificatory purposes of a Linnaeus, but to serve the ordinary non-classificatory purposes of ordinary speakers (indeed, the use of 'mental state', as well as its differences from 'state of mind', are worthy of careful investigation).

Fourthly, there should be no presumption that a given psychological concept or phenomenon that *is* subsumable under one or other of these general categories is subsumable under *only* one. The psychological verbs have manifold uses. 'Being gloomy', for example, may signify an occurrent mental state with genuine duration, an enduring dispositional state or a character trait. 'Expecting' may signify an occurrent mental state, a belief or supposition ('I expect he'll be there'), or a demand ('I expect you to be there!').

Fifthly, categorial classification may sometimes be positively useless for the purposes of a comparative overview. 'Knowing, believing, hoping, fearing, etc. are such different kinds of concepts', Wittgenstein wrote, 'that a classification, arranging them in different drawers, is of no use for us. But we want to recognize the differences and similarities between them' (MS 137, 89b). Being told, for example, that knowledge is an ability, whereas belief is not will not shed much light upon the complex relationships between the two concepts, upon the language-games in which they are at home, and upon their point.

With these provisos, Wittgenstein was now willing to go along with existing classifications. 'I don't want to produce some sort of final classification of psychological concepts,' he wrote, 'but rather to show to what extent the existing one can be justified, and also to show that uncertainty clings to any such classification. The classification should be used only to emphasize rough differences between concepts' (MS 137, 89b).[32] Consequently, his categorial observations are more often than not *negative*: meaning something is *not* a mental act or activity; understanding is *not* a mental state or process, but more akin to an ability; thinking is *not* generally an activity, and even when it approximates one, it is logically altogether unlike a physical activity (and that does not merely mean: it is mental, not physical).

At the end of 1947 (at the same time as he drew up his plan for the treatment of psychological concepts), Wittgenstein wrote that he felt that he should write 'about "psychological phenomena" in general. As it were, about the different ways the different psychological categories come into being' (MS 134, 98). It is clear from the sequel that he did not mean the very general categories of (mental) states, processes, acts and activities, etc., but the more specific categories such as perceptions, sense-impressions, emotions, and so forth. What had caught his attention was, for example, the question of how one arrived at the thought that seeing, hearing, tasting, smelling, etc. belong together (MS 136, 131b). The suggestion that they all inform us about 'the external world' he brushes away, rather surprisingly, as superficial. We should imagine a language, he suggests, without the general term 'perception', but with words such as 'see', 'hear', 'smell', 'taste', etc. And now examine the affinities and differences between the senses—the complex web of connections—and these concepts immediately drift much further apart than one might expect. The connections that warrant classifying them together are far more complex and subtle than might initially seem.

The description of affinities (both similarities and connections) and of differences is a hallmark of Wittgenstein's method in philosophy of psychology. The surface grammar of psychological verbs and nouns is especially misleading

---

[32] A conclusion strikingly similar to Ryle's some years later. Having placed far too much emphasis on the notion of a category-mistake in *Concept of Mind* (1949), in *Dilemmas* (Cambridge: Cambridge University Press, 1953), p. 9) Ryle came to the conclusion that 'this idiom [of categories] can be helpful as a familiar mnemonic with some beneficial associations. It can also be an impediment, if credited with the virtues of a skeleton-key. I think it is worthwhile to take some pains with this word "category", but not for the usual reason, namely that there exists an exact professional way of using it, in which, like a skeleton-key, it will turn all our locks for us; but rather for the unusual reason that there is an inexact, amateurish way of using it in which, like a coal-hammer, it will make a satisfactory knocking noise on doors which we want opened to us. It gives answers to none of our questions but it can be made to arouse people to the answers in a properly brusque way.'

(MS 134, 126). The concepts are disguised (MS 134, 125). Countless psychological verbs that look so alike in their surface grammar 'have a barely comparable mode of application. Once that is realized, the investigation of the particular case becomes much easier' (MS 129, 178). How is one to combat the illusions of homogeneity generated by surface grammar? In three ways:

First, 'direct your interest to the language-games' (MS 130, 151) in which the concept is at home—the *behaviour* with which the word meshes, and the *occasion* on which it is appropriate (MS 134, 126). If one is baffled by the misleading similarities between seeing something and imagining something, then one should attend to the different situations in which these verbs are used, the different forms of behaviour that are appropriate to 'I see (and "He sees") X' and 'I imagine (and "He imagines") X' as well as to 'Look at X!', as opposed to 'Imagine X!'.

Secondly, investigate the ways in which the concept might be taught, for there is a systematic connection between possible ways of teaching and meaning. If one is baffled how dreaming that something is so and perceiving that something is so differ, start by examining how one might teach a child to prefix 'I dreamt' to a description. If one is puzzled how a person can 'know what he intends', investigate how one might teach a child the use of 'I'm going to . . .'. The primitive language-games here involved are not the ground-floor of a theory, but poles of a description (RPP I §633).

Thirdly, one must overcome the misleading features of surface grammar by description of the kinships and differences of concepts (MS 135, 73). Importantly, one should not look merely for similarities in order to justify a concept (i.e. a classification), 'but also connections. A father gives his name to his son, even though his son is altogether unlike him' (MS 134, 125 = RPP I §923). Seeing and imagining are *connected*, but contrary to Hume, not by *similarity*, and their distinctness is not a matter of relative vivacity. Seeing and tasting are both forms of sense perception, but not because they are alike.

How are kinships and differences of concepts to be discerned? Apart from language-game contextualization, surely by careful examination of usage. We need to examine the dozens of familiar paths leading off in different directions from a given concept. It is possible to say something quickly or slowly, but not to mean something quickly or slowly. One can be interrupted in one's state of concentration, but it makes no sense to say that one was interrupted in knowing or believing. 'He believes that p, but it is false that p' makes sense, but 'I believe that p, but it is false that p' does not. And so on. Each such grammatical observation is part of the profile of the constituent concepts, and an appropriate ordering of such observations depicts a distinctive feature in the landscape of psychological concepts.

However, the geography of psychological concepts is exceptionally irregular. Ridges that appear connected are separated by sudden crevasses, bodies of water that seem separate are connected by channels, and fog lies on the swamps and bogs. The perils of misdescription are accordingly great:

> Mere description is so difficult because one believes that one needs to fill out the facts in order to understand them. It is as if one saw a screen with scattered colour-patches, and said: the way they are here, they are unintelligible; they only make sense when one completes them into a shape.—Whereas I want to say: Here *is* the whole. (If you complete it you falsify it.)   (RPP I §257; cf. §723)

Surface grammar in this domain is so deeply misleading because the forms of grammar make profoundly different concepts appear much more similar than they are. We think of knowledge as a state (like ignorance[33]), of meaning something as a mental act or activity (like saying something), of seeing something as a mental episode, like hallucinating, only with a cause that corresponds to the content of the episode. In all such cases, we are misled by surface grammar. So we make the wrong comparisons. But, 'What appears at first sight to be homologous, we must not, if we seek for a deeper understanding, consider to be homologous. And we must be able to see as homologous things which, to a superficial appearance, do not appear to be' (MS 130, 83). Interestingly, he observes that this is also a method of mathematics. Presumably what he had in mind is, for example, that in topology a pyramid is more like a sphere than a doughnut is, or that in geometry a parabola is more like a circle than like a line. One must compare what looks like a jawbone with a foot (MS 134, 125)—thinking, not with talking to oneself, but with the expression with which one talks; meaning something, not with saying something, but with intending; knowing what one wants, not with knowing what another wants, but with having decided, and so on.

Often philosophers introduce a new use for a familiar word without even being aware of having done so, for example, by assimilating its use to that of another word (e.g. 'want' to 'wish'), or they construct certain uses for words—ascribing to them a far more elaborate use than they have (e.g. 'attitude'). Sometimes they try to follow up certain features of the ordinary use of a word to make it 'more consistent' (MS 130, 116 = RPP I §§51 f.)—thereby falsely representing it (e.g. thinking to find an epistemic use for 'I know I am in pain', or supposing that the reason we do not say that whatever we see we also seem to see is because it is too obviously

---

[33] As when we say 'She is in a blissful state of ignorance'. But ignorance is not a *mental* state, and knowledge is not a state of any kind. (One can be in a paralysed state, but not in a state of being able to walk.)

true to be worth saying). Philosophers commonly admit that the use they are introducing, of 'knowledge' for example, does not accord with ordinary usage, but insist that it is more important and more interesting than ordinary usage. 'But the philosophical concept', Wittgenstein noted, 'is derived from the common one through a variety of misunderstandings, and it reinforces those misunderstandings. It is not in the slightest bit interesting, except as a warning' (MS 136, 94b = RPP II §289).

'We must take a concept as one finds it, and not want to refine it', Wittgenstein wrote (MS 137, 15a), 'Because it is not our business to modify it, to introduce a concept appropriate for certain purposes (as it is done in the sciences); rather, it is to understand it, that is, not to draw a false picture of it'. The goal is not a theory—how could it be? what would be the observations grounding such a philosophical theory? and what evidence would verify it (what *experimentum crucis* would confirm or disconfirm the existence of 'qualia', for example)? The task in philosophy of psychology is to give an overview of the conceptual scheme that we have, not to introduce an alternative one. It is to present the methods and techniques of comparing and contrasting concepts and language-games. It is to teach us to find our way around this irregular landscape, and to fend for ourselves when confronted with conceptual unclarities and problems—in philosophy of psychology, in psychology itself, and in cognitive neuroscience.

6. Surveyable Representations and Philosophical Method

When reflecting on Wittgenstein's writings on philosophy of psychology after 1945, one must bear in mind the fact that one is looking at work in progress, not at finished work. With the exception of MS 144 and the lost typescript made from it (TS 234, the so called Part II of the *Investigations*), the materials are not even ordered. In fact what we have is raw material for a book, the scope and shape of which we do not know. We have little, if any, idea how Wittgenstein might have decided to arrange his materials or what guiding principle of arrangement he might have adopted—and perhaps he too had little idea. Nevertheless, the privilege of seeing the work in progress is instructive and illuminating.

One striking contrast between these materials, and the finished work of the *Philosophical Investigations*, is that, as already noted, the *Investigations* was Janus-faced. It is no coincidence that Wittgenstein would have liked to see it published in a single volume together with the *Tractatus*, so that his new thoughts could be seen in the right light by contrast with, and against the background of, his old way of thinking—in which he now recognized grave mistakes (PI, Preface p. x). This dialectic, of course, provided a principle of arrangement for a significant part of the book. No such principle is in play in the reflections on the philosophy of psychology. He is not confronting his old ways of thinking about problems in the philosophy of psychology (that had already been done in the reflections on understanding, thinking, intentionality, and meaning in the *Investigations*). Rather, he was exploring the field of psychological concepts, partly for their intrinsic interest, partly to resolve some deep problems and puzzles that caught his interest (like Moore's paradox of belief, or the paradoxes of aspect perception), and partly to extirpate a range of endemic errors and misconceptions. There is no evidence to suggest that after 1946 he saw any need to modify the conception of the goals and methods of philosophy that he had advanced in the *Investigations*. So we can assume, at least as a working hermeneutical hypothesis, that his raw writings on philosophy of psychology, despite their incompleteness and tentative character, exemplify his conception of the methods, limits and goals of philosophical investigation—not, of course, by way of finished work, but rather by way of procedure. That in turn serves to illuminate contentious aspects of his methodology and conception of philosophy.

Looked at from this point of view, it is evident that in his writings on the philosophy of psychology

(i) there are no theories (PI §109)—on the model of the hypothetico-deductive theories that characterize the natural sciences. Rather, his grammatical remarks sketch out fragments of the logical geography of locations and environments within the landscape of psychological concepts.

(ii) there are no theses (PI §128)—which assert that things *must* be thus and so as a condition of the possibility of our thinking or reasoning, on the model of the *Tractatus* and of Waismann's *Thesen* for the Vienna Circle that were based on it. Of course, his grammatical remarks are not *theses*—they describe *the nature* of the psychological phenomena under scrutiny. So, they are expressions of rules for the use of the constituent words, or, as one might also say, for the use of the concepts expressed (cf. PI §§371–3). Only gross misunderstanding would lead one to think that these are exclusive (cf. PI §370).

(iii) there is nothing hypothetical (PI §109), that might stand in need of empirical confirmation or disconfirmation, or that might be more or less probable. The investigation is wholly a priori, and so too are the grammatical remarks the arrangement of which resolves philosophical problems. It is not a *hypothesis* that pain is a sensation, or that one can experience an aspect change without anything in the object perceived changing, or that one can speak quickly or slowly but cannot mean something quickly or slowly.

(iv) the only explanations are grammatical, i.e. the calling to mind (PI §127) of familiar rules for the use of words.

(v) nothing that is hidden from view plays any role in the grammatical explanations or elucidations (PI §126)—for were anything hidden from view, it could not play a role in the guidance, justification, correction, and criticism of linguistic behaviour. The sense-determining rules for the use of expressions could no more be unknown to those who use them than what they see could be invisible to them. For what is unknown cannot fulfil the guiding, justifying, and critical function that is intrinsic to rules. But there may well be *comparative features* of familiar rules for the use of words that one had not *realized*.

(vi) everything *in the grammar of psychological concepts* is left as it is (PI §124)—it is not the task of philosophy in general, or of philosophy of psychology in particular, to reform language or to introduce a novel (logically more perfect) language. (Of course, that does not *preclude* introducing new *classificatory concepts* in terms of which to order our existing psychological concepts, although, as we have seen, at the end of the day, the only novel concept Wittgenstein brought into play is that of 'genuine duration'.) What is *not* 'left as it is' are the conceptual confusions rife in philosophy of psychology, on the one hand, and in empirical psychology on the other (PPF §371)—these are ruthlessly exposed.

(vii) the methods of clarification are descriptive (PI §109)—the uses of psychological expressions that are, for one reason or another, problematic is described, the presuppositions of their use teased out, the contexts of their use elaborated, and the language games in which they are embedded characterized. To be sure, the choice of the grammatical propositions selected is constrained by the philosophical, conceptual, problems at hand.

(viii) the problems are solved by the *arrangement* of what we already know (PI §109), namely the relevant rules for the use of the words that are the source of our difficulties. The arrangement of grammatical remarks is guided by the goal of giving us an overview of the grammar of the problematic concept in its conceptual field, enabling us to see affinities and differences of which we may well have been unaware. That is why, whereas the appropriate response to a scientific discovery may be 'Goodness me, who would have thought of that!', the response to a philosophical insight should be 'Of course! I should have thought of that'.

(ix) the ordering of grammatical remarks is neither arbitrary nor person-relative, but rather problem-relative. It is guided by the goal of providing a *surveyable representation* of the problematic concept that will provide the key to the solution or dissolution of the problems or puzzles that arise.

We should view Wittgenstein's struggles with the philosophy of psychology between 1946 and 1949 as the endeavour to collect grammatical materials for surveyable representations of problematic psychological concepts. These do not add to our knowledge of the world, but only to our understanding of the forms of our thought and talk about the world. They provide us with a map of Treasure Island. But the only treasure is the island—and the map.[34]

[34] I am grateful to Hanoch Ben-Yami, Yuval Lurie, and Joachim Schulte for their comments on an earlier draft of this paper.

14

Concepts: Between the Subjective and the Objective

HANS-JOHANN GLOCK

1. Introduction

The term 'concept', its equivalents and cognates are employed not just in a variety of disciplines but also in numerous different ways. My primary concern is with the ordinary use. This ordinary use includes everyday uses. (Quotidian contexts are particularly significant for the German *Begriff*, since the humdrum verb *begreifen* covers all types of comprehension.) Ordinary use also includes, however, the established uses of 'concept' in specialized forms of discourse such as history of ideas, psychology, logic, and philosophy. Peacocke has rejected this kind of analysis on the grounds that 'concept' is 'something of a term of art' which lacks 'a unique sense that is theoretically important'. His evidence is a Woody Allen movie in which a character from the entertainment industry says: 'Right now, it's only a notion, but I think I can get money to make it into a concept, and later turn it into an idea'.[1] In my view, by contrast, the quote is funny precisely because it presupposes a distinction between concept, notion, and idea that we do not recognize in everyday speech, and which we suspect to be obscure even to the speaker himself. What we should concede is that the everyday use of 'concept' may involve different strands, something which obviously holds of specialized uses. Furthermore, some of these uses may not just be distinct but downright incompatible. That would be all the more reason, however, to disentangle these different strands. Furthermore, current technical uses of 'concept', including those which are allegedly stipulative, are

---

[1] C. Peacocke, *A Study of Concepts* (Cambridge, Mass.: MIT Press, 1992), pp. 1–2.

part of philosophical or psychological theories that purport to explain cognitive and semantic phenomena that are described in terms of concepts by laypeople and specialists alike. This makes it imperative to chart the similarities and differences between novel and established senses of the term, since we need to clarify whether the novel theories even address the phenomena they aspire to explain.

Philosophers and logicians talk of comparative (x is warmer than y), quantitative (x is 20 $^{\circ}$C), individual (the author of 'Wuthering Heights'), logical (negation, implication), spatial, and temporal concepts. In line with the philosophical mainstream, my focus will be on concepts that correspond to general terms of a particular kind, namely one-place predicates formed with the help of verbs, adjectives or count-nouns (x runs, x is radioactive, x is a tool, etc.). It is relatively uncontroversial that such concepts are involved when rational creatures entertain thoughts like:

(1) Dogs bark.

The nature of this involvement remains controversial, however. Concepts have been regarded as

- universals or properties: doghood, barking
- components of the proposition that dogs bark
- meaning(s) of linguistic expressions like 'dog' and 'bark'
- 'modes of presentation': how the subject conceives of dogs or barking
- psychic or neurological processes in the head of a subject who thinks that dogs bark.

In spite of this variety, one can detect a pervasive contrast between two fundamentally opposed approaches.[2] According to *objectivist* or *logical* conceptions, concepts exist independently of individual human minds, e.g. as self-subsistent abstract entities or as abstractions from linguistic practices. According to *subjectivist* or *psychological* conceptions, concepts are mental phenomena, entities or goings-on in the mind or in the head of individuals.

My essay explores this contrast both historically and substantively. I shall be partly guided by two thinkers on whom Anthony Kenny has shed invaluable light—Frege and Wittgenstein. But I shall also draw on Kenny's seminal reflections on abilities and their role in a proper understanding of the mind.

---

[2] See e.g. A. Kenny, *The Metaphysics of Mind* (Oxford: Clarendon Press, 1989), p. 136.

If we are to situate concepts within this subjective/objective spectrum, it is useful to distinguish at least five philosophical questions that can be raised about them:

> *Definition* question: What are concepts?
> *Individuation* question: How are concepts individuated?
> *Possession* question: What is it to have a concept?
> *Function* question: What is the role of concepts?

Once we keep apart these four questions, one further question arises:

> *Priority* Question: Which of these questions—definition, individuation, possession, or function—is the most fundamental?

Sections 2 and 3 concern the definition question. I shall argue that concepts are neither mental particulars, as subjectivism has it, nor properties or meanings, as objectivists maintain. These inconclusive results lend succour to an indirect approach to concepts, one which tackles their nature not head-on, but through exploring one of the other questions (Section 4). My favoured indirect approach is inspired by Wittgenstein and starts out from the possession question. Section 5 defends the view that concept-*possession* is an ability. Section 6 rejects the Wittgensteinian proposal that *concepts themselves* can be equated with abilities and Section 7 does the same with Wittgenstein's own suggestion that they can be equated with techniques or rules, while tentatively defending the neo-Fregean idea that concepts are ways of thinking. The final section returns to the subjective/objective contrast and argues that concepts are objective in that they exist independently of individual minds, subjective in that this existence derives from the cognitive capacities and achievements of rational creatures.

2. Are Concepts Mental Particulars or Mental Representations?

The most prominent contemporary version of subjectivism is the 'representational theory of mind' championed by Fodor and his followers. According to this theory, so-called propositional attitudes like belief and desire are mental states, and they 'are constituted by relations to mental representations', namely 'thoughts'.[3] Concepts are 'the constituents of thoughts'.[4] They constitute a

---

[3] Fodor, *Hume Variations* (Oxford: Clarendon Press, 2003), n. 8, pp. 141, 10.
[4] Fodor, *Concepts: Where Cognitive Science Went Wrong* (Oxford: Clarendon Press, 1998), n. 7, p. 25.

kind of 'mental representation' and hence a 'kind of mental particular'. As mental *particulars*, they are 'objects in the mind' or 'in the head' of individuals; they are 'concrete' rather than abstract; and they have causes and effects in the physical world.[5] As mental *representations*, they have 'representational content'. They contribute to the content of our propositional attitudes, to what we believe, desire, etc. They do so by determining the conditions under which our beliefs are true and our desires satisfied.

Any form of subjectivism immediately faces a Fregean objection: concepts cannot be phenomena in the minds or heads of individuals, since they can be *shared* between different subjects. Now, 'sharing' and its cognates are used in a variety of ways. One paradigm is that of *dividing* an object into parts, which themselves are not shared, as in sharing a banana. But there is another, equally basic paradigm which does not imply division and extends well beyond material objects. Different people can share bicycles, predilections, insurance companies, heads of states, the credit for an invention, beliefs, etc. It is in this sense that concepts are shareable. Two individuals *A* and *B* can both *have the same concept*, which means that they both have mastered that concept and can employ it.

For Frege a concept is the 'referent' (*Bedeutung*) of a 'concept-word' or predicate; but it is the 'senses' of predicates rather than concepts that are components of the senses of sentences, i.e. of propositions (*Gedanken*).[6] The sense of an expression is the 'mode of presentation' of its referent. Roughly speaking, the sense of a sentence is the thought expressed by it, the sense of a proper name is determined by the features which an object must possess to be the referent of the name, the sense of a concept-word is determined by the features which objects must possess to fall under the concept-word.

Frege's most explicit statements on shareability concern not concepts themselves, but these senses. The sense of a sign 'may be the common property of many people, and so is not a part or a mode of the individual mind'. That is to say, different people 'are not prevented from grasping the same sense'.[7] In the current context, however, Frege's distinction between the senses of predicates and concepts does not matter. He himself occasionally used 'concept' for the sense of concept-words.[8] More importantly, Frege's point about the shareability of senses extends directly to concepts; and this extension is very

---

[5] Fodor, *Concepts*, pp. 3, 7–8, 22; Fodor, *Hume Variations*, p. 13+n.

[6] 'Letter to Husserl 24.5.1891', in M. Beaney (ed.), *The Frege Reader* (Oxford: Blackwell, 1997), p. 149.

[7] 'On Sense and Meaning' (1892), pp. 29–30. [References for Frege's published articles are to the original pagination reproduced in Beaney (ed.), *The Frege Reader*.]

[8] *Posthumous Writings* (Oxford: Blackwell, 1979), p. 253; Frege, 'Negation' (1918), p. 151.

much part of his frequent insistence that concepts are objective in that they 'confront everyone in the same way'.[9] According to Frege, the shareability of senses/concepts can be guaranteed only by treating them as abstract entities, entities which are what Frege calls 'non-actual' (by contrast with material objects) yet 'objective' (by contrast with mental phenomena like ideas).

Shareability is a feature of the concept of a concept in both everyday life and in disciplines like psychology and the history of ideas. One central use we make of 'concept' and terms that are equivalent in the relevant contexts (like 'conception', 'idea', or 'notion') is in claims about different individuals or even groups of individuals either sharing a concept, or failing to do so. For instance, different political and religious traditions may or may not share concepts like those of freedom or of guilt. Such claims are equally central to intellectual history, e.g. when it comes to comparing the Greek concept of *eudaimonia* with our concept of happiness.

Appeals to established use would normally be given short shrift by Fodor. Yet even he accepts as a 'non-negotiable condition on a theory of concepts' that 'concepts are public; they're the sorts of things that lots of people can, and do, share'.[10] The obvious difficulty is that Fodor's mental particulars contrast with concepts in that they *are* modes of individual minds or heads, and hence private to their owners.[11] But Fodor thinks that he can easily overcome this difficulty and reject Frege's anti-subjectivist argument by introducing a distinction between type and token. Fodor's 'language of thought hypothesis' treats mental representations as symbols of a 'language of thought' or 'Mentalese'. Thoughts, the larger wholes formed by concepts, are the sentences of Mentalese, physical tokens of computational types. When we engage in conceptual thought, Mother Nature inscribes words of a computer programme into our brains. And concepts are nothing other than the token-words of Mentalese.

---

[9] *Grundgesetze der Arithmetik*, vol. i (Jena: Pohle 1893), p. xviii; see also *Grundlagen der Arithmetik* (1886), p. x; 'Thought' (1918–19), pp. 66–7.

[10] Fodor, *Concepts*, p. 28.

[11] Frege used the term 'idea' (*Vorstellung*) to signify what Fodor calls a mental particular. And he assumed that ideas are private in the same innocuous sense as smiles: the ideas of two individuals may be qualitatively identical but must be numerically distinct (e.g. *Grundgesetze der Arithmetik*, pp. xviii–xix). That assumption was questioned by Wittgenstein, who challenged the possibility of distinguishing qualitative and numerical identity in the case of sensations, visual impressions, and mental images. Nevertheless such a distinction is imperative. For instance, even if *A* and *B* have the 'same' pain as regards location and hedonic qualities, it is possible to get rid of one of them (through *A* taking an analgesic) without getting rid of the other. See H. J. Glock, *A Wittgenstein Dictionary* (Oxford: Blackwell, 1996), p. 306 and W. Künne, 'Wittgenstein and Frege's Logical Investigations', in H. J. Glock and J. Hyman (eds), *Wittgenstein and Analytic Philosophy: Essays for P. M. S. Hacker* (Oxford: Oxford University Press, 2009), pp. 38–9. In any event, Frege's anti-subjectivist argument would stand even if he were wrong about the privacy of ideas, since its crux is that the mental particulars invoked by subjectivists are unshareable, unlike concepts.

Consider the scenario in which Anne and Sarah both believe that dogs bark and (improbably) utter 'Dogs bark' in close succession. In that case we have two tokens of a single type-sentence 'Dogs bark', and two tokens of a single type-word 'bark'. Similarly, according to Fodor, in Anne's brain there occurs one neural token-sentence, and in Sarah's brain there occurs another neural token-sentence. Yet Anne and Sarah both believe the same thing, namely that dogs bark, since both tokens instantiate the same Mentalese type-sentence DOGS BARK. Finally, they share the concept DOG, because both have tokens of one and the same Mentalese type-word.

This position can account for shareability. It does so at a price, however. The type/token distinction cannot be used to invalidate Frege's argument, since it implies abandoning the claim that concepts themselves are particulars. After all, even on Fodor's own account Anne and Sarah do not have a Mentalese token-word in common, what they have in common is that their distinct token-words are of the same type. What can be shared between different individuals are representation-types; and these types, as Fodor duly acknowledges, are 'abstracta' rather than mental particulars. To be more precise, types are repeatable universals and hence abstract. Conversely, what can qualify as mental particulars are representation-tokens; and these tokens are confined to each individual rather than shareable. This leaves Fodor's response to the Fregean argument in tatters. On the one hand, the non-negotiable constraint on concepts, namely that they be *shareable*, is satisfied only by the *abstract types* which are neither particulars (mental, physical, or otherwise) nor concrete. On the other hand, his central claim, namely that concepts are *concrete particulars*, applies only to the *tokens* which are not shareable. If Fodor persistently kept apart types and tokens, he would be forced to abandon the subjectivist credo that concepts are mental particulars that can enter into causal relations. Instead he would have to concede that concepts themselves—the things that can be shared by different individuals—are *not* particulars.

As far as the Fregean argument against subjectivism is concerned, concepts might yet be mental *representations*, namely of the type- rather than token-variety. This is in line with Fodor's contention that 'concepts are [Mentalese] symbols'.[12] But at the same time he is driven to the claim that concepts are something that 'mental representations . . . express', namely 'word meanings'.[13] Accordingly, he is committed to the inconsistent idea that concepts are both mental words and the meanings of those very same words. This inconsistency is no coincidence. For Fodor needs to situate concepts at the level of things

---

[12] Fodor, *Concepts*, n. 7, p. 28.   [13] Fodor, *Concepts*, n. 7, p. 2; *Hume Variations*, n. 2, p. 13.

represented. After all, like his objectivist opponents he invokes concepts in order to account for the fact that different people can entertain the same thoughts. For both, concepts must be shareable because they are components of what people believe, of shareable thoughts or 'propositional contents'. But as their components, concepts can no more be representations or signs than propositions themselves—they must rather be something represented by representations or signs. This is in line with the commonsensical idea that concepts are *expressed* by signs (the concepts at issue in this essay by one-place predicates).[14]

3. Are Concepts Properties or Meanings?

Let us turn to two alternative candidates that are non-actual yet objective in Frege's sense, and with which he or other objectivists have identified concepts. There is a venerable yet vibrant tradition of treating concepts as universals and the latter as properties. Often, moreover, the latter are in turn identified with meanings of predicates, but the thesis that concepts are meanings can also be upheld independently of that claim.

Frege's main positive contention about concepts is that they are functions from objects to truth-values and hence entities of an 'unsaturated' kind. He also identifies concepts with properties, though somewhat in passing.[15] Finally, he thinks that a singular term, being saturated, can refer only to a saturated entity—an object—and not to an unsaturated entity—a concept. For this reason he embraces the notoriously paradoxical claim that the concept *horse* is not a concept. But since identity is a relation between objects, this also means that the identity relation is 'conceivable' only 'with respect to objects, not with respect to concepts'.[16] By this token, there cannot be any criteria of identity for concepts, strictly speaking. In so far as there can be, moreover, it would appear that concepts are no more finely individuated than the extensions of predicates. For concepts are the 'meanings', i.e. referents, of predicates; and predicates with the same referent are those that apply to all and only the same things. By contrast, most lay people, philosophers, and logicians would insist that, for example, the concept of having a kidney differs from that of having a heart. Arguably, concepts should be individuated more finely even than properties and just as finely as Fregean senses: although 'equilateral triangle'

---

[14] My 'Concepts: Where Subjectivism Goes Wrong', *Philosophy* 84 (2009) elaborates these objections to Fodor.

[15] Frege, 'Funktion und Begriff' (1891), p. 201.   [16] Frege, *Posthumous Writings*, p. 120.

and 'equiangular triangle' apply necessarily to all and only the same objects, they do not express the same concept, since they are not synonymous.[17]

The claim that concepts are the referents of predicates rather than their senses is also problematic for other reasons. The proposition

(1) Dogs bark

does not refer to, and is not about, the concept of a dog or the concept of barking. By the same token, someone who thinks that dogs bark is thinking about dogs, or barking, at a pinch. But she is not thinking about the concepts of a dog or of barking. Irrespective of what concepts turn out to be, predicates do not denote concepts in the way in which singular terms denote objects: rather, concepts are what predicates *express*.[18]

For Frege's most famous pupil Carnap, concepts are the 'intensions' or senses of predicates instead of their extensions or referents. He also individuates them more finely: two predicates express the same concept if and only if they are logically equivalent, i.e. have the same extension across all 'possible worlds'. At the same time, Carnap explicitly identifies concepts with properties. He uses 'concept' as a generic term for properties, relations, and individual concepts. The label is to be understood in an 'objective' rather than 'mental sense', that is: it refers not 'to a process of imagining, thinking, conceiving, or the like, but rather to something objective that is found in nature'.[19]

Pedigree and popularity notwithstanding, however, the identification of concepts with properties is at odds with important features of the ordinary use of 'concept', even if one leaves aside the aforementioned difference concerning criteria of identity. The most obvious difference is that to have or possess a concept *F* is not the same as to have or possess the property of being *F*. Indeed, 'concept' and 'property' are not even substitutable *salva significatione*, let alone, *salva veritate*, in such contexts.

(2) Sarah possesses the property of benevolence

and

(3) Sarah possesses the concept of benevolence

can obviously differ in truth-value.

[17] See my 'Concepts: Representations or Abilities?', in E. Di Nucci and C. McHugh (eds), *Content, Consciousness and Perception* (Cambridge: Scholars Press), pp. 57–9.

[18] See W. Künne, 'Properties in Abundance', in P. F. Strawson and A. Chakrabarti (eds), *Universals, Concepts and Qualities* (Burlington: Ashgate, 2006), p. 254, n. 31.

[19] R. Carnap, *Meaning and Necessity* (Chicago: University of Chicago Press, 1956), pp. 27, 21.

One cannot dismiss this contrast as a semantically insignificant detail of ordinary use. For it is partly constitutive of both properties and concepts that they can be possessed, and the fact that this *amounts to something different* in each case marks an important contrast between the two. To possess the property of being F is to instantiate it, or simply to be F; by contrast, to possess the concept of an F is to master that concept. Proponents of the identification might try to turn this point to their advantage by insisting that the failure of intersubstitutability is due to an ambiguity of the predicate 'x possesses y' or the auxiliary 'have'. Now, according to a criterion accepted by otherwise disparate philosophers, a term is ambiguous if and only if in one and the same context it can make for both a true and a false statement.[20] It is far from clear that 'have' is ambiguous by this standard. For instance, replacing 'possesses' in (2) by 'has mastered' results in

(2′) Sarah has mastered the property of benevolence

which is arguably nonsensical rather than either true or false. Admittedly, if instead we replace 'possesses' by 'instantiates' we obtain two sentences that are logically equivalent:

(2*) Sarah instantiates the property of benevolence
(3*) Sarah instantiates the concept of benevolence.

Yet this does not show that 'concept' and 'property' are logically equivalent, let alone synonymous. For they fail the test of intersubstitutability *salva veritate* in other contexts.

(4) Wittgenstein was fond of the concept of nonsense

is true, for instance, while

(5) Wittgenstein was fond of the property of being nonsensical

is false.

Nobody would stoop to diagnosing an ambiguity of 'is fond of' in these cases. Indeed it is obvious that the contrast between (4) and (5) derives instead from a difference between 'concept' and 'property'. To be fond of the concept F is, roughly speaking, to be fond of thinking or speaking of things as F; whereas to be fond of the property of being F is to be fond of, *pro tanto*, things which are F. The moral is clear. Properties are in fact objective somewhat in the sense intended by Carnap; they are possessed by entities of all kinds.

---

[20] BB 58; W. V. O. Quine, *Word and Object* (Cambridge, Mass.: MIT Press, 1960), pp. 241–2, §27; B. Rundle, *Grammar in Philosophy* (Oxford: Oxford University Press, 1979), §3.

Concepts, by contrast, are possessed by rational subjects who think or speak about things according to the properties the latter possess, notably by classifying them according to these properties.

A different category mismatch looms when we identify the meaning of a predicate with the property expressed by it. When we say of Socrates that he is courageous, we ascribe to him the property of being courageous, but not the meaning of 'courageous'.[21] But why not bypass properties and identify concepts with linguistic meanings, or at least the meanings of general terms?

One reason is that Socrates satisfies or falls under the concept of being courageous, yet he cannot be said to satisfy or fall under the meaning of 'courageous'. Another reason is that conceptual thinking is not tied to either overt or silent speech (see Section 6). A final reason arises from the need to distinguish between the meaning of a sentence on the one hand, and what is said by the use of a sentence—the proposition expressed by the sentence—on the other.[22] Propositions, in the sense of what is or could be said, are what we convey by the use of sentences, not their meanings. Unlike the meaning of a sentence, for example, what is said (believed, etc.) can be true or false, implausible or exaggerated. Furthermore, far from being identical with sentence-meanings, what is said on a particular occasion depends on sentence-meaning and context of utterance. But in so far as concepts are components of propositions (see Section 7), we must also distinguish between concepts and word-meanings. Just as propositions are sayables and thinkables, concepts are predicables, but this does not hold of word-meanings.

4. The Priority Question

Given the failure of paradigmatic answers to the definition question from both the subjectivist and the objectivist camp, it is time to consider the priority question. Perhaps the nature of concepts is best approached indirectly, through one of the other questions on our list. In that case these questions would be prior to the definition question, at least from a methodological point of view.

The idea of such an indirect approach to philosophical 'What is'-questions has powerful sources in both Frege and Wittgenstein. Frege tackles some questions of the form 'What are Fs' by elucidating the criteria for the identity

---

[21] Künne, 'Properties in Abundance', p. 289, n. 76.

[22] See my *Quine and Davidson on Language, Thought and Reality* (Cambridge: Cambridge University Press, 2003), pp. 153–4.

of *F*s. Thus he suggests that the most helpful way of explaining what a direction is is to elucidate under what conditions two lines have the same direction. And the most propitious way of explaining what a cardinal number is may be to scrutinize the conditions under which two sets have the same number of members.[23] In both cases we switch from nouns to adjectives, from something abstract to something palpable, and from something elusive to something familiar.

Wittgenstein's indirect approach goes in a different direction. It is also immediately linked to the topic of concepts, since he develops it with respect to the notions of meaning, explanation, and understanding.

What is the meaning of a word? Let us attack this question by asking, first, what is an explanation of the meaning of a word; what does the explanation of a word look like. The way this question helps us is analogous to the way the question 'how do we measure a length?' helps us to understand the problem 'what is length?'. The questions 'What is length?', 'What is meaning?', 'What is the number one?' etc. produce in us a mental cramp. We feel that we can't point to anything in reply to them and yet ought to point to something.   (BB 1; see PG 68–9)

Finally, this move to the explanation of meaning draws in its wake a further widening of the horizon, namely to linguistic understanding. The meaning of '*X*' is both what is explained by an explanation of '*X*' and what one understands when one understands '*X*' and its explanation (BT 11; PG 45, 60; PI §560). And like the capacity to use '*X*', the capacity to explain '*X*' is a criterion for understanding '*X*'. That is why in lectures from the thirties Wittgenstein utilized the question 'What is it to understand a general term such as "plant"?' as one of the remedies against the urge to reify meanings.[24]

The move from linguistic meaning to linguistic understanding has parallels in a later move urged by Peacocke, namely from a theory of concepts to a theory of concept-possession.[25] Leaving aside the theoretical aspirations, Wittgenstein should welcome this strategy. The dictations to Waismann proffer as 'the real doctrine of concepts' (*die eigentliche Lehre vom Begriff*): 'the meaning of a word is constituted by the rules for its employment'. And they occasionally switch not just from word-meaning to concept but also from understanding words to understanding concepts, notably regarding the concept of an integral, which obviously cuts across different natural languages (VW 142, 466).[26]

---

[23] *Grundlagen der Arithmetik*, §§62–70.

[24] See J. Wisdom, 'Ludwig Wittgenstein, 1934–1937', *Mind* 61 (1952), p. 258.

[25] Peacocke, *A Study of Concepts*, pp. viii, 4–6.

[26] For a more detailed account of Wittgenstein's replacement strategy and its relation to contemporary theories of concepts, see my 'Wittgenstein on Concepts', in A. M. Ahmed (ed.), *Critical Guide to*

Wittgenstein's strategy with respect to meaning is one of *replacement*. First, he switches from the original explanandum to another notion which is not offered as a direct explanans, but which is illuminatingly related to the former, let's call it the *illuminans*. In our case, he switches from meaning to explanation and understanding. Secondly, he operationalizes the illuminans and thereby the explanandum. So we move not just from 'What is length?' to 'What is it to measure the length of a body?', but from there to 'How do we measure the length of a body?'. Analogously, we move not just from 'What is meaning?' to 'What is it to explain the meaning of a word?' and 'What is it to understand the meaning of a word', but from the latter to 'How do we explain the meaning of a word?' and 'How do we establish whether someone understands the meaning of a word?'.

If we extend the replacement strategy to concepts, we arrive at the following contrast. On the one hand, we have a *direct* or *Socratic* approach. It seeks explicit definitions through questions like

> What is the meaning of an expression?
> What are concepts?
> What is X?

On the other hand, we have a *contextualist* or *Wittgensteinian* approach which switches to analogous questions like:

> What is it to understand the meaning of an expression?
> What is it to have a concept?
> What is it to know X?

As a response, it expects implicit or contextual definitions of the original explanandum.

Socratic 'What is . . . ?' questions have a notorious tendency to lead to *aporiai*. What is more, this tendency seems to be unaffected by the switch from the material mode, i.e. questions of the form 'What is the essence or nature of F', to the formal mode, i.e. questions of the form 'What does "F" mean?'. But what grounds do we have for hoping that the indirect approach might fare better? Consider the following pair of questions:

> (6)   What is a mortgage?
> (6*) What is it for a house to have a mortgage on it?

Wittgenstein's 'Philosophical Investigations' (Cambridge: Cambridge University Press, 2009). For the connections between meaning, explanation, and understanding see G. P. Baker and P. M. S. Hacker, *Wittgenstein: Understanding and Meaning* (Oxford: Blackwell, 2005), chs II, XVII.

(7)   What is a legal obligation?

(7*)   What is it for someone to be legally obliged to do something?

Wittgenstein hints at two reasons why the contextualist questions are easier to answer than the 'What is...?' questions. First, the noun-phrases derive their content from non-nominal constructions. We talk about legal obligations because agents face expectations and sanctions of a certain kind. Secondly, and relatedly, the contextualist move 'takes us back to the rough ground' (PI §107). Unlike legal obligations, agents being subjected to expectations and sanctions is something concrete and directly observable.

Let us return to Wittgenstein's indirect approach to meaning/concepts. Its first step—the replacement—introduces an illuminans with an epistemic dimension—understanding and concept-possession respectively. This epistemic dimension in turn provides a rationale for the second step—the operationalization. Understanding or concept-possession manifest themselves in behaviour and hence can be ascertained by ordinary speakers. Unfortunately, this idea is resisted by cognitive scientists on the one hand and realist semanticists on the other. Thus Fodor suspects that the insistence on the manifestability of understanding is fuelled by 'atavistic sceptical anxieties about communication'.[27] But this suspicion ignores the fact that at least in our case the explanandum itself has an intrinsic epistemic dimension, one to which the illuminans draws attention.

It is part and parcel of the established notion of linguistic meaning that the meaning of an expression is known to competent speakers who have mastered that expression. This need not mean that they can spontaneously proffer an optimal explanation of that expression. But it means two things: they must be capable of explaining it in some way, e.g. by exemplification or analogy; and they must be capable of recognizing an explanation if it is offered to them by discerning linguists or conceptual analysts.[28]

Its current popularity notwithstanding, the idea that meaning might transcend what competent speakers are capable of manifesting in behaviour ignores the dependence of meaning on practice. Words do not have linguistic meaning intrinsically, as a matter of arcane factors accessible exclusively to scientists, but only because speakers use and explain them in a certain way (see BB 27–8). Therefore it is simply absurd to suggest that our term 'teddy-bear', for instance, has a real meaning, and might, for all normal speakers know, refer to a type of super-nova. The meaning of an expression simply is what competent

---

[27] Fodor, *Concepts*, p. 5.

[28] See my *Quine and Davidson on Language, Thought and Reality*, pp. 244–9.

speakers understand by the expression, and what they explain to neophytes when they explain what it means. By a similar token, what speakers say in using expressions simply is what those who understand their utterances grasp. Any account which opens the floodgates to semantic scepticism straightforwardly misses the concept of meaning. Hidden factors are idle wheels, semantically speaking. Those who hanker for them are really after the causes of our beliefs and utterances, which may indeed be unknown.

As regards concepts, this Wittgensteinian line of reasoning can be summarized as follows. It is part of the concept of a concept that concepts are known (mastered or grasped) by those who possess and employ them. Furthermore, what concepts people possess or employ is manifest in their cognitive and linguistic operations and achievements, especially in how they employ and explain the corresponding terms. Therefore we can establish what concepts a person possesses or employs by looking at her cognitive and linguistic activities and at the way she justifies and explains them. At a more general level, we can establish what it is to possess a concept by looking at the grounds on which we ascribe mastery of concepts to people, at our criteria for concept-possession.

5. Concept-Possession

These criteria clearly suggest that having a concept is the possession of an ability, capacity, or disposition. We credit subjects with concept-possession and linguistic understanding not on the basis of (mental or neurological) goings-on, processes accompanying intelligent behaviour or communication, but on account of what they are capable of doing.

Wittgenstein elaborates these points in the context of his discussion of linguistic understanding. His negative line of reasoning is familiar.[29] First, conceptually speaking, neither mental nor physical processes or states are either necessary or sufficient for understanding. Secondly, even in cases in which speakers or hearers typically associate a given expression with specific mental images or with other symbols, these accompaniments do not determine what they mean by an expression or how they understand it.

Wittgenstein's alternative, however, is less clear-cut. In the dictations to Waismann, he seems happy to contend that understanding is a disposition, while wavering on the question of whether that disposition is a state of a person, such as a physiological state of his brain. He characterizes understanding a word as 'a disposition to use this word' (VW 358, 368, 440). This suggests a

---

[29] See my A Wittgenstein Dictionary (Oxford: Blackwell, 1996), pp. 179–84, 372–6.

behaviourist position susceptible to the obvious objection that one can under-stand a word—for instance an obscenity or faddish slogan—without being in the least disposed to use it. In other passages, Wittgenstein goes on to explain the idea that understanding is a disposition in a more fruitful fashion, namely as a *Vermögen* (capacity) or *Können* (ability), something linked to the auxiliary 'can'. More circumspectly still, he settles for the claim that 'there is a kinship between the grammar of "can", "is able to" and that of "understands the meaning"'. 'The question "Do you understand this word?" is much closer to "Can you operate with this word?" than to "What process occurs in you on hearing the word?"' (VW 356–8, 440–2, 464–5; see also AWL 92; PLP 346). 'Understand-ing a word can mean: knowing how it is used; being able to apply it' (PG 47).

This avenue is congenial to the mature later work. Thus Wittgenstein maintains that the grammar of 'know' is 'evidently closely related' to that of 'can' and 'is able to' on the one hand, and of 'understand' on the other, as well as the pregnant suggestion in parenthesis that the latter is '"mastery" of a technique' (PI §150). Understanding a word is, or is akin to, an ability, one which manifests itself in three ways: (i) how one uses it; (ii) how one responds to its use by others; (iii) how one explains what it means when asked (see PI §§75, 317, 363, 501–10; LFM 19–28).

Wittgenstein now denies that understanding is a 'mental state' with genuine duration,[30] even though the pertinent passage from the *Investigations* is mis-leading. But his attitude towards the claim that understanding is a disposition remains ambivalent. On the one hand, in PI §149 he explicitly relegates dis-positions to physiological states of the subject underlying its performances, and denies that understanding is such a state. On the other hand, he continues to assimilate understanding to a disposition in order to highlight the contrast with 'states of consciousness', that is, states that possess genuine duration and which can be avowed authoritatively by the subject without spot-checking (Z §§72, 82, 672–5; RPP II §§45, 57, 243).

Be that as it may, in both the intermediate and the later period Wittgenstein approaches concept-possession along the same lines as linguistic understanding. Negatively, this applies to the contrast with mental representations. There may be representations (*Vorstellungen*) that typically accompany understanding a particular expression—Wittgenstein is primarily thinking of mental images here. But these do not determine what speakers understand. They do not even distinguish 'concepts' from sentences. 'The truth of the matter is that a representation can represent a concept on one occasion, a sentence on another' (VW 460). Positively, it applies to linking concept-possession with an

---

[30] See Baker and Hacker, *Wittgenstein: Understanding and Meaning*, pp. 371–5.

ability. More specifically, Wittgenstein links concept-possession with mastery of language-games. 'Whoever cannot play this game [establishing the colour of an object by looking at it] doesn't have this [colour] concept' (ROC III §115, see §§112–24). As in the case of understanding, moreover, Wittgenstein stresses that this ability is acquired through teaching and learning—a point obvious to everyone save inveterate nativists.

Even though Wittgenstein ultimately fails to clarify the tricky relationship between disposition and ability, in the context of characterizing concept-possession as a disposition he commits himself to treating both as a 'possibility' (VW 360). In Aristotelian terms, concept-possession is a power or potentiality rather than an actuality. That much is accepted, willy-nilly, even by representationalists who profess to disagree with Wittgenstein on this score. Concept-possession must belong to the category of a potentiality. Unlike concept-exercise, concept-possession is enduring or static rather than episodic or occurrent. A subject can possess a concept at time t without exercising the concept at t. At the same time, concept-possession manifests itself in certain episodes, in the employment of concepts, notably in overt or silent classification or inference.[31] Even representationalists admit that the idea of concept possession as an ability or capacity is 'initially attractive'. But they are wont to add 'until one starts to figure out what kind of ability it might be'.[32]

This is indeed a challenge, and not just because one needs to specify the proper actualization or exercise of concept-possession.[33] It is also because concept-possession is not a straightforward kind of disposition or ability. Concept-possession is not a disposition in the everyday sense of that term.[34] In ordinary parlance, human dispositions include character traits which are halfway between abilities and action, between a capacity and its actualization. They are neither realized automatically nor simply subject to the will. Furthermore, to have the disposition to be generous, for instance, it does not suffice to be capable of being generous; one must also have a tendency to do so in propitious circumstances.

At the same time, in a vaguely technical sense, dispositions are one-way powers to be contrasted with abilities. Typical abilities of human beings are what Kenny calls 'two-way powers'. Unlike 'one-way' or 'natural powers', these two-way powers are not automatically exercised given certain antecedent conditions. Rather, their possessors can exercise them or refrain from exercising

[31] A. Kenny, *Will, Freedom and Power* (Oxford: Blackwell, 1975), p. 106.

[32] T. Crane, 'Something Else, Surely', *Times Literary Supplement*, 7 May 2004, p. 4.

[33] I attempt to meet this challenge in 'Concepts: Representations or Abilities?', pp. 51–7.

[34] See Kenny, *Metaphysics of Mind*, pp. 83–5; Baker and Hacker, *Wittgenstein: Understanding and Meaning*, pp. 373–5.

them at will. Greenhouse gases have the power to trap light reflected from the surface, and will inevitably do so given certain conditions. By contrast, I can choose whether or not to exercise my ability to cycle to work.

But now, neither understanding nor concept-possession are two-way powers. Their exercise is not (uniformly) subject to the will. I might be able to decide not to employ certain concepts actively in a complex train of thought. And I can refrain from exercising my linguistic understanding actively, by performing or responding to certain utterances. But as Kenny points out, passive understanding is not subject to the will: 'Looking up at the flashing lights of the advertisements in Piccadilly Circus, one cannot prevent oneself from understanding their message. (How much more beautiful they would be, G. K. Chesterton once remarked, if only one could not read!)'[35] Similarly, while we can decide whether or not to take a look, once we do look, we cannot decide whether or not to see something within our field of vision. By the same token, conceptually gifted creatures cannot decide whether or not to conceptualize what they see, in the sense of recognizing it as being of a certain kind. At most, they can try to reconceptualize what they see by thinking of less obvious categories that also apply to it.

On the other hand, it has been held in the wake of Davidson that attributions of dispositions lack normative force: a possessor that fails to act in accordance with a disposition is not subject to correction. From this perspective, concept-possession, like some other intellectual abilities, occupies a halfway position. By contrast to two-way powers it is not subject to the will, and by contrast to mere dispositions or one-way powers its exercise is subject to normative assessment: conceptual classifications are susceptible to criticism and correction. This intermediate status is further confirmed by the fact that understanding and concept-possession are manifested not just through cognitive operations which are beyond voluntary control, but also through the possession of abilities which are two-way powers. These are precisely the linguistic abilities Wittgenstein emphasizes, namely of explaining and employing a term, and of reacting to its use by others.

6. Concepts and Abilities

Given that concept-possession is an ability (albeit of a special kind), it would seem natural to identify concepts with abilities. Thus, in response to the question 'are concepts entities or are they dispositions?', Price states in no

[35] Kenny, *Metaphysics of Mind*, p. 22; see also p. 70 and *Will, Freedom and Power*, pp. 52–3.

uncertain terms: 'a concept is not an entity...but a disposition or capacity'.[36] In the same vein, and under the influence of Wittgenstein, Geach pronounces that concepts 'are capacities exercised in acts of judgement'.[37]

Geach points out that this identification of concepts and capacities does not fall foul of the constraint that concepts must be shareable. It does not entail that 'it is improper to speak of two people as "having the same concept"', since different individuals can possess the same mental capacities.[38] Furthermore, concepts and abilities alike can be acquired, applied, and lost, and some of them may be innate. Finally, it is tempting simply to infer from the fact that to possess a concept is to possess an ability that concepts themselves are abilities. Such a move would be precipitate. For our linguistic constructions need not comply with the naïve compositionalist recipe having x = having $y \Rightarrow x = y$, since having may amount to something different in each case.

In fact, there are weighty objections against identifying concepts with dispositions, capacities, or abilities. First, one thing we do with concepts is to define or explain them. But to define a concept is not to define or explain a capacity. Secondly, concepts can be instantiated or satisfied by things. But abilities cannot. Thirdly, and relatedly, concepts have an extension (the set of objects which fall under them) and an intension (the features which qualify objects for falling under them); yet this cannot be said of abilities. Insofar as the ability linked to possessing the concept F has an extension, it is not the range of things that are F, but either the range of subjects that possess F, or the range of situations in which these possessors can apply or withhold F. Fourthly, a concept can occur in a proposition or statement, but an ability cannot. Of course, abilities can occur in propositions in the sense of being mentioned in them. But concepts occur in propositions in yet another and more pervasive way. The concept of being sweet occurs in the proposition that

(8) Sugar is sweet

even though there is no mention of an ability.

To some Wittgensteinians, this line of reasoning may smack of reification. For it seems committed to a building-block model according to which small abstract components—concepts—combine to form large abstract wholes—thoughts or propositions. But, the Wittgensteinians are wont to insist, this model is not a truism but a problematic Platonist metaphor. What seems to give content to that metaphor is exclusively the fact that the linguistic expressions of thoughts—namely sentences—have components—namely

---

[36] H. H. Price, *Thinking and Experience* (London: Hutchinson, 1953), pp. 320, 348.
[37] P. T. Geach, *Mental Acts* (London: Routledge, 1957), p. 7; see also p. 13.   [38] Ibid., p. 14.

words.[39] The Platonist picture transposes the part/whole relation from the spatial and temporal sphere—including that of the written or spoken word—to a sphere—that of abstract entities—to which *ex hypothesi* neither spatial nor temporal notions apply.

It should be noted, however, that there is a reason for parsing propositions into concepts which is not fuelled by building-block metaphors. Instead, it relies on the basic rationale for speaking about concepts and propositions. These notions are helpful in accounting for facts like the following: first, different people can think the same—that is, share the same thoughts; secondly, they can entertain thoughts which, though different, stand in logical relations to each other; thirdly, they can do both of these things *without* sharing a language. When a monoglot Anglophone A and a monoglot Germanophone B both believe that

(9) Cats are animals

then they share a thought. Similarly, if A believes that

(10) Cats are mammals

and B believes that

(11) Cats are vertebrates

then what B believes follows from what A believes. These facts are easily explained in terms of propositions and concepts. A and B can both believe that (9) because they have both mastered the concepts that occur in (9), irrespective of the fact that they express them through different words (e.g. 'animal' vs. 'Tier'). What A believes entails what B believes because of the relations that obtain between the concepts that occur in (10) and (11). All of which is in no way undermined by the fact that A and B would express these propositions and concepts through different words (e.g. 'animal' vs. 'Tier').

As will become manifest in the final section, I share the Wittgensteinian aspiration of treating propositions and concepts as logical constructions from linguistic and cognitive abilities and activities. As regards our examples, the idea would be to treat concepts as abstractions from the inferential relations between propositions like (10) and (11), and to explain the latter by reference to our practices of reasoning. But note two things. First, our talk of concepts does not lend itself easily to a meta-linguistic reduction. There is no linguistic expression or language mastery of which is necessary for the possession of the concepts involved in (9). And it is a moot question whether

---

[39] Kenny, *Metaphysics of Mind*, pp. 126–7.

primitive concepts can be possessed by creatures who possess no language whatever. It is also unclear how conceptual relations like those between (10) and (11) are to be analysed in terms that do not presuppose something like concepts. Secondly, even if concepts are nothing but abstractions from linguistic practices, this abstraction drives a real wedge between concepts and abilities. To put it at its least committal, concepts are involved in propositions in a way in which abilities are not. If the logical construction of concepts succeeds, it will mean that a range of abilities on the part of speakers is presupposed (probably in a rather complex and indirect fashion) by the proposition that sugar is sweet. Yet it will not mean that this proposition maintains or implies that sugar has such abilities, even though it clearly maintains or implies that sugar possesses a certain property or satisfies a certain concept.

A final objection starts out from the very observation that seemed to lend succour to the identification of concepts with abilities. If having a concept is an ability, it would seem to be an ability to operate with concepts. In that case, however, the concept itself cannot be identical with the ability. Rather, it is something employed in the exercise of that ability.

7. Techniques, Rules, and Modes of Presentation

Concepts are not identical with abilities, even though to possess a concept is to possess an ability. But perhaps the suggestion that concepts are employed in the exercise of that ability points the way forward. At any rate, it is congenial to remarks Wittgenstein made during the 1940s.[40] Thus he maintained that 'a concept is a technique of using a word' (LPP 50) or 'the technique of our use of an expression: as it were, the railway network that we have built for it' (MS 163: 56ᵛ). To master or possess a technique is to master or possess an ability. Yet techniques are not themselves abilities, but something which the possessor of an ability uses in exercising the ability. There is a difference, for instance, between the ability to skin a rabbit and the various techniques one might employ to this end.

Nevertheless Wittgenstein's suggestive remarks go astray, since they tie concepts too closely to language. Most philosophers influenced by Frege and/or Wittgenstein accept that the possession of concepts requires linguistic

---

[40] I owe the reference to these passages to J. Schulte, 'Concepts and Concept-Formation', in N. Venturinha (ed.), *Wittgenstein after his Nachlass* (London: Palgrave, 2009).

capacities.[41] Even if they are right, however, and it is a substantial if, concepts occur in thoughts that we do not enunciate. A venerable tradition reaching from Plato through Occam to contemporary believers in a language of thought would have it that in such cases we nonetheless use words *in foro interno*, namely either by employing words of a natural language in the imagination, or by employing the words of a language of thought which we can never consciously bring to mind. But this is misguided, for reasons Wittgenstein himself highlighted. Talking to oneself in the imagination is no more necessary or sufficient for thinking than the occurrence of mental images. And the idea of a deeply unconscious language of thought ignores the fact that a linguistic symbol must be used according to rules that a subject can explicate or at least recognize.[42]

Wittgenstein's idea can easily be given a Kantian twist, however, which ties concepts in the first instance to thought or understanding rather than language. Concepts are techniques not just for using words, but for mental operations or mental acts. The capacity for such mental operations may presuppose possession of language, yet it can be exercised by a subject who does not engage in either overt or silent speech at the time. But what kind of mental operation? A plausible answer is that conceptual thought revolves around classification and inference. Accordingly, the proposal currently under consideration is this: a concept is not identical with the capacity to classify or infer, but only with the technique employed by someone who exercises the ability to classify or infer. Next, the term 'technique' needs to be made more specific, in line with both Kant and Wittgenstein. In so far as conceptual thought involves a technique, it is a technique of operating according to a rule or principle. Concepts, the proposal now runs, are rules or principles of classification and/or inference.

Even this modified proposal is threatened by category mismatches. It does not seem that to define a concept is to define a principle or rule. Rather, the principle or rule features in the definition. But perhaps this is just a vagary of our current use of 'definition' without further conceptual import. There is no linguistic infelicity in maintaining that to explain a concept is to explain a principle or rule for operating with the concept. Furthermore, Wittgenstein's

---

[41] Kenny is an exception, since he grants that animals might possess concepts (*Metaphysics of Mind*, pp. 36–7, 128). For a defence of this stance see my 'Can Animals Judge?', *Grazer Philosophische Studien* (2010). If that defence succeeds, however, Kenny is precipitate in maintaining that 'The question "how do our thoughts have content?" is the same as the question "how do our words have meaning?"' (*Metaphysics of Mind*, p. 130), since one can manifest conceptual thought without possessing language, at least in principle.

[42] See P. M. S. Hacker, 'Languages, Minds and Brains', in C. Blakemore and S. Greenfield (eds), *Mindwaves* (Oxford: Blackwell, 1987), pp. 485–505. Also my 'Philosophy, Thought and Language', in J. Preston (ed.), *Thought and Language* (Cambridge: Cambridge University Press, 1997), pp. 151–69.

strategy vis-à-vis meaning can be adapted to this case: a concept is what the explanation of a concept explains, and if to explain a concept is to explain a rule, then this suggests that concepts are rules (even though only a general compositionalist principle would yield this as a definite conclusion).

One qualm would be that principles can be true or false, whereas concepts cannot. Prima facie, rules escape this difficulty, in so far as they are expressed by sentences in the imperative rather than indicative mood. Note, however, that this exemption does not even hold for all regulative rules, not to mention constitutive rules. Thus a regulative rule like

(12) x ought to Φ in condition C

can be prefixed by 'it is true that . . .'.[43]

Furthermore, the question arises what form these principles or rules should take. Here we seem to be facing a dilemma. Either the rules are standards for the employment of concepts. They might, for instance, take the form of the rules Bennett extracts from Kant:[44]

(13) You may apply concept F to x iff x is . . .

In that case the concept F itself is not identical with the rule. It is rather a kind of mental predicate the use of which is governed by the rule. Or the rule specifies another activity, e.g.

(14) You may treat x in way W iff x is . . .

In that case the danger is that we are stuck with two unpalatable options. One is that W is a place-holder for practical activities which may presuppose concept-possession, but which someone who has mastered the concept need not engage in; the other is that W is a place-holder for conceptualization or classification, which would render the account unexplanatory.

Perhaps we can avoid that last impasse by appeal to the Fregean proposal that concepts are senses or 'modes of presentation'. Unfortunately, the latter is no more than a catchphrase, and one Frege himself never elaborated, least of all with respect to concepts, which he regarded as referents rather than senses of predicates. But we can put some flesh on it by treating concepts as *ways of thinking about objects*, though not in the adverbial sense of thinking about them hard or longingly. More specifically, concepts are ways of thinking about or conceiving of objects *as possessing certain properties*, without themselves

---

[43] See my 'The Normativity of Meaning Made Easy', in C. Nimtz and A. Beckermann (eds), *Philosophy and Science*, Proceedings of GAP 5 (Paderborn: Mentis, 2005), pp. 219–41.

[44] J. Bennett, *Kant's Analytic* (Cambridge: Cambridge University Press, 1966), p. 145.

being properties. To render that suggestion viable, we need to avoid literal interpretations of the Fregean idea that a sense is a mode of presenting a referent. Strictly speaking, there can be no way of presenting a referent unless *there is* a referent or extension. In the case of concepts, this would rule out uninstantiated concepts, which is absurd. On my construal, therefore, ways of thinking about objects are directed not just at those objects which possess the relevant properties, but at all objects of which the relevant properties can be predicated *either* truly *or falsely*. To put it differently, a concept is a way of thinking of objects from a suitable range as possessing or lacking certain properties. This reintroduces the idea of classification. Finally, in the spirit of Wittgenstein, we can operationalize ways of thinking as follows: the concept expressed by a predicate is determined by the features by reference to which the subject decides what objects, if any, fall under the concept-word (or would decide, if the question arose).

8. Conclusion

I argued against Fodor that concepts are not representations in the minds of individuals but something represented by linguistic symbols. This position is compatible with Künne's suggestion that concepts are 'representational abstract entities'.[45] As modes of presentation, i.e. ways in which different subjects can think of something, concepts can be both *representanda* of predicates and at the same time *representantia* of properties. They are subjective not in Fodor's individualistic sense, but in the sense of being essentially cognitive.

At least prima facie, like abilities, principles, or rules but unlike concepts, ways of thinking do not occur in all propositions, but only in those which explicitly mention or refer to them. This problem may not be intractable, however. If Strawson is to be trusted, universals like properties can enter a proposition not just in the direct sense that the sentence expressing the proposition contains words or phrases 'referring' to the universal, but also in the less direct sense that the sentence contains words or phrases 'signifying' them.[46] By a similar token, already intimated in Section 5, the sentence contains general terms expressing the concept, even though it does not refer to them. Finally one can extend this courtesy to any otherwise plausible explanans of concepts. Accordingly, the predicate in 'Sugar is sweet' expresses a way of thinking about, or of, substances, namely as possessing the property of being sweet.

[45] Künne, *Abstrakte Gegenstände* (Frankfurt; Kohlhammer 2007), pp. 346–7.
[46] See P. F. Strawson, *Individuals* (Oxford: Oxford University Press, 1959), pt II.

Crucial to this construal is that standard propositions, and by implication our common and garden thinking, are not about concepts. That insight unites enlightened neo-Fregeans like Künne with enlightened mentalists like Price: 'The concept is not *before* the mind as an object of inspection. It is at work *in* the mind, but not as one inspectable content among others . . . It shows itself not as a detectable item of mental furniture, but rather as a guiding force, determining the direction which the series of presented particulars [mental images or words] takes . . .'.[47] It goes back to Aquinas, as illuminated by Kenny. Ideas (*species*) are 'not what is thought of (*id quod intelligitur*) but that by which thinking takes place (*id quo intelligitur*)'.[48]

Yet why should one accept that concepts—conceived as ways or instruments of thinking—feature in all propositions, however indirectly? The answer, I submit, is: because both propositions and concepts are abstract and yet dependent on cognitive subjects capable of thinking and/or speaking. Both notions make sense only by reference to the activities and abilities of such subjects. Propositions are sayables and thinkables; and we identify them by classifying actual or potential utterances according to what they say or would say. By the same token, concepts are predicables, things we can and do predicate of objects, and we identify them by looking at actual or potential predications. To talk of propositions and concepts is not just a *façon de parler*, on my view, and propositions and concepts are not just 'make-believe entities' (to use what is indeed a currently fashionable *façon de parler*). Rather, they are logical constructions in a non-reductive sense. It may prove impossible to paraphrase concepts away. We may need to refer to them in order to describe the practices of creatures with highly evolved cognitive and/or linguistic abilities. At the same time, the existence and nature of concepts becomes unmysterious once their role within that practice and its description is understood. That idea is obviously Wittgensteinian in spirit. Alas, to substantiate it is beyond the scope of this essay.[49]

---

[47] Price, *Thinking and Experience*, p. 342.

[48] A. Kenny, *Aquinas* (Oxford: Oxford University Press, 1980), p. 71.

[49] I wish to thank the editors for helpful comments on a first draft. This material has also profited from discussions in Hatfield, Modena, Reading, Southampton, and Zurich, for which I am grateful.

15

Some Remarks on 'Wittgenstein's Early Philosophy of Mind'

JOACHIM SCHULTE

1. Introduction

When I first came across Kenny's article on Wittgenstein's early philosophy of mind[1] and when, later, I translated it into German[2] I felt that its title was provocative in two respects. The first and more obvious provocation is the suggestion that the early Wittgenstein had a philosophy of mind at all. The second provocation, which is implied by Kenny's use of the word 'early', lies in the idea that part of Wittgenstein's later writings could rightly be called a philosophy of mind. Surely I am not the only person to think that, if what people like Dennett, Dretske, Fodor, and Jackson do is legitimately called 'philosophy of mind', then what Wittgenstein does may be *relevant to* this sort of theoretical enterprise but certainly is not a *contribution* to it. On the first page of his article, however, Kenny clarifies his meaning by saying that a 'philosophy of mind' is 'an analysis of sentences reporting beliefs, judgments, perception and the like'; and while this characterization will leave many people who think they are doing philosophy of mind out in the cold, it surely goes some way towards counting Wittgenstein in.

This takes care of the second provocation. But what about the first one? Here I must confess that I feel unpersuaded by Kenny's arguments. I continue to believe that there is nothing in the *Tractatus* that would deserve to be called 'philosophy of mind', and I do not see any need to think that Wittgenstein

---

[1] Anthony Kenny, 'Wittgenstein's Early Philosophy of Mind' (1981), reprinted in Kenny's book *The Legacy of Wittgenstein* (Oxford: Blackwell, 1984), pp. 1–9. Simple page references in the present article refer to this reprint.

[2] 'Wittgensteins frühe Philosophie der psychologischen Begriffe', in J. Schulte (ed.), *Texte zum Tractatus* (Frankfurt am Main: Suhrkamp, 1989), pp. 155–64.

must have made certain assumptions about the nature of mental phenomena. Kenny's remarks concern two sections of the *Tractatus*. The first one consists of propositions 3ff., the second of 5.541–5.5423. Here I will discuss only the first section. One of its many remarkable features is that it begins and ends with statements to the effect that a thought is not just a thought, but something that seems to be entirely different. In 3 Wittgenstein says that a thought is a logical picture. In TLP 3.5 he claims that a thought is an applied and thought-out (*gedachtes*) propositional sign. And in 4 he declares that a thought is a proposition with a sense. What is lacking is a remark to the effect that a thought is something mental.

In view of this textual evidence it seems reasonable to wonder whether what Wittgenstein had in mind when speaking of *Gedanken* (thoughts) was something non-mental. Accordingly, Kenny asks: 'Is the *Gedanke* of the 3s a psychological matter at all? May it not have more in common with Frege's Platonic entity than with the topic of Russell's theory of judgment?' (p. 1) Clearly this is a legitimate question, although it may be advisable not to restrict the set of plausible candidates for the position of a *Gedanke* to the thoughts considered by Frege and Russell. We may surely ask ourselves if what Wittgenstein is talking about has anything to do with the kind of mental phenomena studied by a scientific psychologist such as Wilhelm Wundt or William James. Or does it have anything to do with what people mean when in the ordinary course of things they employ words like 'think' and 'thought'? It is likely that most readers of TLP 3–4 would after some reflection reply, No, these remarks seem to be far removed from what either psychologists or laypeople tend to mean when speaking of thoughts. Of course, Wittgenstein's familiarity with Frege's work and terminology is an additional good reason for suspecting that in talking about thoughts he did not mean to refer to mental acts or their substrates. Frege wanted to separate the world of *Gedanken* from that of *Vorstellungen*. These mental or psychological phenomena were to be banished from the realm of what can be true or false. And it was in this vein that Frege declared that a thought is the sense of a name of a truth-value, i.e. of a proposition—a *Satz*. This is a use of the word '*Gedanke*' to which Wittgenstein was very well accustomed; and it is a use which can be spelled out, adopted, and modified without buying into Frege's Platonic ontology of what he called the 'third realm'.

2. The Letter to Russell

So why should one in spite of all the evidence to the contrary opt for the idea that Wittgenstein's *Gedanken* in the 3s are mental entities in the sense of states or processes attributable to the minds of individual thinkers? Kenny's answer to this question is that there is one piece of evidence that eclipses all competing evidence. This overwhelming evidence is supplied by two passages from a letter Wittgenstein wrote to Russell towards the end of his stay in the prisoners of war camp at Monte Cassino. These passages are often cited in the literature relevant to the questions discussed in Kenny's article. A prominent example is Miss Anscombe's book on the *Tractatus*,[3] which is taken into account by Kenny.

Considering the importance generally ascribed to this letter, it will certainly be appropriate to have a fresh look at this material. When Russell, who had been sent Wittgenstein's own copy of his *Abhandlung* from the camp, had read the typescript twice, he wrote to Wittgenstein. In his letter he not only expressed his opinion that Wittgenstein's work was a '*book of first-class importance*' but also set out various points of criticism and doubt. In addition, he attached to his letter a separate sheet with queries, hoping that Wittgenstein might enlighten him on these questions. In his reply, however, Wittgenstein initially shows himself to be rather unwilling to comply with Russell's request for clarification.[4] After having finished his letter, Wittgenstein adds a PS, saying that he feels 'tempted after all to answer some of [Russell's] simpler points'. Two of these nine points are directly relevant to the issues discussed by Kenny, who quotes Wittgenstein's words. Russell had written: 'But a Gedanke is a Tatsache: what are its constituents and components, and what is their relation to those of the pictured Tatsache?' Wittgenstein replied:

(2) I don't know *what* the constituents of a thought are but I know *that* it must have such constituents which correspond to the words of Language. Again the kind of relation of the constituents of thought and of the pictured fact is irrelevant. It would be a matter of psychology to find it out.[5]

The second relevant point bears the number (4), and here Wittgenstein, after having repeated Russell's question 'Does a Gedanke consist of words?', goes on to say: 'No! But of psychical constituents that have the same sort of relation to reality as words.' This passage, Kenny says, 'is unequivocal'; that is, he regards it as incontrovertible evidence for the view that in Wittgenstein's early work a *Gedanke* is something psychological. On the other hand, he does raise doubts about the reliability of the letter as a whole when he proceeds to mention the fact that the first explanation given by Wittgenstein in this

---

[3] See Anscombe, *An Introduction to Wittgenstein's Tractatus* (London: Hutchinson, 3rd edn, 1967), e.g. pp. 28 and 88.

[4] His reasons for his unwillingness have a certain bearing on the question how to weigh the evidence supplied by Wittgenstein's letter and will be mentioned below.

[5] 9 August 1919. Printed in Brian McGuinness (ed.), *Wittgenstein in Cambridge* (Oxford: Blackwell, 2008), pp. 98–9.

letter 'is notoriously difficult to reconcile with the actual text of the *Tractatus*' (p. 2). In the sequel, Kenny gives additional reasons for believing that in the *Tractatus* a thought is something psychological, but these reasons are clearly less unambiguously in favour of that belief. Still, after an examination of the relevant passages from the letter to Russell I will move on to a discussion of Kenny's argument.

As I said, Kenny mentions one reason for being sceptical about the reliability of Wittgenstein's words as known to us from the letter to Russell: his clarification of the meanings of '*Sachverhalt*' and '*Tatsache*' is difficult to reconcile with the actual text of his book. It seems, however, that Kenny could easily have made more of this objection. After all, there is a general methodological point lurking in the background: there is a great difference between the text of a book that claims, in its preface, to offer, 'on all essential points, the final solution of the problems', and the text of a letter containing information on how the text of that book is to be read. Probably very few people will want to dispute the soundness of the maxim that this sort of extraneous information ought to be treated with great circumspection, in particular if this information is in conflict with the letter or the spirit of the work it is ostensibly meant to elucidate.

This is a general point, and here I wish to content myself with stating that exegetical work might have profited from taking this point more seriously. Besides this general point there are several specific ones that can easily be seen to speak in favour of the view that the letter to Russell should be treated with a great deal of caution. The first of these specific points is obvious: at the time of writing the letter Wittgenstein had been a prisoner of war for nearly ten months, and most of this time had been spent in conditions of extreme hardship. The distractions and worries of camp life could go a long way towards explaining inaccuracies and mistakes.

Three further points that I want to underline are mentioned in the letter itself. The first is the fact that at the time of writing the letter Wittgenstein did not have a copy of his *Abhandlung*; it had been sent to Russell.[6] So it was materially impossible for him to look at the typescript to refresh his memory of what he had actually written. The second point is his general disinclination to write about questions discussed in his book, especially if 'a very lengthy answer' was required. The third point—whose significance should not be

---

[6] According to previous letters to Russell and Keynes the typescript was sent in early June and reached Keynes and subsequently Russell towards the end of that month. This means that for at least ten weeks Wittgenstein had had no possibility of looking at his typescript. And of course it is not unlikely that, even before sending the typescript, he had not spent much time reading it since his return to the front towards the end of September or in early October 1918.

underestimated—is the fact that just before writing to Russell Wittgenstein had received a letter from Frege[7], to whom a copy of the book had been sent from Vienna and who now expressed his failure to 'understand a word of it all', as Wittgenstein puts it. Of course, Frege's reaction was a great disappointment to Wittgenstein. He may well have been desperate. It is unlikely, however, that he was chagrined by Frege's lack of understanding of certain details of the *Abhandlung* or by his complaints about what he regarded as Wittgenstein's terminological inconsistency and sloppiness. What must have frustrated him was Frege's inability to see the point of the whole enterprise—the 'ethical' point as he famously called it in a letter to Ludwig von Ficker.[8] I am sure that this was one reason why he not only emphatically repeated (one version of) the 'main point' of his work but went on to implore Russell to be open to the ideas of the book: 'So my only hope is to see *you* soon and explain all to you, for it is VERY hard not to be understood by a single soul!'

No doubt these facts are more than sufficient to cast doubt on the reliability of Wittgenstein's explanations as given in this letter if they stand in conflict with letter and spirit of the book. But what may be more relevant is the likelihood that they affected, not so much the reliability, but the straightforwardness of Wittgenstein's words. Any thorough interpretation of the relevant passages from the letter to Russell will have to take the facts mentioned into account.

3. The 'Main Point'

But no matter to what degree these facts may influence our opinion of the reliability and straightforwardness of Wittgenstein's words, they constitute only the less substantial part of what in my view should make us reconsider the significance of the two passages quoted by Kenny. The more substantial part can suitably be introduced by what I have called Wittgenstein's repetition of his 'main point'—the point regarding which he is afraid that Russell may have failed to grasp it just as Frege had evidently failed to grasp it: 'my main contention, to which the whole business of logical prop[osition]s is only a corollary'. I quote:

[7] Frege's letters to Wittgenstein are printed in *Grazer Philosophische Studien* 33/34 (1989), pp. 5–33. The letters concerning Wittgenstein's *Abhandlung* are numbers 18–21, written between 28 June 1919 and 3 April 1920.

[8] Written in October or November 1919, printed in Wittgenstein, *Briefe*, ed. Brian McGuinness and Georg Henrik von Wright (Frankfurt am Main: Suhrkamp, 1980), pp. 96–7. An English translation of the relevant passage can be found in McGuinness, *Wittgenstein: A Life: Young Ludwig (1889–1921)* (London: Duckworth, 1988), p. 288.

The main point is the theory of what can be expressed (gesagt) by prop[osition]s—i.e. by language—(and, which comes to the same, what can be *thought*) and what can not be expressed by prop[osition]s, but only shown (gezeigt); which, I believe, is the cardinal problem of philosophy.

Obviously, the quoted sentence concerns more philosophically significant questions than can be discussed in one paper. But the importance of the passage as a whole lends additional weight to the part that interests us in the present context. This part is contained in the words 'what can be expressed (gesagt) by prop[osition]s—i.e. by language—(and, which comes to the same, what can be *thought*)'. Mind you, this is part of the formulation of Wittgenstein's chief point in the same letter in which he is supposed to have said that thought is miles away from language! At any rate, these words should be borne in mind when trying to arrive at an adequate understanding of Wittgenstein's answers to Russell's questions.

What do the three sentences making up the above-quoted answer (2) amount to? Wittgenstein says that he does not know anything about the nature of the constituents of thought; he also says that he does know that a thought must have constituents that correspond to the words of 'Language'.[9] How can he claim to know this if at the same time he professes to know absolutely nothing about the nature of those constituents? A straightforward answer suggested by Wittgenstein's formulation of his main point is that talking about thoughts comes to the same thing as talking about propositions: the only sort of complexity we can confidently attribute to thoughts is the complexity of propositions expressing these thoughts. The kinds of relation possibly obtaining between the constituents of thoughts, and hence of propositions, on the one hand and the constituents of pictured facts on the other are irrelevant to philosophy.[10] They may be of interest to an empirical science like psychology. And such a science would presumably have nothing to go by except for the words uttered by people to whom thoughts are ascribed. To speak of the constituents of a thought would only be another way of speaking of the words of a proposition expressing the thought in question.

This line of reasoning is continued in answer (4). Of course a thought does not consist of words: If it consists of anything at all, then its components will

---

[9] It may well be significant that in this passage Wittgenstein spells 'Language' with a capital L. If one wishes to argue that this is probably just a slip, I would like to reply that it is a slip of the same order as his writing (or rather dictating) 'If a word creates a world' (NB, p. 104). In TLP 5.123 this has of course become 'If a god creates a world'.

[10] Here it is important to remember that while Wittgenstein mentions relations between psychic entities and the facts, he does not mention any relation between propositions (words) and psychic entities.

suitably be called mental ('psychical') elements. About these elements nothing is known except for the fact that they stand in the same relation to (the elements of) reality as the words making up the propositions expressing our thoughts. The mental is simply the reverse of language. All I can say about it will have to be expressed in terms of language or, ultimately, in terms of picturing.

If Wittgenstein's answers are read along these lines, they do not involve any assumptions about mysterious mental entities. What they do involve, however, is a strong claim about the primacy of the linguistic—of 'Language' with a capital L. And such a claim is surely in keeping with the overt strategy of the book.

4. Propositional Signs

In Kenny's view Wittgenstein's letter to Russell is not the only evidence we have for supposing that a mentalistic conception of thought plays an important role in the *Tractatus*. He says that the 3s contain a number of clues that, if read against the background of the *Prototractatus* (a manuscript draft of what became the *Tractatus*), add up to a picture according to which thought does a kind of work that is quite independent of language. One line of argument developed by Kenny takes its start from the observation that there appears to be a contradiction between 3.1 and 4: in the former remark Wittgenstein says that a proposition expresses a thought; in 4 thought and 'sense-full'[11] proposition are identified: 'A thought is a proposition with a sense.' So, if thought and proposition are the same, how can it be right to claim that the former is expressed by the latter?

Kenny says that there is a fairly easy way out of the difficulty raised by him. This way out involves paying particular attention to a distinction drawn by Wittgenstein himself—the distinction between proposition and propositional sign. If I understand Kenny's argument correctly, he suggests that 'proposition' is the right word in 4, whereas in 3.1 Wittgenstein should have written 'propositional sign'. Kenny finds evidence for holding this view in the fact that the *Prototractatus* talks about *Satzzeichen* in 3.1 and various other places where the *Tractatus* speaks of *Sätze*. Wittgenstein's claim that a proposition expresses a thought (3.1) should hence be rectified to read that propositional *signs* express thoughts. The wording of 3.1 is in Kenny's words due to 'verbal carelessness: like every great philosopher Wittgenstein was inconsistent in his

---

[11] Kenny's expression, p. 3.

use of his own technical terms' (p. 3). I agree that Wittgenstein was not always consistent in his use of terminological expressions. But first of all I am not sure about the extent to which this is due to carelessness; and, secondly, I am even less sure whether the relevant terminological distinctions can really be drawn in the way suggested by Kenny.

Another term which may be seen to play a crucial role in this context is the verb '*ausdrücken*' ('express'). We remember that according to Kenny's account 3.1 says that a proposition expresses a thought, and that in 3.12 Wittgenstein asserts that a propositional sign expresses a thought. Well, this is *roughly* what these propositions of the *Tractatus* say. But a close look at the text reveals that Wittgenstein went out of his way to bring out nuances that are not always easy to capture by English words. In fact, neither 3.1 nor 3.12 states that a proposition or a propositional sign expresses a thought. 3.1 says (in a literal if unidiomatic translation) that in a proposition a thought expresses itself (in a perceptible way). The translators have tried (quite successfully, I think) to render this by saying that 'In a proposition a thought finds an expression that can be perceived by the senses'. What is inevitably lost is the peculiar impersonal style of the German reflexive phrase 'sich ausdrücken', which recalls the central expression '*sich zeigen*'. 3.12 on the other hand emphasizes that *we*—language-users—express thoughts by means of certain signs: 'I call the sign with which we express a thought a propositional sign.' At any rate, as a first result of this consideration, it may be stated that Wittgenstein's formulations in 3 and 3.12 are *not* parallel. As a second result we may note that neither formulation instantiates the pattern 'proposition *p* expresses *t*'. What we do not know yet is whether either result is of the slightest importance to the question discussed by Kenny.[12]

In his view we are dealing with a clear-cut (ontological) distinction between *mere* propositional signs, propositions, and thoughts. Seen from this perspective, a propositional sign is, as it were, less than a proposition: it is a mere sign that requires an additional ingredient to develop into a full-blown proposition. This extra is supplied by thought. Thus, Kenny writes: 'The propositional sign, plus the thought, is the proposition; the thought is what gives the proposition its sense [. . .]' (p. 3). This sounds reasonable enough, but what the quoted passage asserts is not easy to reconcile with Wittgenstein's text.

One problem is obvious but none the less important. The English word 'proposition', which, as far as the *Tractatus* is concerned, is generally used to render Wittgenstein's '*Satz*', behaves quite differently from its presumed German counterpart. First of all, in the relevant sense 'proposition' is not an

---

[12] As will be seen below (§§5 and 7 (c)) I do think that this point *is* of a certain importance.

ordinary word of English, and its very artificiality makes it suitable for technical uses as a terminological expression. None of this is true of the German word '*Satz*'. This is a very ordinary word with a great variety of meanings. In many cases of its use context makes it clear what is intended. But in many other cases of its ordinary use various distinguishable meanings shade into one another and admit only of artificial and precarious clarification: there are many ordinary uses of '*Satz*' where an English-speaking philosopher would be hard put to disambiguate the intended meaning by means of supposedly more well-defined expressions like 'statement', 'assertion', 'proposition', 'utterance', 'remark', 'sentence', 'sentential symbol', or 'what was said'. On the other hand, there are various technical uses of the philosophical term 'proposition' that cannot plausibly or naturally be rendered by the German word '*Satz*'.

There are at least two points to be added to this. First, it was obviously a deliberate decision on Wittgenstein's part to ignore the technical terminology he was well acquainted with from his reading of Russell's and Frege's writings and his conversations with both logicians. He chose a word that is as ambiguous and as vague as a word can be without becoming useless. On the other hand, it is a word which, also because of its many ordinary uses and in contrast with a word like 'proposition', is extremely sensitive to contextually determined nuances and resonates with allusions and indirect references. Here I shall refrain from speculating about the question why Wittgenstein chose the word '*Satz*' to bear the weight it evidently does have to bear. But every reader of the *Tractatus* will be well advised to remember that Wittgenstein's choice of words was a peculiar one—a choice which is not easy to reconcile with an author's intention to write as clearly and unambiguously as possible.

The second point may be more directly relevant to the questions raised by Kenny. In most uses of the word '*Satz*' that interest us it would be extremely unnatural to read it as signifying a 'disembodied' entity. Even in those cases where its meaning chiefly corresponds to 'assertion', 'statement', or 'proposition', a German reader would not be inclined to think of a *Satz* as something which is not, or not yet, a sign or which might be given independently of a sign.[13] Kenny reads Wittgenstein's distinction between *Satz* and *Satzzeichen* as amounting to a distinction between something that is *merely* a sign, on the one hand, and something that has been turned into or has 'become' (p. 5) a real proposition (a *Satz*), on the other. It is said to *become* a real proposition through the good offices of thought.

---

[13] So, the word '*Satz*' could not be used to translate standard phrases like 'express the same proposition by different words' into German.

No doubt the distinction *can* be drawn in this way, and drawing it in this way is surely in accord with an established terminological tradition. But does it accord with Wittgenstein's use of words and his philosophical intentions? An alternative to the view defended by Kenny would not involve the claim that a *Satzzeichen*, a propositional sign, is something that needs to be supplemented by an extra element if it is to become a proposition in the full sense of the word. According to such an alternative reading, to speak of a propositional sign is at the same time a way of speaking of a proposition. The term 'propositional sign' serves, not to indicate a chrysalis stage of what can develop into a full-grown proposition, but to emphasize a certain aspect of something that is a proposition anyway.

5. Propositions and Projection

It will be useful to examine some of Kenny's exegetical arguments against the background of the two alternative readings just sketched. He writes:

In 3.12 Wittgenstein introduced the term '*Satzzeichen*' ('propositional sign') for the perceptible state of affairs—the holding of a relation between written or spoken words or code-signs in more substantial hardware (3.143[14])—which expresses the thought. So far as it expresses a thought, the propositional sign is a projection of a possible state of affairs (3.11–12). (p. 3)

As was pointed out above, in this passage (3.11–12) Wittgenstein does not really say that a propositional sign expresses a thought but that *we* do so by means of the sign. At first sight the difference may seem a minor one, but considering the context and the specific words used by Wittgenstein one will notice that the difference may matter. One point worth noting is that the two remarks we are talking about (3.11–12) are structurally alike. Both consist of two sentences, and the first sentence of each speaks of what *we* do while the second is an impersonal statement. The first sentence of 3.11 says that we use the perceptible sign of a proposition; the first sentence of 3.12 says that we express thoughts by means of propositional signs. So, what Wittgenstein is discussing is the *use* of signs; and here it would have been decidedly odd to use the word '*Satz*', which in other contexts can easily capture the sign aspect of *Sätze*. Had Wittgenstein said 'We use the perceptible *Satz*', he would naturally have been taken to mean that there is a stock of *Sätze* from which we choose some for a given purpose. (That is, by speaking of the use of

---

[14] The text has '3.1433' but surely '3.143' is meant.

a *Satz* he would have described a situation analogous to that of picking a suitable motto from the *Oxford Book of Quotations* or a similar publication.) But that is clearly not what Wittgenstein wants to say. Accordingly, he makes his meaning explicit by writing that we use signs. This, however, does not imply that we use *mere* signs. The signs we use may well be signs of full-blown *Sätze*. And it may equally well be that Wittgenstein would not speak of a propositional sign unless the sign were meant to be the sign of a real proposition.

One central idea of the remarks that Kenny focuses on is the notion of projection. Unfortunately—and characteristically—Wittgenstein's observations are not unequivocal. If an image *a* is projected onto a screen *S*, the result of this process is an image *b* on the screen. Either image may be referred to as 'what is projected', but unless an attempt at disambiguation is made, we do not know whether *a* or *b* is meant. This is a problem that comes up in 3.13. An analogous ambiguity affects the noun 'projection' and hence 3.11: Is the projection mentioned there a process of projecting something onto something else? Or is it the result of such a process? Kenny says that 'a propositional sign can only be a proposition if projected by a thought on to the world' (p. 3). But if this is, perhaps among other things, meant to throw light on 3.11, one wonders if it is really true to Wittgenstein's words.

Let us disregard the mention of 'a thought' in the quotation from Kenny, and suppose 'projection' is taken in the sense of a process of projecting something. Why, then, should the propositional sign be projected onto the world? If it is taken to be a *mere* sign, it is quite unclear what could be meant by this. Suppose we are dealing with the mere propositional sign 'The cat is on the mat': Do we project 'the cat' onto a particular cat, 'the mat' onto a particular mat, and 'is on' onto the relation of *x*'s being on *y*? But of course we do not know what we are supposed to do if the signs are taken as mere signs. So, let's ignore this reading and suppose that the sign has developed into a proper proposition which can be understood as consisting of parts that can be projected onto elements of the world. But what is not really clear is why we should think that this is the right direction of projection. Why should we suppose that the proposition(al sign) is to be projected onto the *world*?

To be sure, this *is* the right direction when what is at issue is verification, that is, when we want to compare our propositions with reality (2.223, 4.05). But 3.11–13 concern sense and hence projection in the nature of the presentation or representation of (possible) states of affairs (*Sachverhalte*) or situations (*Sachlagen*) mentioned for example in 2.11, 2.201, 2.202, 2.221, and 4.031. To the extent the world comes into play at all—and in 3.12 it does come into play when a proposition is said to be 'a propositional sign in its projective relation to the world'—the direction of the projection indicated by Kenny seems to be the right one (or one of the right ones): a proposition, or perhaps rather its sense, may be compared with, and hence projected onto, the world. But when it is a question of sense—the *independent* sense of a proposition—the only directions of projection that appear to play any role at all are those between a proposition and possible states of affairs or a situation (and while possible situations—or possibilities of the obtaining of states of affairs—may be constitutive of sense, they are not constitutive of the world[15]).

There is another problem connected with the notion of projection that comes to the fore when one tries to make clear sense of 3.11. Here Wittgenstein says that we 'use the perceptible sign of a proposition [...] as a projection of a possible situation'. This seems to suggest that the sign, the perceptible sign, is used as a screen onto which a possible situation is projected. But this reading does not look particularly helpful; it is not clear in which way this idea could serve to explain anything. Another possibility of reading the first paragraph of 3.11 is this: that propositional signs are used for the purpose of projecting possible states of affairs. Naturally, this reading will tend to call forth questions about what these possible states of affairs are to be projected onto. And it is not easy to see how such questions could be answered without elaborating on particular situations in which signs are used.

But perhaps this is precisely the route we should take to find an instructive reading of our remarks. And if we do take this route, we should begin by taking the following two steps: First, it is to be acknowledged that Wittgenstein is talking about the use of perceptible signs and in doing so does not hesitate to conceive of these signs as signs of full-blown propositions: normally, using a propositional sign is not to be distinguished from entertaining, uttering, or thinking about a proposition. Second, it is important to get away from a too narrow understanding of the idea of projection. The notion of a mapping, of projecting *a* onto *b* or vice versa, is surely a central one. But it is likely that Wittgenstein, in speaking of projection, means to cover a wide range of uses that are or can be made of pictures.

Projection, taken in such a broad sense of the word, comprises a variety of eminently public and teachable and clarifiable practices. And speaking of projection in this sense does not involve anything particularly mentalistic: it does not bring in any occult powers of the mind whose private exercise is supposed to bestow meaning on our signs. This is emphasized in the second paragraph of 3.11: 'Thinking the sense of the proposition is the method

---

[15] Even under an idealist interpretation of the *Tractatus* world the difference between possible states of affairs or situations and actual ones (= facts) has to be respected.

of projection.'[16] Apparently this statement has been misunderstood by some authors to mean that the method used to effect projections of the relevant type consists in our performing certain mental acts—in the taking place of private, inaccessible processes of thinking.

But what Wittgenstein wants to say and does say is that thinking the sense of a proposition is applying a certain method of projection; and this method is one which is applied by using, e.g. by uttering or writing down the signs of propositions. 'And a proposition is a propositional sign in its projective relation to the world' (3.12). This means that a proposition is a sign that is used in accordance with the rules we have learned to apply in talking about the world. Again, a thought is what we express by using a propositional sign. That is, expressing a thought is the same thing as expressing a proposition. And to the extent we understand the idea of thinking the sense of a proposition, the idea of thinking can become intelligible to us if we conceive of it as an application of the same rules we follow in uttering or writing down propositions. All these remarks of the *Tractatus* are steps on the way towards Wittgenstein's identification of an applied, thought (or 'thought out')[17] propositional sign with a thought (3.5), which in its turn is identified with a proposition with a sense (4).[18]

No doubt a reading of the *Tractatus* that does not require the assumption of thoughts that project propositions onto the world and thereby lend sense to propositional signs has the advantage of harmonizing much better with the rest of the book than readings that do require such an assumption. There is, however, one passage which seems to raise great difficulties for a reading of the kind favoured by me. This is 3.13, which plays a crucial role in Kenny's article, where it is elucidated by an ingenious argument. This argument will now be summarized, and then an attempt will be made to find out (a) whether the argument can be accepted and (b) whether the problems posed by the passage in question cannot be overcome by an interpretation along the lines recommended here.

---

[16] This translation of 'Die Projektionsmethode ist das Denken des Satz-Sinnes' is taken from Brian McGuinness, 'The Supposed Realism of the *Tractatus*', repr. in *Approaches to Wittgenstein* (London: Routledge, 2002), p. 91. Reasons for changing the original Pears-McGuinness translation were given by Rush Rhees in his *Discussions of Wittgenstein* (London: Routledge, 1970), p. 39. (Rhees also suggested italicizing the 'is'.) Cf. McGuinness, *Approaches*, p. 97. The same translation is used by Norman Malcolm in *Nothing is Hidden* (Oxford: Blackwell, 1986), pp. 66 and 73, but the interpretation he gives is very different from the one favoured by the present writer.

[17] It is clear that on my reading the thought involved in thinking a propositional sign presupposes neither any operations of mysterious mental powers nor the existence of 'psychic entities' corresponding to the linguistic signs we use.

[18] The importance of this identification is acknowledged by Kenny when he writes that 'thought seems to be related so closely to a proposition as to be capable of being identified with it' (p. 2).

6. Kenny's Exegetical Argument

Tractatus 3.13 consists of five short paragraphs. Here I shall follow Kenny and quote the German original of this remark and the Pears-McGuinness translation in full. For ease of reference I add '(a)' to '(e)':

(a)	*Zum Satz gehört alles, was zur Projektion gehört; aber nicht das Projizierte.*	A proposition includes all that the projection includes, but not what is projected.
(b)	*Also die Möglichkeit des Projizierten, aber nicht dieses selbst.*	Therefore, though what is projected is not itself included, its possibility is.
(c)	*Im Satz ist also sein Sinn noch nicht enthalten, wohl aber die Möglichkeit ihn auszudrücken.*	A proposition, therefore, does not actually contain its sense, but does contain the possibility of expressing it.
(d)	*(,,Der Inhalt des Satzes" heißt der Inhalt des sinnvollen Satzes.)*	('The content of a proposition' means the content of a proposition that has sense.)
(e)	*Im Satz ist die Form seines Sinnes enthalten, aber nicht dessen Inhalt.*	A proposition contains the form, but not the content of its sense.

From their position in the *Prototractatus* and the fact that (except for a vague echo of NB 21.10.14 [4] in 3.13c) no earlier versions of these remarks can be found in the manuscripts before PTLP it can safely be concluded that this material belongs to an early stage of the composition of the book.[19] As Kenny points out, in the penultimate manuscript version the paragraphs constituting 3.13 were placed in a later context (PTLP 3.211–3.214). When it came to producing the final version of the *Abhandlung* Wittgenstein decided to move these five paragraphs to their present position, where they are surrounded by remarks about *Satzzeichen* while they themselves only speak of *Sätze*. According to Kenny, Wittgenstein must have noticed that PTLP 3.211ff. fitted the *Satzzeichen* context better and therefore moved them to their present location. In the process, however, he omitted or forgot to change the word '*Satz*' to '*Satzzeichen*' and thereby rendered 3.13 unnecessarily difficult to comprehend.

---

[19] For details of the genesis of MS 104 (= the material basis of PTLP) and the various *Abhandlungen* that can be extracted from it see McGuinness, 'Wittgenstein's 1916 "Abhandlung"', in R. Haller and K. Puhl (eds), *Wittgenstein and the Future of Philosophy* (Vienna: öbv & hpt, 2002), pp. 272–82.

But this description of the genesis of this part of the book *presupposes* the correctness of Kenny's characterization of the relation between propositional sign and proposition. As I want to challenge the validity of this characterization, I would prefer a more neutral description, e.g. the following one: the five paragraphs concerned were indeed moved, but the wider context to which they were relocated speaks of *Sätze* as well as of *Satzzeichen*. Actually, as the 3.14s show, Wittgenstein uses these two expressions indiscriminately, freely moving back and fro between '*Satz*' and '*Satzzeichen*' in accordance with the aspect he wishes to underline.

Kenny does not claim, however, that all occurrences of '*Satz*' in 3.13 ought or need to be changed to '*Satzzeichen*'. In his view, paragraphs a and b can be made sense of if '*Satz*' is read as 'proposition' in his sense. He writes:

> The proposition includes not only the propositional sign, but also the projecting thought; it does not include the state of affairs which is projected (if the proposition is false there is no such state of affairs for it to include) but it includes the possibility of that state of affairs (because of its pictorial form, which is the possibility that things are related to one another in the same way as the elements of the picture, 2.151).

Bringing in 'projecting thought' seems quite unwarranted, though. What is involved in both proposition and projection is explained by remarks introduced by two consecutive occurrences of 'therefore': the first one (3.13b) specifies that the common element is the possibility of what is projected. However this idea will be spelled out, it is not clear why it should imply anything about 'projecting thought'.

It is striking that Kenny decides to drive a wedge between the two occurrences of 'therefore': the first one (3.13b) is supposed to go with 'proposition'; the second one (3.13c), however, can in Kenny's opinion only be understood if it is read as being about propositional signs. His main reason for holding this view is the following. If one reads '*Satz*' in the sense of 'proposition', the statement made by 3.13c sounds very odd. After all, it is a characteristic feature of propositions to express a sense. Then why should Wittgenstein say that a *Satz* contains the *possibility* of expressing its sense? This oddity, says Kenny, is easy to remove if one reads '*Satz*' as 'propositional sign': 'a propositional sign, without the projecting thought, will not have a sense; but being capable of being projected, it will be capable of expressing that sense' (p. 5).

According to Kenny, in addition to facilitating a smooth interpretation of 3.13c the suggestion to read '*Satz*' as 'propositional sign' has the further virtue of making 3.13d–e intelligible. For then the 'content' which is there being talked about can be understood in terms of the sense which is added to a propositional sign upon its becoming a proposition. And the distinction between form and content of the sense of a *Satz* (3.13e) can be elucidated in terms of the difference between a kind of objects contained in a proposition and a kind of objects not contained in it:

> The content of the propositional sign, *when it becomes a proposition*, is its sense; the content of the sense of the proposition are the objects of the possible state of affairs which the proposition depicts; the proposition as a whole—the proposition which is propositional sign plus thought sense—contains the form but not the content of its sense: it is made up of objects which are not identical with, but formally congruent with, the objects in the possible state of affairs.   (p. 5)

In spite of the complexity and ingenuity of the argument it fails to convince me. My reasons for remaining unimpressed are twofold. First, I see a number of great if not insurmountable difficulties for Kenny's reading as an interpretation of Wittgenstein's actual words. Second, it is possible to give an interpretation of 3.13 which avoids these difficulties and conforms better with letter and spirit of the work. It will accordingly be unnecessary to saddle Wittgenstein with the mentalist machinery brought to bear by Kenny, and we shall gain the additional advantage of removing a formidable element of discontinuity between the early and the later Wittgenstein.[20]

7. Difficulties for Kenny's Argument

To begin with, I shall mention a few difficulties that stand in the way of a successful application of Kenny's reading. The first problem is connected with the two occurrences of 'therefore' in 3.13b and c, to which I have already drawn attention. The second paragraph (3.13b) consists of an incomplete sentence and must be read as being governed by the predicate of 3.13a ('includes'). The 'therefore' in 3.13b is consequently to be read as introducing an elucidation of the statement made in 3.13a. And this elucidation amounts to saying that, while what is projected is not included in a proposition, the possibility of what is projected is so included. But what about the second 'therefore' (in 3.13c)? This would ordinarily be taken to introduce another elucidatory consequence, this time also relying on the immediately preceding paragraph (3.13b). But if we follow Kenny's suggestion, 3.13c deals with propositional signs lacking a sense, whereas 3.13a and b are assumed to *have* sense. If one accepts this,

---

[20] I mention this because tracing the continuities in Wittgenstein's thought is one of Kenny's abiding concerns. See *Legacy*, p. viii, and the last chapter (entitled 'The Continuity of Wittgenstein's Philosophy') of his book *Wittgenstein* (1973), rev. edn (Oxford: Blackwell, 2006), pp. 173–83.

Wittgenstein's '*also*' ('therefore') becomes completely bewildering. Assuming Kenny's terminological distinction between proposition and propositional sign one would ask oneself: In what way could the claim that a propositional sign lacks sense be seen to follow as an elucidatory consequence from the statement that a proposition includes the possibility of a projected state of affairs but not the state of affairs itself? The only way out of this difficulty would be to claim that Wittgenstein's 'therefore' in 3.13c is gratuitous and should be disregarded.

The second difficulty is connected with the nature of the states of affairs brought into play by Kenny. He says that a proposition of the kind mentioned in 3.13a and b projects, but does not include, a certain state of affairs. Then he goes on to say that no such state of affairs obtains if the proposition is false. But presumably a false proposition too projects something, e.g. a possible state of affairs which happens not to obtain. If this is right, however, we seem to be confronted with an asymmetry which is hard to account for: the sort of states of affairs projected by true propositions is said not to be available in the case of false propositions. Accordingly, true propositions are said to project a different kind of states of affairs (viz. real ones) from those projected by false ones (presumably possible ones). This cannot be right, and I suspect that this untenable if implicit claim is due to some confusion over Wittgenstein's notion of sense.

This notion of sense is relevant to the third difficulty, which affects the central part of Kenny's argument. He says that we cannot make sense of 3.13c unless we take '*Satz*' as 'propositional sign' (in his narrow sense of the word); for only then will it be possible for us to avoid the oddity inherent in claiming that a proposition (which presumably expresses a sense) does not contain its sense but only the possibility of expressing it. The problem is that 3.13c *can* be made sense of without reading '*Satz*' as 'propositional sign' (in Kenny's narrow sense). One way of making sense of it will be sketched below. Here I just want to hint at the following points:

(a) Wittgenstein is talking about the *content* of *Sätze* (or *Satzzeichen*), and to talk about content as Wittgenstein understands it does not automatically amount to talking about sense.

(b) It is at least conceivable that one may want to speak of the content of a proposition independently of a particular situation of utterance without thereby speaking only of a (mere) propositional sign.

(c) Most importantly, the possibility of expressing a certain sense intended by Wittgenstein need not be the *proposition*'s possibly expressing that sense (as Kenny seems to assume); it may for example be its offering *me* the means to express a certain sense. That is, it is important to distinguish different uses of the phrase 'express a sense'. Naturally one can say that a sign or a combination of signs expresses a certain sense. But one can also say that speakers express a certain sense (by means of certain signs). To use a seemingly paradoxical formulation, one may want to say that a proposition (a *Satz*) expressing a given sense contains the possibility (= enables me) to express a certain sense, which may but need not agree with that expressed by the proposition considered in itself. Of course, a defender of a very narrow notion of a proposition will hardly be in a position to say that, but Wittgenstein's use of the word '*Satz*' is surely not such a narrow one.

The fourth difficulty concerns Kenny's way of formulating his reading of 3.13e. He says that the idea of the content of the sense of a proposition can be elucidated by appealing to 'objects which are not identical with, but formally congruent with, the objects in the possible state of affairs' (p. 5). He goes on to support this claim about what in a previously cited passage he has called 'psychic elements' by referring to 3.2, which says: 'In a proposition a thought can be expressed in such a way that elements of the propositional sign correspond to the objects of the thought [*den Gegenständen des Gedankens*].' In Kenny's view the phrase 'objects of the thought' is ambiguous between (a) objects that are being thought about and (b) objects constituting a thought. And he continues by saying that the changes Wittgenstein made when reformulating PTLP 3.14[21] in a way that yielded *Tractatus* 3.2 show that he moved from a wording clearly expressing (a) to one more suggestive of (b).

This is just a mistake. Of course there has been a considerable change in the wording of this passage. But even though the transition from '*Gegenstände der Wirklichkeit*' to '*Gegenstände des Gedankens*' can surely be made out to be significant, the phrase just cannot mean 'constituent of (a) thought'. Maybe the English phrase 'objects of the thought' is ambiguous in the way indicated by Kenny; the corresponding German words are not. I too think that the change from the *Prototractatus* to *Tractatus* 3.2 is significant; and I agree that the later wording is the result of trying to get away from a (too) clear expression of a (too) simple picture. But even though the remark has become more complex and perhaps vaguer, it has not become a remark about constituents of thought: it is about what one thinks (or talks) about. This attempt to support the idea that in 3.13e Wittgenstein is (implicitly) speaking of 'psychic' constituents of thought is and will remain unsuccessful.

---

[21] 'Im Satzzeichen entsprechen den Gegenständen der Wirklichkeit die einfachen Zeichen' ('In a propositional sign the simple signs correspond to the objects of reality').

8. An Alternative Account

In conclusion I want to round off my discussion with a brief account of 3.13, which will rely heavily on what was said in the previous section of this paper. By way of introduction I shall make another observation on '*Satz*' and '*Satzzeichen*'. In my view it is hard to believe that Wittgenstein on the one hand wanted to draw a radical distinction between these two terms in the way Kenny suggests and on the other hand forgot to change the wording of 3.13 (with its five occurrences of '*Satz*') in accordance with this distinction. For one thing, the compound noun is a very clumsy neologism and a homonym of the ordinary German word for 'punctuation mark' to boot. You do not simply forget about it once you have introduced it. Apparently, Wittgenstein did not mind using the word, but he did change a few occurrences of it between the *Prototractatus* and the *Tractatus* to '*Satz*' without intending any great shift of meaning of the whole remarks in question.

Moreover, there are various passages where the two expressions occur in the same context with no indication of a substantial difference in meaning. To mention just one example: In 3.2 Wittgenstein moves smoothly from '*Satz*' to '*Satzzeichen*'. 3.201 refers back to '*Satzzeichen*' in 3.2 and says that simple signs are elements of *propositional signs* and that, once you have arrived at these elements, you are confronted with a completely analysed *proposition*.[22] These simple signs—names—are such that no one has ever seen or heard one, and presumably no one ever will. So what are these entities doing in a 'physical' sign?[23] Then Wittgenstein goes on to repeat the substance of 3.201, but this time he speaks of propositions: 'The simple signs employed in propositions are called names' (3.202). And so on and so forth. Evidently Wittgenstein made no clear distinction between '*Satz*' and '*Satzzeichen*', nor could he consistently have drawn one without finding himself in a conflict with the implicit and explicit identifications pronounced in 3.12, 3.2, 3.5–4, and other places. I conclude that there is no textual basis for ascribing to Wittgenstein the radical distinction between *Satzzeichen* and *Satz* attributed to him by Kenny. Wittgenstein's reasons for switching back and fro between these two terms are matters of emphasis and German idiom.

[22] Cf. 4.02 and 4.021, where Wittgenstein speaks of understanding the sense of a *Satzzeichen* in the same way as of understanding the sense of a *Satz*.

[23] This is important because, if fully analysed propositions and their signs are not to be perceived, then 3.1 ('In a proposition a thought finds an expression that can be perceived by the senses') will need some qualification.

Accordingly, in my opinion Wittgenstein could have used 'Satzzeichen' to formulate 3.13 but chose not to do so. In a way 3.13 begins by repeating what was said about pictures in general in 2.1513: 'a picture [. . .] also includes the pictorial relationship, which makes it into a picture'. 3.13a and b do not add much to that. It is important to remember that pictures represent or project independently of their truth or falsehood (2.22) and that what they represent or project is their sense (2.221). Furthermore, as was pointed out above, it is important not to drive a wedge between 3.13a–b and c, which is connected to the two immediately preceding paragraphs by another 'therefore' and makes it explicit that it is the sense of pictures that we are talking about. The interesting claim made in 3.13c is that sense is not included in a picture, a proposition. This in turn may serve to clarify earlier statements about what is *contained* in a picture or a thought (2.203, 3.02). There are at least two ways of reading the claim made in 3.13c. One was indicated above (§7 (b)): If we want to consider a proposition independently of a particular situation of using its sign, we will refrain from attributing to it the sense it may acquire through a use of its sign. But in my view this reading is too fussy and too difficult to bring into accord with the rest of the text.

A more promising reading of 3.13c will connect it with what was said in 2.15 about structure and form of pictures. Structure is the way the elements of a picture are related to one another, and this structure represents that things are related to each other in a certain way. The possibility of this sort of structure is pictorial form. What is represented by the structure of a picture corresponds to what is projected by a proposition. But what is represented or projected by these structured arrangements is clearly not an internal feature of these arrangements. What is represented is a 'situation [. . .] constructed by way of experiment', in other words: what is represented or projected is a sense (4.031). The pictorial form, however, which is the possibility of structure, *is* an internal feature of the picture. In particular, it is a feature which it can have in common with other pictures and with reality. Similarly, in 3.13c Wittgenstein says that sense—what is projected by a proposition—is not an internal feature of the proposition. Its possibility, however, is such an internal feature. And, as I suggested above, this feature is something that can offer us as speakers and thinkers the means to express an actual sense.

Now one may want to object that this reading cannot be reconciled with Wittgenstein's parenthetic statement that what he says about the content of a proposition concerns the content of propositions that have sense. But this remark poses a difficulty only if one construes '*sinnvoll*' as meaning that the sense is *contained* in the proposition.[24] But that is not the meaning. Just as talking about a restful sleep does not mean that the sleep 'contains' rest—after all, it is the *sleeper* who is rested—so speaking of a '*sinnvollen Satz*' does not imply that sense is part of the proposition's content. What Wittgenstein's remark amounts to is that there is no contradiction involved in saying that a proposition with a sense does not *contain* that sense. The content of a proposition may comprise all kinds of things (e.g. syntactic and semantic features conducive to expressing a sense) without including sense as a proper part.

3.13e reformulates what has already been said and does so in the terminology of 'form' and 'content'. The internal features of a proposition include those that enable it to express a sense (*form*) but not what is projected when a sense is actually expressed (*content*).

Of course, this is just a sketch of an interpretation which, in order to become fully convincing, would require a good deal of contextual embedding as well as support drawn from other parts of the book. Still, together with my earlier remarks it may suffice to persuade some readers, especially those who feel uncomfortable about the prospect of burdening our interpretation of the *Tractatus* with mentalistic paraphernalia, which in their turn remain completely undiscussed in the text.

Even such readers, however, may have qualms about one particularly outstanding characteristic of Wittgenstein's remarks, viz. his identification of things that seem to be quite different:[25] logical picture, thought, propositional sign, proposition. But I think that there is no real difficulty here. What the champion of the *Prinzip der Vertretung* (4.0312) had in mind was that it is possible for one thing or person to stand in, to deputize, to go proxy for another thing or person as far as a particular function normally fulfilled by that other thing or person is concerned. In short, if you can play my role as *X* and I can play your role as *X*, you and I can be the same as far as playing that role *X* is concerned. And this way of looking at the matter is particularly relevant if one is not so much interested in the identity of who or what is doing a certain job but in how the job is done. Something like this way of looking at the matter informs Wittgenstein's discussion: to the extent thought, picture, proposition, and propositional sign can be seen as playing the same role we need not distinguish between them. On the contrary, seeing identities of function may help us to understand how certain functions are performed.

---

[24] Something like that seems to be implied by Kenny's rendering 'sense-full', see §4 above, n. 11.

[25] Frege, for example, protested that using different expressions to mean the same thing ought to be proscribed (28 June 1919). In his next letter (16 September) he expressed his disappointment at having to see that Wittgenstein's book was not so much a scientific but rather an artist's work: 'what is said disappears behind the way in which it is said'.

This way of looking at the matter is characteristic not only of Wittgenstein's early philosophy; it is a continuous trait of his thinking early and late. This is shown by remarks like the statement that it is essential to mathematics that its signs are also employed in mufti (RFM V, §2, 1942) or the invitation to compare our notion of the meaning of a word with that of 'the "function" of an official. And "different meanings" with "different functions" ' (C §64, 1949–50). In an analogous way we can imagine Picture putting on a different hat or a different tunic and turning around to do its job as Thought or Proposition. If the jobs prove to be structurally similar or identical, we will have learned something that goes well beyond a description of these jobs.

16

A Tale of Two Problems: Wittgenstein's Discussion of Aspect Perception

SEVERIN SCHROEDER

Between 1946 and 1949 Wittgenstein occupied himself intensely with the topic of aspect perception or seeing-as. It is one of his main concerns in the typescripts and manuscripts that have now been published as *Remarks on the Philosophy of Psychology* and *Last Writings on the Philosophy of Psychology*, and it is discussed at considerable length in the selection of remarks Wittgenstein culled from those volumes in 1949 (MS 144; TS 234), and which was eventually printed under the title 'Part II' of *Philosophical Investigations*.[1] Half a century later it is probably still true to say that 'Wittgenstein's treatment of aspect perception continues to be one of the least explored and least understood of the major themes in his later philosophy'.[2]

In his 1949 selection Wittgenstein begins the discussion of aspect perception with the following distinction:

Two uses of the word 'see'.

The one: 'What do you see there?'—'I see *this*' (and then a description, a drawing, a copy). The other: 'I see a likeness in these two faces'—let the man to whom I tell this be seeing the faces as clearly as I do myself.

What is important is the categorial difference between the two 'objects' of sight.

---

[1] In the 4th edition of the *Philosophical Investigations*, ed. P. M. S. Hacker and Joachim Schulte (Oxford: Blackwell, 2009) this text is renamed *Philosophy of Psychology—A Fragment* (abbreviated 'PPF') and the remarks are numbered. Hence what used to be *PI* II. xi (pp. 193–229) is now: PPF §§111–366. My references will be to this new edition, followed by the page numbers from the old one: *Philosophical Investigations*, ed. G. E. M. Anscombe and R. Rhees, trans. G. E. M. Anscombe, 2nd edn (Oxford: Blackwell, 1958).

[2] S. Mulhall, 'Seeing Aspects', in H. J. Glock (ed.), *Wittgenstein: A Critical Reader* (Oxford: Blackwell, 2001), p. 246.

I observe a face, and then suddenly notice its likeness to another. I *see* that it has not changed; and yet I see it differently. I call this experience 'noticing an aspect'.   (PPF §§111, 113; p. 193)

Seeing a likeness between two faces [A], however, is only the first of a number of examples Wittgenstein considers. Others are:

(B) Seeing a geometrical drawing as a glass cube or as an inverted open box, or as three boards forming a solid angle (PPF §116; p. 193); or again, seeing a triangle as a triangular hole, as a solid, as a geometrical drawing; as standing on its base, as hanging from its apex; as a mountain, as a wedge, as an arrow or pointer, as an overturned object which is meant, for example, to stand on the shorter sight of the right angle, as a half parallelogram, etc. (PPF §162; p.200).

(C) Seeing an ambiguous puzzle picture in one way, e.g. seeing a rabbit's head in what at first glance looks just like the drawing of a duck's head (PPF §118; p. 194); or a human figure where there were previously branches (PPF §131; p. 196).

(D) Suddenly recognizing a familiar object in an unusual position or lighting (PPF §141; p. 197); or recognizing an old acquaintance (PPF §§143–4; p. 197).

(E) Seeing three-dimensionally (PPF §148; p. 198).

(F) Seeing a sphere in a picture as floating in the air (PPF §169; p. 201); or seeing a horse in a picture as galloping (PPF §175; p. 202).

(G) Aspects of organization: seeing a row of four equidistant dots either as two groups of two dots or as two dots in the middle bracketed by a dot on each side (cf. PPF §§220–1; p. 208).

What is the point of Wittgenstein's persistent discussion of such cases? Whence this tenacious interest in those phenomena?

1. Continuous and Episodic Aspect Perception

It is true that in the course of Wittgenstein's discussion of seeing-as certain philosophical theories of visual perception are criticized and rejected; but, as Stephen Mulhall rightly notes, the attraction and defects of those theories, however important to bring out, cannot fully explain Wittgenstein's abiding fascination with the topic. According to Mulhall's own interpretation, Wittgenstein wants to teach us that aspect perception is a ubiquitous phenomenon: everything we perceive, we perceive in its relevant aspects: in a picture we immediately see what it represents and respond to it accordingly, just as we always see artefacts as what they are for us, what roles they play in our lives, or again, we generally experience words as having a certain meaning. That is, we always take up the attitude towards objects that Heidegger calls *readiness-to-hand* [*Zuhandenheit*].[3]

There is indeed textual support for Mulhall's interpretation. Wittgenstein emphasizes the distinction between knowledge of an aspect—say, what a picture represents—and actually seeing it:

When should I call it just knowing, not seeing?—Perhaps when someone treats the picture as a working drawing, *reads* it like a blueprint.   (PPF §192; p. 204)

That is *not* our attitude towards a portrait or a photograph. We do not just read off it some information about the visual appearance of a person, we see the person in the picture:

we *view* the photograph, the picture on our wall, as the very object (the man, landscape and so on) represented in it.   (PPF §197; p. 205)

Of course, that is not to say that we uncritically accept every portrait as accurate. We may, for example, have grave doubts whether Shakespeare really looked like the man in the Flower portrait. Wittgenstein's point, however, is that when looking at that portrait we see a man with a moustache (the picture's 'internal subject'),[4] and don't just apprehend pieces of information about the appearance of a man, e.g. that he has a moustache. It is noteworthy that here Wittgenstein applies the 'seeing-as' locution to ordinary and unambiguous pictures, and not only to puzzle pictures that can be seen first as one thing and then as another. In the latter case we may suddenly notice new aspects (which 'light up'), whereas the former can be called the 'continuous seeing' of an aspect (PPF §118; p. 194). Mulhall's claim is that in spite of the fact that most of the time Wittgenstein appears to discuss cases of aspect change, the concept of *continuous* aspect perception—and the general attitude it characterizes—is his real concern.[5] The same view was expressed some twenty years earlier by P. F. Strawson:

the striking case of the *change* of aspects merely dramatizes for us a feature (namely seeing as) which is present in perception in general.[6]

---

[3] S. Mulhall, *On Being in the World: Wittgenstein and Heidegger on Seeing Aspects* (London: Routledge, 1990), pp. 15–28, 106 ff., 126 ff.; cf. Mulhall, 'Seeing Aspects'. Cf. M. Heidegger, *Being and Time* [*Sein und Zeit*, 1927], trans. J. Macquarrie and E. Robinson (Oxford: Blackwell, 1962), §15, p. 98.

[4] Cf. J. Hyman, 'Language and Pictorial Art', in D. E. Cooper (ed.), *A Companion to Aesthetics* (Oxford: Blackwell, 1992), pp. 261–8; p. 263.

[5] Mulhall, 'Seeing Aspects', p. 255.

[6] P. F. Strawson, 'Imagination and Perception', in his *Freedom and Resentment* (London: Methuen, 1974), p. 58.

This interpretation may be strengthened further by the following: It is no coincidence that Wittgenstein begins the discussion of aspect perception in his 1949 selection of remarks (PPF) with the case of seeing a likeness, because all the other examples can be regarded as variations of this theme. Aspect perception, in general, involves noticing a similarity. 'In all those cases one can say that one experiences a *comparison*' (RPP I §317). An object is seen as a variation, or derivation, or copy, of another one (RPP I §508). When I see something *as* X I am aware of a similarity between it and X, be it a glass cube, the head of a rabbit, or a galloping horse.[7] But then, it can be argued that virtually *all* seeing is or involves seeing resemblances. When I see a tree, for example, and realize that it is a tree, I see its resemblance with other trees. In general, seeing that something is of a certain kind involves seeing its likeness, in relevant respects, with other, familiar, objects of that kind. And even when looking at an arrangement of shapes and colours I cannot make out what it is or represents, I will at least be able to identify certain shapes and colours, which again means: seeing in what way they are like other shapes and colours I've seen before. To the extent to which 'to see' is a verb of epistemic success, every seeing involves identification of kinds of objects or appearances, which means seeing them as similar to others of that kind.[8]

It is true that Wittgenstein mentions the inappropriateness of saying 'Now I see it as . . .' in cases of ordinary perception. For example, as long as I haven't realized the ambiguity of the duck-rabbit drawing, but simply see it as the drawing of a duck's head, the 'seeing as' locution would make as little sense for me as to say at the sight of a knife and fork 'Now I see this as a knife and fork'. Nevertheless someone else could correctly say of me: 'He sees the picture as a duck' (PPF §§120–2; pp. 194 f.). Similarly, although normally with a conventional picture or photograph there is no question of seeing it *as* something, and so the expression is out of place, the question can be raised when, by way of contrast, one considers anomalous attitudes towards a picture. Thus, Wittgenstein imagines people who would be repelled by small black and white photographs, and would perhaps be unable to see human faces in them (PPF §198; p. 205). By contrast with such people we can then meaningfully say that '*we* view a portrait as a human being' (PPF §199; p. 205).[9]

---

[7] When I recognize an old acquaintance, I see a resemblance between a face in front of me and one I remember. When I see three-dimensionally, I latch on to a resemblance between the visual appearance of what I see and the visual appearances of familiar three-dimensional objects.

[8] This applies even if I can answer the question 'What do you see?' only by producing a drawing (cf. PPF §111b; p. 193). For in that case I am aware that what I see looks *like* this →.

[9] Cf. Strawson, 'Imagination and Perception', p. 58.

However, there is a considerable number of passages in Wittgenstein that appear to contradict Mulhall's interpretation (and Strawson's claim). Not that Wittgenstein would have denied the ubiquity of aspect perception as a continuous, dispositional attitude; it is only that there are many parts of the discussion where that is clearly not his main interest. The contrast between two different concepts of seeing-as—one dispositional, one episodic—is brought out in the following remark:

I say: 'We view a portrait as a human being'—when do we do so, and for how long? *Always*, if we see it at all (and don't, say, see it as something else)?
  I might go along with this, and thereby determine the concept of viewing a picture.—The question is whether yet another concept, related to this one, also becomes important to us: that, namely, of a seeing-as which occurs only while I am actually concerning myself with the picture as the object represented.   (PPF §199; p. 205)

The answer to this question is clearly: yes. The concept of an ephemeral *experience* (*Erlebnis*) of seeing-as—as opposed to a general attitude—plays a prominent role in Wittgenstein's thoughts:

The phenomenon we are talking about is the lighting up of an aspect.   (LW I §429)

Of aspect perception in this episodic sense Wittgenstein says that it is essentially an 'unstable state' (RPP II §540).[10] Only in the change of aspect does one become *conscious* of an aspect (LW I §169). And it is this sudden experience of change, Wittgenstein says, that he is interested in (LW I §173). The experience of aspect perception is like the experience of recognition, which also does not last all the time I know who somebody is. Wittgenstein draws this analogy with recognition in a lecture:

Do I always see a thing *as* something, although only puzzle-pictures bring this out? . . .
  Suppose I show it to a child. The child says, 'It's a duck' and then suddenly, 'Oh it's a rabbit.' So he recognizes it as a rabbit. This is an experience of recognition. So if you see me in the street and say, 'Ah, Wittgenstein.' But you haven't an experience of recognition all the time. The experience only comes at the moment of *change* from duck to rabbit and back. In between, the aspect is as it were dispositional. . . .
  Geach: Couldn't I say at any time how I see it—not just when it changes?
  Wittgenstein: Only if you are concentrating on it . . .   (LPP 103–4)

Thus, although Wittgenstein is prepared to speak of continuous aspect perception when using the term in a dispositional sense, in other passages, using the term in an episodic sense, as denoting a particular experience, he denies the ubiquity of aspect perception (RPP I §§24, 860; LW I §§170, 454). *Pace*

[10] Cf. LW I §§438, 518, 588; RPP I §1021; PPF §237; p. 210.

Strawson, the feature that interested Wittgenstein in aspect change is not present in perception in general.

Aspect perception is concept-laden. Seeing something as an X presupposes mastery of the concept of an X. For example to see a row of six equidistant dots as two groups of three dots requires familiarity with the concept of a group of things, of things 'belonging together' (PPF §221; p. 208). And only someone who has mastered the psychological concept of happiness can see a circle with two dots and four curved lines in it as a happy face. Thus a logical condition of one's having an experience of aspect perception is that one has mastered a certain technique (PPF §§222–4; pp. 208–9). This is something that struck Wittgenstein as paradoxical:

> But how odd for this to be the logical condition of someone's having such-and-such an *experience*! After all, you don't say that one only 'has toothache' if one is capable of doing such-and-such.   (PPF §223; p. 208)

Here, again, it is very clear that (*pace* Mulhall) Wittgenstein is concerned with the concept of a *momentary experience* of seeing-as; for the observation that mastery of a technique should manifest itself, dispositionally, in—and be presupposed by—a certain attitude towards a picture is not in the same way puzzling.

In short, Wittgenstein appears to shift between two different accounts of aspect perception, and Mulhall's interpretation may well fit one account, but not the other one. The fact is, I think, that Wittgenstein occupied himself with two connected, but distinct conceptual problems in this area and was not always careful to keep them separate, moving from one to the other and back again. The two problems are:

(1) Are visual aspects (resemblances) actually *seen* or are they only *thought* of in an interpretation?

(2) How (or in what sense) is it possible to *experience* an aspect (a thought, the meaning of a picture) in an instant?[11]

I shall try to unravel the discussion, especially in the relevant sections in the 1949 typescript on philosophy of psychology, by expounding those two discussions in turn.

---

[11] It has been suggested that Wittgenstein's main concern in discussing aspect change was to dissolve the following paradox: 'when looking at a picture-object we can come to see it differently, although we also see that the object itself remains unchanged. It seems to have changed and yet seems not to have changed' (H.-J. Glock, *A Wittgenstein Dictionary* (Oxford: Blackwell, 1996), p. 37; cf. Mulhall, 'Seeing Aspects', p. 247). However, if this is a paradox, it is dissolved at the very beginning of the discussion by Wittgenstein's remark that there are two uses of the word 'see' and hence two 'objects' of sight (PPF §111; p. 193). Once we note this ambiguity it is not surprising that what we see (in one sense) can change while what we see (in another sense) remains the same. What remains puzzling, of course, is that in the former case, too, we use the word 'see'; which is what I presented as problem (1).

2. Seeing or Interpreting?

(1) Are visual aspects actually *seen* or are they only *thought* of in an interpretation? (PPF §§140, 144, 148, 149, 169, 175, 181 f., 187, 190, 248.) Of course we commonly *say* that we see aspects (as the opening remark PPF §111, quoted above, shows), but one may suspect that that is only a conventional figure of speech, a derivative (metonymical) use of the word 'see' (PPF §169; p. 201; cf. §190; p. 204). Just as one speaks of marrying money, although of course one does not literally marry money, but rather a rich spouse (LW I §765). Again, consider Wittgenstein's analogy with the phenomenon of 'secondary meaning': Under certain circumstances we are prepared to apply colour words to vowels (PPF §177; p. 202); or the words 'fat' and 'meagre' to days of the week (PPF §§274–8; p. 216). But we are always prepared to add that this is just a quirk of language: of course the letter 'e' is not *really* yellow; and Wednesday is not really fat. Similarly, it might be held that an aspect is not really seen, but only thought of or associated with one's vision. Thus, Berkeley insists 'that the ideas of space, outness, and things placed at a distance, are not, strictly speaking, the object of sight'.[12] All we actually see are configurations of colour; anything else can only be 'suggested to the mind by the mediation of some other *idea* which is itself perceived in the act of seeing'.[13]

Against Berkeley and, more generally, against the view that aspects are only interpretations Wittgenstein makes the following points:

(i) 'To interpret is to think, to do something; seeing is a state' (PPF §248; p. 212). That is, seeing has genuine duration: one can ask for how long one saw the drawing as a duck before it changed to a rabbit, whereas it sounds incongruous to ask for the duration of an interpretation (LPP 330).[14]

(ii) 'When we interpret we form hypotheses, which may prove false', whereas ' "I see this figure as a . . ." can be verified as little as (or only in the same sense as) "I see a bright red" ' (PPF §249; p. 212).—This, however, is problematic. For one thing, seeing too tends to involve taking something to be true, which may conceivably turn out to be false (e.g. if it is an illusion or hallucination). And my seeing-as can also turn out to be true or false: for instance, when in the dark I see as a suspicious human figure what in truth

[12] G. Berkeley, *An Essay Towards a New Theory of Vision* [1709], in *A New Theory of Vision and other writings* (London: Dent 1969), §46; cf. LPP 109.
[13] Berkeley, *New Theory*, §16; cf. PPF §211; p. 207: '[In aspect perception] it is as if an *idea* came into contact, and for a time remained in contact, with the visual impression'.
[14] Cf. RPP I §§882, 1025; RPP II §§43, 388. Note, however, that this criterion is not as easily applicable to the dispositional sense of 'seeing-as', discussed above.

is only a bush. Or, to take one of Wittgenstein's examples, I suddenly seem to recognize an old friend, seeing his former face in an older one (PPF §143; p. 197)—but then it turns out that it wasn't him after all. Of course, seeing something *as* X need not involve any belief that it actually *is* X, but then, similarly, one can retreat from hypothesizing to mere imagining. That is, both on the side of vision and on the side of thinking one can distinguish between taking something to be true and merely toying with an idea. Thus, the fact that many cases of seeing-as belong to the latter category may show that they cannot be construed as interpreting, yet, more importantly, it is not enough to set them apart from thinking and vindicate them as proper seeing.

(iii) If seeing something as X were only an interpretation (assertorical or fictional), superimposed on what is actually seen, it should be possible to describe what is actually seen, the uninterpreted data; but typically we cannot. Saying 'I see it as . . .' is not just an indirect description of the visual experience, that could be replaced by a more direct one. It is the most appropriate report of what I see (PPF §117; pp. 193f.; RPP I §318). Or, in some cases, it would perhaps be possible to replace the expression of an aspect perception (e.g. the three-dimensional impression of a landscape, or a facial expression) by a Berkeleian description in terms of mere colours and shapes, but only after special instruction and practice (PPF §148; p. 198; LPP 110).

(iv) As already explained above: when we see a picture as representing something, we do not *read* it like a blueprint, but respond to it as to the object represented (PPF §§192–9; pp. 204 f.). The aspect is directly perceived and not only thought or known to be there as the result of an interpretation. This experience of actual perception is also manifest in certain emphatic expressions, such as: 'The sphere [in the picture] seems to float', 'One sees it floating', 'It floats!' (PPF §169; p. 201), or, of an eye represented by a dot: 'See how it's looking!' (PPF §201; p. 205).

(v) Finally, as already noted, seeing-as is essentially noticing a resemblance, an internal relation between an object and other objects, real or imagined (PPF §247; p. 212). But the act of noticing a visual resemblance cannot be construed as distinct from that of seeing (the resemblance). Of course you can see the same object without noticing the resemblance, but the noticing (when it occurs while looking) is not a mental operation distinct from seeing. Rather, it *is* seeing (LW I §511).[15]

---

[15] Could one notice a visual resemblance without seeing it? Yes, indirectly: When on two occasions I write down a description of what I've seen, and then later deduce from the similarity of the descriptions that the two objects must have looked alike in certain respects, although I didn't realize at the time. Again, by feeling two objects with my hands in the dark I may notice similarities in shape that could also be seen.

Those are the conceptual justifications for calling visual aspect perception 'seeing'. The observation invoked in the last point (v)—namely that in aspect perception one experiences a comparison (RPP I §317)—serves also to dissolve two apparent objections to calling it 'seeing', which focus on the way aspect perception can change:

The first objection is that since when I suddenly see something differently (e.g. switch from seeing a drawing as a duck to seeing it as a rabbit) the object itself remains unchanged, the change can only be one of interpretation. The lighting up of an aspect is essentially a subjective experience (*Erlebnis*) and not a truthful cognition of an object; even though it is reported as if it were a visual perception (PPF §137; p. 197).

A second objection to accepting seeing-as as a proper case of seeing is that, unlike veridical perception, it is subject to the will. 'There is such an order as... "Now see the figure like *this*!"; but not: "Now see this leaf green!"' (PPF §256; p. 213; cf. RPP II §544).

However, once we appreciate the essentially relational character of aspect perception (i.e., that it involves an awareness of a resemblance between what is seen and something else (RPP I §317)), it is no wonder that aspects can change although the object remains the same; just as Socrates can without undergoing any intrinsic change be found first tall and then short—depending on whom we compare him with. And of course, respects of comparison can be changed at will. Nonetheless, aspect perception can be said to identify an objective feature of the object, namely a relation of likeness between it and some other object, even if the latter is arbitrarily chosen (PPF §254b; p. 213; cf. §247; p. 212). Hence, in as much as it picks out an actual resemblance it is of course a form of perception. Seeing-as is seeing all right, but a kind of seeing that is particularly concept-laden, typically more so than seeing shapes and colours.

That, however, was denied by the Gestalt psychologist Wolfgang Köhler, who argued that what we see, in the strictest sense of the word, is not only colours and shapes, but also 'organization'. It is a 'sensory fact' that usually in our visual field the contents of certain areas 'belong together' as circumscribed units from which their surroundings are excluded.[16] Thus, when we see a puzzle picture first as a duck, then as a rabbit, each time we experience a different 'visual reality'. The aspect is seen just like shapes and colours.[17]

Wittgenstein disagreed with Köhler (cf. LPP 110). He was not in general opposed to saying that at the lighting up of a new aspect (when looking at

---

[16] W. Köhler, *Gestalt Psychology* (London: G. Bell, 1930), p. 114.   [17] Cf. LPP 100 ff.

a puzzle picture, for example) the 'organization' of one's visual impression changes. The expression sounds phenomenologically apt enough. The question is, however, what exactly it is supposed to mean. If one regards the 'organization' as a feature on a par with colour and shapes (as a 'visual reality') one is treating the visual impression as an inner object, as some kind of mental representation (PPF §134; p. 196). The actual drawing remains the same, yet *something* in one's vision changes; so that must be one's inner picture. But note that a change of aspect is not an illusion: one is not under the wrong impression that the drawing does in fact change. Rather, the change of aspect goes together with an awareness that the drawing itself remains unchanged. Hence, if seeing it is construed in terms of awareness of an inner picture (one's visual impression), that inner picture must both change its 'organization' and remain unchanged!

> Of course, this makes this object chimerical; a strange vacillating entity. For the similarity to a picture is now impaired.   (PPF §134; p. 196)

In fact, a visual impression is not a picture, nor can it always be accurately represented by a picture. For take any picture you like, it can always be seen in different ways. In other words, the way a picture is seen, cannot—on pain of an infinite regress—be determined by another picture; for that again could be seen in different ways, and so on and so forth. So, when after an aspect change my visual impression has a different 'organization', the pictures I draw to represent my visual impressions before and after the change may be the same (PPF §131; p. 196). Perhaps only a three-dimensional model could bring out the difference in visual impression (PPF §135; p. 196). 'And this suffices', Wittgenstein concludes, 'to dispose of the comparison of "organisation" with colour and shape in the visual impression' (PPF §136; p. 196). The colour and shapes in the visual field can always be represented by an image, whereas 'organization' cannot: sometimes it can only be represented by further means of expression, such as a three-dimensional model, or perhaps a description of what is seen in terms of concepts that are not literally applicable to the object (e.g. seeing a triangle as fallen over). What this brings out is that many aspects are not 'organizational' in Köhler's sense: that is, seeing them requires not only taking certain elements of the visual impression together, as foreground, but essentially involves one's imagination—surrounding the object with some fiction (PPF §234; p. 210)—and some knowledge of what other things look like; for example, my noticing that somebody resembles his absent father; or that the duck-rabbit figure resembles a rabbit's head (PPF §§211, 216 f.; p. 207).

To conclude: visual aspect perception may well be called 'seeing', although it is often more concept-laden than seeing just shapes and colours. An important result of the discussion so far is that one's visual impression cannot be construed as an inner picture. One crucial consideration for Wittgenstein to justify calling visual aspect perception 'seeing' is that it involves a certain *attitude* towards an object, especially the internal object of a pictorial representation (PPF §193; p. 205). Here, seeing-as is taken not only in an episodic sense, but also as a continuous and largely dispositional stance.

But then there is the more specific phenomenon of the lighting up of an aspect, already touched upon in this discussion, which occasions Wittgenstein's other major concern:

3. The Instantaneous Experience of an Aspect

(2) How (or in what sense) is it possible to *experience* an aspect in an instant? This is a variant of a philosophical problem that had occupied Wittgenstein already in the *Philosophical Investigations* ('Part I'), underlying, for example, the famous rule-following considerations. Understanding, intention, expectation, remembering, and other such mental occurrences, can have remarkably rich and complex contents. It may take very long to spell out completely what exactly someone understood, intended, expected, or remembered on a given occasion. And yet, it appears that the understanding, intending, expecting, or remembering can occur instantaneously: in a flash. How is it possible for some incredibly complex contents to be experienced in one moment?

Consider, for example, that the meaning of a word is its use, which can be very complicated and difficult to describe. How on earth can such a complicated grammatical description be instantaneously present to one's mind?

When someone says the word 'cube' to me, for example, I know what it means. But can the whole *use* of the word come before my mind, when I *understand* it this way? (PI §139)

Surely not, and yet it is possible to have such an instantaneous understanding. The puzzle recurs repeatedly in the *Investigations*:

A writes series of numbers down: B watches him and tries to find a law for the sequence of numbers. When he succeeds he exclaims: 'Now I can go on!'—So this capacity, this understanding, is something that makes its appearance in a moment.   (PI §151)

I want to remember a tune and it escapes me; suddenly I say 'Now I know it' and sing it. What was it like to suddenly know it? Surely it can't have occurred to me *in its entirety* in that moment!   (PI §184)

There is no doubt that I now want to play chess, but chess is the game it is in virtue of all its rules (and so on). Don't I know, then, which game I want to play until I *have* played it? or are all the rules contained in my act of intending?   (PI §197)

This is *the paradox of the instantaneous experience of complex contents: The contents must all be there in a flash,* for I can correctly avow that *at a particular moment* I have understood, I intend, I expect, or remember. Yet, of course, *the contents are not all there in a flash,* for I am not really aware of all the details: all possible uses of the word; all numbers of an arithmetic series; all notes of a melody; all rules of chess; they are not all in front of my mind at the same time. That is particularly obvious in the case of understanding an arithmetical series, where the object of understanding is literally infinite.

So how is it possible to experience such complex contents in a moment?—It isn't. If to experience the meaning of a word, say, is to have an account of it in one's mind, a mental representation, then no such instantaneous experiencing occurs; and likewise with other intentional mental phenomena. Hence, even God, had he 'looked into our minds he would not have been able to see there whom we were speaking of' (PPF §284; p. 217), or what it was we understood or remembered. The mental representation we feel compelled to postulate in such cases is an illusion. That is the upshot of the discussions of the paradox of the instantaneous experience of complex contents in the *Investigations*: the rejection of a wrong philosophical picture (cf. PI §115).[18]

One may well feel that this entirely negative result is not the whole story. After all, in such cases there *is* an experience of sorts, and surely, it can be correct to report: 'Now I understand!' Wittgenstein himself felt that there remained some unfinished business and he thought further about the puzzling phenomenon of instantaneously 'experiencing' a complex content, especially the meaning of a word, during the years 1946 to 1949 (cf. LPP 347).

While in the *Philosophical Investigations* ('Part I') Wittgenstein asks 'How is it possible to experience the meaning of a word (for example) in an instant?' and returns a negative answer ('It isn't' (cf. Z §180)), in those later writings he pursues the follow-up questions: 'Why do we (feel compelled to) say so then?' and 'What are we to think of that odd kind of experience?' The phenomenon is particularly poignant in the case of ambiguous words. The word 'till', for example, can be uttered and heard as a verb, as a noun, or as a conjunction (PPF §8; p. 175). That is, even when the word is spoken in isolation we can *hear* it in either of its different meanings; although there is really nothing in such

---

[18] Cf. S. Schroeder, *Wittgenstein: The Way Out of the Fly-Bottle* (Cambridge: Polity, 2006), chs 4.5–4.6.

an experience that could possibly determine the meaning of the word. Oddly enough, the 'experience of meaning' has no actual content (RPP I §105).

A philosophical puzzle is not so much to be solved as to be *dis*solved. 'The only way to deal with the puzzle is to get someone to see it's *not* a puzzle' (LPP 347).[19] Sometimes that can be achieved by reminding oneself that what strikes us as odd is in fact not as rare and peculiar as we thought:

> The particular peace of mind that occurs when we can place other similar cases next to a case that we thought was unique, occurs again and again in our investigations... (BT 416)

For example, Augustine found it puzzling how we could measure time:

> That I measure time, I know; and yet I measure not time to come, for it is not yet; nor present, because it is not protracted by any space; nor past, because it now is not. What then do I measure?[20]

He should have reminded himself that other things too are measured while not being present in their entirety. Length is sometimes measured while the object is passing by (e.g. by counting the wagons of a railway train). Then the case of measuring time loses its disquieting uniqueness, its appearance of anomaly, and begins to look once more as common as it is.

This methodological device is explicitly brought up again in the context of the discussion of strangely meaningful experiences:

> Philosophy often solves a problem merely by saying: "*Here* is no more difficulty than *there*."
>> That is, just by conjuring up a problem, where there was none before.
>> It says: 'Isn't it just as remarkable that...', and leaves it at that. (RPP I §1000)

And what Wittgenstein invokes as 'just as remarkable' as experiencing the meaning of a word is, amongst other things,[21] the experience of instantaneous aspect perception (the 'lighting up' of an aspect). At one point he explains that his interest in the discussion of aspect perception is indeed largely due to his hope that it might shed some light on his older problem of instantaneous experiences of word meaning (PPF §261; p. 214). Does it? That is far from obvious. To begin with, aspect perception provides not only another variant of a known type of problem, it brings up some fresh conceptual problems of its own (as illustrated above). Indeed, in some respects it might appear even more

---

[19] Cf. ibid. ch. 4.3.

[20] Augustine, *The Confessions* [*Confessiones*, 400], trans. E. B. Pusey (London: Dent, 1907), Bk XI, §xxvi, pp. 271 f.

[21] Other objects of comparison are: remembering (PPF ch. xiii; p. 231) and momentary intending (PPF §§279 ff.; pp. 216 ff.; RPP I §178).

puzzling than experiences of meaning. It was noted earlier that Wittgenstein found it odd that a logical condition of one's having an experience of aspect perception is that one has mastered a certain technique, whereas the parallel phenomenon that experiencing the meaning of a word presupposes a mastery of that meaning does not appear equally odd.—Still, it may be worthwhile to consider the analogy further.

Wittgenstein's next move was to inquire after the importance and role in our lives of the kind of experience he found puzzling. The importance an experience has in our lives can be thrown into relief by considering the imaginary case of people lacking that experience. Thus, Wittgenstein introduces the idea of a 'meaning-blind' person: somebody who understands the meanings of words, and is also able to use homonyms according to their different meanings, but never has the experience of hearing a word, in isolation, as having one meaning or another (RPP I §§202, 232, 239, 242, 247, 250). The question is: 'What would someone be missing if he did not *experience* the meaning of a word?' (PPF §261; p. 214). Would this be a serious handicap? And again, in the analogous case of aspect perception:

Could there be human beings lacking the ability to see something *as something*—and what would that be like? What sort of consequences would it have?—Would this defect be comparable to colour-blindness, or to not having absolute pitch?—We will call it 'aspect-blindness'—and will now consider what might be meant by this. (A conceptual investigation.)   (PPF §257; p. 213)

Is an experience of aspect perception perhaps not only conditioned by certain abilities, but also a condition for certain abilities? Does one, under certain circumstances, need to *see* something in a particular way in order to be able to do something—not only dispositionally: that one takes it, responds to it, in a certain way, but as an occurrent experience? Wittgenstein suggests that that may indeed be so, for instance in aesthetic contexts (PPF §178; p. 202), or when following a geometrical demonstration (PPF §§179–80; p. 203). However, his remarks on this point are only tentative and suggest merely that aspect perception may *help* one's understanding, not that it is an absolute precondition. According to other remarks, what an experience of aspect perception is likely to manifest itself in, is not so much new abilities as new dispositions, that is, inclinations to react or comment in a certain way: What I expect from someone who sees the duck-rabbit as a duck will be different from what I expect from someone who doesn't (PPF §196; p. 205). He may for example find the beak too long.

Unfortunately, Wittgenstein's intention to investigate the concept of aspect-blindness is not really carried out. In the remainder of the quoted remark (PPF

§257), he notes that an aspect-blind person would still be able to recognize similarities. Then there follow only three more remarks on the topic—in which none of the questions raised are satisfactorily answered—before Wittgenstein links it up with, and moves back to, the parallel issue of experiencing the meaning of a word (PPF §261; p. 214).[22] After that there is no more mention of the topic of aspect perception. In the remainder of this paper I shall try to continue where Wittgenstein left off and investigate the concept of aspect-blindness a little further, to see whether it can shed any more light on the phenomenon of experiencing a meaning.

4. Aspect-Blindness, Emotional Seeing-As, and the Experience of Meaning

Could there be a generally aspect-blind person? No. As suggested earlier, whenever something is seen (and not only looked at inanely or absent-mindedly) *some* aspect of it must be noticed, be it only certain shapes or colours. Of course for any particular aspect of an object it may be imagined that an onlooker fails to see it; but then, as long as it is to be granted that the person sees the object at all, there must be some other visual aspects of it that he does notice. Thus, if you fail to see the face in a puzzle picture, you see, say, only leaves, or perhaps some arabesque patterns. And if when looking at a bookcase you don't see it three-dimensionally, you see it as an arrangement of different coloured rectangles on a flat surface; and can describe it as such.

Wittgenstein seems to suggest a distinction between noticing a shape in a drawing and seeing the drawing *as* one of that shape:

is [the aspect-blind man] supposed not to recognize that the double cross [which can be seen as white cross on black ground or as black cross on white ground (PPF §212; p. 207)] contains both a black and a white cross? So if told 'Show me figures containing a black cross among these examples', will he be unable to manage it? No. He should be able to do that... (PPF §257; p. 213)

But in that case it is hard to deny that he can see the drawing *as* one of a black cross on white ground (or vice versa). Again, someone may not be able to see a schematic drawing of a cube (cf. PPF §116) three-dimensionally, as a cube, but only as a two-dimensional geometrical drawing of a square and two rhomboids. But then such a person would hardly be able to observe the relevant resemblance between the drawing and a cube. For once he notices

---

[22] Experiencing the meaning of a word was already discussed earlier in PPF, in section ii: §§7–17.

that resemblance, does he not *ipso facto* see the drawing *as* (a drawing of) a cube? Or again, if while looking at

(a) ●●●●

you bring to mind the resemblance between it and

(b) ●● ●●

do you not *thereby* see (a) as two pairs of two dots? It seems that at least in some simple cases seeing an aspect consists in nothing more than noticing a certain resemblance. Hence it would appear inconsistent to suggest that somebody may be blind to that aspect and yet perfectly capable of noticing the resemblance in question.

It was noted that Wittgenstein is particularly interested in the episodic experience of aspects. Perhaps, then, his idea is that the aspect-blind person cannot see the *lighting up* of an aspect, even though he may be able to see aspects continuously:

> The aspect-blind man is supposed not to see the A aspects [i.e., the two aspects of the double cross] change. . . . he will not be supposed to say: 'Now it's a black cross on a white ground!'   (PPF §257; p. 213)

> . . . for him [the schematic cube] would not switch from one aspect to the other.   (PPF §258; pp. 213 f.)

However, elsewhere Wittgenstein denies explicitly that it is merely blindness to aspect *change* that he has in mind:

> Of course it is imaginable that someone might never see a change of aspect, the three-dimensional aspect of every picture always remaining constant for him. But this assumption *doesn't interest us.*   (RPP II §480)

Moreover, that assumption too is problematic. Given, as Wittgenstein seems to allow of the aspect-blind person, that one can be made to see first the black cross in the double cross figure (perhaps by being shown a straightforward black cross as an object of comparison) and later can be made to see the white cross, it is hard to imagine that once one has realized that the drawing consists of both a black cross and a white cross interlinking one should not be able to switch from one to the other. (It may be different with a more complex puzzle picture where the aspects are not so easily located and conceptualized—as black cross and white cross—and hence may be much more difficult to retrieve.) And even if one doesn't experience a change of aspect while looking, remembering that one saw a different cross the last time would be enough to allow one to say: '*Now* it's a black cross'.

It would appear, then, first, that the idea of general aspect-blindness is inconsistent. Secondly, considering the example of the double cross, Wittgenstein's idea that blindness to certain aspects may be compatible with normal vision and intelligence, in particular with a capacity to spot the relevant resemblances, seems to be equally unworkable.

At this point, however, it may be useful to distinguish between different kinds of visual aspects. For one thing, there is an obvious difference between pictorial aspects and others. Seeing-as may be seeing something as a picture of something else, for example, as the drawing of a duck, or of a cube. On the other hand, seeing a row of equidistant dots as grouped in a certain way; seeing a black cross on white ground; or seeing something as a three-dimensional object—is not seeing what a picture represents. These are non-pictorial aspects.

Some of Wittgenstein's remarks suggest that he is particularly interested in pictorial aspects, and they are perhaps what we should focus on when trying to get a grip on the idea of aspect-blindness:

The 'aspect-blind' will have an altogether different relationship to pictures from ours. (PPF §258; p. 214)

But it seems to me that the class of pictorial aspects needs to be further subdivided in order to make sense of some of Wittgenstein's ideas. The remark above relates back to Wittgenstein's claim that 'we *view* the photograph, the picture on our wall, as the very object (the man, landscape and so on) represented in it' (PPF §197; p. 205). That, however, is not applicable with equal plausibility to *all* pictures. A photograph of a loved one is a very different matter from a schematic drawing of a cube or a face. I see this: ☺ as a face, but I do not relate to it as to a real person. So we need to distinguish between schematic or very stylized drawings, on the one hand, and fairly elaborate paintings and photographs, on the other. Hence, we can now distinguish three classes of visual aspects:

1. Non-pictorial aspects
2. Schematic pictorial aspects
3. Elaborate pictorial aspects

With the first two classes there is nothing more to seeing an aspect than recognizing a shape or arrangement, or noticing a resemblance. Hence, in such cases Wittgenstein's suggestion that one might be able to see the relevant resemblances and yet be blind to the aspect is unconvincing. With elaborate pictorial aspects (3), however, a more demanding concept of aspect perception gets a foothold. Here it is indeed possible to notice the relevant resemblances without yet seeing the aspect, because aspect perception in this fuller sense requires also that the picture is experienced as transparent for a certain imaginative engagement with the object depicted. 'We view a portrait as a human being' (PPF §199; p. 205); just as we view an actor as Henry V, and a mere stage cockpit as the vasty fields of France. In such cases it is easy to imagine somebody unable to adopt the required attitude. Indeed, for most people full absorption into the represented or fictional scene is only ever fairly brief: 'a picture is not always *alive* for me while I am seeing it' (PPF §200; p. 205), and a theatregoer's experience of seeing *Henry V* is likely to be interrupted by thoughts about the quality of the acting or salient features of the production, or indeed by the distracting noises made by a school class in the auditorium. It seems certainly possible that someone may well understand the practice of dramatic representation on stage, notice the relevant similarities between the actors and the characters they are meant to impersonate, and yet not be able to enter into the game of make-believe: Instead of seeing the people on stage as French and English soldiers in combat, he only ever sees them as actors wearing historical costumes and imitating the motions of a battle. Such a person could be called aspect-blind, in a sense of the word that is not applicable to the cases of non-pictorial or schematic pictorial aspects.

Thus the only kind of aspect perception that allows of aspect-blindness (as envisaged by Wittgenstein) is the experience of a picture or theatrical representation as transparent for an imaginative engagement with the object depicted. In such cases seeing-as is not so much a cognitive achievement as an imaginative and emotional experience. The aspect-blind person is not deficient in his understanding of what is represented, nor does he actually see less, he merely lacks a certain emotional response; a response that others experience at most intermittently, when momentarily fully engrossed in the representation.

And it is only this kind of aspect perception, the *emotional seeing-as* of pictorial representations, that affords Wittgenstein the desired analogy with the phenomenon of experiencing the meaning of a word. Sometimes, hearing a word we experience it as having a familiar face, as having 'taken up its meaning into itself' (PPF §294; p. 218). This experience may accompany our understanding of a word, but it is not itself an act of understanding. Because, for one thing, it is an illusion to think that we experience a representation of the linguistic meaning on which our capacity to use the word correctly could be based. As noted above, Wittgenstein argued repeatedly that no such complex contents are in fact experienced in such a case. For another thing, most of the time we use and understand words in ordinary conversation we do not, in this sense, experience their meaning at all (PPF §272; pp. 215 f.). The meaning-blind person is not lacking in linguistic competence (cf. PPF §8;

p. 175), but merely in his emotional attachment to words (PPF §294; p. 218). Such a person would feel about language in roughly the way we feel about recently learnt code words:

Suppose I had agreed on a code with someone; 'tower' means bank. I tell him 'Now go to the tower'—he understands me and acts accordingly, but he feels the word 'tower' to be strange in this use, it has not yet 'taken on' the meaning.   (PPF §263; p. 214)

Similarly, the aspect-blind person understands that a certain actor represents Henry V, yet he never experiences him to *be* Henry V, to have 'taken on' the character.

It has been argued above that only one of Wittgenstein's concerns with aspect perception was the question whether seeing-as can properly be regarded as a case of seeing. That that is not the full story of Wittgenstein's discussions can be highlighted once more by reverting to that initial question. Wittgenstein discusses it mainly with respect to non-pictorial and schematic pictorial aspects, and he presents good reasons for an affirmative answer. Seeing a geometrical drawing as a cube, for example, is indeed a case of seeing, not only of interpreting. But what about elaborate pictorial aspects and emotional seeing-as? Is emotional seeing-as really seeing? Arguably not. When someone smiles tenderly at a photo, relating directly to the person depicted, he doesn't *see* anything the aspect-blind person fails to see. In particular, it is not as in other cases of aspect perception that somebody who sees an aspect notices a resemblance which somebody else who doesn't see the aspect misses. No, both parties see the likeness and understand the representational purpose. The difference lies in their emotional responses. One of them may, for example, feel a glimpse of his daughter's presence while looking at her picture, whereas the other one experiences only an inanimate photograph. It was argued above (359(iii)) that aspect perception was not only an interpretation imposed on what was really seen since, typically, one cannot give a more direct description of what one sees. This case is different. When emotionally relating to a person while looking at his photograph one can easily syphon off the extra element of the experience and describe what is actually seen, namely a mere photograph. After all, emotional seeing-as is not a form of illusion: in spite of one's emotional engagement one remains fully aware that what one sees is only a representation. So, whereas earlier, in the discussion of non-pictorial and schematic aspect perception, Wittgenstein argued, with certain qualifications, that we do see aspects, here the thrust of his remarks points in the opposite direction. Emotive aspects are not really seen, but only felt. And that provides an illuminating model for the phenomenon of experiencing the meaning of a word.

To say that a word is heard to be 'filled with its meaning' is only a figurative expression (PPF §265; p. 215). The meaning of a word is its rule-governed use (PI §43)[23] and cannot literally be discerned in its sound, nor mentally represented while hearing the sound. It can only *feel* to us as if it were there, owing to the familiar association of the word with its use; just as the name 'Schubert' can feel to us to have taken on the atmosphere of Schubert's music (PPF §270; p. 215). However, that is not self-evident. There is, on the contrary, a strong temptation to think that somehow it must be possible after all to experience the meaning of a word when hearing it, which when we consider the difficulty of compressing it into a momentary impression, produces a paradox. Wittgenstein's own long-lasting occupation with the topic indicates how strongly he himself must have felt that temptation. Hence, a comparable phenomenon where the imaginary character of what we experience is obvious might help to dispel the air of paradox. With emotional seeing-as it is obvious that the object of our experience is not really there. What in fact we see is only a *portrait* of a person or a theatrical *representation* of certain events, not the person or the events themselves. And yet, at least momentarily it feels as if we were experiencing the real thing. Thus the analogy between emotional seeing-as and the experience of meaning proves useful after all. It might help us to accept that in the latter case, too, we engage imaginatively with something that is not actually present. The sound of a word is associated with its meaning, but the meaning is not really present in the sound of the word, nor in our experience of that sound, even if that is the way it sometimes feels to us.[24]

---

[23] Cf. Schroeder, *Wittgenstein*, ch. 4.4.

[24] I am grateful to John Cottingham, David Dolby, Maximilian de Gaynesford, Peter Hacker, Stephen Mulhall, Angus Ross, and Constantine Sandis for comments on earlier versions of this paper.

Bibliography of the Works of Anthony Kenny

A. Authored Books

1963: *Action, Emotion and Will* (London: Routledge & Kegan Paul; 2nd edn 2003).

1964: *St Thomas Aquinas, Summa Theologiae: Volume 22: Dispositions for Human Acts (Ia2ae.49–54)* (London: Blackfriars and Eyre & Spottiswoode).

1968: *Descartes: A Study of His Philosophy* (New York: Random House; (reprint by Garland 1987; by Thoemmes Press in 1993).

1969: *The Five Ways* (London: Routledge & Kegan Paul; new edn 2003).

1972: & H. C. Longuet-Higgins, J. R. Lucas, and C. H. Waddington, *The Nature of Mind: the Gifford Lectures 1971–2* (Edinburgh: Edinburgh University Press).

1973: & H. C. Longuet-Higgins, J. R. Lucas, and C. H. Waddington, *The Development of Mind: the Gifford Lectures 1972–3* (Edinburgh: Edinburgh University Press).

1973: *The Anatomy of the Soul* (Oxford: Blackwell).

1973. *Wittgenstein* (London: Allen Lane; Cambridge, Mass.: Harvard University Press; paperback 1975, Penguin Books; Spanish 1974, Dutch 1974, German 1974, French (garbled) 1975, Italian 1984).

1975: *Will, Freedom and Power* (Oxford: Blackwell).

1978: *Freewill and Responsibility* (London: Routledge & Kegan Paul; paper 1981).

1978: *The Aristotelian Ethics* (Oxford: Clarendon Press).

1979: *The God of the Philosophers* (Oxford: Clarendon Press).

1979: *Aristotle's Theory of the Will* (London: Duckworth (hard & paper)).

1980: *Aquinas* (Oxford: Oxford University Press; New York: Hill and Wang; several reprints; Italian 1980, Portuguese 1981, Czech 1983, Hungarian 1986, Romanian 1998, Polish 1999, German 1999, Dutch 2000, Korean 2000).

1981: *The Computation of Style* (Oxford: Pergamon Press).

1982: & Norman Kretzmann & Jan Pinborg (eds), *The Cambridge History of Later Medieval Philosophy*.

1983: *Thomas More* (Oxford: Oxford University Press; repr. 1992; Spanish 1987).

1983: *Faith and Reason* (New York: Columbia University Press).

1984: *The Legacy of Wittgenstein* (Oxford: Blackwell (hard & paper); Spanish 1990).

1985: *The Logic of Deterrence* (London: Firethorn Press; Chicago: University of Chicago Press).

1985: *The Ivory Tower: Essays in Philosophy and Public Policy* (Oxford: Blackwell).

1985: *A Path from Rome*. London, Sidgwick and Jackson (Oxford (paper), 1986).

1985: *Wyclif* (Oxford: Oxford University Press).

1986: *A Stylometric Study of the New Testament* (Oxford: Clarendon Press).

1986: *Rationalism, Empiricism, and Idealism* (ed.) (Oxford: Clarendon Press).

1986: *The Road to Hillsborough* (Oxford: Pergamon Press).

1987: *Reason and Religion: Essays in Philosophical Theology* (Oxford: Blackwell).

1987: *The Heritage of Wisdom* (Oxford: Blackwell).

1988: *God and Two Poets: Arthur Hugh Clough and Gerard Manley Hopkins* (London: Sidgwick & Jackson).

1988: *The Self* (Milwaukee: Marquette University Press).

1989: *The Metaphysics of Mind* (Oxford: Clarendon Press; Spanish 2004).

1990: *The Oxford Diaries of Arthur Hugh Clough* (ed.) (Oxford: Clarendon Press).

1991: *Computers and the Humanities* (British Library).

1991: *Mountains: An Anthology* (London: John Murray).

1992: *Aristotle on the Perfect Life* (Oxford: Clarendon Press).

1992: *What is Faith?* (Oxford: Oxford University Press; Czech 1995).

1993: *Aquinas on Mind* (London: Routledge; Japanese 1994; Czech 1997; Spanish 2000).

1994: *The Wittgenstein Reader* (ed.) (Oxford: Blackwell; German 1996).

1994: *The Oxford Illustrated History of Western Philosophy* (ed.) (Oxford: Oxford University Press; reissued without illustrations as *The Oxford History of Western Philosophy* OUP 2000; German 1995).

1995: *Frege* (London: Penguin Books; reissued Blackwell 2000; Spanish 1997; Italian 1999).

1997: *A Life in Oxford* (London: John Murray).

1998: *A Brief History of Western Philosophy* (Oxford: Blackwell; Portuguese 1999; Korean 2003; 2nd illustrated edn 2006).

2001: *Essays on the Aristotelian Tradition* (Oxford: Clarendon Press).

2002: *Aquinas on Being* (Oxford: Clarendon Press).

2004: *The Unknown God* (London: Continuum).

2004: *A New History of Western Philosophy*, Volume I. *Ancient Philosophy* (Oxford: Clarendon Press).

2005: *Arthur Hugh Clough: The Life of a Poet* (London: Continuum).

2005: *A New History of Western Philosophy*, Volume II. *Medieval Philosophy* (Oxford: Clarendon Press).

2006: *What I Believe* (London: Continuum).

2006: *A New History of Western Philosophy*, Volume III. *The Rise of Modern Philosophy* (Oxford: Clarendon Press).

2006: *Life, Liberty and the Pursuit of Utility* (with Charles Kenny) (Exeter: Imprint Academic).

2007: *A New History of Western Philosophy*, Volume IV. *Philosophy in the Modern World* (Oxford: Clarendon Press).

2007: *Can Oxford be Improved?* (with Robert Kenny) (Exeter: Imprint Academic).

2008: *From Empedocles to Wittgenstein: Historical Essays in Philosophy* (Oxford: Clarendon Press).

B. Editions and Edited Collections

See Section C for abbreviations of titles of collected papers.

1962: *The Responsa Scholarum of the English College, Rome, Part One: 1598–1621* (London: Catholic Record Society).

1963: *The Responsa Scholarum of the English College, Rome, Part Two: 1622–1685* (London: Catholic Record Society).

1969: *Aquinas; A Collection of Critical Essays* (ed.) (London: Macmillan; Doubleday; Notre Dame, Ind: University of Notre Dame Press, 1976).

1970: *Descartes: Philosophical Letters* (trans. and ed.) (Oxford: Clarendon Press; paperback 1981: Minneapolis: Minnesota University Press).

1971: *Objects of Thought*, by A. N. Prior, ed. with P. T. Geach (Oxford: Clarendon Press; Italian 1981; French 2002).

1974: & Rush Rhees. Edition and Translation of *Philosophical Grammar* by L. Wittgenstein. (Oxford: Blackwell; Berkeley and Los Angeles: University of California Press; paperback Blackwell 1980).

1976: & P. T. Geach. Edition of *The Doctrine of Propositions and Terms*, by A. N. Prior (London: Duckworth).

1985: *On Universals* (translation of John Wyclif's *Tractatus de Universalibus*) (Oxford: Clarendon Press).

1986: *Wyclif in his Times* (ed.) (Oxford: Clarendon Press).

1991: & J. Cottingham, R. Stoothoff, and D. Murdoch. *The Philosophical Writings of Descartes*, Volume III. *The Correspondence* (Cambridge: Cambridge University Press).

2001: *The History of the Rhodes Trust* (ed.) (Oxford: Oxford University Press).

C. Articles

Many of the essays listed below have been reprinted in one or other of eight volumes of collected papers. The collections are referred to by the following abbreviations.

AS	*The Anatomy of the Soul* (Oxford: Blackwell, 1973).
LoW	*The Legacy of Wittgenstein* (Oxford: Blackwell, 1984).
IT	*The Ivory Tower* (Oxford: Blackwell, 1985).
RR	*Reason and Religion* (Oxford: Blackwell, 1987).
HW	*The Heritage of Wisdom* (Oxford: Blackwell, 1987).

AT   *Essays on the Aristotelian Tradition* (Oxford: Clarendon Press, 2000).
UG   *The Unknown God* (London: Continuum, 2004).
EW   *From Empedocles to Wittgenstein* (Oxford: Oxford University Press, 2008).

1958: 'Was St John Chrysostom a Semi-Pelagian?' *Irish Theological Quarterly* [reprinted in RR].

1959: 'Aquinas and Wittgenstein', *Downside Review* 77.

1962: 'Counterforce and Countervalue', *Clergy Review*, 47: 721–31 [reprinted in IT].

1962: 'Necessary Being', *Sophia* [reprinted in RR].

1964: 'The Use of Logical Analysis in Theology', in *Theology and the University* (ed. John Coulson), pp. 220–35. (London: Darton, Longman and Todd) [reprinted in RR].

1966: 'God and Necessity' in *British Analytical Philosophy* (ed. Bernard Williams and Alan Montefiore), pp. 131–52 (London: Routledge and Kegan Paul) [reprinted in RR] [Italian version, 'Il concetto di Dio e di necessità', in *Filosofia Analytica Inglese* (Roma: Lerici, 1967), pp. 165–90].

1966: 'The Practical Syllogism and Incontinence', *Phronesis* [reprinted in AS].

1966: 'Aristotle on Happiness', *Proceedings of the Aristotelian Society* [reprinted in AS].

1966: 'Cartesian Privacy', in *Wittgenstein: Modern Studies in Philosophy* (ed. G. Pitcher) (Doubleday, 1966). [Italian version, 'il privato cartesiano', in *Capire Wittgenstein*, ed. D. Marconi (Genoa: Marietti) pp. 252–68.]

1968: 'Intention and Purpose in Law', in *Essays in Legal Philosophy* (ed. Robert S. Summers), pp. 146–65 (Oxford: Blackwell).

1968: 'A Self out of Season', in *Good Talk: An Anthology from BBC Radio* (ed. Derwent May), pp. 199–206 (London: Gollancz) [reprinted in HW].

1969: 'Descartes' Ontological Argument', in *Fact and Existence* (ed. Joseph Margolis), pp. 18–35. (Oxford: Blackwell) [reprinted in HW].

1969: 'Mental Health in Plato's Republic', *Proceedings of the British Academy* [reprinted in AS].

1970: 'The Cartesian Circle and the Eternal Truths', *Journal of Philosophy* 67: 685–99 [reprinted in HW].

1971: 'The Homunculus Fallacy', in *Interpretations of Life and Mind* (ed. Marjorie Grene), pp. 65–74 (London: Routledge and Kegan Paul) [reprinted in LoW, also in *Investigating Psychology*, ed. John Hyman (Routledge, 1991); Italian 1994].

1971: 'The Verification Principle and the Private Language Argument', in *The Private Language Argument* (ed. O. R. Jones), pp. 204–28 (London: Macmillan) [Spanish version 1979].

1972: 'Divine Foreknowledge and Human Freedom', in *Logical Analysis and Contemporary Theism* (ed. John Donnelly) (New York: Fordham University Press).

1972: 'Descartes on the Will', in *Cartesian Studies* (ed. R. J. Butler), pp. 1–31 (Oxford: Blackwell) [reprinted in AS].

1974: 'The Ghost of the *Tractatus*', in *Understanding Wittgenstein* (ed. Godfrey Vesey), pp. 1–13 (London: Macmillan; German, 1989). [reprinted in LoW].

1974: (With R. M. Hare) 'What Use Is Moral Philosophy?', in *Philosophy in the Open* (ed. Godfrey Vesey), pp. 45–53 (Milton Keynes: Open University Press).

1975: 'Thomas von Aquin über den Willen', in *Thomas von Aquin im philosophischen Gesprach* (ed. W. Kluxen) (Freiburg: Alber).

1976: 'Direct and Oblique Intention and Malice Aforethought in Murder', *Kingston Law Review*, 6: 28–335 [reprinted in IT].

1976: 'From the Big Typescript to the Philosophical Grammar', *Acta Philosophica Fennica* 28: 41–53 [reprinted in LoW].

1976: 'The Stylometric Study of the Aristotelian Writings', *CIRPHO* [reprinted in AT].

1977: 'Handlungen und Relationen', in *Analytische Handlungstheorie*, vol. i (ed. Georg Meggle), pp. 265–281 (Frankfurt: Suhrkamp).

1977: 'Intention and *Mens Rea* in Murder' in *Law, Morality, and Society* (ed. P. M. S. Hacker and J. Raz), pp. 161–74 (Oxford: Clarendon Press) [reprinted in IT].

1979: 'Wittgenstein über Philosophie', in *Wittgenstein Schriften: Beiheft 3*, pp. 9–34 (Frankfurt: Surhkamp). [English version 'Wittgenstein on the Nature of Philosophy', listed below under 1982.]

1979: 'The First Person', in *Intention and Intentionality* (ed. Cora Diamond and Jenny Teichman), pp. 3–14 (Brighton: Harvester) [reprinted in LoW].

1979: 'Duress *per Minas* as a Defence to Crime', *Law and Philosophy*, I: 197–206 [reprinted in IT, also in *Law, Morality and Rights* (ed. M. A. Stewart), pp. 345–55 (Dordrecht: Reidel, 1983)].

1981: 'Wittgenstein's Early Philosophy of Mind', in *Perspectives on the Philosophy of Wittgenstein* (ed. I. Block) (Oxford: Blackwell 1981) [reprinted in LoW]. [Italian version in *Capire Wittgenstein* (ed. D. Marconi), (Genoa: Marietti) pp. 252–68.]

1981: 'Language and the Mind', *Philosophical Transactions of the Royal Society* [reprinted in LoW].

1982: 'Wittgenstein on the Nature of Philosophy', in *Wittgenstein and his Times*, ed. Brian McGuinness (Chicago: University of Chicago Press), pp. 1–26 [reprinted in LoW]. [Italian version in *Capire Wittgenstein* ed. D. Marconi (Genoa: Marietti) pp. 209–28.]

1982: 'Reform and Reaction in Elizabethan Balliol, 1559–1588', in *Balliol Studies* (ed. John Prest), pp. 17–52 (Oxford: Leopard's Head Press).

1983: 'The Expert in Court', *Law Quarterly Review* 99: 197–216 [reprinted in IT].

1983: 'A Stylometric Comparison between Five Disputed Works and the Remainder of the Aristotelian Corpus', in *Zweifelhaftes im Corpus Aristotelicum* (ed. Paul Moraux & Jurgen Weisner), pp. 342–66 (Berlin: De Gruyter) [reprinted in AT].

1983: 'The Cartesian Spiral', *Revue internationale de philosophie*.

1984: 'Better Dead than Red', in *Objections to Nuclear Defence*, ed. Nigel Blake and Kay Pole, pp. 12–27 (London: Routledge and Kegan Paul) [reprinted in IT].

1984: 'Aquinas: Intentionality', in *Philosophy through its Past* (ed. Ted Honderich), pp. 78–96 (Harmondsworth: Penguin Books) [reprinted in LoW].

1984: 'Philosophy of Mind in the Thirteenth Century', in *L'Homme et son univers au Moyen Âge* (Louvain-la-Neuve).

1986: 'The Logic and Ethics of Nuclear Deterrence', in *Ethics and International Relations* (ed. Anthony Ellis), pp. 92–104 (Manchester: Manchester University Press).

1986: 'Anomalies of Section 2 of the Homicide Act 1957', *Journal of Medical Ethics*, 12: 24–7

1986: 'Wyclif: A Master Mind', *Proceedings of the British Academy*.

1987: 'Defence without Deterrence', in *Peace Studies: The Hard Questions* (ed. Elaine Kaye), pp. 83–105 (London: Rex Collins).

1987: 'The Definition of Omnipotence', in *The Concept of God* (ed. Thomas V. Morris), pp. 125–33 (Oxford: Oxford University Press).

1987: 'Medieval Philosophy', in *The Great Philosophers* (ed. Bryan Magee), pp. 56–75 (Oxford: Oxford University Press/BBC; Portuguese, 1988).

1987: 'Aquinas on Knowledge of Self', in *Language, Meaning and God* (ed. Brian Davies), pp. 104–19 (London: Geoffrey Chapman). [reprinted in HW].

1987: Contribution (pp. 303–16) to *Choices: Nuclear and Non-Nuclear Defence* (ed. O. Ramsbotham), (London: Brasseys).

1987: 'Abortion and the Taking of Human Life', in *Medicine in Contemporary Society* (ed. Peter Byrne), pp. 84–98 (Oxford: Oxford University Press for the King's Fund) [reprinted in RR].

1988: 'Cosmological Explanation and Understanding', in *Perspectives on Human Conduct* (ed. Lars Hertzberg and Juhani Pieteraninen), pp. 72–88 (Leiden: Brill).

1988: 'Aristotle on Moral Luck', in *Human Agency: Language, Duty and Value* (ed. Jonathan Dancy et al.), pp. 105–19 (Stanford, Calif.: Stanford University Press) [reprinted in HW, also in *Modern Thinkers and Ancient Thinkers* (ed. R. W. Sharples), pp. 157–71 (London: UCL Press)].

1988: 'The Problem of Evil and the Argument from Design', in *Teodica Oggi* (ed. M. M. Olivetti), pp. 545–56 (Padua: Cedam).

1990: 'Anselm on the Conceivability of God', in *l'Argomento Ontologico* (ed. M. M. Olivetti), pp. 71–80 (Padua: Cedam) [reprinted in UG].

1990: 'Quale autonomia per la scienza?' in *Scienza ed ettica nella centralità dell'uomo* (ed. Paolo Cattorini), pp. 157–66 (Milan: Franco Angeli).

1990: 'Newman as a Philosopher of Religion', in *Newman: A Man for Our Time* (ed. D. Brown), pp. 98–121 (London: SPCK) [reprinted in UG].

1990: 'An Interview with Anthony Kenny', *Cogito*, 4: 3–8.

1991: 'Technology and Humanities Research', in *Scholarship and Technology in the Humanities* (ed. May Katzen), pp. 1–10 (London: Bowker Saur).

1991: 'Form, Existence and Essence in Aquinas', in *Peter Geach: Philosophical Encounters* (ed. Harry A. Lewis), pp. 65–76. (Dordrecht: Kluwer) [reprinted in HW].

1991: 'Can Responsibility Be Diminished?' in *Liability and Responsibility* (ed. R. G. Frey and Christopher Morris), pp. 13–31 (Cambridge: Cambridge University Press).

1991: 'The Nicomachean Conception of Happiness', in *Oxford Studies in Ancient Philosophy: Aristotle and the Later Tradition* (ed. H. Blumenthal and Howard Robinson), pp. 67–80 (Oxford: Oxford University Press) [reprinted in AT].

1991: 'Metaphor, Analogy and Agnosticism', *Archivio di filosofia 60* [reprinted in UG].

1992: 'Introduction to *Computers and the Humanities* (ed. J-P Genet and A. Zampolli,) pp. xi–xvi (Dartmouth Publishing Company for the European Science Foundation).

1992: 'Victorian Values: Some Concluding Thoughts', in *Victorian Values* (ed. T. C. Smout), pp. 217–24 (Oxford: Oxford University Press for the British Academy).

1993: 'The Kingdom of the Mind', in *Humanity, Environment and God* (ed. Neil Spurway), pp. 174–211 (Oxford: Blackwell) [reprinted in AT].

1993: 'The Metamorphosis of Metaphysics', *Proceedings of the American Philosophical Society* 137: 669–79.

1995: 'Philippa Foot on Double Effect', in *Virtues and Reasons* (ed. Rosalind Hursthouse et al.), pp. 77–88 (Oxford: Clarendon Press) [reprinted in AT].

1995: 'The Ineffable Godhead', in *The Warburton Lectures 1985–1994*, pp. 61–72 [reprinted in UG].

1995: 'Wittgenstein on Mind and Metaphysics', in *Wittgenstein: Mind and Language* (ed. Rosaria Egidi), pp. 37–46 (Dordrecht: Kluwer) (Italian, 1996) [reprinted in UG].

1995: Keynote Address, in *Networking in the Humanities* (ed. Stephanie Kenna & Seamus Ross), pp. 1–14 (London: Bowker Saur).

1995: 'Aristotle's Ideals of Life', in *The Good Idea* (ed. John A. Koumoulides), pp. 95–118 (New Rochelle, A. D. Caratzas).

1996: 'Scotus and the Sea Battle', in *Aristotle in Britain during the Middle Ages* (ed. John Marenbon), pp. 145–56 (Turnhout: Brepols) [reprinted in AT],

1996: 'History of Philosophy: Historical and Rational Reconstruction', *Acta Philosophica Fennica*, 61: 67–82.

1997: Translation of Second Alcibiades, in *Plato, Complete Works* (ed. John Cooper), pp. 596–608 (Indianapolis: Hackett).

1998: Foreword to *Towards the Digital Library*, pp. 5–9 (London: British Library).

1999: 'Scholarship and Information Technology', in *Information Technology and Scholarship* (ed. Terry Coppock), pp. 1–6 (London: The British Academy).

1999: 'Aquinas on Aristotelian Happiness', in *Aquinas's Moral Theory* (ed. S. McDonald & Eleonore Stump), pp. 15–27 (Ithaca, NY: Cornell University Press) [reprinted in AT].

1999: 'Body, Soul and Intellect in Aquinas', in *From Soul to Self* (ed. James C. Crabbe), pp. 33–48 (London: Routledge) [reprinted in AT].

1999: 'Frege', in *The Philosophers* (ed. Ted Honderich), pp. 203–11 (Oxford: Oxford University Press).

2000: 'Descartes the Dualist', in *Descartes: Reception and Disenchantment* (ed. Y. Senderowicz & Y. Wahl,) pp. 89–100 (Tel Aviv: University Publishing Projects) [reprinted in AT].

2000: 'The National Perspective of Legal Deposit', in *The People's Heritage*, pp. 27–32 (London: The British Library).

2001: 'The Immortality of the Book', in *The Next Communication Civilization*, pp. 83–90 (Hania: The International STEPS Foundation).

2001: 'Beyond a Warm Feeling', in *The Discovery of Happiness* (ed. S. McReady), pp. 222–37 (London: MQP Press).

2001: Introduction to A. Trollope, *South Africa* (2 vols) (London: The Trollope Society).

2001: 'Intentionality: Aquinas and Wittgenstein', in *Thomas Aquinas: Contemporary Philosophical Perspectives* (ed. B. Davies), pp. 243–56 (Oxford: Oxford University Press).

2002: 'St Thomas Aquinas on the Virtue of Humility', in *Bene Scripsisti* (ed. J. Benes et al.), pp. 25–30 (Praha: Filosofia) [reprinted in UG].

2002: 'On Teleology and Design', in *Simply Philosophy* (ed. B. Wilson), pp. 172–4 (Edinburgh: Edinburgh University Press).

2003: 'The Reception of *Aeterni Patris*', in *La Filosofia cristiana tra ottocento e novecento*, pp. 389–93 (Città del Pieve: Arcidiocesi di Perugia).

2003: Replies to T. Irwin and J. Cooper, in *Plato and Aristotle's Ethics* (ed. R. Heinaman), pp. 109–16, 148–53.

2004: 'Philosophy only states what everyone admits', in *Wittgenstein at Work* (ed. E. Ammereller and E. Fischer), pp. 173–82 (London; Routledge) [reprinted in EW].

2004: 'Stump's Aquinas', *Philosophical Quarterly* 54: 457–62.

2004: 'Seven Concepts of Creation', *Proceedings of the Aristotelian Society*, suppl. vol 78: 81–92 [reprinted in EW].

2004: 'Oxford's Chancellor', in *Roy Jenkins, A Retrospective* (ed. A. Adonis and Keith Thomas), pp. 253–70 (Oxford: Oxford University Press).

2005: 'A Brief History of Wittgenstein Editing', in *Wittgenstein: The Philosopher and his Works* (ed. A. Pichler et al.), pp. 341–55 (Bergen: University of Bergen Press) [reprinted in EW].

2005: 'Les Categories chez les Pères de l'Église Latin', in *Les Categories et leur histoire* (ed. O. Bruun et L. Corti), pp. 121–33 (Paris: Vrin [English version in EW]).

2005: 'The Philosopher's History and the History of Philosophy', in *Analytic Philosophy and History of Philosophy* (ed. Tom Sorell and G. A. J. Rogers), pp. 13–25 (Oxford: Clarendon Press).

2007: 'Worshipping an Unknown God', in *The Meaning of Theism* (ed. John Cottingham), pp. 59–70 (Oxford: Blackwell).

2007: 'Knowledge, Belief and Faith', *Philosophy* 82: 381–97 [reprinted in EW].

2007: 'Aquinas Medallist's Address, and Thomas Aquinas and the Beginning of Individual Human Life', *Proceedings of the American Catholic Philosophical Association*, 80: 23–38 [reprinted in EW].

2008: 'The Beginning of Individual Human Life', *Daedalus* (Winter 2008), pp. 15–22.

D. Reviews

1962: Van der Meer, *Augustine the Bishop* (*Catholic Herald*, 19 Apr.).

1963: Copleston, Frederick, *A History of Philosophy VII: Fichte to Nietzsche* (*The Tablet*, 24 Aug.).

1965: De la Bedoyere, Michael. *Objections to Roman Catholicism* (*New Statesman*, 1 Jan.).

1965: Taylor, Charles, *The Explanation of Behaviour* (*Oxford Magazine*, 18 Feb.).

1965: Vivian, Frederick, *Human Freedom and Responsibility* (*New Statesman*, 21 Apr.).

1968: Barnstone, Willis, *The Poems of St John of the Cross* (*MHRA Quarterly* 65: 4210).

1969: Berlin, Isaiah, *Four Essays on Liberty* (*Listener*, 15 May).

1971: Flew, Antony, *An Introduction to Western Philosophy* (*Journal of Theological Studies*).

1972: Luscombe, D. E., *Peter Abelard's Ethics* (*Journal of Theological Studies*).

1973: Quinton, Anthony, *The Nature of Things* (*Listener*, Feb.).

1973: Lucas, John, *A Treatise on Time and Space* (*Theology*, pp. 487–9).

1976: Cooper, David, *Philosophy and the Nature of Language* (*Notes and Queries*, July).

1982: Hare, R. M., *Moral Thinking*; Williams, Bernard, *Moral Luck*; Midgley, Mary, *Heart and Mind* (*Observer*, 24 Jan.).

1984: Gray, John, *Hayek on Liberty* (*Listener*, 25 Oct.).

1985: Bossy, John, *Christianity in the West 1400–1700* (*Listener*, 8 Aug.).

1985: *The New Jerusalem Bible* (*Listener*, 19 Dec.).

1986: Caute, David, *The Espionage of the Saints* (*Listener*, 6 Feb.).

1986: Nagel, Thomas, *The View from Nowhere* (*New York Times Book Review*, 23 Feb.).

1986: Mackillop, Ian, *The British Ethical Societies* (*Listener*, 27 Mar.).

1986: Chadwick, Henry, *Augustine* (*Listener*, 15 May).

1986: Harman, Geoffrey, *Bitburg in Moral and Political Perspective* (*TLS*, 21 July).

1988: Courtenay, William, *Schools and Scholars in Fourteenth Century England* (*Renaissance Quarterly*, pp. 195–8).

1991: Duff, R. A., *Intention, Agency and Criminal Liability* (*Mind*, pp. 378–9).

1991: Martz, Louis, *Thomas More: The Search for the Inner Man* and Rex, Richard, *The Theology of John Fisher* (*Journal of Ecclesiastical History*).

1998: Ackroyd, Peter, *The Life of Thomas More* (*The Tablet*, 14 Mar.).

1999: John Paul II, *Fides et Ratio* (*The Tablet*, 26 June).

1999: Cornwell, John, *Hitler's Pope* (*National Post*, 6 Nov.).

1999: Marius, Richard, *Martin Luther: the Christian between God and Death*.

2000: Coleman, Janet, *A History of Political Thought* (*TLS* 8 Dec.).

2000: Armstrong, Karen *The Battle for God* (*National Post*, 22 Apr.).

2000: Wills, Gary, *Papal Sin: Structures of Deceit* (*National Post*, 24 June).

2001: Gottlieb, Anthony, *The Dream of Reason* (*TLS*, 6 Jan.).

2002: Nielsen, Kai, *Naturalism and Religion* (*TLS*, 18 Jan.).

2002: Moynahan, Brian, *If God Spare My Life* (*Tablet*, 29 June).

2002: McCabe, Herbert, *God Still Matters* (*TLS*, 20 Dec.).

2003: Macfarlane, Robert, *Mountains of the Mind* (*The Tablet*, 14 June).

2005: Cross, Richard, *Duns Scotus on God* (*TLS*, 28 Oct.).

2005: Kirsch, Arthur, *Auden and Christianity* (*The Tablet*, 26 Nov.).

2006: McGrath, Francis, *The Letters and Diaries of John Henry Newman X* (*TLS*, 15 Dec.).

2007: Larsen, Timothy, *Crisis of Doubt* (*TLS*, 1 June).

2007: McGrath, Alister, *The Dawkins Delusion* (*TLS*, 17 Aug.).

2007: Cornwell, John, *Darwin's Angel* (*The Tablet*, 15 Sept.).

2007: Hare, John E., *God and Morality* (*TLS*).

Notes on the Contributors

JONATHAN BARNES read Greats at Balliol College Oxford where he was one of Anthony Kenny's first pupils. Later he taught philosophy at Oriel College (where he is an Honorary Fellow) and at Balliol (where he is an Emeritus Fellow). Towards the end of his career he was Professor of Ancient Philosophy at the University of Geneva and the Sorbonne. He is a Fellow of the British Academy. His most recent books are *Truth, Etc.: Six Lectures on Ancient Logic* (2007) and *Coffee with Aristotle* (2008).

SARAH BROADIE is a Wardlaw Professor of Philosophy at the University of St Andrews, and taught previously at the universities of Edinburgh and Texas at Austin; also at Yale, Rutgers, and Princeton. She has mainly published on Aristotle's natural philosophy and on his ethics, and her books include *Nature, Change, and Agency in Aristotle's* Physics (1982) (as Sarah Waterlow); *Ethics with Aristotle* (1991); and *Aristotle*, Nicomachean Ethics, *with Translation, Introduction, and Commentary* (2002) (translation by Christopher Rowe).

DAVID CHARLES is Research Professor in Philosophy and Fellow of Oriel College, Oxford. His books include *Aristotle's Philosophy of Action* (1984) and *Aristotle on Meaning and Essence* (2000). He has published articles on ancient philosophy, Wittgenstein, and contemporary philosophy of mind.

DESMOND M. CLARKE is a member of the Royal Irish Academy and Professor Emeritus of Philosophy at the National University of Ireland, Cork. He has written extensively on seventeenth-century philosophy; recent publications include *Descartes's Theory of Mind* (2003), and *Descartes: A Biography* (2006). He has been co-general editor of *Cambridge Texts in the History of Philosophy* since its inception, and has edited *George Berkeley: Philosophical Writings* (2008) for that series.

JOHN COTTINGHAM is Professor Emeritus of Philosophy at the University of Reading and an Honorary Fellow of St John's College, Oxford. His books include *Philosophy and the Good Life: Reason and the Passions in Greek, Cartesian and Psychoanalytic Ethics* (1998), *On the Meaning of Life* (2003), The *Spiritual Dimension* (2005) and *Cartesian Reflections* (2008). He is co-translator of *The Philosophical Writings of Descartes* and his edited collections include *Western Philosophy* (2nd edn, 2007). He is editor of *Ratio*, the international journal of analytic philosophy.

BRIAN DAVIES is Professor of Philosophy, Fordham University, New York. His publications include *The Thought of Thomas Aquinas* (1992), *Aquinas* (2002), and

The Reality of God and the Problem of Evil (2006). He is co-editor (with Brian Leftow) of *The Cambridge Companion to Anselm* and *Aquinas, Summa Theologiae, Questions on God* (2006).

STEPHEN GAUKROGER is Professor of History of Philosophy and History of Science at the University of Sydney, and Professor of Philosophy at the University of Aberdeen. He is author of: *Explanatory Structures: Concepts of Explanation in Early Physics and Philosophy* (1978); *Cartesian Logic: An Essay on Descartes' Conception of Inference* (1989); *Descartes, An Intellectual Biography* (1995); *Francis Bacon and the Transformation of Early Modern Philosophy* (2001); *Descartes' System of Natural Philosophy* (2002); and *The Emergence of a Scientific Culture: Science and the Shaping of Modernity, 1210–1685* (2006).

HANS-JOHANN GLOCK is Professor of Philosophy at the University of Zurich and Visiting Professor at the University of Reading. He is the author of *A Wittgenstein Dictionary* (1996), *Quine and Davidson on Language, Thought and Reality* (2003), and *What is Analytic Philosophy?* (2008). He has edited *The Rise of Analytic Philosophy* (1997), *Wittgenstein: A Critical Reader* (2001), and *Strawson and Kant* (2003), and co-edited (with Robert L. Arrington) *Wittgenstein's Philosophical Investigations* (1991), *Wittgenstein and Quine* (1996), and (with John Hyman) *Wittgenstein and Analytic Philosophy: Essays for P. M. S. Hacker* (OUP 2009). He has published numerous articles on the philosophy of language, the philosophy of mind, and the history of analytic philosophy.

PETER HACKER is an Emeritus Research Fellow at St John's College, Oxford, where he was a Tutorial Fellow from 1966 to 2006. His main interests lie in the philosophy of Wittgenstein, the history of analytic philosophy, philosophy of mind, and philosophy and cognitive neuroscience. Among his recent books are: *Wittgenstein's Place in Twentieth-Century Analytic Philosophy* (1996); *Wittgenstein: Connections and Controversies* (2001); *Philosophical Foundations of Neuroscience* (co-authored with M. R. Bennett; 2003); *History of Cognitive Neuroscience* (co-authored with M. R. Bennett; 2008); and *Human Nature: the Categorial Framework* (2007), which is the first volume of a projected trilogy on human nature.

JOHN HALDANE is Professor of Philosophy, and Director of the Centre for Ethics, Philosophy and Public Affairs in the University of St Andrews. He has published widely in the philosophy of mind, philosophy of religion, and history of philosophy, and his books include *Atheism and Theism* (with J. J. C. Smart, 1996, 2nd edn 2002). His next publication is *Reasonable Faith*, a companion volume to *Faithful Reason* (2006).

TERENCE IRWIN is Professor of Ancient Philosophy in the University of Oxford and a Fellow of Keble College. From 1975 to 2006 he taught at Cornell University. He is the author of *Plato's Gorgias* (translation and notes, 1979), *Aristotle's Nicomachean Ethics* (translation and notes, 2nd edn, 1999), *Aristotle's First Principles* (1988), *Classical Thought* (1989), *Plato's Ethics* (1995), and *The Development of Ethics* (vol. i, 2007; vol. ii, 2008; vol. iii, 2009).

DAVID S. ODERBERG is Professor of Philosophy at the University of Reading. He is the author of *The Metaphysics of Identity over Time* (1993), *Moral Theory* (2000), *Applied Ethics* (2000), and most recently *Real Essentialism* (2007). He has published widely on metaphysics, philosophical logic, ethics, philosophy of religion, and other subjects.

MARLEEN ROZEMOND teaches at the University of Toronto. Her research area is the early modern period, including its relationship to Aristotelian scholasticism. She works primarily on issues around the mind–body problem: the nature of mind, body, their union and interaction, the nature of mechanistic explanation. She is the author of *Descartes's Dualism* (1998) and various articles about Descartes, Locke, Leibniz, and the Clarke–Collins correspondence.

JOACHIM SCHULTE teaches at the University of Zurich. He has published numerous articles and four books on the philosophy of Wittgenstein. He is co-editor of critical editions of Wittgenstein's *Logisch-philosophische Abhandlung* (1989, 2nd edn 2001) and of the critical-genetic edition of the *Philosophische Untersuchungen* (2001). In collaboration with Peter Hacker, he has produced the 4th edition and modified English translation of the *Philosophische Untersuchungen* (2009).

SEVERIN SCHROEDER is Lecturer in Philosophy at the University of Reading. He is the author of three books on the philosophy of Wittgenstein: a monograph on the private language argument (*Das Privatsprachen-Argument*, 1998), *Wittgenstein: The Way Out of the Fly-Bottle* (2006), and *Wittgenstein Lesen* (2009). He is the editor of *Wittgenstein and Contemporary Philosophy of Mind* (2001) and *Philosophy of Literature* (2009).

CHRISTOPHER SHIELDS is Tutor and Fellow of Lady Margaret Hall and Professor of Classical Philosophy in the University of Oxford. He is the author of *Order in Multiplicity: Homonymy in the Philosophy of Aristotle* (1999), *Classical Philosophy: A Contemporary Introduction* (2003), *Aristotle* (2007), and, with Robert Pasnau, *The Philosophy of Thomas Aquinas* (2003). He is the editor of *The Blackwell Guide to Ancient Philosophy* (2002) and the forthcoming *Oxford Handbook of Aristotle*. Also forthcoming is his edition of *Aristotle's De Anima, Translated with Introduction and Notes*.

Index

Printed and bound by CPI Group (UK) Ltd, Croydon, CR0 4YY